Communications
in Computer and Information Science   1540

More information about this series at https://link.springer.com/bookseries/7899

Isidoro Gitler · Carlos Jaime Barrios Hernández ·
Esteban Meneses (Eds.)

High Performance Computing

8th Latin American Conference, CARLA 2021
Guadalajara, Mexico, October 6–8, 2021
Revised Selected Papers

 Springer

Editors
Isidoro Gitler ⓘD
Centro de Investigación y de Estudios
Avanzados
Mexico City, Mexico

Carlos Jaime Barrios Hernández ⓘD
Universidad Industrial de Santander
Bucaramanga, Colombia

Esteban Meneses ⓘD
Centro Nacional de Alta Tecnología
San José, Costa Rica

ISSN 1865-0929   ISSN 1865-0937 (electronic)
Communications in Computer and Information Science
ISBN 978-3-031-04208-9   ISBN 978-3-031-04209-6 (eBook)
https://doi.org/10.1007/978-3-031-04209-6

This Springer imprint is published by the registered company Springer Nature Switzerland AG
The registered company address is: Gewerbestrasse 11, 6330 Cham, Switzerland

Preface

CARLA, the Latin American High Performance Computing Conference, is an international academic meeting aimed at providing a forum to foster the growth and strength of the High Performance Computing (HPC) community in Latin America and the Caribbean through the exchange and dissemination of new ideas, techniques, and research in HPC and its application areas. Started in 2014, CARLA has become the flagship conference for HPC in the region. One of its principal goals is to spread, together with the international community, the advances on both HPC and HPC&AI (convergence between HPC and Artificial Intelligence), as those two key areas are becoming the predominant engine for innovation and development.

In the last few years CARLA has offered two main tracks: HPC and HPC&AI. The latter highlights the convergence of HPC with modern machine learning methods and their application to multiple areas. CARLA also has become a fundamental forum to disseminate, discuss, and learn about new international trends on advanced computing. The 2021 edition addressed topics from advanced computer science applications, which generated a new distinctive track for the 2022 edition. It has become clear for the HPC Latin American community that after these eight editions CARLA has matured and has consolidated its organization, showing the strength of the academic network behind its organization.

The 8th Latin American High Performance Computing Conference (CARLA 2021) was, for a second time, a fully remote event, which meant an opportunity to be more inclusive and flexible with the participation of the community. The conference was held during October 6–8, 2021, and hosted by the University of Guadalajara (UDG), the Laboratory for Applied Mathematics and HPC from CINVESTAV (ABACUS), the Advanced Computing System for Latin America and the Caribbean (SCALAC), the Mexican Network for HPC (REDMEXSU), and the University Corporation for Internet Development (CUDI).

In addition to the conference days there were seven workshops (October 4–5) and 11 tutorials: fundamental tutorials (September 27 – October 1) and advanced tutorials (October 11 – October 15) all within the framework and scope of the CARLA conference. The website (http://www.ccarla.org) provides relevant information on these activities.

CARLA 2021 had 888 registered attendees from 25 countries. Out of the total number of attendees, 828 came from 10 Latin American countries and 60 from 15 other countries (in Europe, Asia, Africa, and Oceania). The board committee gathered more than 40 colleagues in 13 committees and seven workshop committees, representing more than 30 institutions in Latin America. The board committee had over 45 meetings during the organizing year. CARLA 2021 had the sponsorship of four important high technological companies and six academic institutions or societies.

CARLA 2021 had four keynote speakers: Satoshi Matsuoka, Katherine Yelick, Frank Würthwein, and Walfredo Cirne. In addition, each track had two invited speakers: Jose E. Moreira and Lucia Drummond for the HPC track and Natasa Przulj and Nayat Sanchez for the HPC&AI track. The HPC track had 11 accepted author contributions and the

HPC&AI track had four accepted author contributions. Also, there were five accepted poster contributions. Additionally, there were seven industrial talks given by various sponsors. The conference had two panels with 13 international panelists: the first panel's theme was "Africa-Latin American HPC and AI Cooperation"; the second panel's theme was "Public Policies on Network infrastructures HPC and AI Services". Furthermore, the seven workshops featured 10 invited speakers and 11 tutorials (with 494 attendees).

This book contains 18 papers selected from 45 submitted manuscripts, comprising the 15 papers accepted for the main conference tracks along with three outstanding papers from the workshops. All papers were peer reviewed by at least three different members of the Program Committee. The paper by Fernando Furusato, Eduardo Miqueles, Matheus Sarmento, Luciano Zago, and Gustavo Aranha, "TEPUI: High-performance computing infrastructure for beamlines at LNLS/Sirius", was selected for the Best HPC Paper Award. The paper by Maria Pantoja, Christina Monahan, Alexander Garcia, Evan Zhang, and Dimitry Timokhin, "Distributed Artificial Intelligent Model Training and Evaluation", was selected for the Best HPC&AI Paper Award. It is noteworthy to mention that since 2018, the impact of article citations in the CARLA conference volumes has visibly increased.

March 2022

Isidoro Gitler
Carlos Jaime Barrios Hernández
Esteban Meneses
Sergio Nesmachnow
Andrei Tchernykh

Organization

Program Chairs

Isidoro Gitler	CINVESTAV-ABACUS, Mexico
Carlos Jaime Barrios	Universidad Industrial de Santander, Colombia
Esteban Meneses	Centro Nacional de Alta Tecnología, Costa Rica
Sergio Nesmachnow	Universidad de la República, Uruguay
Andrei Tchernykh	Centro de Investigación Científica y de Educación Superior de Ensenada, Mexico

Program Committee

Nicolás Wolovick	Universidad Nacional de Córdoba, Argentina
Antonio Tadeu Gomes	Laboratório Nacional de Computação Científica, Brazil
Esteban Clua	Universidade Federal Fluminense, Brazil
Lola Bautista	Universidad Industrial de Santander, Colombia
Javier Montoya	Universidad de Cartagena, Colombia
Harold Castro	Universidad de los Andes, Colombia
Cristian Mateos Diaz	ISISTAN-CONICET and UNICEN, Argentina
Benjamin Hernandez	Oak Ridge National Laboratory, USA
Bruno Raffin	Inria, France
Ricardo Barrientos	Universidad Católica del Maule, Chile
Pedro Silva	NVIDIA, Brazil
Jesús Carretero	Universidad Carlos III de Madrid, Spain
Esteban Mocskos	Universidad de Buenos Aires, Argentina
Juan Carlos Cajas García	ENESMérida UNAM, Mexico
Juan Manuel Ramírez	Universidad de Colima, Mexico
Esteban Meneses	Centro Nacional de Alta Tecnología, Costa Rica
Luiz Angelo Steffenel	Université de Reims Champagne-Ardenne, France
Silvio Rizzi	Argonne National Laboratory, USA
Federico Silla	Universitat Politecnica de Valencia, Spain
Guilherme Peretti-Pezzi	ETH Zurich and CSCS, Switzerland
Javier Iparraguirre	Universidad Tecnológica Nacional, Argentina
José M. Cecilia	Universitat Politecnica de Valencia, Spain
Jose M Monsalve Diaz	Argonne National Laboratory, USA
Robinson Rivas-Suarez	Universidad Central de Venezuela, Venezuela
Ulises Moya Sanchez	Gobierno de Jalisco, Mexico

Contents

High Performance Computing

High Performance Computing and Artificial Intelligence

High Performance Computing Applications

High Performance Computing

TEPUI: High-Performance Computing Infrastructure for Beamlines at LNLS/Sirius

Fernando S. Furusato[1,2]([⊠]), Matheus F. Sarmento[1,2],
Gustavo H. O. Aranha[1,2], Luciano G. Zago[1,2], and Eduardo X. Miqueles[1,2]

[1] Brazilian Synchrotron Light Laboratory/CNPEM, Campinas, Brazil
`{fernando.furusato, eduardo.miqueles}@lnls.br`
[2] Scientific Computing Group/Data Acquisition and Processing Division,
Campinas, Brazil

Abstract. We describe the main infrastructure for data processing of Sirius (the 4th generation Brazilian Synchrotron) beamlines, the Throughput Enhanced Processing Unit – TEPUI. Most of the beamlines are fundamentally supported by proper scientific instrumentation that requires fast data processing of n-dimensional arrays. In this sense, an appropriate set of hardware was selected in order to maximize the data throughput related to an expanding set of beamlines. Access to the HPC and storage is granted for beamlines in an exclusive way, without interfering the science under development; even though it is also granted for users related to a research within the CNPEM campus. Managing an HPC cluster can take great advantage of repetitive task automation. In this manuscript we present some tools that were developed to automate the scheduling of HPC users and monitor their usage, associated to each beamline.

Keywords: HPC Infrastructure · Monitoring · Sirius · Synchrotron

1 Introduction

Some of Sirius beamlines act as large digital signal generators, and some of these signals are multidimensional digital arrays. All of them are obtained through the interaction of synchrotron light with some object (usually referred to as a sample), which is the study object from some scientific case. When passing through the sample, the signal suffers interference and is detected in a plane perpendicular to the incident wavefront, where the detector is placed. These detectors then transform the propagated signal into a digital signal, which is stored in different formats in a processing unit. The vast majority of detected signals are two-dimensional, which is why we refer to the signal as an image and each image is composed of pixels, which can vary in quantities, both horizontally and vertically, and this is initially a characteristic of the detector that is being used the in scientific experiment. Normally, the number of horizontal pixels equals the number of vertical

© Springer Nature Switzerland AG 2022
I. Gitler et al. (Eds.): CARLA 2021, CCIS 1540, pp. 3–18, 2022.
https://doi.org/10.1007/978-3-031-04209-6_1

pixels, but that is not a rule - for simplicity we'll refer to this number as n. Thus, detectors are able to generate images that contain propagation information and are stored in different dynamic ranges allowing the researcher or algorithms to distinguish more information in the measured sample. Different dynamic ranges can be used for pixel information, depending on the detector characteristics. For Sirius sensors (either commercial or in-house developments), the detected images operate at $b = 12$, $b = 16$ or $b = 24$ bit-depths, and at different frame-rates. The number of images is what determines a 3D experiment, and is peculiar to the type of experiment for a given beamline. Engineering developments, which support scientific experiments, handle more than 1000 FPS acquisition (for example, running a sample at an experiment in micro/nano tomography). This means that at least $1000bn^2/8$ bytes of information are acquired per unit of time. Some other parameters of the experiment can cause this amount of bytes to be variable, such as the exposure time. Therefore, in the worst case, we can have n images measured in a few seconds and thus $bn^3/8$ bytes of measured information. Not all data is collected quickly, and this is a characteristic of the scientific experiment running at the beamline. However, fast experiments are the ones that consume the most processing power, and this is directly linked to the computation capability available to process the information. Thus, in the worst case, we can have data of more than 80 Gigabytes acquired within few seconds, and a beamline usually do hundreds of these experiments, which yields a total consumption that easily

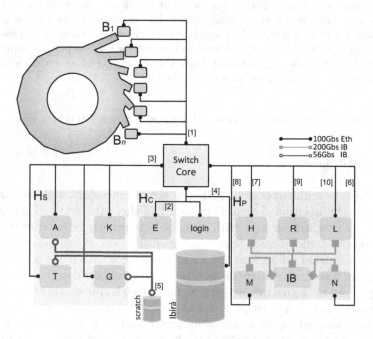

Fig. 1. High-performance computing topology available for data processing associated to beamlines $\{\mathbf{B_1}, \ldots, \mathbf{B_n}\}$ and also users within CNPEM, starting at 2021.

Table 1. Hardware specifications for the cluster at LNLS/Sirius.

Server	CPU cores	Mem.(TB)	Arch. GPU	GPU Boards	Cuda cores	Subsystem
A	64	768	V100	1	5120	H_S
G	32	512	K80	6	14976	
T	48	512	K80	4	9984	
K	48	256	T4	1	2460	
E	448	6046	–	–	–	H_C
M	256	1024	A100	8	55296	H_P
R	256	1024	A100	8	55296	
L	256	1024	A100	8	55296	
N	256	1024	A100	8	55296	
H	256	1024	A100	8	55296	
Storage	Capacity (TB)	Filesystem				
IBIRA	2048	Lustre				
SCRATCH	140	GPFS				

reaches the order of terabytes on Sirius central storage. The hardware supporting Sirius beamlines processing demands, are divided into three processing subsystems, which we denote by H_P, H_S and H_C, referring to processing, segmentation/visualization and computing, respectively. These are: (a) Processing nodes within set H_P are dedicated to data processing similar to those performed on local servers (attached to detectors and placed at the beamline), but which may need to be repeated with other boundary conditions, following user research needs. These are primarily GPU based and with an equally CPU intensive capacity. These set of nodes are commonly referred to as a clusters of GPUs; (b) Processing nodes belonging to H_S are dedicated to users that are dependent on a graphical user interfaces. Typical tasks used in these nodes are data quantification (with commercial software), visualization, data annotation and data inference (from machine learning) using internal tools developed by LNLS; and (c) Processing nodes H_C are used for massive calculation involving a strong CPU parallelism and intensive use of shared memory, such as molecular dynamics, protein crystallography, Monte-Carlo simulations, wavefront propagation simulation, among others. We refer to pool H_C as being a fat node of CPU.

The current hardware topology is shown in Fig. 1 - with servers indicated by letters {T,G,A,K,H,N,L,M,R,E} - and whose detailed description are presented in Table 1. The hardware is logically administrated by the scientific computing group of LNLS, which is also responsible for providing high performance algorithms for data processing and data segmentation solutions for images generated at the beamlines. The cluster has a total capacity of 1 PFlop and is expandable in each of the subsystems H_C, H_P, H_S and global storage IBIRA (*tree* in Tupi-Guarani), according to Sirius beamlines needs. The scientific network was chosen with the ethernet protocol of 100 Gbs bandwidth (expandable to 400 Gbs), being the core switch (with duplication) able to receive experimental data - in a parallel form - from a

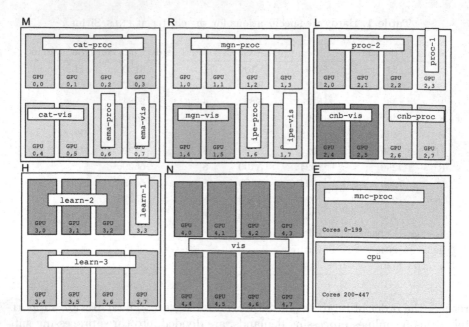

Fig. 2. Queues availables for 6 initial beamlines starting in 2021, with exclusive data processing and visualization.

maximum of $n = 40$ beamlines. Subsystem $\mathbf{H_P}$ has an Infiniband HDR 200 Gbs switch, allowing fast data communication between servers {H,R,L,M,N}.

Some of the main synchrotrons in the world also adopt their respective data processing and storage policies, according to [4,14,17] for ESRF, APS and SOLEIL respectively, as well as different monitoring schemes [9,13]. Growth of HPC infrastructure can be estimated based on history and demand; with the amount of data that Sirius is capable of producing, and based on the demand of each beamline and types of users, a powerful HPC and storage infrastructure must be prepared. It is also unavoidable that the processing infrastructure ends up being segmented in order to provide computing access to different experimental techniques. The data generation is also a subject of virtually endless discussions and can only be estimated, taking into account the size and complexity of LNLS' potential data producers, their demands and history. Thus, just like HPC processing, storage infrastructure should enable easy expansion. For the current demand – and a reasonable amount of time – the solution presented for HPC and storage infrastructure must suffice (Fig. 2).

2   Cluster Subsystems

We divided the cluster into two large units, the high-performance servers and storage, as indicated by Fig. 1. The scenario presented here can easily support Sirius' first 6 beamlines starting in 2021, and can be expanded as the computing demands increase. Each beamline has a detector coupled to a server, with an equally large computational capacity and also supported by GPU [16]. In this way, the processing of measured data is balanced between local servers and the main cluster.

2.1 High-Performance Computing

The subsystem **H_S** is dedicated to running commercial software or those developed internally by the scientific computing group for the purpose of data analysis, mainly data segmentation using artificial intelligence. They are human interactive dependent, which typically rely on graphical interfaces, granted through suitable tools (such as VNC for example). In this class of subsystems, software on demand by the user are executed. As they are machines equipped with GPU and with adequate RAM, they can allocate more than one user simultaneously. Once the access is approved by a formal committee – via research proposal – the user is granted with a share of the server, for a limited amount of time, which guarantees a percentage of memory, CPU cores and at least one GPU device. Servers G,A,T have a connection to an old legacy storage SCRATCH (see Fig. 1) through an Infiniband protocol with a maximum bandwidth of 56 Gbs to a GPFS file system. Normally, servers available for subsystem **H_S** are accessed after an imaging experiment has been through a complete cycle. In fact, data measured for imaging setup are processed during the beamtime (e.g., reconstructed in the case of tomography, coherent-diffraction experiments or ptychography), but it is very unlikely that the data analysis after reconstruction can be done during the beamtime. The servers within set **H_S** can then be remotely accessed by the same group comprised by the research proposal. The clearance to access the set **H_S**, after the beamtime, is granted for a period of six months, where users can use the tools, provided by the LNLS staff, to process the measured/reconstructed data. Referring to Fig. 1 and Table 2, we note that using the set **H_S**, the stored data is transferred from IBIRA to the memory server, processed and stored again. This is true for data annotation tasks, where users can use in-house development [19] to provide a proper input for machine learning purposes. Quantification follows the same pattern, using commercial and free-software requested *a priori* by the user team. Machine learning tasks follow a different scheme in these servers; in fact, once data is annotated, a training model runs on a different server (H), lying on the set **H_P** and using a proper queue.

Table 2. Usage for processing subsystem **H_S**.

Server	Task	Flux of data	Beamline usage	Scheduling
{A,G,T}	Quantification	[4-3-4]	Available	Available
	Annotation	[4-3-4]		
	Learning	[4-7-4]		

The set $\mathbf{H_C}$ contains a single fat node E, dedicated to running external software or software developed internally by the scientific computing group, in order to support parallel processing with intensive use of CPU cores and memory. This server has 28 cores per processor, with a total of 8 processors, providing a total of 448 cores (with hyperthread enabled). A physical expansion of the set $\mathbf{H_C}$ is possible within the data center, adding more cores connected through a specific hardware connection. This server handles tasks using the job scheduler Slurm [1] and is the main hardware for processing the data collected at the Manacá beamline (MNC), dedicated for protein crystallography. It is connected to the IBIRA storage through the switch core with a Lustre 100 Gbs bandwidth connection. Protein crystallography runs the XDS software [7] using a maximum of 200 cores from server E. This software runs on an exclusive queue, as indicated by Table 3, using the back-end provided by the MXCUBE interface [5]. In this case, the collected data is automatically sent from the detector interface to the storage, where reconstruction using the reciprocal space information takes place. As it is well known from the crystallography user community, more powerful servers provide faster reconstructions. Server E shares resources with a second queue cpu, available either for users on the same technique, but running different models after beamtime, or users non related to the Manacá beamline. This is the case for intensive parallel software as SRW [6] for wavefront propagation simulation, or software FLUKA [3] for simulating radioactive decay.

Table 3. Usage for processing subsystem $\mathbf{H_C}$.

Server	Task	Flux of data	Beamline usage	Scheduling
E	Protein crystallography	[1-4-2-4]	mgn-proc	NA
	CPU intensive	[1-4-2-4]	NA	cpu

The subsystem $\mathbf{H_P}$ is dedicated to running mostly in-house software developed by the scientific computing group with the purpose of processing data measured at the beamline. In this subsystem, for each GPU in a queue, it is also available a proportional portion of the server resources – 128 GB of RAM and 32 threads. Here, algorithms that take advantage of the GPU can perform better with a proper code development and data partitioning. This is the case of tomography [12] for the Mogno beamline (MGN), ptychography [2] and fluorescence tomography [11] for the Carnaúba beamline (CNB), and coherent-diffraction imaging [10] for the Cateretê beamline (CAT). Each one of these reconstructed volumes can take advantage of the corresponding processing queue as well their associated visualization queues vis. Each visualization queue is fundamentally supported by INDEX/NVIDIA [18] software allowing fast data rendering through multi-GPUs. This is done in such a way that the user can have a smooth experience, i.e., measurements $\overset{(i)}{\rightarrow}$ data processing $\overset{(ii)}{\rightarrow}$ visualization. Here, we can have two main drawbacks (Table 4):

Table 4. Usage for processing subsystem $\mathbf{H_C}$.

Server	Task	Flux of data	Beamline usage	Scheduling
M,R,L	Tomography	[1-9-4]	`mgn-proc, mgn-vis`	NA
	Coherent-diffraction	[1-8-4]	`cat-proc, cat-vis`	
	Ptychography	[1-10-4]	`cnb-proc,cnb-vis`	
	Spectroscopy	[1-9-4]	`ipe-proc, ipe-vis`	
	Extreme conditions	[1-8-4]	`ema-proc, ema-vis`	
N	Visualization	[4-6]	`vis`	
H	Training models/AI	[4-7-4]	`learn-1, learn-2, learn-3`	Available
L	General processing	[4-6]	`proc-1, proc-2`	Available

(i) *Transferring data*: Large volumes can have a transfer latency from the detector to storage, or from detector to the computing node. Whenever sent directly to storage, the application will have to wait reading a large volume before starting data processing. There are several applications where reading data is inevitable, such as 4D tomography [15], where a sequence of volumes is acquired per units of second; or even in the case of XPCS [8] where large bursts of 2D images are acquired for long time stamps. The scientific computing group has decided to adopt, whenever possible, modern solutions as RDMA or GPU direct to improve data transfer from storage to the processing server;

(ii) *Processing data*: There exist some experimental conditions that require a more complex processing, which can consume more computing time; this is the case for advanced iterative reconstructions techniques. As long as the data processing is done within a low computational time – bounded by the scanning acquisition time – the flow (i),(ii) will not be impacted. Also, since queues are exclusive for the experiment, users do not have to wait for another user job to finish before their own starts.

We use the Slurm [1] resource management system for submitting jobs on systems $\mathbf{H_C}$ and $\mathbf{H_P}$. Here, the login system supports a large amount of concurrent users (as predicted by Table 5, see Sect. 2.2). When access is granted, the user submits their processing job to the queue indicated for his type of data.

2.2 Storage

The main storage system is composed by two units with optimized performance in writing and reading, SCRATCH and IBIRA. The first is a legacy of the old UVX particle accelerator machine from LNLS and has a nominal write rate of 56 Gbs on the infiniband protocol using the GPFS file system. With the installation and migration of the computing system to the new data center room, located in Sirius, all the old data was migrated to the IBIRA storage, ensuring that the old one remains as a cold data storage unit. The SCRATCH operates - if necessary - at optimized rates mainly with servers G,A,T (see Fig. 1) due to the infiniband

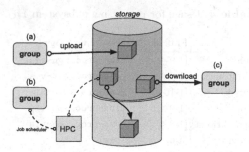

Fig. 3. Group actions for users at Sirius/LNLS impacting the Storage

switch connected to two physical hosts operating several virtual machines (for Sirius beamline projects). The IBIRA storage system - from HPE supplier - with a total capacity of 2PB, works with the Clusterstor E1000 appliance, capable of operating in Lustre, NFS and CIFS file systems. The impact of data on storage is due to the following groups: beamline, researchers, internal users, and external users. Each of these groups generates data at a rate per unit of time, which can be estimated *a priori* by an upper bound based on the facility's usage history and Sirius usage expectation. Most of these groups interact with some type of high-performance machine, generating data from measurements at LNLS internal facilities. The usage according to each group follows the division presented below:

Table 5. Upper bound for percentages in actions (a), (b), (c) according to LNLS experience (see Fig. 3) for 6 starting beamlines in 2021 and an generic beamline BL.

Action	CAT	MNC	MGN	CNB	EMA	IPE	BL	LNLS	INTERNAL USR	EXTERNAL USR
(a)	50	50	50	50	50	50	50	40	10	10
(b)	40	40	40	40	40	40	40	40	80	50
(c)	10	10	10	10	10	10	10	20	10	40
Daily access	100	100	100	100	100	100	100	100	100	100

1. *Beamline*: there is a daily generation rate (order of Terabytes at maximum operating capacity), which is sent to storage in two situations: data already processed by the high-performance server located at the beamline or to be processed by the cluster within the data center.
2. *Support and Research*: Internal facilities can generate data with size similar to beamlines. For example, data that is already stored and will be processed afterwards (following some processing queue) in the cluster significantly increases storage space consumption;
3. *Users*: Two types of users are identified, internal and external. Both use data already collected and stored for computational processing, generating more data that consumes the total storage capacity

For each group above, there are three actions that move the data stream into storage as illustrated in Fig. 3; these are (a) uploading data to the storage (b) processing data allocated in the storage, and (c) downloading data. These three actions occur at random within the dynamics of Sirius' beamlines. Ideally, read and write rates vary for each action (a), (b) and (c); for example, the write rate is greater than the read rate in action (a), while the opposite must be true for (b). Based on LNLS experience, the percentage assigned to each action for each usage group is as shown in Table 5. Here, we assume that the beamlines are divided equally between upload and cluster processing through job scheduler, directly impacting storage. This is no longer true for groups of users who do not upload but download processed data. Each group has a maximum number of people and servers; just as each server uses a different type of protocol for storage access. The operating systems commonly used by groups for data access are Unix and Windows, which affect the storage access system. As shown in Table 5, we assume an upper limit of 100 users per day accessing storage, according to each group; generating a global access amount of at least 1000 users per day, within the dynamics presented in Fig. 3. The total number of users accessing the computing system since 2018 is presented in Fig. 4(a) and (b).

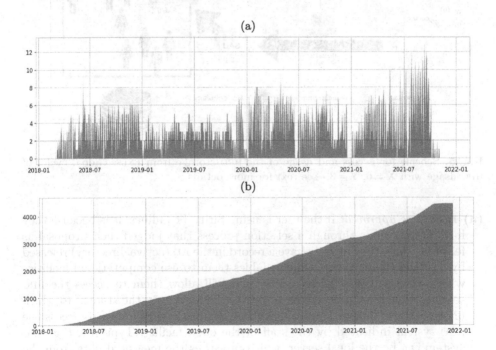

Fig. 4. (a) Total number of schedules for the HPC system since 2018. (b) Cumulative histogram for user scheduling.

3   System Access

The access to Sirius high-performance computing infrastructure is always associated to a beamline proposal, or internal research from LNLS/Sirius experimental stations. The users supporting system office (SAU) provide the access to servers in two situations, described below, and only after approval from a proper committee:

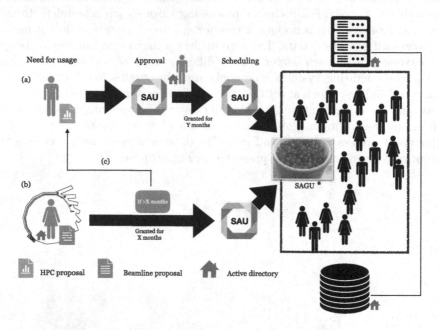

Fig. 5. Scheme for access and usage of the HPC/storage from LNLS. Global cycles of HPC usage with X = 6, Y = 3 - see text for more details.

(a) *Beamtime approved*: If the user is using Sirius beamlines, it is because they have already gone through a selection process that judged their proposal as feasible. Thus, they already have a record in the AD (active directory) released by SAU and the IT group, which enables them to use computational facilities within the CNPEM. This record is what will allow them to access the HPC servers, as well as indicate the respective folder within the storage to which his research is linked. During beamtime, the user will be able to access the HPC system indicated by the staff of the open facility. Typically, this HPC system can be the local server, which processes the measured data from the beamline, or some convenient computing node in the cluster. After beamtime, access to the HPC system is granted for X months. This means that during this time, they can always contact SAU to reschedule machine time in order to complete their data processing. After these X months, the user must submit a technical report to SAU, indicating what results were obtained with access to the HPC and pointing out any improvements. If the research still needs HPC resources, the user can submit a new proposal to SAU, for the use of machines, and if approved, a new global cycle of appointments for Y months is rescheduled.

(b) *Non-existent Beamtime*: If the internal user is not using Sirius beamlines, but needs computational resources to advance some research, she/he can write a proposal for use of HPC, submitting it for analysis through SAU. If approved, it will have an overall time for appointments of the order of Y months; having to submit a technical report to SAU after the end of this period. New cycles of Y months can be scheduled, after the submission of new proposals and approved by SAU internal rules.

The information described above is outlined in Fig. 5. Each proposal (with or without associated beamtime) must always have an associated principal investigator (PI), responsible for the research. As an example, consider a proposal submitted by Marie Curie, containing researchers Albert Einstein and Paul Erdös. After analysis and approval by the responsible committee, an AD group is formed with an identifier containing the letter p and the year of submission, followed by 4 other random numbers; for instance p20210987. In the same AD, the identifiers up.mcurie, up.aeinstein and up.perdos are registered (first letter of name followed by surname). Regardless of whether it is beamtime or HPC time requested by this team, a directory in the storage is created with the identifier 20210987/ preceded by the path that points to the corresponding quota of the installation being used. Only the proposal group has permission to manipulate (writing and read) the data stored within 20210987/; certain LNLS support groups can have permission access under this directory, in order to help users with data manipulation.

SAGU (as an acronym in portuguese for *user scheduling system*) is a software developed by the scientific computing group with the purpose of scheduling the HPC system for data processing. It is used by SAU in order to provide user access to a given computing node. This service uses a MONGODB database located on a virtual machine, containing the following information per schedule: proposal number, author name, start date, end date, software needed, server name.

If a license is requested in the schedule, the SAGU system is responsible for enabling users of the proposal on the FlexNet license server, with the requested software and the number of license tokens needed. When using the software, a query is made to the license server and if there are tokens available for the user's proposal, the software will be able to run. There is a daemon for SAGU, running on all servers available for scheduling. Its job is to consult (daily basis) the database and enable access for each user of the proposals scheduled on that server, and remove users without access permissions on that day. The user access is then performed through SSH. Each proposal will have a limited amount of resources (CPU, Memory and GPU) equally to the other proposals scheduled on the same server in the same period of time.

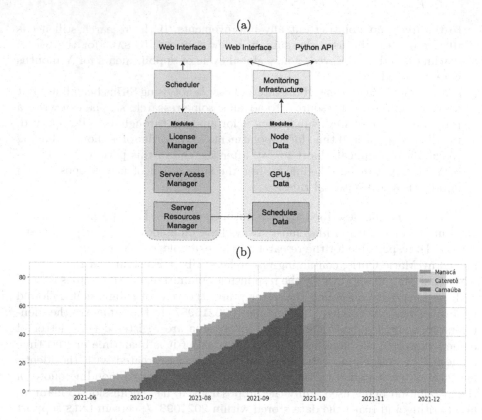

Fig. 6. (a) General system overview for scheduling users at the HPC infrastructure. (b) Cumulative histogram for HPC user proposals associated to three new Sirius beamlines.

3.1   Scheduling System

The scheduling system uses PHP and Javascript technologies for the web interface, MONGODB for the scheduling database and Python to release the schedules on the servers, as presented in Fig. 6. Compartmentalization of computational resources available on servers, in order to attend proposals, is done using Linux Control Groups (cgroups). It allows the software to reserve, limit and record the use of computational resources on a Linux operating system, that is present in all high performance servers. That is, each proposal has its computational resource reserved during the scheduling period. Thus, there is no competition for use in different proposals. we will only use the `libcgroup` library to manage these settings. The `cgroup` allows us to limit and/or register the use of CPU, RAM, devices, network, IO and number of processes. The web service tool for user scheduling at SAGU is shown in Fig. 7. Figure 6 presents a cumulative histogram for the total of HPC user proposals using SAGU system, indicating the efficiency of the scheduling methodology.

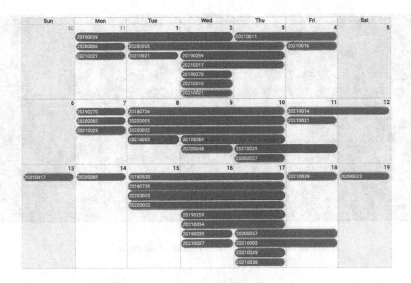

Fig. 7. SAGU user scheduling web service.

4   Monitoring System

We have developed a system for monitoring the usage of HPC/Sirius research proposals users related to each high performance server (SALMAO), presented in Fig. 8. In addition to facilitating the detection of bugs and instabilities, monitoring allows us to extract information about the usage of servers and how users are taking advantage of their resources.

4.1   Infrastructure

The use of a monitoring system allows one to obtain data on availability, latency, performance and efficiency, resulting in faster response to emergencies and assisting in planning future expansions. The tools used in our system were Prometheus and Grafana, both free software developed in the Go language. Both are the state of the art in observability and scalability in monitoring systems [20]. They allow support for heterogeneous systems, such as different types of server architectures and data sources, in addition to visualizing data in an easy way.

In comparison, old tools like Nagios and Zabbix do not support the monitoring of complex systems as a large-scale and heterogeneous HPC environment, as they are characterized as Black Box monitoring systems, which focuses on monitoring basic system resources, compared to monitoring applications with a White Box system. Another important feature is to alert system administrators about failures and warnings, obtain general metrics of the machines, such as CPU, RAM, GPU, network, temperature and energy usage. As well as specific information for each schedule, that is, how many resources were used by each research proposal.

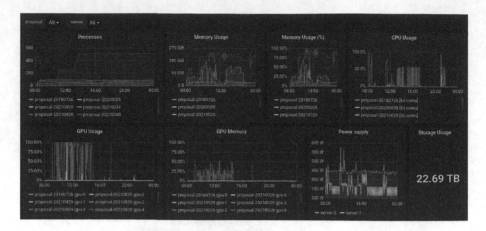

Fig. 8. SALMAO monitoring dashboard.

In addition to the specific requirements of our ecosystem, there are requirements inherent to a modern data center, such as scalability, high availability and automation. The system consists of combining Prometheus tools, a time series database, specific for application monitoring, and Grafana, a customizable data viewer with a web interface, using exporters specific to our needs.

An *exporter* is software that runs on servers and exports specific metrics on a certain port. The exporters `node exporter`, `DCGM exporter` and `Slurm exporter` were used, which handle general machine metrics, NVIDIA GPUs metrics and Slurm scheduler metrics, respectively. As there was no *exporter* in the community to obtain metrics generated by *cgroups*, it was necessary to develop the *Cgroups exporter*. This custom exporter was developed with Python, using the `lark-parser` library, to read the configuration files of *cgroups*, `nvidia-ml-py` to get the metrics from GPU and `prometheus_client`, to facilitate the export of metrics in the Prometheus format. The metrics exported are the usage of CPU, RAM, GPU and the number of processes, for each *cgroup* (equivalent to each proposal). A Python API was also developed to retrieve data from our monitoring database and use with data science frameworks, such as Pandas, as presented in Script 1.1.

Listing 1.1. Python API for data extraction from server H from HPC/SALMAO database

```
from sscSalmao import tools

ID = "20201134"
S = "-30m"
E = "now"
step = "60"

p = tools.gpu(proposal=ID, server="H", start_time=S, end_time=E,
    step=step)
p = tools.gpu_memory(proposal=ID, server="H", start_time=S, end_time=E,
    step=step)
p = tools.cpu(proposal=ID, server="H", start_time=S, end_time=E,
    step=step)
p = tools.ram(proposal=ID, server="H", start_time=S, end_time=E,
    step=step)
p = tools.processes(proposal=ID, server="H", start_time=S, end_time=E,
    step=step)
p = tools.energy(server="H", start_time=S, end_time=E, step=step)
```

```
# Scheduling
s = tools.get_scheduled_proposals(day="today")
s = tools.get_proposal_users(proposal=ID)
s = tools.get_available_servers(day="today")
```

5 Conclusion

With all the schematics and politics in order for usage, a demand was created to manage user access in an automated way. Automation generally reduces human errors and can be traced through well generated logs. Since it was not possible to find a tool that would be able to: receive input from a front end web interface; send data to a database, which would be used to schedule user on servers – we developed our own. SAGU is the system created to fill in that gap. And an advantage is that we would be able to generate and store usage data and statistics which could be visualized afterwards. Fortunately, there is a variety of monitoring and data visualization systems available. This is how our monitoring system, SALMAO came into place. With monitoring data available, and the help of tools such as Grafana and Prometheus, it is possible to generate and visualize statistical data, which can be used to predict – to some extent – the need for expansion or data cleanup, for instance.

Acknowledgments. Special thanks to the IT group from CNPEM - *Dennis Massarotto Campos, Sergio Carrare* and *Felipe Campos* - responsible for the implementation of the high-performance network available for Sirius beamlines.

References

1. SLURM. https://slurm.schedmd.com. Accessed 15 June 2021
2. Baraldi, G.L., Dias, C.S.B., Silva, F.M.C., Tolentino, H.C.N., Miqueles, E.X.: Fast reconstruction tools for ptychography at Sirius, the fourth-generation Brazilian synchrotron. J. Appl. Crystallogr. **53**(6), 1550–1558 (2020)
3. Battistoni, G., et al.: The fluka code: description and benchmarking. In: AIP Conference Proceedings, vol. 896, pp. 31–49. American Institute of Physics (2007)
4. Dimper, R., Götz, A., de Maria, A., Solé, V., Chaillet, M., Lebayle, B.: ESRF data policy, storage, and services. Synchrotron Radiat. News **32**(3), 7–12 (2019)
5. Gabadinho, J., et al.: MxCuBE: a synchrotron beamline control environment customized for macromolecular crystallography experiments. J. Synchrotron Radiat. **17**(5), 700–707 (2010)
6. He, A., et al.: Parallel performance of "synchrotron radiation workshop" code: partially coherent calculations for storage rings and time-dependent calculations for XFELs. In: Advances in Computational Methods for X-Ray Optics V, vol. 11493, p. 114930H. International Society for Optics and Photonics (2020)
7. Kabsch, W.: XDS. Acta Crystallogr. Section D: Biol. Crystallogr. **66**(2), 125–132 (2010)
8. Leheny, R.L.: XPCS: nanoscale motion and rheology. Curr. Opin. Colloid Interface Sci. **17**(1), 3–12 (2012)

9. Llopis, P., Lindqvist, C., Høimyr, N., van der Ster, D., Ganz, P.: Integrating HPC into an agile and cloud-focused environment at CERN. In: EPJ Web of Conferences, vol. 214, p. 07025. EDP Sciences (2019)
10. Mandula, O., Elzo Aizarna, M., Eymery, J., Burghammer, M., Favre-Nicolin, V.: PyNX. Ptycho: a computing library for X-ray coherent diffraction imaging of nanostructures. J. Appl. Crystallogr. **49**(5), 1842–1848 (2016)
11. Miqueles, E.X., De Pierro, A.R.: Iterative reconstruction in X-ray fluorescence tomography based on radon inversion. IEEE Trans. Med. Imaging **30**(2), 438–450 (2010)
12. Miqueles, E.X., Martinez Jr, G., Guerrero, P.P.: Fast image reconstruction at a synchrotron laboratory. In: Proceedings of the 2020 SIAM Conference on Parallel Processing for Scientific Computing, pp. 24–34. SIAM (2020)
13. Nieke, C., Lassnig, M., Menichetti, L., Motesnitsalis, E., Duellmann, D.: Analysis of cern computing infrastructure and monitoring data. In: Journal of Physics: Conference Series, vol. 664, p. 052029. IOP Publishing (2015)
14. Ounsy, M., Gagey, B.: SOLEIL data management policy. Synchrotron Radiat. News **32**(3), 23–24 (2019)
15. Pak, T., de Lima Luz, L.F., Tosco, T., Costa, G.S.R., Rosa, P.R.R., Archilha, N.L.: Pore-scale investigation of the use of reactive nanoparticles for in situ remediation of contaminated groundwater source. Proc. Natl. Acad. Sci. **117**(24), 13366–13373 (2020)
16. Sanfelici, L., et al.: Solutions for the SIRIUS'beamlines in a nutshell. In: AIP Conference Proceedings, vol. 2054, p. 030033. AIP Publishing LLC (2019)
17. Schwarz, N., Veseli, S., Jarosz, D.: Data management at the advanced photon source. Synchrotron Radiat. News **32**(3), 13–18 (2019)
18. Spina, T.V., Miqueles, E.X.: High-throughput 3D image reconstruction, visualization, and segmentation of large-scale data at the sirius synchrotron light source (2020). https://developer.nvidia.com/gtc/2020/video/s21278-vid. GTC Nvidia Developer
19. Spina, T.V., Peixinho, A.Z., Bernardi, M.L.: High performance volumetric image visualization and segmentation for large data sets. In: AI-enabled Advances in Materials Imaging and Analysis XXIX. International Materials Research Congress (2021)
20. Sukhija, N., Bautista, E.: Towards a framework for monitoring and analyzing high performance computing environments using kubernetes and prometheus. IEEE SmartWorld, April 2019

Energy Consumption Studies of WRF Executions with the LIMITLESS Monitor

Andres Bustos[1]([✉]), Alberto Cascajo[2], Antonio Juan Rubio-Montero[1],
Elena García-Bustamante[3], José A. Moriñigo[1], David E. Singh[2],
Jesus Carretero[2], and Rafael Mayo-Garcia[1]

[1] Technology Department, CIEMAT, Av. Complutense 40, 28040 Madrid, Spain
{andres.bustos,antonio.rubio,josea.morinigo,rafael.mayo}@ciemat.es
[2] Computer Science and Engineering Department, Universidad Carlos III de Madrid,
Avenida Universidad 30, Leganés, 28911 Madrid, Spain
{cascajo,dexposit,jcarrete}@inf.uc3m.es
[3] Energy Department, CIEMAT, Av. Complutense 40, 28040 Madrid, Spain
elena.garcia2@ciemat.es

Abstract. We present a study of the performance of the Weather Research and Forecasting [WRF] code under several hardware configurations in an HPC environment. The WRF code is a standard code for weather prediction, used in several fields of science and industry. The metrics used in this case are the execution time of the run and the energy consumption of the simulation obtained with the LIMITLESS monitor, which is the main novelty of this work. With these results, it is possible to quantify the energy savings of WRF run configurations, which include variations in the number of computing nodes and in the number of processes per node. It is found out that a slight increase in the computing time can drive to a noticeable reduction in the energy consumption of the cluster.

Keywords: HPC optimization · WRF · LIMITLESS

1 Introduction

The optimal use of hardware resources is one of the major issues in Computer Science and in particular in High Performance Computing (HPC). Usually, the optimization of code executions targets the minimization of the computing time, setting aside other criteria. However, the study of the energy consumed in the computations is of particular interest from the environmental and economical points of view. Such an evidence has become cornerstone with the advent of the exascale infrastructure in which a kind of trade-off between computational and energy efficiencies is pursued. Examples of this trend nowadays can be found in the literature. Thus, a study of the performance and energy consumption of HPC workloads on a cluster can be found in [19], an auction mechanism model for energy-efficient HPC is detailed in [6], or even theoretical approaches

© Springer Nature Switzerland AG 2022
I. Gitler et al. (Eds.): CARLA 2021, CCIS 1540, pp. 19–33, 2022.
https://doi.org/10.1007/978-3-031-04209-6_2

for achieving a sustainable performance while reducing energy consumption [10] demonstrate the actual necessity for successfully combining both performance and energy issues.

A timely research line such as artificial intelligence is being used for improving this trade-off as well. Driven holistic approaches to reduce the power usage effectiveness (PUE) [30] or swarm optimized greedy algorithm [13], just to mention a few, are recent developments on this topic.

However, there is a lack of understanding of the power consumption characteristics of HPC jobs that run on production HPC systems [23]. The gap is being filled by studies applied to different codes widely used, see for example [7] for an energy-efficiency tuning of lattice Boltzmann simulations, [29] for stencil-based application on Intel Xeon scalable processors, or [11] for molecular dynamics calculations executed on hybrid and CPU-only supercomputers with air and immersion cooling.

Following this line of work, we study both the computing time and the energy consumption of two different simulations of the WRF (Weather Research and Forecasting) code, widely used in forecasting predictions and climate evolution. There is in the literature a vast number of references related to the evaluation of the WRF code in what respects their physical results applied to different areas in the world, but scarce information about its computational and energy efficiencies in ultimate processors to the authors' knowledge.

To carry out this study, we test WRF together with a new performance monitor for HPC clusters called LIMITLESS already developed by the authors. LIMITLESS presents an easy deployment and configuration to gather data with a low overhead from any hardware element in the HPC cluster.

The reminder of this paper is organized as follows. We start with a brief introduction to WRF and the simulations carried out in the experiments in Sect. 2. Then we describe the main characteristics of LIMITLESS and the methodology followed in the performance studies in Secs. 3 and 4. We show the results in Sect. 5 and present our conclusions in Sect. 6. The main results are that diverse deployments of WRF with small variations in the execution time can lead to important variations in the power consumption.

2   WRF: The Standard for Weather Simulations

The Weather Research and Forecasting [WRF] simulation code is a well-established tool in weather prediction since 2007 [18]. It is a massive parallel code that solves the atmosphere dynamics, considering many physical and multiscale phenomena. The lowest 1–3 km region of the atmosphere within the troposphere, characterized by friction and turbulent mixing is called *planetary boundary layer* (PBL) [28]. The PBL plays an important role in the transportation of energy (including momentum, heat and moisture) into the upper layers of the atmosphere and acts as a feedback mechanism in wind circulation. Mesoscale models, as WRF, include different schemes for convection, planetary boundary layer turbulence, radiation, cumulus and land-surface processes which is a complete description of the behavior of the atmosphere both in hind-cast and forecast. The PBL parametrization implemented in the mesoscale models is important for accurate simulations of turbulence, wind, wind power, air quality and, in general, any process occurring in the lower layers of the atmosphere. WRF is used in many industrial and research activities, including weather forecasting and wind power.

The two kind of WRF simulations presented in this work differ in the mesoscale model:

- The non-local-K scheme from Yonsei University, denoted by *YSU* [16].
- The model with local turbulence kinetic closure from Mellor-Yamada Nakanishi and Niino, Level 2.5, denoted by *MYNN* [22].

Some recent studies were reported in literature regarding the use of these two settings e.g. [12,14,15,17,31]. In particular, the WRF model is widely used to generate wind resource maps. These wind atlases are usually made by simulating several years at high horizontal and vertical resolution, for which the computational cost is very high. Therefore, the WRF model is usually run in HPC in a distributed way, i.e., a long simulation is run in each group of nodes. In the *New European Wind Atlas* (NEWA) project [1], it was decided to run simulations of 7 days plus a 24 h spin-up period, which overlaps with the last day of the preceding weekly run. An advantage of the weekly runs is that the simulations are independent of each other and can be integrated in parallel. This reduces the total wall clock time needed to complete a multi-year climatology at a decent computational overhead. Figure 1 shows the temperature at 2 m above ground level in the whole Mediterranean Sea using the WRF model with a weekly run. The PBL *MYNN* parametrization was used in this case.

Fig. 1. Temperature at 2 m above ground level for a weekly run simulation in the Mediterranean area.

For each weekly run, in the domain of the Fig. 1 (6,213,460 grid points), 4 nodes in Xula (160 cores, see Sect. 4) are used and the computational time is around 6 h, i.e., 960 core hours. With 52 weeks/year for 30 years simulated, 1,497,600 core hours will be needed if 4 nodes are used (just the half when 8 nodes are used and so on). As for many medium-size supercomputers, the amount of nodes that are accessible by a user is limited, the logical consequence is that the same simulation is performed several times in a kind of parameter sweep calculation. At this point is where a trade-off between the simulation walltime and the energy consumed is interesting to be analyzed (see below in the results section). Even more when the WRF scalability is not optimal, i.e., a computational and energy cost-effective execution is of even greater importance.

In the present work, we have executed shorter test WRF simulations with the two parametrizations aforementioned for our performance studies. Depending on the number of computing nodes involved and the MPI configuration, those simulations take 20–40 min to complete in a standard HPC infrastructure and produce 53 GB of output data. Because the problem size is always constant for each input configuration (*YSU/MYNN*), all scaling studies presented here refer to strong scaling.

3   The LIMITLESS Monitor

In this work, data from the system have been collected using the LIMITLESS monitor. LIMITLESS [9] is a highly scalable framework for monitoring and application scheduling that is able to work under near-to-second sampling rates with low overheads. However, this sampling interval can be established from hours to less than a second. LIMITLESS is fully integrated with other system software like the scheduler, and other runtimes that allow it to enhance some goals such as application-level monitoring, I/O interference awareness, and scalability. In a previous work [8], a description of the monitoring architecture, as well as a practical example of its use for enhancing the application scheduling, are shown.

LIMITLESS includes a monitoring tool designed to provide performance information for generic purposes in large-scale systems. It consists of the following components: one *LIMITLESS* Daemon Monitor (LDM) per node, that periodically collects the performance metrics; a set of *LIMITLESS* Daemon Aggregators (LDAs), that are responsible for forwarding the information from the LDMs to other aggregators or servers, and the *LIMITLESS* Daemon Server (LDS), which gathers and stores the monitoring information in an ElasticSearch database. The LDS is also able to send the information to other processes involved in the monitoring or to store it locally for future local exploitation like, for instance, in-transit processing.

The monitoring information collected by LIMITLESS includes, but is not limited to, different metrics related to CPU, main memory, I/O and communication network utilization, as well as temperature and energy consumption. The monitor collects many of these metrics directly from the kernel performance counters. However, the energy consumed is measured by means of the *Intelligent Platform Management Interface* (IPMI).

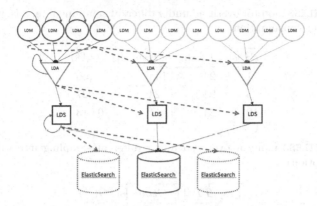

Fig. 2. Example of deployment with Triple Modular Redundancy and watchdog processes in the first monitoring branch.

Figure 2 shows a generic deployment of LIMITLESS with fault-tolerance mechanisms enabled for the LDMs, LDAs and LDSs. The purpose of replicating these components is to enhance the monitor's scalability and resilience. The techniques applied are *Triple Modular Redundancy* (TMR) and *Watchdog processes* (WD). The first one allows each component to forward the information to three other components (instead of one). TMR includes two configurations: with replication and without it. When replication is enabled, each component sends the same information to the three linked components. Alternatively, if replication is not enabled, the component sends the information to the first linked component and waits for confirmation. If there is no confirmation, it sends the information to the second linked component and waits again. If there is no confirmation, it repeats the process with the third option. Note that in this last approach, once a confirmation has been received, the data replication is avoided in order to reduce the communication overhead. On the other hand, WD is a process that executes an application as a service, checking if the managed components are running or not. In case of failure, WD restarts the component with the same configuration. Note that Fig. 2 shows a generic topology that does not necessarily fit with the monitoring framework topology used in this work.

LIMITLESS monitor has been selected to provide the performance information due to its reduced overhead (shown in Table 1) with values less than 1 %. This overhead does not include the overhead of collecting energy consumption through IPMItool and the state of the InfiniBand network. Table 2 shows the overheads of monitoring with those two features, which are higher for those sampling intervals because of the syscall-related overheads. The columns identified by SI indicate the sampling interval; TT shows the total execution time while the monitor is running; $Ctime$ is the number of CPU seconds that the monitor dedicates to collect the information; finally, the O columns show the CPU overhead in percentage.

Table 1. LIMITLESS monitor overhead under different sampling intervals, without measuring the power consumption.

SI [s]	TT [h]	$Ctime$ [s]	$O(\%)$
1	24	144	0.166
5	24	24	0.027
10	24	11	0.013

Table 2. LIMITLESS monitor overhead under different sampling intervals (including power consumption).

SI [s]	TT [h]	$Ctime$ [s]	$O(\%)$
1	24	2350	2.72
5	24	475	0.55
10	24	243	0.28

We can observe that the monitor overhead is very low, which is important in production clusters to keep monitor interference with other applications as small as possible.

The topic of monitoring in distributed systems has been extensively addressed in previous works. However, monitoring is a crucial component that has to be adapted to new technology improvements related to HPC platforms. There are solutions based on frameworks that combine various components to offer global views (for example Ganglia [4,20], Nagios [3] or Slurm [32]). Those frameworks are well known and used in HPC. However, simpler and lighter monitors also have a place, as in the case of Collectd [5], which works as a local monitoring daemon.

The advantage of using LIMITLESS is that is easily adaptable and reconfigurable to multiple platform configurations. LIMITLESS is also able to select different metrics of interest and process the results with a minimum impact on the platform performance.

4   Methodology

The simulations presented in this work were run on the Xula facility, located at the data center at CIEMAT, Madrid, Spain. This HPC cluster is in production since November 2019 and it is currently adhered to the Spanish Supercomputing Network (RES) [2]. The cluster is divided into several InfiniBand islands with different hardware installed, which correspond with partitions in the batch system. In this work, the first partition was used, which is precisely the offered to the external users belonging to the RES. This allows better reproducibility and the profiting of the results, because many of them make use of WRF in their research. The island is composed of computing nodes with double Intel(R)

Xeon(R) Gold 6148. In total there are 40 cores at 2.40 GHz per node (hyper-treading is disabled). Inside the island, the connectivity is based in 4xEDR Infini-Band (100 Mbps), without blocking among nodes, but with 2:1 blocking against the LUSTRE storage servers.

Moreover, the nodes used in this work were reserved and removed temporally from the execution queues to improve the accuracy of the measurements. Thus, no other software was using the hardware that might influence on our experiment, with exception of the shared storage. Similarly, turbo-boost is disabled on the island. Thus, allocating in the nodes the maximum of 40 MPI tasks will not disrupt the measurements.

We configured the LDM in LIMITLESS to measure every 5 s and dump the data from all involved nodes into a text file in the central server. The information is sent via Ethernet to the LDA/LDS, which runs in an independent server in the cluster, so the monitor does not overload the MPI communications. We used Python to integrate, analyze and plot all the results.

In the experiments, we carried out several WRF simulations with the two different input configurations (*YSU* and *MYNN*), described at the end of Sect. 2. For each input file, we measured the execution time and energy consumption in different deployments: varying the number of nodes involved and the number of processes per node [*np*]. Every simulation case, defined by the input file, the number of nodes and *np*, is executed at least three times in order to have a more robust estimation of the computing time and energy consumption (see below for a deeper explanation about reproducibility and errors). In this way, we can estimate the variation in our results due to the use of the cluster by other users that can occupy neighboring nodes or make intensive use of the storage system. Thus, we present the mean values and all error bars correspond to the standard deviation.

We completed a total of 166 simulations in the Xula cluster and found that typically the dispersion in the measurements is very small. We observe those the errors correspond to a standard deviation below 3% in almost 90% of the cases in the results of the next Section (Figs. 3, 4 and 5), showing the previously mentioned good reproducibility. In this sense, it should be pinpointed that taking a t-Student confidence interval of 95% and the previous standard deviation value, moving from a set of three repetitions to six would simply reduce the final error associated to the measurement from 1.14% to 0.07%, with the consequent additional energy consumption and CO_2 emission made by the cluster. Hence we can say that the experiments are reproducible in most cases.

5   Results

The main objective of these experiments if to find out the relation between the strong scaling of an MPI application, such as WRF, with its energy consumption. This is shown in the following figures of this Section, starting with a generic scaling study, increasing the number of cores/nodes, and later relating them to the energy consumption.

In Fig. 3 we plot the execution time of WRF using the *YSU* input file using a single node with 40 CPUs and varying the number of processes, *np*. We can see that the minimum execution time is obtained using $np = 20$, indicating that the scaling is not very good above those *np*. This is a known behavior of a certain type of MPI applications [24, 27, 33]. MPI operations are optimized for process communication between nodes, not for efficient intra-node communications, where context changes, protocols, and intermediate libraries overload the CPUs and increase the latency. For those reasons, if the application cannot use threads (e.g. OpenMP), the MPI processes are distributed in the cluster [21] to measure both the strong and weak scaling.

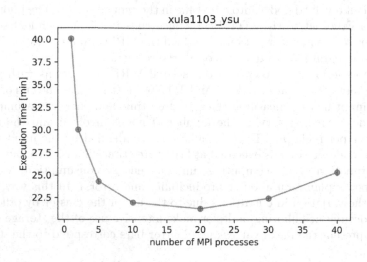

Fig. 3. Execution time of WRF with *YSU* input file, using a single Xula node [named xula1103], as a function of the number of MPI processes.

We chose to compare the maximum distribution of MPI processes between CPUs ($np = 2$, one process per CPU) and the optimal concentration ($np = 20$), varying the number of nodes and consequently the total number of MPI tasks. This is shown in Fig. 4, where we plot the execution time versus *np*. As can be seen, although for $np = 2$ each process has all hardware resources available, WRF does not scale well for more than 4 nodes. On the other hand, there are no improvements if we use more than one node if they execute 20 processes.

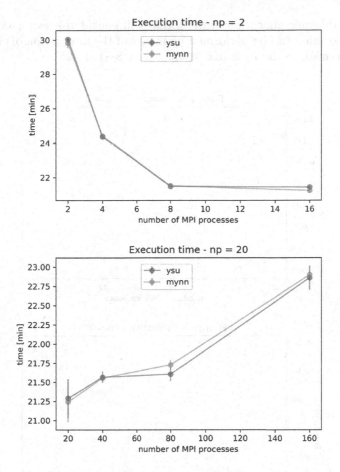

Fig. 4. Execution times of WRF runs for *YSU* and *MYNN* input configurations. *np* is the number of processes per node, so 1, 2, 4 and 8 nodes are used to obtain the total number of MPI processes in each execution.

The energy consumption in the previous cases does not show promising results. As can be observed in Fig. 5, increasing the number of nodes produces a monotonously increase, close to linear, in the energy consumption. Concentrating processes in nodes implies, in principle, some energy savings, but it occupies all the cores that can be eventually utilized by other users. So, from the power consumption point of view, it is advisable neither to use more than one node nor launching few MPI processes per node. As it is known, policies regarding processes location, spreading, and/or consolidation must be properly evaluated in the context of the Resource Management System (Slurm in the present work) at the same time of considering the utilization profile (CPU utilization, average number of cores, average requested memory, etc.) by users. In this sense, the current work for characterizing the WRF execution profile opens the door to perform dynamic allocation of tasks that will benefit this evaluation. Such a dynamic allocation can be performed by means of the integration of checkpointing mechanisms into the Resource Management System [25].

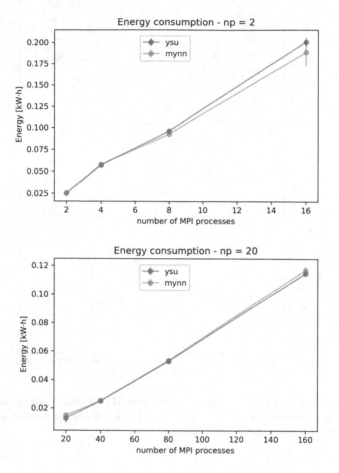

Fig. 5. Energy consumption of WRF runs. np is the number of processes per node, so 1, 2, 4 and 8 Xula nodes are used.

In Fig. 6 we show a scatter plot of the energy consumption versus the execution time for all 166 simulations considered. In this set of simulations, we include those from Figs. 4 y 5 and additional ones performed with different np. Since, as we previously said, we repeat every setting at least three times, we observe in the small clusters the typical dispersion of the measured quantities. We also observe a huge variability in the energy consumption, whereas the computing time is more bounded.

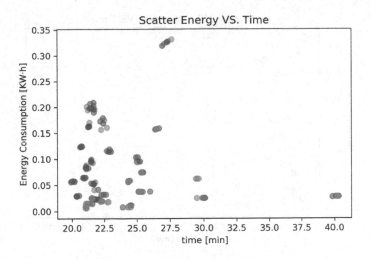

Fig. 6. Scatter plot of energy consumption and execution time for all numerical experiments (blue = *MYNN*, orange = *YSU*). (Color figure online)

Similarly, in Fig. 7 we show another scatter plot with the number of MPI processes versus the execution time, confirming the reduced scaling of the WRF run with the number of MPI processes.

Finally, in Table 3 we show the best cases, those that minimize the energy consumption or execution time, of all WRF executions. We can observe that:

- With *MYNN* input, increasing computing time 6% reduces energy consumption a factor of 9.
- With *YSU* input, increasing computing time 20% reduces energy consumption a factor of 7.

The use of the fastest settings indicated in Table 3 imply an excessive occupation of hardware resources, that is unaffordable because of the small gain in execution time.

Nevertheless, and taking into account that the presented results are obtained in a shared cluster used by a wide set of different users and computational requirements, there are several combinations of *np* and the number of nodes grouped altogether below 0.1 kW·h in Fig. 7 and also below 50 MPI processes in Fig. 6, with execution times smaller than 25 min. Consequently, it is possible to define executions of WRF that balance the cluster occupation, the duration of the run, and the power cost, i.e., to find out say sub-optimal configurations that obtain a close-to-optimal trade-off for these three variables.

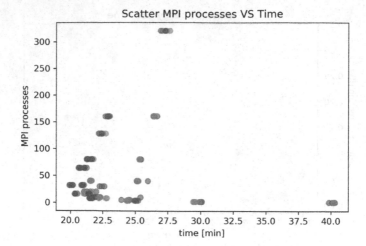

Fig. 7. Scatter plot of the number of MPI processes and execution time for all numerical experiments (blue = *MYNN*, orange = *YSU*). (Color figure online)

Table 3. Cases with minimum execution time and energy consumption. See the text above for estimation of the errors.

Input	Nodes	np	Ex. time	Energy
MYNN	8	32	**19.9 min**	0.0560 kW·h
MYNN	1	16	21.0 min	**0.0063 kW·h**
YSU	8	32	**19.9 min**	0.0569 kW·h
YSU	1	5	23.9 min	**0.0081 kW·h**

6   Conclusions and Future Work

It is not unusual that codes such as WRF are run on a daily basis, in particular, to execute weather forecasting jobs in several geographical locations. This represents significant expenses in terms of human, material, and energy resources, which are also difficult to quantify. This is due to the nature of WRF and other similar codes, that scale differently in execution time and energy consumption in relation to the total number of processes generated and occupied nodes.

We have performed a preliminary study of the execution time and energy consumption for two input configurations of WRF, changing the number of nodes and the number of processes in each node. We have characterized the strong scaling of WRF, its consumption and resource usage in a modern HPC cluster.

In the WRF cases here documented, the energy consumption grows linearly with the number of nodes used, whereas the computing time is barely reduced, or even increases when each node executes the maximum number of MPI processes allowed. However, reducing the number of processes per node does not imply a smaller consumption, but only a smaller cluster occupation.

Hence, it has been found that in this dedicated infrastructure there are several sub-optimal deployments that compensate execution time, energy usage, and cluster occupancy. Among them, we see that is possible to drastically reduce the energy consumption of the nodes, with the corresponding refrigeration savings, at the expense to slightly increase the computing time. As previously commented, this outcome can profit from a dynamic allocation of tasks mechanism (based on checkpointing capabilities) that will optimize this trade-off. Even when of much interest, to find out the algorithm that rules this dynamic allocation of tasks taking also into account the infrastructure being exploited is out of the scope of this work. Such an endeavor will require of the application of artificial intelligence methodologies to design a scheduling algorithm that would optimize the use of a shared cluster as Xula is accordingly to the users' demands and historic behavior.

This article is then the first step for such a future work in which a deeper study must be performed. Hence, an increase in the number of executions, code configurations, number of iterations even when a good reproducibility has been already obtained, consideration of the idle power consumption on additional nodes (when executing all processes in the same node), etc. ought to be performed. This bunch of experiments could be then complemented with the design of a new scheduling algorithm for an optimal use of the cluster that could profit from the available study of the researchers exploiting Xula [26].

At the same time, the achieved experience paves the way for future studies with other codes suitable in HPC job planning in the context of energy efficiency. In this sense, the previous conclusions and their potential extension to codes with a near-perfect performance scaling should be confirmed or not in order to check if there are less possibilities of energy savings as the power consumption will follow a linear behavior with the use of resources used.

Acknowledgments. This work was partially funded by the Comunidad de Madrid CABAHLA-CM project (S2018/TCS-4423), the ADMIRE project Grant Agreement number 956748 (H2020-JTI-EuroHPC-2019-1), and the ENERXICO project Grant Agreement number 828947 (H2020-FETHPC-2018).

References

1. New European Web Atlas. https://www.neweuropeanwindatlas.eu. Accessed June 2021
2. Red Española de Supercomputación. https://www.res.es/. Accessed June 2021
3. Nagios - The Industry Standard In IT Infrastructure Monitoring (2018). https://www.nagios.org/. Accessed June 2021
4. Ganglia Monitoring System (2018). http://ganglia.sourceforge.net/. Accessed June 2021
5. Collectd - The System Statistics Collection Daemon (2018). https://collectd.org/. Accessed June 2021

6. Ahmed, K., Tasnim, S., Yoshii, K.: Simulation of auction mechanism model for energy-efficient high performance computing. In: Proceedings of the 2020 ACM SIGSIM Conference on Principles of Advanced Discrete Simulation, SIGSIM-PADS 2020, pp. 99–104. Association for Computing Machinery, New York (2020). https://doi.org/10.1145/3384441.3395991

7. Calore, E., Gabbana, A., Schifano, S.F., Tripiccione, R.: Energy-efficiency tuning of a lattice Boltzmann simulation using MERIC. In: Wyrzykowski, R., Deelman, E., Dongarra, J., Karczewski, K. (eds.) PPAM 2019. LNCS, vol. 12044, pp. 169–180. Springer, Cham (2020). https://doi.org/10.1007/978-3-030-43222-5_15

8. Cascajo, A., Singh, D.E., Carretero, J.: Performance-aware scheduling of parallel applications on non-dedicated clusters. Electronics 8, 982 (2019). https://doi.org/10.3390/electronics8090982

9. Cascajo, A., Singh, D.E., Carretero, J.: LIMITLESS - LIght-weight MonItoring tool for LargE scale systems. In: Proceedings - 29th Euromicro International Conference on Parallel, Distributed and Network-Based Processing, PDP 2021, pp. 220–227. Institute of Electrical and Electronics Engineers Inc., March 2021. https://doi.org/10.1109/PDP52278.2021.00042

10. Cerf, S., Bleuse, R., Reis, V., Perarnau, S., Rutten, É.: Sustaining performance while reducing energy consumption: a control theory approach. In: Sousa, L., Roma, N., Tomás, P. (eds.) Euro-Par 2021. LNCS, vol. 12820, pp. 334–349. Springer, Cham (2021). https://doi.org/10.1007/978-3-030-85665-6_21

11. Dlinnova, E., Biryukov, S., Stegailov, V.: Energy consumption of MD calculations on hybrid and CPU-only supercomputers with air and immersion cooling. Adv. Parallel Comput. 36, 574–582 (2020). https://doi.org/10.3233/APC200087

12. Dörenkämper, M., et al.: The making of the new European wind atlas - part 2: production and evaluation. Geosci. Model Dev. 13(10), 5079–5102 (2020). https://doi.org/10.5194/gmd-13-5079-2020

13. Dupont, B., Mejri, N., Da Costa, G.: Energy-aware scheduling of malleable HPC applications using a particle swarm optimised greedy algorithm. Sustain. Comput.: Inform. Syst. 28, 100447 (2020). https://doi.org/10.1016/j.suscom.2020.100447

14. Garrido, J.L., González-Rouco, J.F., Vivanco, M.G., Navarro, J.: Regional surface temperature simulations over the Iberian Peninsula: evaluation and climate projections. Clim. Dyn. 55, 3445–3468 (2020). https://doi.org/10.1007/s00382-020-05456-3

15. Hahmann, A.N., et al.: The making of the new European wind atlas - part 1: model sensitivity. Geosci. Model Dev. 13(10), 5073–5078 (2020). https://doi.org/10.5194/gmd-13-5053-2020

16. Hong, S.Y., Noh, Y., Dudhia, J.: A new vertical diffusion package with an explicit treatment of entrainment processes. Mon. Weather Rev. 134(9), 2318–2341 (2006). https://doi.org/10.1175/MWR3199.1

17. Jiménez, P.A., Dudhia, J.: Improving the representation of resolved and unresolved topographic effects on surface wind in the WRF model. J. Appl. Meteor. Climatol. 51, 300–316 (2012). https://doi.org/10.1175/JAMC-D-11-084.1

18. Kerbyson, D., Barker, K., Davis, K.: Analysis of the weather research and forecasting (WRF) model on large-scale systems. In: Proceedings of Parallel Computing, PARCO 2007. Parallel Computing: Architectures, Algorithms and Applications. Advances in Parallel Computing, Juelich, Germany, vol. 15, pp. 89–98 (2007)

19. Mantovani, F., et al.: Performance and energy consumption of HPC workloads on a cluster based on arm ThunderX2 CPU. Futur. Gener. Comput. Syst. 112, 800–818 (2020). https://doi.org/10.1016/j.future.2020.06.033

20. Massie, M.L., Chun, B.N., Culler, D.E.: The ganglia distributed monitoring system: design, implementation, and experience. Parallel Comput. **30**(7), 817–840 (2004)
21. Moríñigo, J.A., García-Muller, P., Rubio-Montero, A.J., Gómez-Iglesias, A., Meyer, N., Mayo-García, R.: Performance drop at executing communication-intensive parallel algorithms. J. Supercomput. **76**(9), 6834–6859 (2020). https://doi.org/10.1007/s11227 019 03142-8
22. Nakanishi, M., Niino, H.: An improved Mellor-Yamada level-3 model with condensation physics: its design and verification. Boundary-Layer Meteorol. **112**, 1–31 (2004). https://doi.org/10.1023/B:BOUN.0000020164.04146.98
23. Patel, T., Wagenhäuser, A., Eibel, C., Hönig, T., Zeiser, T., Tiwari, D.: What does power consumption behavior of HPC jobs reveal?: demystifying, quantifying, and predicting power consumption characteristics. In: 2020 IEEE International Parallel and Distributed Processing Symposium (IPDPS), pp. 799–809 (2020). https://doi.org/10.1109/IPDPS47924.2020.00087
24. Rodríguez-Pascual, M.A., Moríñigo, J.A., Mayo-García, R.: Effect of MPI tasks location on cluster throughput using NAS. Clust. Comput. **22**(4), 1187–1198 (2019). https://doi.org/10.1007/s10586-018-02898-7
25. Rodríguez-Pascual, M., Cao, J., Moríñigo, J.A., Cooperman, G., Mayo-García, R.: Job migration in HPC clusters by means of checkpoint/restart. J. Supercomput. **75**(10), 6517–6541 (2019). https://doi.org/10.1007/s11227-019-02857-y
26. Rodríguez-Pascual, M., Rubio-Montero, A.J., Moríñigo, J.A., Mayo-García, R.: Execution data logs of a supercomputer workload over its extended lifetime. Data Brief **28**, 105006 (2020). https://doi.org/10.1016/j.dib.2019.105006
27. Shainer, G., Lui, P., Liu, T., Wilde, T., Layton, J.: The impact of inter-node latency versus intranode latency on HPC applications. In: Proceedings of the IASTED International Conference on Parallel and Distributed Computing and Systems, pp. 455–460 (2011). https://doi.org/10.2316/p.2011.757-005
28. Stull, R.B.: An Introduction to Boundary Layer Meteorology. Kluwer Academic Publishers, Dordrecht, Boston, London (1988)
29. Szustak, L., Wyrzykowski, R., Olas, T., Mele, V.: Correlation of performance optimizations and energy consumption for stencil-based application on Intel Xeon scalable processors. IEEE Trans. Parallel Distrib. Syst. **31**(11), 2582–2593 (2020). https://doi.org/10.1109/TPDS.2020.2996314
30. Tracey, R., Hoang, L., Subelet, F., Elisseev, V.: AI-driven holistic approach to energy efficient HPC. In: Jagode, H., Anzt, H., Juckeland, G., Ltaief, H. (eds.) ISC High Performance 2020. LNCS, vol. 12321, pp. 267–279. Springer, Cham (2020). https://doi.org/10.1007/978-3-030-59851-8_17
31. Vegas-Cañas, C., et al.: An assessment of observed and simulated temperature variability in the sierra de Guadarrama. Atmosphere **11**(9), 985 (2020). https://doi.org/10.3390/atmos11090985
32. Yoo, A.B., Jette, M.A., Grondona, M.: SLURM: simple Linux utility for resource management. In: Feitelson, D., Rudolph, L., Schwiegelshohn, U. (eds.) JSSPP 2003. LNCS, vol. 2862, pp. 44–60. Springer, Heidelberg (2003). https://doi.org/10.1007/10968987_3
33. Zhang, C., Yuan, X.: Processor affinity and MPI performance on SMP-CMP clusters. In: IEEE International Symposium Parallel and Distributed Processing, Atlanta, USA, pp. 1–8 (2010). https://doi.org/10.1109/IPDPSW.2010.5470774

Improving Performance of Long Short-Term Memory Networks for Sentiment Analysis Using Multicore and GPU Architectures

Cristiano A. Künas[1]([⊠]) [iD], Matheus S. Serpa[1] [iD], Edson Luiz Padoin[2] [iD], and Philippe O. A. Navaux[1] [iD]

[1] Federal University of Rio Grande do Sul, Porto Alegre, Brazil
{cakunas,msserpa,navaux}@inf.ufrgs.br
[2] Regional University of Northwestern Rio Grande do Sul, Ijuí, Brazil
padoin@unijui.edu.br

Abstract. A massive amount of data is generated on the Internet through websites, blogs, and social networks, with all kinds of content, including comments about companies and their products. Sentiment analysis (SA) is the interpretation of emotions in texts. It is essential for different companies as it helps identify customer's opinions. It is also beneficial to understand people's responses to new content, providing audience insights to help make decisions. However, current technological advances enable us to efficiently store and retrieve these immense amounts of data to better insight into different application areas. Companies use this information to make marketing decisions. In response, we propose a performance optimization LSTM for SA using multicore and GPUs to keep the accuracy. To validate our proposal, we have applied it over a public database with 50,000 film records. The results showed a performance improvement of 3.17 times on the multicore and 12.15 on the GPU.

Keywords: Artificial intelligence applications · Sentiment analysis · Natural language processing · Recurrent neural networks · Multicore · GPUs

1 Introduction

Knowing people's opinions about something has always been important to most people during a decision making [18]. Acquiring a product or brand, or knowing a specific place, are examples of activities that can be done based on the experiences reported by other people. Opinion content has become an indispensable tool for companies looking for new business opportunities, market their products, and managing their reputations. In this sense, companies have been showing increasing interest in automating the mining process on what is being said about them in order to understand and identify relevant content, which

I. Gitler et al. (Eds.): CARLA 2021, CCIS 1540, pp. 34–47, 2022.
https://doi.org/10.1007/978-3-031-04209-6_3

allows taking specific actions, projecting the improvement in the services offered and consequently the improvement in their market positioning [22].

Opinions play a fundamental role in almost all human activities because they are indicators of behavior. Whenever a decision is about to be made, the opinions of others are heard and are of great importance [11]. In recent years, more and more users have begun to share their feelings freely in the form of opinions on a wide variety of topics, resulting in an enormous amount of data. People and companies are increasingly using the content available in these media for decision-making. However, analyzing this data and filtering the relevant information in it is challenging due to the rapid dissemination of texts. Each site usually contains a huge volume of opinionated content, which is not always structured and ready for use. Thus, intelligent systems capable of automating the process of sentiment analysis are fundamental.

For sentiment analysis (SA), several approaches based on natural language processing and machine learning have been used in the past. However, methods based on deep learning (DL) are becoming very popular due to their high performance in recent times [28]. Recurrent Neural Networks (RNNs) are better adapted to modeling problems such as time-series data and analysis regarding the application domain. There are several variations of models based on RNN. Most of these models differ mainly due to their ability to memorize input data. In general, basic RNN models can handle short-term dependencies on sentences. However, they encounter problems with long-term dependencies. These dependencies considerably influence the meaning and the polarity of a document. Long Short-Term Memory (LSTM) [7] based models solve this long-term dependency problem by introducing a memory into the network, being able to learn from past data. The LSTM model can produce better performance, outperforming the other classifiers, including RNN, Support Vector Machine (SVM), and Naive Bayes [14].

The main objective of SA is to define automatic techniques capable of extracting subjective information from texts in natural language in order to create structured knowledge to be used in support systems or decision-makers. The essential question in the SA is to identify how feelings are expressed in the texts and whether the expressions indicate positive (favorable) or negative (unfavorable) opinions towards the subject. Therefore, this article compares the accuracy and training time of RNN models based on LSTM to analyze the sentence sentiment polarity. The rest of this paper is organized as follows. Section 2 discusses the related works. Section 3 describes the implementation methodology, tools used and the execution environment. Section 4 discusses our results. Finally, Sect. 5 concludes the paper and points future work.

2 Related Work

Sentiment analysis is an essential topic for different companies, as it helps to identify customer opinions and understand people's responses to new content, providing audience insights to help in decision making. In this context, various approaches are explored. Pan et al. [17] and Kolekar et al. [10] focus on Convolutional Neural Network (CNN) models, some papers explore the use of Word

Embedding [6,13,21], Kalaivani et al. [9] and Widayat et al. [27] explore LSTM architectures, and others combine CNN+LSTM [5,21,29].

Pan et al. [17] have proposed a method for analyzing emotions in medical comment text using a character vector combined with CNN. They manually tracked and labeled 5,298 comments (2,892 positive and 2,406 negative) from a professional medical consultation service platform as a training dataset. In addition, 2,426 comments (1,408 positive and 1,018 negative) were tracked as a test dataset. In the actual task of sentiment analysis of medical texts, the model's accuracy reaches 88.2%.

Kolekar et al. [10], the authors conducted two different experiments. In the first experiment, they compared the proposed CNN on GPU and CPU. They obtained 90% accuracy on the dataset on CPU and GPU. The training time on GPU and CPU was 81 s and 114 s, respectively. The second experiment compared GPU performance with data set sizes 2,000, 4,000, and 6,000. They obtained times of 33 s, 81 s, and 139.8 s respectively. They used a tweet dataset that contains opinions about airline services with a size of 4,000. The batch size is 30, the number of epochs is 10, the dataset was split in the proportion of 80% for model training and 20% for model testing.

Kalaivani et al. [9], the authors compared three deep learning architectures CNN, simple RNN and LSTM for document-level sentiment classification. They report that LSTM has superior performance when compared to the other two networks in terms of accuracy. Stochastic Gradient Descent, RMSprop, Adam and Adagrad are used as optimizers, and their performance is evaluated. LSTM with Adam optimizer shows the best performance.

Widayat et al. [27], the authors used a simple architecture LSTM on the IMDb Movie Review dataset. They used 100 LSTM units, dropout of 0.2, Adam optimizer, 5,000 features, batch size of 64, 3 epochs and the sequence size at 500. Word embedding was used with dimensions of 32, 50, 60, 64, 70, 80, 100 and 128. Using the K80 GPU for training, they obtained 87.86% accuracy for the best case (word embedding of 32), with a training time of 550 s on average.

Abdalraouf Hassan and Ausif Mahmood [6] proposed a neural network architecture model named ConvLstm. The neural network architecture model is a combination of the CNN model and the LSTM model. In the architecture designed, the LSTM layer is used instead of the pooling layer found on CNN. The LSTM layer is used to keep information from long input sequence sentences or commonly called long-term dependencies. In contrast, the convolution layer contained in CNN is used to reduce the loss of local information from each sentence input sequence. The ConvLstm architecture model experimented on two sentiment datasets, and there are the IMDB Movie Review dataset and the Stanford Sentiment Treebank dataset (SSTb). This research using the pre-trained feature from word2vec. At the same time, just a simple and little tuning hyperparameter used in this architecture provides a very satisfying accuracy, which is estimated at 88.3%.

Ch'ng et al. [3], they developed and evaluated a GPU-accelerated social media data processing system based on the premise that the future of meaningful information visualization requires big data processing in real-time. They report that although the system is computationally expensive, they achieved a speed capable of receiving real-time inputs from Twitter, reaching about 43,057 lines per second. At the same time, only 6,000 tweets are generated every second on average.

Celesti et al. [2] they studied the accuracy of user opinions by comparing different Machine Learning approaches, including Bayesian, Linear, SVM and decision tree classifiers with Twitter data. In particular, the goal was to compare performance in terms of accuracy. They used Word Embedding Glove. The experimental result showed that the accuracy of each technique depends on the approach used; that is, for bag-of-words Logistic Regression has the highest accuracy value, while Linear Support Vector Classification (LinearSVC) is the most accurate considering the word embedding approach.

Most previous proposals focus on the accuracy of LSTM-based models for Sentiment Analysis. Differently, we focused on improving the training performance of LSTM-based models for Sentiment Analysis by increasing batch size, using multicore and GPUs to keep the accuracy.

3   Implementation

The proposed solution is the development of RNN for Sentiment Analysis in texts or posts. Our approach focuses on using RNN with Long Short-Term Memory. RNN has the function of analyzing an input text (review) and predicts how positive or negative the sentiment expressed is. RNN's training is performed both in CPU and GPU architecture. Finally, the trained RNN models can be applied in sentiment analysis, allowing us to analyze the results.

3.1   Technical Specifications

The implementation of RNN of this work is done using Python [25] programming language. This was chosen because of its simplicity and the many well-documented modules that help from pre-processing data to applying machine learning models. In this work, the main modules used are: Keras [15], Tensorflow [1] and Scikit-Learn [19].

Keras is used to model the RNN. This is a high-level API written in Python. It was developed with a user focus to allow fast experimentation. It supports several network configurations and works with both CPU and GPU. Tensorflow is Keras's standard back-end. This is an open-source software library for numerical computing using data flow graphs. The flexible architecture allows you to deploy computing for one or more CPUs (Central Processing Unit) or GPUs (Graphics Processing Unit) with a single API. It also allows a fast and easy interface with CUDA (Compute Unified Device Architecture) [16] which is an extension of the C language and enables the use of parallel computing. Tensorflow was developed initially for deep neural network research purposes, but the system is general enough to be applicable in a wide variety of other domains.

To split the data, in training and testing, Scikit-Learn is used. This is a machine learning module for Python created on top of SciPy [8] which is a Python ecosystem for scientific computing.

3.2 Training Data Pre-processing

The database used in the experiments of this work was elaborated in the work of [12]. This base has a collection of 50,000 IMDb[1] ratings. The built data set is balanced, containing an even number of analyses in 2 possible classes: positive (pos) and negative (neg). This means that the sentences are well distributed among the classes. There is no class with a much larger number of sentences than the other. Thus, the sentiment classification in this dataset can be interpreted as a binary classification problem. The set consists of sentences written in English and is used in several works dealing with sentiment analysis [4,5,20,23,26]. This data can be easily found on the Internet.

The pre-processing is done in stages. These aim at removing noise present in the sentences and coding the texts so that they can be used in LSTM-based model training: i) Special characters and punctuation marks are removed; ii) All words are written in lower case; iii) Stopwords – words that do not add much meaning to the text, usually are articles, conjunctions and prepositions – are removed; iv) Sequences are limited to a fixed size (300 words). The dataset was split into two: 80% for training and 20% for testing.

3.3 Model and Training

i) **Model creation:** The creation of the data models is defined as a sequence of layers. This facilitates creating a model by simply adding layers one by one until we are satisfied with the network architecture. There are two main types of models in Keras: the Sequential model and the Functional API Model class. In this work, we use the functional API for modeling. Our base model is defined by a total of six layers, being: input layer, embedding layer, LSTM layer and three dense layers, the last being the model's output. Each layer receives as input the output of the previous layer. Figure 1 shows the RNN architecture used in this work, simulated in TensorBoard [24].

The input layer receives as a parameter the maximum size of the sequences. That is, each review present in the dataset is reduced to a fixed size in order to standardize the input. In our experiments, we defined this size to 300 words. For the embedding layer, we defined the maximum amount of words to keep in the vocabulary (20,000), the dimension of word embedding (128) and the size of the sequences defined in the first layer. Word embedding gives us a way to use a representation in which similar words have similar coding. The embedding dimension is defined according to the size of the data set. A higher dimensional

---

[1] https://www.imdb.com/.

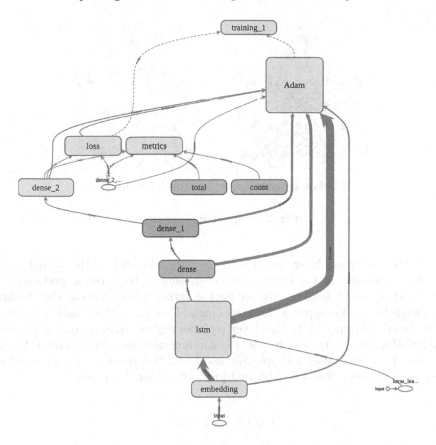

Fig. 1. RNN architecture presented in TensorBoard.

embedding can capture refined relationships between words but requires more data to learn.

In the LSTM layer, we established the dimensionality of the output space with 128 internal units. We have defined the fraction of the units to be discarded for the linear transformation of the inputs (dropout). The dropout value varies in the interval [0, 1], and the higher the rate, the fewer neurons are adjusted during net training. This causes the few remaining neurons to learn ways to suppress the absence of the others. This creates a system of redundancy where one neuron can respond to another. Figure 2 shows the dropout application on an RNN. The dropout value used in the experiments is 0.2. Also, we determine the fraction of the units to be eliminated for the linear transformation of the recurrent state (*recurrent_dropout*).

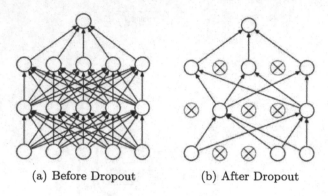

(a) Before Dropout   (b) After Dropout

Fig. 2. Dropout application

For the first dense layer, we defined the dimensionality of the output space with the same value as the LSTM layer, decreasing to 64 in the second and to 2 in the last. *Uniform* is the initializer for the kernel weight matrix. For the first two Dense layers, we apply a *Rectified Linear Unit* (ReLU) activation function of the layer's output, Eq. 1. This layer replaces any negative outputs with zero. The ReLU activation is used in order to introduce non-linearity into the network. The last dense layer uses a simple *Sigmoid* activation function, Eq. 2, to adjust the output between 0 and 1. The final product is a single output.

$$f(x) = max(0, x) \tag{1}$$

$$f(x) = \frac{1}{1 + e^{-x}} \tag{2}$$

ii) **Compilation of the model:** The Compilation of the model configures the learning process. It defines the loss function, the optimizer and a list of metrics. The Keras library has a complete set of all these predefined items and calls the back-end when appropriate. The loss function calculates the logarithmic loss between actual and predicted labels. In this work, since it is a binary classification problem, we use the *binary_crossentropy* function. *Adam* is the optimizer, a gradient descent algorithm, based on the adaptive estimation of first and second-order moments. The list of metrics is used to judge the performance of the model. In our experiments, we use *accuracy* to calculate how often forecasts are equal to labels. It is defined by the sum of True Positive (TP) and True Negative (TN) samples correctly classified, divided by the Total of Samples (TS) of the evaluated series, Eq. 3.

$$Accuracy = \frac{TP + TN}{TS} \tag{3}$$

iii) **RNN training:** The training of the model is done by calling the *fit()* function, dividing the data into batches (number of instances for each gradient update), and repeatedly iterating throughout the data set for a certain number of epochs (5 was used). The returned object *"history"* keeps a record of loss values and metrics during training. We insert the training data (expressions and their labels) and the validation data so that the model can evaluate the metrics defined at the end of each season. Other parameters used are: *shuffle*, which shuffles the training data before each epoch; *verbose*, developer feedback (0 = silent, 1 = progress bar, 2 = detailed; *callbacks*, callback list, *tensorboard_callback* is used to log events in TensorBoard, a visualization tool provided with Tensorflow.

iv) **Evaluating the model:** The model can be evaluated in the test data through the *evaluate()* function. This function will generate a prediction for each input and output and collect scores, calculate the average over the loss value, and any other metric configured. In our model we define the *"accuracy"* metric. The returned object *"scores"* keeps the record of accuracy and loss that our model obtained.

The execution environment is composed of a device with an Intel Core i7-9750 processor with six cores (12 threads) of 2.60 GHz frequency. This equipment has 16 GB DDR4 RAM, NVIDIA GeForce GTX RTX 2060 GPU with 6GB of GDDR6 memory and 1920 CUDA cores, used the Linux operating system Ubuntu 18.04.2 LTS with kernel version 4.15.0-96-generic. The NVIDIA CUDA Compiler version used was 10.0.130.

4 Results

In this section, we present the results. First, we analyze the accuracy obtained with different batch sizes and whether this variation negatively affects the model accuracy. Next, we evaluate the training performance gain with varying batch sizes and the speedup between architectures.

4.1 Accuracy of the Sentiment Analysis Model

The precision (y-axis) achieved with the training data set (40,000 records), with different batch sizes, in CPU and GPU runs is shown in Fig. 3. It is noticed that as the number of instances for each gradient update increases, the accuracy of the model is reduced; that is, less the RNN weights are updated and consequently, the loss rate increases.

The precision (y-axis) obtained from the validation dataset with $10,000$ records is shown in Fig. 4, also varying the *batch_size* and running on CPU and GPU. The validation accuracy informs the percentage that our model has right in the prediction concerning the label. These tests prove that the implementation accuracy remains stable, varying between 87–89%.

4.2 Performance Improvements

The training times according to the defined *batch_size* are shown in Fig. 5. It can be seen that as the batch size increases, the runtime is reduced considerably

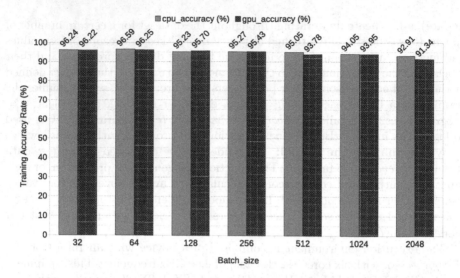

Fig. 3. Accuracy obtained from CPU and GPU executions from training data.

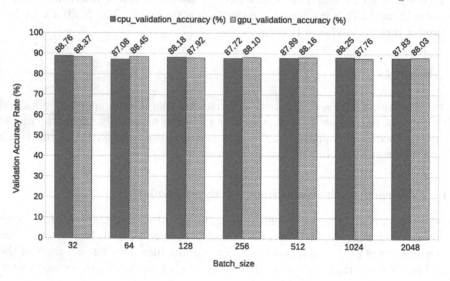

Fig. 4. Accuracy obtained from CPU and GPU executions from validation data.

on both architectures. CPU runs showed a gain of 3.17 times. This reduces the execution time from 1066.02 s to 336.64 s. In GPU executions, the gain reached 12.15 times, jumping from 2098.66 s to 172.73 s. This represents a gain of 91.8%. The gain is very expressive if compared to CPU. However, on executions with smaller *batch_size*, it is possible to notice that the execution time on the GPU increases substantially compared to the CPU time. This is due to the GPU taking more time for data transfer than for training itself. When the number of instances increases, it is possible to use more of the GPU's capacity.

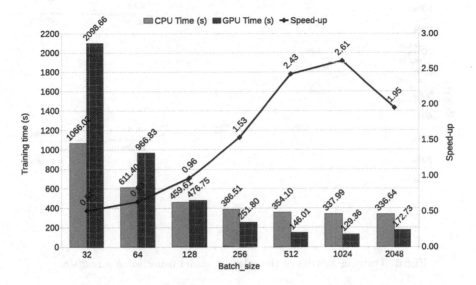

Fig. 5. Time and speed-up of RNN training on CPU and GPU architectures.

The speed-up of the application is also demonstrated in Fig. 5, presenting its best case in training using *batch_size* = 1024. This represents a gain of 2.61 times over the CPU, reducing the CPU runtime from 337.99 s to 129.36 s on the GPU. This is due to the GPU devoting more resources to training instead of prioritizing data transfer. However, when the computational resources limit is reached, it also causes loss of performance, as can be seen by increasing the *batch_size* to 2048. This occurs due to having more processes running and dividing the computational resources.

4.3   Proposal Validation

The trained model that presented the lowest loss rate and the highest accuracy rate, both values obtained from the validation dataset, was selected to validate the proposal. This resulted in the GPU trained model with *batch_size* = 2048. Figure 6 shows the metrics for each training epoch of the selected model, with an accuracy of 88.03% and a loss rate of 28.98%.

RNN loads the model, and then the inputs are submitted for testing. The new entries are random reviews obtained from the official IMDb page about the film *Wonder Woman (2017)*. Ten reviews were chosen and inserted as input for RNN.

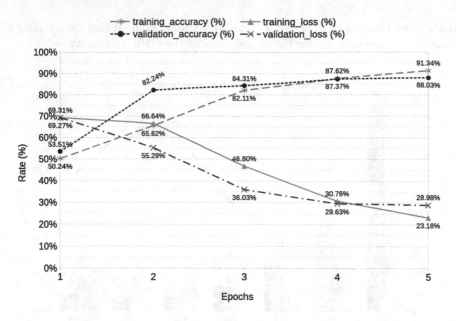

Fig. 6. Training metrics of the selected model using *batch_size* 2048.

The results obtained are shown in Table 1. The first column indicates the selected review. The second column is the number of stars indicated by the author of the review, considering as a negative opinion the evaluations between 1 and 5, and positive opinion the evaluations between 6 and 10. The last column indicates the prediction made by our model. This prediction is a probability

Table 1. Results of proposal validation in the movie Wonder Woman (2017). Considering as a negative opinion the evaluations between 1 and 5, and positive opinion the evaluations between 6 and 10. Prediction: negative (neg), positive (pos).

Review	Evaluation	RNN prediction
1	1/10	99.22% neg
2	5/10	99.49% neg
3	7/10	99.83% pos
4	9/10	99.74% pos
5	1/10	99.54% neg
6	10/10	99.71% pos
7	9/10	99.93% pos
8	5/10	99.01% neg
9	8/10	99.50% pos
10	3/10	99.37% neg

distribution. Our model calculates the probability of the content being a positive or negative opinion and then signals to the one with the highest rate. Analyzing the table shows that the RNN model tested was assertive in all cases submitted.

5 Conclusion and Future Works

This work addressed the use of recurrent artificial neural networks Long Short-Term Memory to classify feelings into sentences. Different configurations were used to analyze the performance of the application running on Multicore and GPU architectures. Regarding the accuracy rate, for CPU architecture, the best rate is registered for *batch_size* 32. For GPU architecture, the best rate is obtained for *batch_size* 64. The proposal presented good performance in terms of RNN accuracy.

Runtime is reduced considerably on both architectures by increasing the *batch_size*. Among the most significant gains, CPU runtime gained 3.17 times. The GPU runtime was reduced by 12.15 times. Comparing the architectures, the GPU runtime showed a reduction of up to 61%, which represents a speed-up of 2.61 times over CPU time. These results indicate that GPU use reduces RNN training time, presenting good yields for larger batch sizes.

We selected the model with less loss and greater precision to validate the proposal and ensure that our model could correctly predict the feeling of reviews, even increasing the batch size. We used the IMDb Review Dataset in training, so to validate, we randomly captured 10 reviews of the film Wonder Woman released in 2017 directly from the official IMDb page. The model correctly predicted all new entries.

As future works, a first initiative could be the use of pre-trained word embeddings. In addition, it is possible to study the influence of other hyperparameters, such as Dropout Rate and Activation Function. It is also possible to evaluate more extensive databases and in other languages. Another analysis that can be done is to add other classification classes besides positive and negative, such as very positive, very negative, and neutral. As well as evaluating other data sources like Twitter. Another approach to be studied is a better separation of the dataset in training, validation, and testing.

Acknowledgment. This work has been partially supported by Petrobras (2016/00133-9, 2018/00263-5) and Green Cloud project (2016/2551-0000 488-9), from FAPERGS and CNPq Brazil, program PRONEX 12/2014 and MCTIC/CNPq - Universal 28/2018 under grants 436339/2018-8. This study was financed in part by the Coordenação de Aperfeiçoamento de Pessoal de Nível Superior - Brasil (CAPES) - Finance Code 001.

References

1. Abadi, M., et al.: Tensorflow: large-scale machine learning on heterogeneous distributed systems. arXiv preprint arXiv:1603.04467 (2016)
2. Celesti, A., Galletta, A., Celesti, F., Fazio, M., Villari, M.: Using machine learning to study flu vaccines opinions of twitter users. In: 2019 IEEE Symposium on Computers and Communications (ISCC), pp. 1103–1106. IEEE (2019)
3. Ch'ng, E., Chen, Z., See, S.: Real-time GPU-accelerated social media sentiment processing and visualization. In: 2017 IEEE/ACM 21st International Symposium on Distributed Simulation and Real Time Applications (DS-RT), pp. 1–4. IEEE (2017)
4. Gandhi, U.D., Kumar, P.M., Babu, G.C., Karthick, G.: Sentiment analysis on twitter data by using convolutional neural network (CNN) and long short term memory (LSTM). Wirel. Pers. Commun. 1–10 (2021)
5. Haque, M.R., Lima, S.A., Mishu, S.Z.: Performance analysis of different neural networks for sentiment analysis on IMDb movie reviews. In: 2019 3rd International Conference on Electrical, Computer & Telecommunication Engineering (ICECTE), pp. 161–164. IEEE (2019)
6. Hassan, A., Mahmood, A.: Deep learning approach for sentiment analysis of short texts. In: 2017 3rd International Conference on Control, Automation and Robotics (ICCAR), pp. 705–710. IEEE (2017)
7. Hochreiter, S., Schmidhuber, J.: Long short-term memory. Neural Comput. 9(8), 1735–1780 (1997)
8. Jones, E., Oliphant, T., Peterson, P., et al.: SciPy: open source scientific tools for python, 2001 (2016)
9. Kalaivani, K., Uma, S., Kanimozhiselvi, C.: Comparison of deep learning approaches for sentiment classification. In: 2021 6th International Conference on Inventive Computation Technologies (ICICT), pp. 1043–1047. IEEE (2021)
10. Kolekar, S.S., Khanuja, H.: Sentiment analysis using deep learning on GPU. In: 2018 IEEE PuneCon, pp. 1–5 (2018). https://doi.org/10.1109/PUNECON.2018.8745401
11. Liu, B., et al.: Sentiment analysis and subjectivity. In: Handbook of Natural Language Processing, vol. 2, pp. 627–666 (2010)
12. Maas, A.L., Daly, R.E., Pham, P.T., Huang, D., Ng, A.Y., Potts, C.: Learning word vectors for sentiment analysis. In: Proceedings of the 49th Annual Meeting of the Association for Computational Linguistics: Human Language Technologies, vol. 1, pp. 142–150. Association for Computational Linguistics (2011)
13. Manalu, B.U., Efendi, S., et al.: Deep learning performance in sentiment analysis. In: 2020 4rd International Conference on Electrical, Telecommunication and Computer Engineering (ELTICOM), pp. 97–102. IEEE (2020)
14. Miedema, F.: Sentiment analysis with long short-term memory networks. Vrije Universiteit Amsterdam, vol. 1 (2018)
15. Moolayil, J.: An introduction to deep learning and keras. In: Moolayil, J. (ed.) Learn Keras for Deep Neural Networks, pp. 1–16. Apress, Berkeley, CA (2019). https://doi.org/10.1007/978-1-4842-4240-7_1
16. Nickolls, J., Buck, I., Garland, M., Skadron, K.: Scalable parallel programming with CUDA. Queue 6(2), 40–53 (2008)
17. Pan, Q., Li, H., Chen, D., Sun, K.: Sentiment analysis of medical comments based on character vector convolutional neural networks. In: 2018 IEEE Symposium on Computers and Communications (ISCC), pp. 1–4. IEEE (2018)

18. Pang, B., Lee, L.: Opinion mining and sentiment analysis. Found. Trends® Inf. Retr. **2**(1–2), 1–135 (2008)
19. Pedregosa, F., et al.: Scikit-learn: machine learning in python. J. Mach. Learn. Res. **12**, 2825–2830 (2011)
20. Qaisar, S.M.: Sentiment analysis of IMDB movie reviews using long short-term memory. In: 2020 2nd International Conference on Computer and Information Sciences (ICCIS), pp. 1–4. IEEE (2020)
21. Rehman, A.U., Malik, A.K., Raza, B., Ali, W.: A hybrid CNN-LSTM model for improving accuracy of movie reviews sentiment analysis. Multimed. Tools Appl. **78**(18), 26597–26613 (2019)
22. Sauter, V.L.: Decision Support Systems for Business Intelligence. Wiley, Hoboken (2014)
23. Subramanian, R.R., Akshith, N., Murthy, G.N., Vikas, M., Amara, S., Balaji, K.: A survey on sentiment analysis. In: 2021 11th International Conference on Cloud Computing, Data Science & Engineering (Confluence), pp. 70–75. IEEE (2021)
24. Tensorboard: Tensorboard — tensorflow (2021). https://www.tensorflow.org/tensorboard
25. Van Rossum, G., Drake, F.L.: The Python Language Reference Manual. Network Theory Ltd. (2011)
26. Vielma, C., Verma, A., Bein, D.: Single and multibranch CNN-bidirectional LSTM for IMDb sentiment analysis. In: Latifi, S. (ed.) 17th International Conference on Information Technology–New Generations (ITNG 2020). AISC, vol. 1134, pp. 401–406. Springer, Cham (2020). https://doi.org/10.1007/978-3-030-43020-7_53
27. Widayat, W., Adji, T.B., et al.: The effect of embedding dimension reduction on increasing LSTM performance for sentiment analysis. In: 2018 International Seminar on Research of Information Technology and Intelligent Systems (ISRITI), pp. 287–292. IEEE (2018)
28. Yadav, A., Vishwakarma, D.K.: Sentiment analysis using deep learning architectures: a review. Artif. Intell. Rev. **53**(6), 4335–4385 (2019). https://doi.org/10.1007/s10462-019-09794-5
29. Yenter, A., Verma, A.: Deep CNN-LSTM with combined kernels from multiple branches for IMDB review sentiment analysis. In: 2017 IEEE 8th Annual Ubiquitous Computing, Electronics and Mobile Communication Conference (UEMCON), pp. 540–546. IEEE (2017)

A Methodology for Evaluating the Energy Efficiency of Post-Moore Architectures

Pablo Josue Rojas Yepes[1](✉)(iD), Carlos Jaime Barrios Hernandez[1](✉)(iD), and Luiz Angelo Steffenel[2](✉)(iD)

[1] Universidad Industrial de Santander, Cl. 9 # Cra 27, Bucaramanga, Colombia
pablo2198162@correo.uis.edu.co, cbarrios@uis.edu.co
[2] Université de Reims Champagne Ardenne, LICIIS – LRC CEA DIGIT Laboratory, Reims, France
angelo.steffenel@univ-reims.fr

Abstract. The improvement of computational systems has been based on Moore's law and Dennard's scale, but for more than a decade it has started to fall to a standstill. To maintain the improvement new technologies are proposed, this has established a Post-Moore era. Currently there are different methodologies to evaluate emerging devices and technologies, but the results of these methodologies end up being particular solutions. This paper presents a methodology that can evaluate Post-Moore devices or technologies in an agile way, characterizing an application, choosing a device that meets its needs, selecting tests and parameters that are executed to meet the objectives set by the methodology. The results show how to evaluate the energy efficiency of these new technologies, but the scope of the methodology can cover other needs.

Keywords: Evaluation methodology · Embedded system · Benchmark · Low-cost computing · Edge computing · Many-core · Heterogeneous computing

1 Introduction

Measuring the performance of computer systems was an art in its beginnings, with the passage of time certain agreements were reached. Among the approaches that were adopted to measure the performance of a computational architecture are the time it took to complete a specific task or the number of operations performed, one of the main metrics that emerged due to this was FLOPS. One of the main tools to perform these measurements was HPL [1]. Due to its constant use it became the basis of measurement of the main HPC machines [2] until it became a standard for HPC hardware.

At the same time, Moore's law was established as the main driver of computational growth, but its progress started to stagnate in the last decade [3, 4]. To overcome this barrier, different approaches were presented to address the problem, which triggered a "Cambrian explosion" [5] of hardware and dubbed the current era as the Post-Moore era [6]. One of the most dominant approaches states that applications determine the

© Springer Nature Switzerland AG 2022
I. Gitler et al. (Eds.): CARLA 2021, CCIS 1540, pp. 48–60, 2022.
https://doi.org/10.1007/978-3-031-04209-6_4

right hardware to run them [6]. Based on this proposition, the premise is formulated: Applications Choose Devices Carefully.

This paper assumes the proposed premise, presents a methodology to evaluate the traditionally manufactured Post-Moore architectures. This methodology is called **"Applications Choose Devices Carefully"** or **ACDC** for short. This methodology analyzes applications or devices, characterizes and proposes a workflow to evaluate them. In the case study, embedded and low-cost devices are selected.

The second section presents some of the state of the art of evaluation methodologies, the third section shows the functioning scheme of the ACDC methodology and describes each of the steps of the scheme, the fourth section presents a use case of the ACDC methodology and finally the conclusions of the work are presented.

2 State of the Art

After reviewing the extensive state of the art, three contributions stand out in the last three years in reference to the evaluation of Post-Moore architectures.

The first contribution [7] studies the applicability of FPGAs to accelerate the core of the Spectral Element Method (SEM) in many computational fluid dynamics (CFD) applications. This is evaluated using Stratix 10 GX series FPGAs versus systems such as ARM ThunderX2, NVIDIA Tesla/Pascal/Volta/Ampere series boards and general purpose many-core CPUs. The methodology consists of configuring the SEM on the FPGA and using languages such as OpenCL [8, 9] or OpenACC [10] to configure the SEM on the GPUs and CPUs, the development of the test methodology is implicit in the development of the work.

The second contribution [11] proposes a comprehensive open source methodology for evaluating emerging technologies. To demonstrate its effectiveness, the methodology is used to perform end-to-end simulation and analysis of heterogeneous architectures using CNFETs, TFETs and NCFETs, along with multiple hardware designs. The methodology consists of four main levels of modeling: device models, logic gates, logic and memory blocks, and architecture. This methodology evaluates CNFET, TFET and NCFET devices using hardware designs of varying complexity and provides the means to assess the high-level impact of emerging technologies.

Finally, the third contribution [12] presents a testbed [13–16] covering networking, identity management, resource scheduling and tools along with techniques they have developed to manage these Post-Moore devices. More than a methodology, it presents several methods to evaluate different Post-Moore architectures with different tests. This generates particular evaluation methodologies for different devices. With this brief presentation, the ACDC methodology will be outlined.

3 ACDC Methodology Outline

As discussed above, one of the main focusses of the Post-Moore era is that the applications determine the hardware on which they will be deployed. Furthermore, with the "Cambrian explosion" [5], it is possible to adopt a methodology to evaluate the applications and the possible hardware that can execute them.

Another approach of the Post-Moore era is that the hardware integrates multiple specific purpose chips, tailored to the needs of the application [6]. It should be noted that the hardware to be used for the development of the work is based on traditional manufacturing. Hardware for neuromorphic computing, quantum computing [17] or 3D-Chips will not be taken into account for this methodology. Also note that the methodology will not use FLOPS as a metric, even though it is the most reliable metric to measure performance, the methodology intends to evaluate different types of operations, not only floating operations. The evaluation will take into account the number of operations completed in a defined time, their energy consumption, among others.

Figure 1 is a outline of how the implementation of the ACDC methodology would be carried out. It consists of nine sequential steps but the penultimate step presents a loop that may point to step three or four depending on the situation.

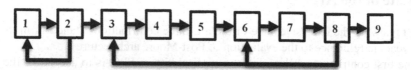

Fig. 1. ACDC methodology outline

The steps of the ACDC methodology are the following:

Step 1. Selection of the application and definition of its primary needs.
Step 2. Post-Moore device selection.
Step 3. Test settings optimization.
Step 4. Parameterization of the test.
Step 5. Preparation of miscellaneous needs.
Step 6. Running the test and data capture.
Step 7. Data labeling and storage.
Step 8. Repeat the test, select a new test or end the test.
Step 9. Data analysis.

3.1   Description of the ACDC Methodology

3.1.1   Selection of the Application and Definition of its Primary Needs

In this step two cases can be presented, in the first case the application is to be evaluated on a Post-Moore architecture of traditional manufacturing, in the second case a device is to be evaluated and its capabilities are to be known. Therefore, step one and two can be interchanged.

The backbone of the methodology is: applications choose the most suitable devices to deploy them, getting the best performance and efficiency. The application can be a code, benchmark, methodology, testbed, etc. As a **result** of this step, a documentation is generated that lists the characteristics and description of the application, giving an understanding of the functional needs. These are some of the general characteristics:

- Multi-platform or cross-compiled.
- Define the hardware required by the application (CPU, GPU, NPU, FPGA, etc.).
- Identification of the dependencies.
- Types of data the application works with.
- Classification of instructions (RISC or CISC).

3.1.2 Post-Moore Device Selection

In the previous section the application was chosen. To satisfy these needs, it is necessary that the devices contain the necessary hardware, the application and software needs are compiled for the architecture and the Operating System (OS) is optimized, this simplifies the selection process. This reduces implementation time, improves the performance and efficiency of the application.

As a **result**, a documentation with the description, performance and theoretical efficiency of the device is presented. In addition, the execution of the application on the device is guaranteed.

3.1.3 Test Settings Optimization

In this step there are two possibilities to perform the evaluation:

- **Perform synthetic testing**: If a set of synthetic tests is chosen, the bottlenecks are simulated. The **metrics** are mainly the number of iterations of the test during a given time or the amount of time it takes to perform a given number of operations.
- **Running the application**: the actual behavior of the application on the device is verified, profiling is performed to determine the bottlenecks. In this case, the **metrics** focus on execution time.

The test configuration can be performed in several ways, multiple tests can be organized with different resource allocations, the configuration that generates the highest performance can be chosen, or depending on what is sought in the evaluation, parameters are defined in the application configuration. As a **result**, preliminary tests are performed to get an idea of the behavior of the test to be performed on the chosen devices and a list of parameters is generated.

3.1.4 Parameterization of the Test

With the generated parameter list the tests are adjusted to the evaluation needs, this fine-tunes the tests to meet the objectives of the evaluation, study or research. As a **result**, it is up to the tester to choose the settings and parameters that are important for testing on the device.

3.1.5 Preparation of Miscellaneous Needs

Miscellaneous needs arise from the moment the metrics are set. In many cases, metrics require cross-referencing different data. This data is obtained from internal and external monitors that are run before, during and after testing. As a result, a list of miscellaneous data capture miscellaneous is created.

3.1.6 Running the Test and Data Capture

Before running the test, a checklist should be run to simplify and mechanize the work:

1. Configure the test.
2. Run external monitors.
3. Run internal monitors.
4. Run the test.

It is not advisable to run the tests after powering up the device as the OS may be running processes in the background. Monitors should be tracking the device before the test is run, this way a baseline behavior of the device can be established when it is not in use.

3.1.7 Data Labeling and Storage

The captured data must be processed to facilitate its analysis. It is necessary to generate a list of tags, to segment the data and facilitate its analysis, in the process of tagging ideas may arise that add more value to the results. It is recommended that the data be stored in the cloud or in secure and reliable media, loss of data can delay the research or cancel it. Data can be stored in matrices or dictionaries for easy management. As a **result**, a mechanism for labeling the data is generated, facilitating its management.

3.1.8 Repeat the Test, Select a New Test or End of the Test

This step is a trifurcation in which one must choose between the following paths:

- **Repeat the Test** occurs when the amount of data is insufficient to identify a pattern of behavior. Tests can be repeated as many times as necessary; the number of repetitions is at the discretion of the tester. **Return to step six.**
- **Select a New Test** occurs when it is deemed that it is no longer necessary to repeat a test. The test is repeated with new configurations or a new test is chosen. In this way it is possible to mechanize the process and speed up the acquisition of test data. **Return to step three.**
- **End of the Tests** occurs when it is considered that there is an acceptable amount of data and all tests have been performed. **Go to data analysis**, generating conclusions that point to the objectives set for the evaluation.

3.1.9 Data Analysis

The data collected are processed to generate results to meet the objectives of the evaluation or research.

The next section proposes the implementation of the ACDC methodology.

3.2 Case Study: Implementation of the ACDC Methodology

3.2.1 Step 1 and Step 2

To simplify the use case, a testbed application is proposed [19], the application is compiled for ×86 and ARM architectures, it is written to use the maximum number of available resources, it uses only CPU, its installation can be done through package managers and handles different types of data.

The selected tests are:

- **Pthread**: The test generates multiple pthreads (POSIX threads) at runtime.
- **Malloc**: During the test execution allocate, reallocate and free memory with malloc, calloc, realloc and free calls dynamically.
- **Cfloat**: The computation operations it performs are floating number ones.

To evaluate the methodology, the following objectives are established:

- Measure the performance of the selected devices.
- Measure the energy efficiency of the devices.

In this case, an Nvidia Jetson Nano [18] and a desktop PC are selected. These devices are considered Post-Moore because they have many cores and heterogeneous. Both have an Nvidia GPU but for the use case it is not necessary and is not considered.

In the Table 1 the **Device** column presents the name of each device, the Jetson Nano is labeled Nano and the desktop PC is named PC. The **CPU** column describes the CPU of each device, the **GPU** column explains the GPU of each device, the GPU of the PC is a GTX 1050ti with 4 GB of independent memory, while the Nano shares its memory between the CPU and GPU. The **RAM** column details the memory in both devices.

Table 1. Devices selected

Device	CPU	GPU	RAM
Nano	ARM Cortex-A57 Quad-Core @~1.5 GHz	Nvidia Maxwell 128 CUDA-Cores ~921 MHz	4 GB LPDDR4 @1600 MHz
PC	AMD Ryzen 5 3600 Hexa-Core @3.6–4.2 GHz	Nvidia Pascal 768 CUDA-Cores 1350–1800 MHz	16 GB DDR4 @3200 MHz

3.2.2 Step 3

For this case, the option of synthetic tests is taken, so that focused tests can be performed. The following synthetic tests are proposed:

- **Pthread:** start N workers that iteratively creates and terminates multiple pthreads (the default is 1024 pthreads per worker). In each iteration, each newly created pthread waits until the worker has created all the pthreads and then they all terminate together.
- **Malloc:** start N workers continuously calling malloc, calloc, realloc and free. By default, up to 65536 allocations can be active at any point. Allocation, reallocation and freeing are chosen at random; 50% of the time memory is allocation (via malloc, calloc or realloc) and 50% of the time allocations are free'd. Allocation sizes are default size being 64K. The worker is restarted if it is killed by the out of mememory (OOM) killer.
- **Cfloat:** 1000 iterations of a mix of floating point complex operations

Test results are presented as Operations or **Ops**. One facility offered by the testbed is that they can be run for a given amount of time. Preliminary tests show that the number of Ops per second or **Ops/s** remains the same independent of the time allotted. As a result of this behavior, Ops/s is defined as a metric and the number of cores is considered as a parameter to measure the scalability of the application. Previous tests also show that Pthreads and Malloc consume all available resources on the device. The Cfloat test allows the number of cores to be varied. This covers one of the objectives of the evaluation, to measure the performance of the chosen devices.

3.2.3   Step 4
See Table 2.

Table 2. Test parameters.

Tests	Parameters
Pthread	4 jobs and 1024 threads per job
Malloc	4 jobs, 64K in size and 65536 allocations
Cfloat	1, 2, 3 and 4 jobs

Setting more resource-intensive parameters for Pthread and Malloc generates negative impacts. Cfloat only uses the resources allocated to it. The Ops/s are constant, so it is not necessary to mention the time allocated to the tests.

3.2.4   Step 5
The second objective of the evaluation is to determine the energy efficiency of the devices. To meet this objective, energy efficiency is defined as the amount of energy consumed by the operations performed during a given time or Ops/s.

The consumption (C) of the test is determined by the difference between the consumption during the test (Cp) and the base consumption (Cb) and is identified as W/s.

$$C = Cp - Cb = W/s \tag{1}$$

The energy efficiency for the evaluation is determined by the number of operations over consumption or Ops/W.

$$\frac{Ops/s}{W/s} = Ops/W \tag{2}$$

The energy consumed is determined by a consumption monitor [20], this monitor captures the data during the time the test is performed. This is how the two-evaluation metrics are defined, Ops/s and Ops/W.

3.2.5 Step 6 and Step 7

To run the tests, the consumption monitoring should be started before the tests, it is recommended that the device has been on for some time to avoid consumption peaks. The test is executed with the parameters assigned in step 4, once the test is completed the data obtained must be stored.

The data collected during step 6 are organized as shown in Table 3.

Table 3. Data labeling and storage

Device	Test	Core	Ops	Ops/s	W/s	Ops/W
Nano	Pthread	4	1159500	19325	5,8	349286
Nano	Malloc	4	241772479	4029541	5,2	71109553
Nano	Cfloat	1	268145	4469	1,1	235215
Nano	Cfloat	2	535617	8927	2,1	252650
Nano	Cfloat	3	796733	13279	3,1	257011
Nano	Cfloat	4	793350	13223	3,8	206602
PC	Pthread	4	6987682	116461	41,2	170089
PC	Malloc	4	1595115864	26585264	39,2	40739188
PC	Cfloat	1	296587	4943	14,8	19995
PC	Cfloat	2	590779	9846	19,8	29787
PC	Cfloat	3	884458	14741	24,9	35664
PC	Cfloat	4	1171197	19520	29,0	40340

The **Device** column presents two labels, Nano for the Jetson Nano device and PC for the desktop PC. The **Test** column shows the different tests performed on the devices. The **Core** column lists the number of cores or jobs used in the test. The **OPS** column stores the number of operations performed during the test execution. The **OPS/s** column represents the number of operations performed per second. The **W/s** column shows the average power consumption per second during the test run. Finally, the **OPS/W** column is the relation between OPS/s and W/s. The data obtained is stored in a spreadsheet. It should be clarified that the values shown by Table 3 are averages to save space.

3.2.6 Step 8

The cfloat test is the only one to which resources can be allocated, it is run a total of five times per core to have a good base. The pthreads and malloc tests use all available resources, run fifteen iterations per test to have a base similar to cfloat.

Table 3 shows the averaged results of all tests performed with its respective labels. The standard deviation in the pthread test is 0.752% for the Nano and 0.253% for the PC. For the malloc test it is 0.246% for the Nano and 0.202% for the PC. Finally, the standard deviation in the test cfloat has four results for each device, for the Nano it is 0.032% with one core, 0.015% for two cores, 0.020% for three cores and 0.241% for four cores. For the PC case they are 0.339% with one core, 0.140% for two cores, 0.006% for three cores and 0.124% for four cores. A total of approximately 80 preliminary and final tests were realized.

3.2.7 Step 9 Data Analysis

When analyzing the data, the objectives that were set for the development of the methodology, in this case the following objectives should be remembered: measure the performance of the selected devices and measure the energy efficiency of the devices.

With the data collected in Table 3, graphs are generated to give a better understanding of the conclusions of the work. The graphs are presented pointing to two topics: the performance measurement of the devices is carried out by a comparison between the Ops/s of the Nano and the PC in the different tests, and the measurement of energy efficiency is shown by means of a graph that compares the Ops/W of the two devices. Figure 2 show the performance of the devices in the Pthread.

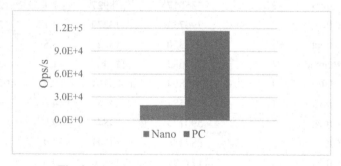

Fig. 2. Devices performance in the Pthread test

The results in Fig. 2 show a performance of about six times higher for the PC. It should be mentioned that the ARM CPU has 4 cores, maximum frequency of 1.5 Ghz, 16 nm lithography and manages to execute 4838 Ops/s while the $\times 86$ CPU has 6 cores, maximum frequency of 4.2 Ghz, 7 nm lithography and manages to execute 19410 Ops/s. It can be assumed that an ARM CPU with the same characteristics as an $\times 86$ would have similar performance. Figure 3 displays the performance in malloc test.

The malloc test (Fig. 3) exercises the memory of the devices, the PC achieves almost 6.6 times the performance of the Nano. As in the previous case, the memory resources

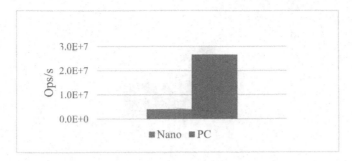

Fig. 3. Devices performance in the Malloc test

on the Nano are much lower, causing this result. It is emphasized that if the Nano had similar capabilities to the PC the results would be very similar. Figure 4 illustrates the performance of the devices in the cfloat test.

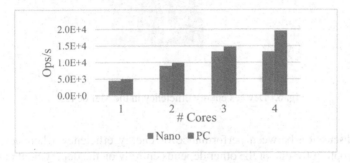

Fig. 4. Devices performance in the Cfloat test

The results in Fig. 4 show the performance of the CPUs when working with float operations. The difference between the ARM and ×86 CPU is 9.6% on cores 1, 2 and 3. The core 4 of the ARM CPU suffers a bigger difference. The drop in core 4 is due to the resource competition between the test and the Operating System (OS) on the Nano.

It is evident that the computational capacity of ARM CPUs are similar to ×86 CPUs even though they have inferior characteristics. It is possible that the Nano OS does not have a good management in the pthreads and malloc tests generating the exposed results, it should also be taken into account that the ARM CPUs have a reduced set of operations and this negatively impacts the results of the tests. With the exposed in the three figures (Figs. 2, 3 and 4) the objective of measuring the performance of the devices is covered. Figure 5 presents the energy efficiency of the devices.

In terms of energy efficiency, the behavior changes, the ARM CPU demonstrates twice the efficiency of the ×86 CPU. This is because the Cortex A57 is focused on giving the best performance for the lowest power consumption. Figure 6 illustrates the energy efficiency of the memory of the devices.

In the malloc test, the efficiency of the Nano is 1.7 times that of the PC, but the performance of the PC is 6 times higher. The same happens in the pthreads test. This

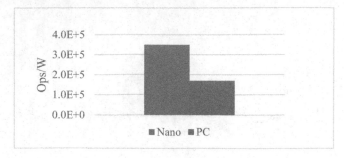

Fig. 5. Devices energy efficiency in the Pthread test

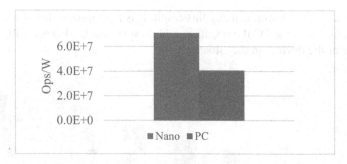

Fig. 6. Devices energy efficiency in the Malloc test

opens the discussion between performance or energy efficiency when deploying an application, opting for one or the other depends entirely on the deployment context. For this reason, a decision is not made in this paper as it is not the objective of this work. Figure 7 presents the energy efficiency of the cfloat test.

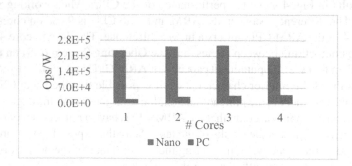

Fig. 7. Devices energy efficiency in the Cfloat test

The difference in energy efficiency of floating point computing of ARM CPUs is abysmal, approximately 11 times higher than that of ×86 CPUs. This tips the balance in favor of embedded devices in the efficiency area. Reinforcing the point made in Fig. 4,

ARM CPUs and embedded devices would be a good choice for implementing applications that have a strong computational component and, if budget or power consumption is a constraint, makes them excellent candidates. But in general, the PC best implements the application. Still the main objective of this paper is not to decide which is better but to demonstrate the benefits of the ACDC methodology.

4 Conclusions

The case study presented shows how the methodology can be adapted to different ways of evaluation, different devices, different metrics, different measurement tools. This facilitates its implementation in other works and different approaches.

As iterations are performed in the ACDC methodology, configurations and parameters are progressively refined to obtain the results. In the end, the data generated will be the best possible and during the process, the performance of the application and how its deployment impacts on the architecture or vice versa will be understood..

The ACDC methodology aims to mechanize the steps to follow to evaluate a Post-Moore architecture, if the ACDC methodology is compared with others, it is much easier to implement different measurement mechanisms. Each step of the methodology generates results that contribute to improve the evaluation results.

The documentation generated by the ADCD methodology can be published as an aid to future work, these documents can be used for best practices, streamlining the implementation of applications on Post-Moore architectures, justification bases for the development of applications on Post-Moore architectures, among others.

Further Works. The work focused only on CPU, in future studies it's intended to extend the synthetic testbed to other types of hardware such as GPU or FPGA. The methodology was tested on single devices, but it's interesting to see its implementation on agglomerated devices. If the catalog of tested embedded devices is increased, implementation guidelines can be developed that simplify the deployment of the application on Post-Moore devices.

References

1. Dongarra, J., Luszczek, P.: LINPACK Benchmark. Encyclopedia of Parallel Computing (2011)
2. Strohmaier, E., Dongarra, J., Simon, H., Meuer, M.: Top 500 the List. Prometeus GmbH. http://www.netlib.org/utk/people/JackDongarra/faq-linpack.html. Accessed 20 May 2021
3. Waldrop, M.M.: The chips are down for Moore's law. Nature **530**, 144–147 (2016)
4. Theis, T.N., Wong, H.-S.P.: The end of Moore's law: a new beginning for information technology. Comput. Sci. Eng. **19**(2), 41–50 (2017)
5. Matsuoka, S.: Cambrian explosion of computing and big data in the post-Moore era. In: Proceedings of the 27th International Symposium on High-Performance Parallel and Distributed Computing (HPDC 2018) (2018)
6. Matsuoka, S., et al.: From FLOPS to BYTES: disruptive change in high-performance computing towards the post-Moore era. In: CF 2016: Proceedings of the ACM International Conference on Computing Frontiers, pp. 274–281 (2016)

7. Karp, M., Podobas, A., Jansson, N., Kenter, T.: High-performance spectral element methods on field-programmable gate arrays: implementation, evaluation, and future projection. In: IEEE International Parallel and Distributed Processing Symposium (IPDPS), pp. 1077–1086 (2021)
8. Kuon, I., Tessier, R., Rose, J.: FPGA Architecture: Survey and Challenges. Now Publishers Inc. (2008)
9. Czajkowski, T.S., et al.: From OpenCL to high-performance hardware on FPGAs. In: 22nd International Conference on Field Programmable Logic, pp. 531–534 (2012)
10. Lee, S., Kim, J., Vetter, J.S.: OpenACC to FPGA: a framework for directive-based high-performance reconfigurable computing. In: 2016 IEEE International Parallel and Distributed Processing Symposium, pp. 544–554 (2016)
11. Vasudevan, D., Michelogiannakis, G., Donofrio, D., Shalf, J.: PARADISE - post-Moore architecture and accelerator design space exploration using device level simulation and experiments. In: IEEE International Symposium on Performance Analysis of Systems and Software (ISPASS), pp. 139–140 (2019)
12. Young, J.S., Riedy, J., Conte, T.M., Sarkar, V., Chatarasi, P., Srikanth, S.: Experimental insights from the rogues gallery. In: IEEE International Conference on Rebooting Computing (ICRC) (2019)
13. Young, J.S., et al.: A microbenchmark characterization of the emu chick. CoRR (2018)
14. Lloyd, S., Gokhale, M.: In-memory data rearrangement for irregular data-intensive computing. Computer **48**(8), 18–25 (2015)
15. Shantharam, M., Iwabuchi, K., Cicotti, P., Carrington, L., Gokhale, M., Pearce, R.: Performance evaluation of scale-free graph algorithms in low latency non-volatile memory. In: 2017 IEEE International Parallel and Distributed Processing Symposium Workshops (IPDPSW), pp. 1021–1028 (2017)
16. Bader, A.D., Berry, J., Kahan, S., Murphy, R., Riedy, E.J., Willcock, J.: Graph500 Benchmark 1 (search) Version 1.2. Graph500 Steering Committee, Tech 211
17. Vetter, J.S., DeBenedictis, E.P., Conte, T.M.: Architectures for the post-Moore era. IEEE Micro **37**(4), 6–8 (2017)
18. Nvidia: Nvidia Jetson Nano. https://www.nvidia.com/es-la/autonomous-machines/embedded-systems/jetson-nano/. Accessed 6 June 2021
19. King, C., Waterland, A.: Ubuntu Manuals, Stress-ng. Canonical Ltd, 22 February 2018. http://manpages.ubuntu.com/manpages/bionic/man1/stress-ng.1.html. Accessed 10 Feb 2021
20. VTA: Manual del Usuario VTA-84630. VTA. https://www.vta.co/wp-content/uploads/2019/09/VTA-84630_manual_bn.pdf. Accessed 15 Feb 2021

Understanding COVID-19 Epidemic in Costa Rica Through Network-Based Modeling

Mariela Abdalah[1]([✉]), Cristina Soto[1,3], Melissa Arce[1], Eduardo Cruz[2], Jöao Maciel[2], Camila Clozato[2], and Esteban Meneses[1,3]

[1] National High Technology Center, San José, Costa Rica
{mabdalah,csoto,emeneses}@cenat.ac.cr, melissa.arcemontero@ucr.ac.cr
[2] Federal Institute of Parana, Paranavaí, Brazil
{eduardo.cruz,joao.maciel,camila.lara}@ifpr.edu.br
[3] Costa Rica Institute of Technology, Cartago, Costa Rica

Abstract. As a result of the critical health situation caused by COVID-19, governments and researchers have acknowledged the significance of epidemic models for understanding a transmissible disease and assessing public policies, in order to determine which ones are truly effective in mitigating its propagation. We apply a modified SEIR model to characterize the behavior of the COVID-19 epidemic in the context of Costa Rica, employing a contact network to simulate the social connections among the inhabitants. Then, we use this model to weigh up the impact of important sanitary restrictions by simulating different scenarios associated to vaccination, authorization for organizing social events, and reopening of the school system. Our validation tests show that the obtained model is precise. In the scenario evaluation, simulations estimate that a constant vaccination reduces the reported cases by 45% and deaths by 42% in the best case where the infection dies out. In contrast, opening the schools with the totality of students increases the number of reported cases by 46% and deaths by 39% in the worst case. Finally, our model predicts that allowing social events causes an increase of 24% in reported infections and 17% more deaths, specially if people gather with close contacts.

Keywords: COVID-19 · Epidemic modeling · Epidemic simulation

1 Introduction

In early March 2020, the first case of the coronavirus disease COVID-19 in Costa Rica was confirmed by the national authorities, situating the country in an alert state to prevent a possible health crisis without precedent. Since the beginning, the government's main actions against the pandemic have been based on non-pharmaceutical interventions (NPI) such as school system and non-essential services closure, social distancing, and the ban of public gatherings. Recently, these containment strategies have been implemented altogether with the vaccination process. Although the adopted measures have been proved to

© Springer Nature Switzerland AG 2022
I. Gitler et al. (Eds.): CARLA 2021, CCIS 1540, pp. 61–75, 2022.
https://doi.org/10.1007/978-3-031-04209-6_5

be successful in slowing down the spread of the virus worldwide, what are their specific outcomes in the Costa Rican scenario? Has the government applied them well enough to prevent the increase of infected cases and lost lives?

Epidemic modeling and simulation are fundamental tools in the process of designing and evaluating interventions for disease outbreaks. Throughout history, scientists have sought to develop high-accuracy but practical models to support public health authorities in an effort to manage global crises such as the COVID-19 pandemic, as well as other prevalent epidemics. In the process of modeling and simulating these phenomena, researchers and health professionals accumulate knowledge and machinery that is helpful to study other epidemics in the future. Also, with a proficient model, the most relevant aspects of a communicable illness are encompassed and, therefore, its dynamics can be reproduced with good accuracy. The above allows researchers to analyze the possible consequences of reducing the infection propagation, which is a major goal in implementing NPIs and the application of a vaccine.

For the purpose of performing such evaluations with epidemic models, a calibration process is needed to assure that reality is genuinely being represented. Models require, at least, minimal information about the population to be calibrated. This implies a dependency between model parameters and the region, given that demographic, geographic, and social characteristics are unique for each population. Other parameters are specific of the disease too. The case of Costa Rica is not an exception, a novel model that comprises its population attributes is necessary to properly assess the measures against the COVID-19 pandemic.

In this paper, we build and calibrate an epidemic model of COVID-19 in the Costa Rican context, using a highly efficient simulation framework [14]. We employ a network-based approach with near 5 million nodes to replicate the inhabitants and their relations at school, work, family, and random degrees. For the epidemiological behavior, we use a modified SEIR (Susceptible-Exposed-Infected-Recovered) compartmental model to estimate the statistics of 81 cantonal geographic divisions. Next, we compare three containment strategies implemented by the government to several scenarios concerning the vaccination process, the schools reopening, and the occurrence of social events.

In brief, the contributions of this paper are:

- An accurate model of the dynamics of the COVID-19 epidemic in Costa Rica (Sects. 3, 4). We believe our methodology for creating this model can be applied to other countries in the region and to other epidemics as well.
- An analysis of the effect of public health policies regarding three important issues: vaccination, school reopening, and restriction of social events (Sects. 3, 4). Our research can help to evaluate which containment policies are more effective.

2 Background

2.1 Epidemic Model Simulation

Sometimes the most relevant characteristics of an epidemic can be captured with simple techniques such as regression. However, it is known that a great number of factors have an impact in the way an epidemic progresses, and these elementary approaches are often not good enough to estimate the possible outcomes for the complex structure of modern society, especially from the standpoint of public health authorities. In consequence, epidemic models have been developed and improved to acquire a better understanding of the spread patterns in epidemics from 1760 until today [9]. The evolution of infection models has been towards compartmental approaches, where the population is divided into several compartments, each composed by individuals with the same characteristics at any point in time. In the classical division (i.e. the SIR model), a subject can be classified into any of the S (Susceptible), I (Infected), or R (Recovered) compartments. Other variations include, for example, the E (Exposed) and the A (Asymptomatic) states [34]. The dynamics may be described through different methods such as differential equations, Monte Carlo methods, or Markov Chains, depending on whether the model is stochastic or deterministic. Although these two forms are complementary, by adding a random effect, the stochastic versions seem to achieve a better description of the natural propagation of a disease compared to their deterministic counterparts [12,41]. However, the costs of simulating stochastic models tend to be higher regarding time and computational resources, because a greater number of executions is necessary to evaluate the overall model output [4].

Despite the fact that classical compartmental models have been useful to represent the behavior of simple epidemics, their limitations are noticeable when more complex scenarios are studied. Assuming homogeneity of the population and immediate contact among individuals is one of the main drawbacks in SIR and similar models. To outweigh these constraints, the compartmental models have been extended to consider singular attributes like age, race, and occupation, as well as population aspects like mobility, births, deaths, and migration [12]. Another valuable extension is to employ weighted graphs for the representation of an individual's contact network and the relevance of each connection, allowing to reproduce a more realistic behavior of subjects and, therefore, the spread path of an illness [6,7,34]. Lately, the utilization of agents has become popular too. Agent-based models are computational approaches of individual behavior, where autonomous agents undergo a ruled decision-making process to perform a certain action that impacts the state of the general system. In the context of epidemics, an agent in an infectious state may help to spread a contagious disease through actions like commuting or visiting crowded places. Some advantages of agent-based modeling are the heterogeneity in the modeled population and the detailed tracking of individuals attributes and actions [1,42].

The outcome of the combination of multiple information layers with compartmental models, either with the use of agents and/or networks, is often a very precise and powerful tool to analyze an epidemic crisis, but also with a considerable gain in complexity, computational demand, and specific data requirements [16].

2.2   Corona++ Simulation Framework

Corona++ is a simulation framework for COVID-19 [14]. The core of the simulator is based on a stochastic form of the SEIR (Susceptible-Exposed-Infected-Recovered) model, extended to handle more compartments and relations between people by employing a heterogeneous dynamic network or population graph. The software was developed in C++ with the aid of the Boost Graph Library to manage graph structures, allowing high-efficiency implementations.

In the typical SEIR model, a subject can be found in one of four possible states and may progressively transition from one to another until reaching a terminal state. If a person is healthy or susceptible (S), it means they are not infected but might be in the future. Someone who is exposed (E) is already infected with the virus but cannot spread it yet. This is the case of people who are in the incubation period. In the infected (I) state, the individual already presents symptoms and is contagious as well. Eventually, the subject recovers and falls in the immune or recovered (R) state. If the person is vaccinated, they transition from susceptible straight to the immune state. Figure 1 demonstrates the compartment diagram for the extended SEIR model in Corona++. An important difference in comparison with the basic SEIR model is that the infected compartment is sub-classified in pre-symptomatic, mild, severe, critical, and asymptomatic. Pre-symptomatic people are capable to spread the virus but have not developed any symptoms yet. Symptomatic individuals may present mild, severe, or critical symptoms, which determines their needs in regard to medical attention. In the model, Intensive Care Units (ICU) and hospital beds are exclusive for subjects in the critical and severe sub-compartments, respectively. When a critical patient improves, his/her state changes to severe. Asymptomatic and subjects that ignore slight symptoms correspond to unreported cases. Finally, Corona++ also takes the deceased into account, who permanently fall in the dead state.

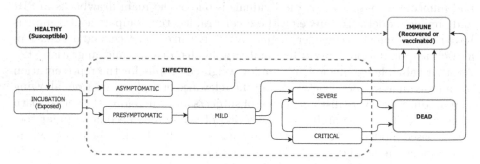

Fig. 1. Compartment diagram for the extended SEIR model in the Corona++ framework.

Another feature of this framework is the use of a social network. Given that every population member is represented with a vertex in the graph, what dictates if a node will be infected is the infection probability of its edges. This probability is determined according to the type of relation between both nodes, their states, and the basic reproductive number r_0 associated, which is defined as the estimated number of secondary cases produced by one contagious subject [11]. The default social connections modeled in Corona++ encompass family, work, school, and random interactions, though other types of connections can be included. The platform allows to simulate pharmaceutical interventions and NPIs, as well as individual events like concerts or soccer games.

2.3 Related Work

The interest in developing high-accuracy models and competent simulation platforms for epidemics has considerably increased. Accordingly, for the COVID-19 disease spread there is a wide research in compartmental [11,18,25,26,31,32,45, 46], network-based [17,24,37], and agent-based modeling in different environments [27,38,40]. There is also variety in the application of simulation frameworks [2,5,8,44]. In the particular case of Costa Rica, a compartmental SEIR model with confinement was implemented in a high-level language and used to simulate the lockdown effects [15]. Another approach is a multi-scale network extension of the SIR model with family, sporadic contacts, and friends among the individual connections. This model is currently implemented in a high-level programming language and has been used by the government as a primary tool in the analysis of projections and possible scenarios of the pandemic in Costa Rica [10]. More straightforward mathematical principles have been applied to analyze general aspects of the COVID-19 disease in Costa Rica and other Central American countries. That is the case of the utilization of logistic regression to approximate the curve of infected cases [43]. To the best of our knowledge, no specific models for Costa Rica have been implemented in a low-level language, neither other scenario studies like the one we present have been published.

The Corona++ framework has been used to study the impact of public health management strategies during the COVID-19 pandemic in Brazil, particularly to evaluate the school reopening plan in the case of the Greater São Paulo metropolitan area [13].

3 Modeling

3.1 Characterization

Geographic and Demographic Data. Costa Rica is geographically divided into provinces, each province into cantons, and cantons into districts. We use a cantonal division for our simulations, although the model can be set up for provinces or districts. Population data is retrieved from the National Institute of Statistics and Census (INEC) database. Since the latest census was performed in 2011, we use the projected data to estimate the population by age group and canton [23]. To be consistent with the input format in Corona++, we carry out a pre-processing step with the Karup-King method to interpolate population data for single ages [19].

Mobility. There is an important area in the country known as the Greater Metropolitan Area (GMA), where the majority of population and economic activities are concentrated. As a result, there is a high mobility in this region, predominantly in the case of commuters. In our model, we consider migration from the surroundings of the GMA to the GMA, inner mobilization between the cities of the GMA, and inner mobilization between the surrounding cities. According to an analysis of the 2011 Census data, the overall mobility in all the country is around 36% [33]. With additional mobility data, we estimated that 1% of people who inhabit the outer cities travel to the GMA for work, while 29% of the people living in the GMA commute to another GMA canton regularly [36].

Health System and COVID-19 Parameters. To calibrate the model, we make use of the official information published by the Health Ministry of Costa Rica [30]. The percentages of severe and critical cases, as well as the mortality rate for severe patients, were approximated from these data. These sources are not clear with respect to the number of available ICUs and beds for severe cases. Given that no deaths caused by lack of appropriate medical attention have been reported, we assume that the health system can manage the number of cases. Mortality rate for critical patients was reported to be 35%, according to different studies [3]. The literature also states that the length of hospital stay varies from less than a week to 2 months in the case of ICUs, and from 1 week to 3 weeks for the rest of hospitalizations [35].

Social, Occupational and Education System Parameters. We assume a gamma distribution for the family and workplace sizes, the number of random connections, and several variables related to the education system. Table 1 shows the main parameters for each distribution.

Table 1. Distribution parameters of interpersonal connections in our model.

Variable	Mean	Standard deviation	Minimum	Maximum
Number of family members	3	2	1	10
Number of employees in a workplace	15	27	2	100
Number of random connections	15	10	5	50
Number of students per school	117	178	2	1943
Number of students per classroom	8	5	2	57
Teacher age	44.2	2.9	20.46	82.5

For the calculation of the workplace and family size distribution parameters, we use data from the Directory of Enterprises and Establishments [20] and the National Household Survey 2020 [22], respectively. A participation rate of 63.4% between ages of 15 and 65 is obtained from the Continuous Employment Survey 2020 [21].

To model transmission inside schools, the simulator requires the definition of several parameters like the number of students, teachers ages, and percentage of school attendance in young people. Education system data is extracted from the Statistic Analysis Department of the Public Education Ministry [28] and the National Institute of Statistics and Census [22]. Other necessary data is provided by the State of the Nation Program (PEN). From these data, we determine that a 96.7% of young people between ages 4 and 17 is currently attending school. Gamma distribution parameters from Table 1 are also calculated from these data.

3.2   Calibration and Scenario Setup

Before exploring the scenarios, we need to recreate the timeline of the pandemic in the country and match the most important variables, namely, reported cases, deaths, and recovered, with their real curves. First, according to the times when the government established new sanitary restrictions, we adjust the weight values of each kind of relation to simulate lockdown, online classes, or working from home.

We took the curve of reported cases as a reference to modify the r_0 parameter and calibrate the model. The model output is obtained by calculating the median of all executions, and the simulation bounds with the 10th and 90th percentiles. To check for consistency with the real data, we compared the official information with the anonymized database, a detailed report of publication date, location, date of recovery, and other specific information about each unidentified patient [29]. The reported and the deceased data are consistent, while the official recovered cases are lower than expected and the official curve shows sudden increments. This implies that the official recovered cases are not instantly reported.

Once the model is calibrated, we proceed to evaluate the scenarios. We focus our analysis on three main issues:

Vaccination Process. The government's strategy has been questioned by the public in general, specially for the lack of constancy in the daily amount of vaccinated individuals. In this plan, the vaccination started in December 2020 and continued under a priority group based criteria. The number of vaccines applied per day is irregular. By the time we performed this study, the majority of immunized people were either healthcare workers or citizens over 58 years old, which are the first two priority groups of this plan. We design alternative scenarios to test other possibilities by using constant vaccination rates. First, we use a realistic conservative number of 5000 people per day; second, we analyze what happens if the health system has the capacity to sustain an exhaustive vaccination of 100,000 per day, a quantity in line with the highest vaccination rates registered. For consistency, in the above scenarios we use the priority group basis to select the candidates for the vaccine. Also, we assume a 95% of vaccine efficacy with a period of 28 days from the first dose for full immunization [39]. These data are valid for the Pfizer-BioNtech vaccine, which has been the most utilized in Costa Rica.

School Reopening. Resuming in-class lessons has been under discussion in Costa Rica because of the social, academic, and economic implications of virtuality, in particular for the most vulnerable families. On the other hand, health authorities are more concerned about the effect that this may cause in the number of infections, not only because about 20% of the population are underage students [23] but because young people tend to have less awareness of potentially contagious situations and practices. Thus, we study two scenarios where the schools are reopened with the 100% of students. We use a different level of intra-school transmission in both cases, in order to assess the outcomes of non observance of measures like social distancing among teachers and students, mask wearing, regular hand washing, and others.

Small Gatherings and Massive Events. Although social gatherings have been strictly forbidden or discouraged by the government, part of the population has shown reluctance to follow these directives. We weigh up the value of this measure by studying two common types of social events. To simulate the effect of organizing small gatherings with contacts like family and friends, we executed 500 events of 5–100 people in random cities for two weekends between day 358 and day 366 since the start of the pandemic, as 15 days is the regular period of time for the health authorities to weigh up the situation and announce new policies. In each gathering, all people are connected and consequently anyone can spread the infection among the attendants. In a similar manner, we perform the simulation of 10 massive events of 4000–11000 people per week for two weeks, from day 358 to 366 as well. Given that people who attend a massive event do not necessarily have a connection with the entire group of attendants, we model their interactions as a circle graph where each person has contact with only the nearest 10 participants.

4 Results

4.1 Experimental Setup

The simulations are executed using Intel Xeon processors with 36 cores @ 3.00 GHz. This node is part of the Kabré Supercomputer, a computer cluster located at the Costa Rica National High Technology Center. Every experiment consists of 3000 repetitions plus results processing, representing a total execution time of 14 h. Memory consumption is about 12.2 GB for each run.

4.2 Validation

Figure 2 shows the results of the simulations for accumulated reported cases, deaths, and recovered cases. Since the main calibration parameter, the r_0 value, is optimized to reproduce the number of reported cases, the model shows a particular good performance for this variable. This is illustrated in Fig. 2a), where the median of all simulations is almost identical to the official data.

As Fig. 2b) shows, we obtain an acceptable approximation of the real number of deaths, but there is a higher deviation compared to the reported cases. In the case of the deceased, the overall mortality rate depends on numerous factors, hence this value is not maintained from one cycle to another. In our model, the

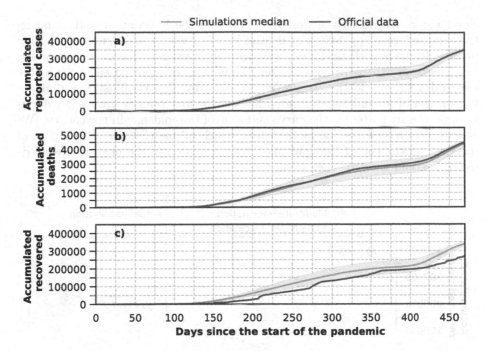

Fig. 2. Simulation results for accumulated a) reported, b) deceased, and c) recovered.

probabilities of dying for severe and critical cases are fixed, specifying a constant mortality rate for all cycles. This is a clear drawback, given that actual mortality can be higher or lower than our parameter for a given cycle. The distribution of the length of hospital stays and the ratio of reported people who are critical or severe are significant parameters that contribute to the observed error too, because we can only approximate them. In spite of these constraints, we consider the model is still proficient concerning the deaths, as in Fig. 2b) the official curve falls inside the shaded area, indicating that the real case is between the 10th and 90th percent of all possible scenarios.

By looking at Fig. 2c) we may conclude that, compared to reality, our model is projecting almost the same amount of recovered but the patients are improving earlier than they should, as the curves have similar shapes but they are separated by a time gap. However, the time difference between our results and the official data could be caused by the delays in the report of recovered people and not necessarily because the simulator is minimizing the recovery time. The above is also noticeable in the shape of the real data, where sudden increments can be observed about every 75 days, suggesting that some reports are behind time.

4.3 Evaluation of Scenarios

Vaccination. The results of the first study are shown in Fig. 3, where the vertical dashed line represents the starting day of the vaccination process. Both simulated strategies have a positive impact on the infection spread, reducing the reported cases by 14% and deaths by 17%, with a moderate vaccination process. In the hypothetical scenario where the government has enough resources to support an exhaustive vaccination, the number of reported cases are a 45% less and a 42% of deaths are prevented. Actually, Fig. 3a) illustrates that the vaccination of around 100,000 individuals of the first priority groups per day is enough to start flattening the curve and control the epidemic in the country. We also observe a slow decline in the cases, which means that for the purpose of speeding up the end of the epidemic, the vaccination of the next groups needs to start sooner than in other scenarios.

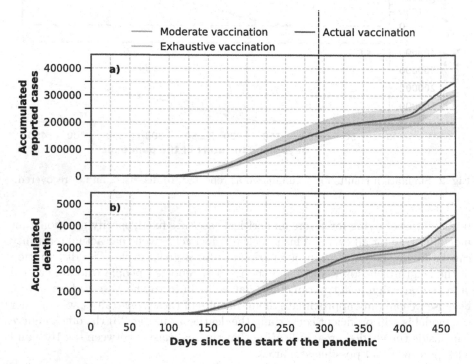

Fig. 3. Projection of accumulated number of a) reported cases and b) deceased for different vaccination strategies.

School Reopening. Figure 4 shows the results of reopening the schools for the totality of students. In this case, the vertical dashed line represents the day when schools were opened. Our model estimates that resuming in-person lessons increases both the number of reported cases and deaths in contrast with the partial opening strategy. The total reopening not only promotes a higher level of contact but also does it for a population with a raised spread capacity, because young people are less watchful of the measures. As a consequence, there are 33% more reported cases and 26% more deaths with schools opened with well respected sanitary measures, which involves a regular intra-school transmission.

The effect can be amplified if teachers and school authorities have a poor observance of the sanitary measures, resulting in a high intra-school transmission. On these terms, our model projects 46% more reported cases and 39% more deaths.

Our simulations also predict that the schools reopening impact is not observed until one or two months. Aside from the incubation periods, students need to get infected themselves first in order to transmit the disease to their family members, causing a belated effect in the general cases. Besides, there is not a substantial raise in the cases at the beginning because young people are modeled to have a remote probability of presenting severe symptoms, which makes them less likely to be reported.

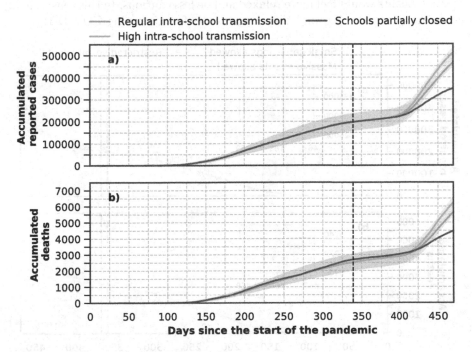

Fig. 4. Projection of accumulated number of a) reported cases and b) deceased for different intra-school transmission levels.

Social Events. In Fig. 5, we see what would happen if the government does not restrict social events for a two-week period. If people are allowed to gather with family and friends, the simulation results in Fig. 5a) show that reported cases increase a 24%. Also, near 17% more deaths are registered, according to Fig. 5b). The model also predicts that the effect of such policy is perceived about a month and a half after it was implemented. This means that even though people are having more contact the cases rise slowly because, based on our results, the probability of getting infected in one of these events is not very high. However, the impact of those few individuals that do get infected is still considerable in their respective contact networks, hence in the general cases.

Our model delivers almost the same results for the massive events scenario. In Fig. 5, we show a zoomed in area where our simulation data ends and where the small differences between the outputs of both scenarios can be discerned. We can consider that attending massive events increases the cases as much as organizing small gatherings but the consequences are slightly milder. This can be explained by the way we modeled the interactions in these events. In public meetings the organizers and the attendants would be more observant of the protocols to minimize contact among strangers, then we can consider these interactions are random. On the other hand, all connections in small meetings are taken as family interactions, which have greater weights than the random ones, because their attendants would feel more relaxed and be less cautious. In this sense, small events are as or more harmful than large events for containing COVID-19.

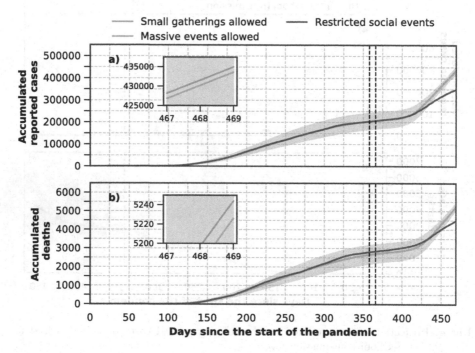

Fig. 5. Projection of accumulated number of a) reported cases and b) deceased in the case of permission to organize small social gatherings and massive events.

5   Conclusions and Further Work

The COVID-19 pandemic has challenged the scientific community and the global health authorities to discover the best containment strategies for a contagious disease. Epidemic modeling and simulations are essential for achieving this goal because they offer the opportunity of assessing a particular policy and its outcomes without real life consequences. We manage to employ a COVID-19 simulation platform to develop an accurate model of the infection spread pattern in

Costa Rica, using a complex contact network. We evaluate the effect of public health measures, determining that reopening schools with the 100% students and authorizing the organization of social events considerably increase the number of reported cases and deaths, specially in the cases where people disregards sanitary practices. In contrast, we show that regularity in the vaccination process slows down the spread even when the number of applications is moderate, and in the case of having enough resources, it could make the infection die out.

We project multiple dimensions in which our work can be extended. First, the modeling and simulation exercise of this paper can be applied to other countries in the region. As long as the same population descriptors can be found for other countries, it is possible to replicate the analysis. Second, we aim at building a wrapper around the simulator to automatically optimize simulation parameters, particularly the basic reproductive number. Third, other epidemiological variables could be incorporated into the simulator. For instance, simulating several concurrent variants of the virus, each with a different contagious degree.

Acknowledgements. This research was partially supported by a machine allocation on Kabré supercomputer at the Costa Rica National High Technology Center.

References

1. Ahmed, A., Greensmith, J., Aickelin, U.: Variance in system dynamics and agent based modelling using the SIR model of infectious disease. In: 26th European Conference on Modelling and Simulation 2012 Proceedings, pp. 9–15. European Council for Modelling and Simulation, Koblenz (2012)
2. Amar, P.: Pandæsim: an epidemic spreading stochastic simulator. Biology **9**, 1–19 (2020)
3. Armstrong, R.A., Kane, A.D., Kursumovic, E., Oglesby, F.C., Cook, T.M.: Mortality in patients admitted to intensive care with COVID-19: an updated systematic review and meta-analysis of observational studies. Anaesthesia **76**(4), 537–548 (2021)
4. Baker, E., et al.: Analyzing stochastic computer models: a review with opportunities. Stat. Sci. **37**(1), 64–89 (2022)
5. Ban, T.Q., Duong, P.L., Son, N.H., Dinh, T.V.: COVID-19 disease simulation using GAMA platform. In: 2020 International Conference on Computational Intelligence (ICCI), pp. 246–251. IEEE (2020)
6. Barrett, C.L., Bisset, K.R., Eubank, S.G., Feng, X., Marathe, M.V.: EpiSimdemics: an efficient algorithm for simulating the spread of infectious disease over large realistic social networks. In: SC 2008: Proceedings of the 2008 ACM/IEEE Conference on Supercomputing, Austin, pp. 1–12. IEEE (2008)
7. Bhatele, A., et al.: Massively parallel simulations of spread of infectious diseases over realistic social networks. In: 2017 17th IEEE/ACM International Symposium on Cluster, Cloud and Grid Computing (CCGRID), Madrid, pp. 689–694. IEEE (2017)
8. Boukanjime, B., Caraballo, T., El Fatini, M., El Khalifi, M.: Dynamics of a stochastic coronavirus (COVID-19) epidemic model with Markovian switching. Chaos Solitons Fractals **141**, 110361 (2020)

9. Brauer, F., Castillo-Chavez, C.: Epidemic models. In: Brauer, F., Castillo-Chavez, C. (eds.) Mathematical Models in Population Biology and Epidemiology. TAM, vol. 40, pp. 345–408. Springer, New York (2012). https://doi.org/10.1007/978-1-4614-1686-9_9

10. Calvo, J.G., Sánchez, F., Barboza, L.A., García, Y., Vásquez, P.: A multilayer network model implementation for COVID-19 (2021)

11. Carcione, J.M., Santos, J.E., Bagaini, C., Ba, J.: A simulation of a COVID-19 epidemic based on a deterministic SEIR model. Front. Public Health **8**, 230 (2020)

12. Chen, D.: Modeling the spread of infectious diseases: a review. In: Analyzing and Modeling Spatial and Temporal Dynamics of Infectious Diseases, pp. 19–42. Wiley (2015)

13. Cruz, E.H.M.: Corona++ (2020). https://gitlab.com/ehmcruz/corona

14. Cruz, E.H.M., et al.: Simulation-based evaluation of school reopening strategies during COVID-19: a case study of São Paulo. Brazil. Epidemiol. Infect. **149**, 1–23 (2021)

15. De-Camino-Beck, T.: A modified SEIR model with confinement and lockdown of COVID-19 for Costa Rica (2020)

16. Duan, W., Fan, Z., Zhang, P., Guo, G., Qiu, X.: Mathematical and computational approaches to epidemic modeling: a comprehensive review. Front. Comput. Sci. **9**(5), 806–826 (2014). https://doi.org/10.1007/s11704-014-3369-2

17. Firth, J.A., et al.: Using a real-world network to model localized COVID-19 control strategies. Nat. Med. **26**(10), 1616–1622 (2020)

18. Giordano, G., et al.: Modelling the COVID-19 epidemic and implementation of population-wide interventions in Italy. Nat. Med. **26**(6), 855–860 (2020)

19. Instituto Nacional de Estadísticas y Censos: Manual de la persona usuaria: Estimaciones y proyecciones de población distritales. Technical report, Instituto Nacional de Estadísticas y Censos (2014)

20. Instituto Nacional de Estadísticas y Censos: Directorio de Empresas y Establecimientos (2020)

21. Instituto Nacional de Estadísticas y Censos: Encuesta continua de empleo al primer trimestre de 2020. Technical report, Instituto Nacional de Estadísticas y Censos (2020)

22. Instituto Nacional de Estadísticas y Censos: Encuesta Nacional de Hogares (2020)

23. Instituto Nacional de Estadísticas y Censos, Centro Centroamericano de Población: Estimaciones y proyecciones de población (2011)

24. Karaivanov, A.: A social network model of COVID-19. PLoS One **15**(10), e0240878 (2020)

25. Lin, Q., et al.: A conceptual model for the coronavirus disease 2019 (COVID-19) outbreak in Wuhan, China with individual reaction and governmental action. Int. J. Infect. Dis. **93**, 211–216 (2020)

26. Liu, Z., Magal, P., Seydi, O., Webb, G.: A COVID-19 epidemic model with latency period. Infect. Dis. Model. **5**, 323–337 (2020)

27. Gharakhanlou, N.M., Hooshangi, N.: Spatio-temporal simulation of the novel coronavirus (COVID-19) outbreak using the agent-based modeling approach (case study: Urmia, Iran). Inform. Med. Unlocked **20**, 100403 (2020)

28. Ministerio de Educación Pública: Información estadística - Autotabulaciones (2021)

29. Ministerio de Salud: Base anonimizada de casos confirmados COVID-19 (2021)

30. Ministerio de Salud, Universidad Estatal a Distancia: Situación Nacional COVID-19 (2021)

31. Nadler, P., Wang, S., Arcucci, R., Yang, X., Guo, Y.: An epidemiological modelling approach for COVID-19 via data assimilation. Eur. J. Epidemiol. **35**(8), 749–761 (2020). https://doi.org/10.1007/s10654-020-00676-7

32. Oliveira, J.F., et al.: Mathematical modeling of COVID-19 in 14.8 million individuals in Bahia. Brazil. Nat. Commun. **12**, 1–13 (2021)

33. Oviedo, L.A.: Movilidad laboral territorial: Un análisis de los desplazamientos por trabajo en Costa Rica. Technical report, Institute for Research in Economic Sciences, San José (2017)

34. Paré, P.E., Beck, C.L., Başar, T.: Modeling, estimation, and analysis of epidemics over networks: an overview. Ann. Rev. Control **50**, 345–360 (2020)

35. Rees, E.M., et al.: COVID-19 length of hospital stay: a systematic review and data synthesis. BMC Med. **18**(1) (2020). Article number: 270. https://doi.org/10.1186/s12916-020-01726-3

36. Sánchez, L.: Diagnóstico sobre la situación del transporte y la movilidad en Costa Rica. Technical report, Programa Estado Nación, San José (2018)

37. Silva, C.J., Cantin, G., Cruz, C., Fonseca-pinto, R., Passadouro, R.: Complex network model for COVID-19: human behavior, pseudo-periodic solutions and multiple epidemic waves. J. Math. Anal. Appl. (2021). https://doi.org/10.1016/j.jmaa.2021.125171. https://www.sciencedirect.com/journal/journal-of-mathematical-analysis-and-applications/articles-in-press?page=2

38. Silva, P.C., Batista, P.V., Lima, H.S., Alves, M.A., Guimarães, F.G., Silva, R.C.: COVID-ABS: an agent-based model of COVID-19 epidemic to simulate health and economic effects of social distancing interventions. Chaos Solitons Fractals **139**, 110088 (2020)

39. Strategic Advisory Group of Experts on Immunization: The Pfizer BioNTech COVID-19 vaccine: what you need to know (2021)

40. Truszkowska, A., et al.: High-resolution agent-based modeling of COVID-19 spreading in a small town. Adv. Theory Simul. **4**, 2000277 (2021)

41. Tulu, T.W., Tian, B., Wu, Z.: Mathematical modeling, analysis and Markov Chain Monte Carlo simulation of Ebola epidemics. Results Phys. **7**, 962–968 (2017)

42. Venkatramanan, S., Lewis, B., Chen, J., Higdon, D., Vullikanti, A., Marathe, M.: Using data-driven agent-based models for forecasting emerging infectious diseases. Epidemics **22**, 43–49 (2018)

43. Villalobos Arias, M.A.: Estimación de población contagiada por Covid-19 usando regresión logística generalizada y heurísticas de optimización (2020)

44. Xie, G.: A novel Monte Carlo simulation procedure for modelling COVID-19 spread over time. Nat. Sci. Rep. **10**(1), 1–9 (2020)

45. Yew, K., Mei, M.: COVID-19: development of a robust mathematical model and simulation package with consideration for ageing population and time delay for control action and resusceptibility. Phys. D **411**, 132599 (2020)

46. Zhao, S., Chen, H.: Modeling the epidemic dynamics and control of COVID-19 outbreak in China. Quant. Biol. **8**(1), 11–19 (2020). https://doi.org/10.1007/s40484-020-0199-0

An Efficient Vectorized Auction Algorithm for Many-Core and Multicore Architectures

Alexandre C. Sena[1]([⊠])⑩, Marcio N. P. Silva[1], and Aline P. Nascimento[2]

[1] Universidade do Estado do Rio de Janeiro, Rio de Janeiro, RJ, Brazil
asena@ime.uerj.br
[2] Universidade Federal Fluminense, Niterói, RJ, Brazil

Abstract. The auction algorithm has been widely used to solve problems in several areas. One important characteristic of this algorithm is that its distributive nature simplifies the adoption of parallel implementations. With its various processing cores and 512-bit vectorized instructions, many-core and multicore machines have the potential to considerably increase the performance of this algorithm. The aim of this work is to efficiently execute the auction algorithm in these architectures. The main contributions of this work are: proposal and implementation of a scalable vectorized version for `AVX-512` instructions; detailed evaluation of vectorized and parallel versions. Results show that vectorization in conjunction with parallelism is capable of harnessing the full potential of many-core and multicore machines. Moreover, the best scalability of a many-core processor, allowed over 750-fold speedup when comparing the proposed parallel vectorized version against the original sequential one.

Keywords: Auction algorithm · Vectorization · Multicore/Many-core

1 Introduction

There are several problems that can be modeled using bipartite graphs, where an optimal match must be found. The problem of pairing bipartite graphs is explored in several areas such as bioinformatics, to verify similarities between proteins [8] and Computer Vision, where the objective is the matching of two images [15]. The auction algorithm [1] has been widely used to solve this problem because it is capable of producing the optimal solution and its distributive nature simplifies the adoption of parallel implementations.

Originally, the auction algorithm was proposed to assign m persons to n distinct objects, where each pair, person-object, has an associated cost that represents its affinity. The aim is to assign a person to the object with greater affinity, maximizing the total sum [4].

To extract the maximum performance from Xeon (multicore) and Xeon Phi (many-core) processors it is necessary to efficiently use the set of SIMD instructions and multiple processing cores available [5]. When compared to multicore

© Springer Nature Switzerland AG 2022
I. Gitler et al. (Eds.): CARLA 2021, CCIS 1540, pp. 76–90, 2022.
https://doi.org/10.1007/978-3-031-04209-6_6

systems, many-core architecture has a larger number of cores with a lower clock frequency to keep energy consumption manageable, although production of Xeon Phi processors was discontinued in 2017. The Xeon processors (i.e. Skylake) have 512 bits registers, as well as the Xeon Phi processors.

In this context, the aim of this work is to propose an efficient scalable vectorization of the auction algorithm for multicore and many-core architectures. To achieve that, a complete vectorized version for 512 bits SIMD register was implemented and evaluated. It is important to highlight that, although it was proposed for AVX-512 architectures, it is essentially scalable and can be easily adapted to new architectures with larger instructions by, basically, changing the name of the intrinsic instructions used. Finally, parallel OpenMP implementation in conjunction with the efficient use of SIMD registers showed that it is possible to exploit the full potential of these architectures, being up to 750 times better than the original sequential version for the many-core machine.

This work is divided as follows: Related works are presented in Sect. 2. Section 3 describes the auction algorithm. Then, Sect. 4 presents the proposed vectorized version. The OpenMP parallel implementation is presented in Sect. 5. A detailed analysis of the proposed vectorized version is presented in Sect. 6. Finally, conclusions are presented in Sect. 7.

2   Related Work

The distributed nature of the auction algorithm allowed different implementations to emerge in different architectures. In the early 90s, parallel synchronous and asynchronous implementations of the auction algorithm were proposed and executed on a real parallel machine [2]. Parallel versions capable of pairing large dense and sparse bipartite graphs were proposed by Sathe 2012 [14] and Kollias 2014 [9]. Experimental results on a Cray XE6 supercomputer showed that the hybrid MPI-OpenMP implementation dramatically reduced the execution time, although no performance analysis has been presented.

Nascimento 2016 [12] implemented and evaluated the performance of an hybrid parallel auction algorithm for multicore clusters. In particular, the article analyzes how the size of the matrix and the number of iterations influence the execution time of OpenMP-MPI version. Vectorized versions of the auction algorithm for multicore system (XEON) were implemented and evaluated in [3]. The work didactically presents only part of the vectorization of the auction algorithm.

3   Auction Algorithm

This section presents the Auction Algorithm and its implementation. Originally, it was proposed to assign m people to separate n objects, where each person/object pair has an associated cost that represents its affinity (in this work matrix A stores the affinity costs). The purpose of the algorithm is to assign a person to the object with greater affinity, maximizing the total sum [1].

Basically, the Auction Algorithm can be divided into two main stages: (1) BID (Algorithm 1(a)), in which people bid for the objects they wish to associate with, and (2) ASSIGN (Algorithm 1(b)), in which the best bid given for each object is selected individually, determining their associations and new prices. The price acts as a regulator of this dynamic process, increased according to the value of the best bid received by the corresponding object.

The algorithm iterates in rounds repeating the two main steps. In the BID phase, each free person, i, will offer a new bid for a object, j, where each bid is calculated as the difference between the prices of the highest and second highest value for a given person (function $max2Max$ in Algorithm 1(a), lines 10 to 21). After bidding, in the ASSIGN phase, one or more objects are then associated with the people who offered the highest bid (function $maxValObj$ in Algorithm 1(b), lines 11 to 19).

At the end of each round, a set of prices and associations is produced (Algorithm 1(b), lines 5 and 6). If all people are satisfied, the algorithm ends, and according to the Equation $l_i = \max_{j=1,...,n} \{a_{ij} - p_j\}$, that returns the highest bid l_i, where a_{ij} is a value of affinity matrix A and p_j is the price associated with the object, each person is necessarily associated with the most valuable object, and there is no free people to make new offers. Otherwise, a new round is started. Thus, as long as there are free people (without associated object), the auction algorithm continues until every person is assigned to an object.

4   Vectorization of the Auction Algorithm for Multicore and Many-Core Architecture

The Xeon and Xeon Phi architectures, in addition to several processing cores, have vectorized instructions that can be used to substantially increase the performance of the application when the same operation can be performed on a data set. Vectorization is the process of converting a scalar implementation of a program to a vector process [11]. This process is essential to extract performance in these architectures, especially in the modern processors that have 512 bits registers that can execute up to 16 instructions at the same time [13].

The compiler itself is able to vectorize the user's program, but only for simple or well-optimized code. This difficulty occurs because, in order to vectorize a program, the compiler must be able to identify the absence of data dependency on operations and, moreover, if access to memory is contiguous [11]. When the compiler is not able to vectorize the code there are two alternatives: explicit vectorization (OpenMP directives) [16] or SIMD instructions programming (intrinsics) [18]. While explicit vectorization consists of providing additional information to help the compiler to vectorize the code, intrinsics is low-level programming that uses SIMD instructions. Although explicit vectorization is less complex, performance depends on the precise use of directives and is limited to the way they were implemented. On the other hand, SIMD instructions programming is more complex, but allows to extract maximum performance.

Before implementing the vectorized auction algorithm, several compilation parameters were tested and no performance gains were obtained. Most important, several simplified parts of the auction algorithm (e.g. find the highest value

```
01 |   int bid(A, l, p, m, n){
02 |      for(i = 0; i < m; i++){
03 |         if (person i is not assigned)
04 |            (l[i].obj,l[i].val) =
                   ↪ max2Max(A[i],p,n)
05 |         else
06 |            (l[i].obj,l[i].val) =
                   ↪ (-1,-1)
07 |      }
08 |   }
09 |
10 |   int max2Max(Ai, p, n){
11 |      (mInd,mVal,smVal) = (0,Ai[0]-p
            ↪ [0],-1)
12 |      for(j = 1; j < n; j++){
13 |         aux = Ai[j]-p[j]
14 |         if (mVal < aux )
15 |            (smVal,mVal,mInd) = (
                  ↪ mVal,aux,j)
16 |         else
17 |            if (aux > smVal)
18 |               smVal = aux
19 |      }
20 |      return (mInd, mVal - smVal + ε)
21 |   }
```

(a) BID phase

```
01 |   int assign(l, p, m, n){
02 |      for(j = 0; j < n; j++){
03 |         (mVal, mInd) = maxValObj(l,j
               ↪ ,m)
04 |         if (there is a new winner
               ↪ for obj j){
05 |            p[j] = p[j] + mVal
06 |            updateAssigment(mVal,
                  ↪ mInd,j)
07 |         }
08 |      }
09 |   }
10 |
11 |   int maxValObj(l, obj, m){
12 |      (mVal,mInd) = (-1,-1)
13 |      for(i = 1; i < m; i++){
14 |         if (l[i].obj == obj)
15 |            if (l[i].val > mVal)
16 |               (mVal,mInd) = (l[i].val
                     ↪ ,i)
17 |      }
18 |      return (mVal, mInd)
19 |   }
```

(b) ASSIGN phase

Fig. 1. Two stages of the auction algorithm

in an array and its index) were tested and in neither cases icc and gcc compilers were able to auto-vectorize the code. To extract the maximum performance from the 512-bit SIMD registers of the multicore and many-core architectures, a complete vectorized version of the auction algorithm was implemented using intrinsics programming. Moreover, the proposed vectorization is scalable, since it takes advantage of maximum size of the instructions available (i.e. 512 bits). More than that, it was designed to exploit the maximum SIMD parallelism available. Thus, if new architectures with even larger SIMD instructions are made available, the proposed vectorization can be easily adapted by simply changing the names of the instructions.

4.1   Vectorization of the BID Phase

The vectorization of the BID phase consisted of optimizing the MAX2MAX function (Algorithm 1(a)), which finds the bid that the person will offer for an object. Basically, it is necessary to find the objects with the highest and second highest values for the person bidding, and the index of the highest value object. The vectorized code, called MAX2MAXVEC, can be seen in Algorithm 2(a).

Initially, the vectorized variables mv and mi that store the highest value and the index of the highest value object are initialized. The command ISET(0) (line 3), initializes all 16 positions of mi with 0, while the command LOAD (v) initializes the 16 positions of mv with the first 16 positions of v (line 4).

The main part of the vectorization process is presented in lines 5 to 21 in Algorithm 2(a). Note that variable i in command **for** (line 5) is incremented by 16, since the vectorized variables of the AVX-512 architectures are capable of storing 16 values when considering integer or single precision numbers. On lines 6 to 8, the vectorized variables $vaux$ and $vaux2$ are initialized with the next 16 positions of v and p, respectively, through the LOAD statement, while vi is

```
01 |    int max2MaxVec (v, p, n){
02 |      // v = A[i] — one line of the
             ↪ affinity matrix
03 |      mi = ISET(0)
04 |      mv = LOAD(v)
05 |      for(i = 0; i < n; i+=16){
06 |        vaux = LOAD(v+i)
07 |        vaux2 = LOAD(p+i)
08 |        vi = ISET(i)
09 |        vaux = SUB(vaux, vaux2)
10 |        vflag = CMP(vaux, mv, >)
11 |        if (!vflag){
12 |          vflag2 = CMP(vaux, smv, >)
13 |          smv = MBLEND(vflag2, smv,
                   ↪ vaux)
14 |        }else{
15 |          smtmp = MBLEND(vflag, vaux,
                   ↪ mv)
16 |          mv = MBLEND(vflag, mv, vaux)
17 |          mi = IMBLEND(vflag, mi, vi)
18 |          vflag2 = CMP(smtmp, smv, >)
19 |          smv = MBLEND(vflag2, smv,
                   ↪ smtmp)
20 |        }
21 |      }
22 |      // Reduction
23 |      STORE(max,mv)
24 |      ISTORE(imax,mi)
25 |      STORE(smax,smv)
26 |      mVal = LOW_VALUE
27 |      for(i = 0; i < 16; i++)
28 |        if(max[i] ≥ mVal){
29 |          mVal = max[i]
30 |          mInd = imax[i]
31 |        }
32 |      max[mInd] = LOW_VALUE
33 |      smVal = LOW_VALUE
34 |      for(i = 0; i < 16; i++)
35 |        if(max[i] ≥ smVal)
36 |          smVal = max[i]
37 |
38 |      for(i = 0; i < 16; i++)
39 |        if(smax[i] ≥ smVal)
40 |          smVal = smax[i]
41 |
42 |      return (mInd, mVal − smVal + ε)
43 |    }
```

(a) Vectorization of MAX2MAX

```
01 |    int maxValObjVec (l, j, m){
02 |      // This code uses two arrays, lObj
             ↪ and lVal, instead of
             ↪ array l with fields obj
             ↪ and val
03 |      vetmVal = SET(LOW_VALUE)
04 |      vetmInd = ISET(−1)
05 |      vObj = ISET(j)
06 |      for(i = 0; i < m; i+=16){
07 |        auxObj = ILOAD(lObj+i)
08 |        mask = CMPEQ(auxObj, vObj)
09 |        if(mask){
10 |          auxPreco = LOAD(lVal+i)
11 |          mask2 = CMP(auxPreco,
                   ↪ vetmVal, >)
12 |          mask = mask & mask2
13 |          vetmVal = MBLEND(mask,
                   ↪ vetmVal, auxPreco)
14 |          auxLeiloeiro = ISET(i)
15 |          vetmInd = IMBLEND(mask,
                   ↪ vetmInd,
                   ↪ auxLeiloeiro)
16 |        }
17 |      }
18 |      // Reduction
19 |      // vMax, iMax (16 positions arrays)
20 |      STORE(vMax, vetmVal)
21 |      ISTORE(iMax, vetmInd)
22 |      mVal = LOW_VALUE
23 |      for(i = 0; i < 16; i++)
24 |        if(iMax[i] ≥ 0 and vMax[i] >
               ↪ mVal){
25 |          mVal = vMax[i]
26 |          mInd = iMax[i]
27 |        }
28 |      return (mVal, mInd)
29 |    }
```

(b) Vectorization of MAXVALOBJ

Fig. 2. Vectorized auction algorithm (Color figure online)

initialized with the value of i through the ISET command. Then, in line 9, the 16 positions of $vaux$ receive the difference between $vaux$ and $vaux2$ using the SUB command. This difference is necessary, since the bid to be offered must subtract the current price being offered for the object, as was shown in Sect. 3. In line 10, the CMP instruction compares which values of $vaux$ are greater than mv and stores it in the bit mask $vflag$. If all values of $vaux$ are smaller than the values of vm then the commands inside **if** will be executed. In this case, only the variable that stores the second highest value should be updated. For this, the CMP instruction stores in the bit mask $vflag2$ all positions of $vaux$ that are greater than smv (line 12). Then, the MBLEND command updates only the positions of smv where the value of $vaux$ is greater (line 13).

Otherwise, the commands inside **else** are executed (lines 15 to 19). In this case, the variables that hold the highest and the second highest values must be updated. For this, the variable $smtmp$ receives the values of $vaux$ or mv through the MBLEND instruction, respecting the bit mask $vflag$ (line 15). That is, $smtmp$ receives values of $vaux$ that are not greater than mv (bits with value 0 in $vflag$) and receives values of mv that are smaller than $vaux$ (bits with a value of 1). On the other hand, line 16, the vectorized variable mv receives the highest values of mv and $vaux$ also through the command MBLEND.

The index of the object for which the highest bid is being placed must also be updated. Then, mi is updated using the IMBLEND command (line 17). Only the positions of mi where the value of $vaux$ is greater are updated, as the mask $vflag$ determines. Finally, to update the variable smv that contains the second highest value, it is necessary to create the bit mask $vflag2$ that receives 1 for positions where the value of $smtmp$ is greater than smv and 0 otherwise, using CMP command (line 18). Then, in line 19, variable smv is updated with the highest values of $smtmp$ and smv.

Right after the end of the **for** command the reduction starts (line 23). That is, reduce the mv, mi and smv vectorized variables that contain 16 values to just one value. Initially, these three variables are stored in arrays of 16 positions using commands STORE and ISTORE (lines 23 to 25). The process of finding the highest bid and the index at which the bid was made is very simple. It is only necessary go through the 16 positions of the array containing the highest values and find the highest value and its index (lines 27 to 31).

On the other hand, to find the second highest bid it is necessary to go through the array that contains the highest values as well as the one that contains the second highest values, since the second highest overall value may be in one of these arrays. To achieve that, it is only necessary to iterate through the 16 positions of the max array and the 16 positions of the $smax$ array to find the second highest value, as can be seen in the lines 33 to 40.

Finally, the algorithm returns the object's index for which the bid will be given and the bid value, which is the difference between the highest and second highest values, plus constant ϵ that deals with convergence in tie cases (line 42).

4.2   Vectorization of the ASSIGN Phase

Vectorized function MAXVALOBJVEC associates the object with the person who offered the highest bid. The code for this function can be seen in Algorithm 2(b). Initially, lines 3 to 5, three auxiliary vectorized variables are initialized through the SET and ISET commands.

The vectorization process takes place from line 6 to 17. As in the BID phase, the variable i in command **for** (line 6) is incremented by 16, since the vectorized variables of the AVX-512 architectures are capable of packing 16 values when considering integer or single precision numbers. In line 7, the ILOAD command stores in the $auxObj$ vectorized variable the objects that the 16 persons in the current iteration bid on. Line 8, on the other hand, compares these 16 objects with the object for which the highest bid is to be found, j, through the CMPEQ command, and stores it in the $mask$ variable. The CMPEQ command stores 1 in the vectorized variable if the comparison is true and 0 if it is false. If all 16 objects compared are different from object j, then variable $mask$ will be equal to 0. Therefore, the commands inside the **if** (line 9) will not be executed.

Otherwise, the execution of the commands inside the **if** stores in *vetmVal* vectorized variable the 16 highest values offered to object j and in *vetmInd* variable the 16 persons who bid. To achieve that, the current 16 values of *lVal* array are stored in the vectorized auxiliary variable *auxPreco* using the LOAD command (line 10). Then, in line 11, the CMP command compares which 16 values stored in *auxPreco* are greater than the values stored in variable *vetmVal*, storing in the *mask2* bit mask 1 if greater and 0 otherwise. As only the bids given to object j are concerned, in line 12 an AND (&) operation is performed between the bit masks *mask* and *mask2*, so that in the end the variable *mask* only has value 1 in the position that is for the object j and the bid given is higher than the previous one. The command MBLEND, line 13, allows a join between the variables *vetmVal* and *auxPreco*, only for positions that have value 1 in variable *mask*. That is, only the positions of the vectorized variable *vetmVal* where the corresponding bit in the variable *mask* has a value of 1 will be updated. Finally, it is also necessary to store the people who bid. For this, the persons of the current iteration are stored in variable *auxLeiloeiro*, using the ISET command (line 14). Then, in line 15, the IMBLEND command updates only the positions of *vetmInd* that the corresponding bit in the *mask* variable has a value of 1.

At the end of all iterations, the *vetmVal* vectorized variable contains the 16 largest values offered to object j. Likewise, variable *vetmInd* contains the index of the 16 persons who offered these values. To finalize the vectorization, it is necessary to reduce these 16 values to just the highest value offered and the index of the person who offered it. To achieve that, the values of the variables *vetmVal* and *vetmInd* must be stored in the 16 positions arrays *vMax* and *iMax* using the commands STORE and ISTORE (lines 20 and 21). Then, it is only necessary to go through the 16 elements of the arrays to find the highest bid and the person's index (lines 22 to 27). It is important to verify if $iMax[i] \geq 0$ (line 24) to ensure that the bid was offered to object j. Finally, on line 28, the value of the highest bid and the index of the person for object j are returned.

In the vectorized codes presented in the Algorithms 2(a) and 2(b) we opted to use mnemonics (alias highlighted in green) instead of the real name of the Intrinsic instruction to make the code easier to read. Thus, the real intrinsics instructions used are: _mm512_load_ps (LOAD), _mm512_load_si512 (ILOAD), _mm512_set1_ps (SET), _mm512_set1_epi32 (ISET), _mm512_store_ps (STORE), _mm512_store_si512 (ISTORE), _mm512_cmp_ps_mask (CMP), _mm512_sub_ps (SUB), _mm512_cmpeq_epi32_mask (CMPEQ), _mm512_mask_blend_epi32 (IMBLEND) and _mm512_mask_blend_ps (MBLEND).

5   Parallelization of the Auction Algorithm

To take advantage of the full potential of multicore and many-core architectures, in addition to the vectorization that maximizes the use of SIMD instructions, it is necessary to use the various processing cores efficiently, through parallelization techniques for shared memory. For this work, the OpenMP [16] parallel programming model was used. As described in Sect. 3, the auction algorithm is a succession of iterations, where in each of these iterations the BID and ASSIGN stages are performed. In the BID phase, the calculation of the bid given by each person for an object does not depend on the bid of another person. Thus, each bid can be carried out in parallel using an openMP `parallel for` directive. In turn, in the ASSIGN phase, each object selects the best bid received and determines its association and new price without depending on the selections of the other objects. Therefore, each object-person association can also be performed in parallel, using an openMP `parallel for` directive. More details on the parallel implementation of the auction algorithm can be found in [12].

6   Experimental Analysis

This section evaluates the results achieved by the vectorized version (Subsect. 6.1) and the vectorized parallel version (Subsect. 6.2) for multicore and many-core architectures. The experiments were carried out on two different machines. The many-core machine has a Intel Xeon Phi 7250 processor with a total of 68 cores (clocked at 1.40 GHz) and 204 GB of memory. In turn, the configuration of the multicore architecture is composed of two Intel Xeon Platinum 8160 processors with a total of 48 cores (base frequency of 2.10 GHz and max turbo frequency of 3.70 GHz) and 187 GB of memory. Both machines have `AVX-512` SIMD instructions and, therefore, are able to use the full potential of the vectorization proposed in this work. Moreover, both machines have `NUMA` (Non-Uniform Memory Access) memory architectures. Finally, all programs used in the experiments were compiled using Intel's icc compiler with `-O3 -xavx` optimization. It is important to point out that exactly the same code were used in both architectures being only necessary to compile it for each machine. Each version of the auction algorithm evaluated in this work for each instance was executed 50 times and the arithmetic average and the coefficient of variation was calculated. The results obtained are quite reliable with a coefficient of variation <2%.

6.1   Experimental Analysis of the Vectorization

This subsection evaluates the performance of the vectorization in multicore and many-core machines. Thus, only one core is used (i.e. no parallel code is used).

Performance Evaluation. For the first experiment, 10 real matrices were used for the problem of matching two images, where the pixels of the first image are represented in the lines, while the pixels of the second image in the columns. Each element of the matrix represents the affinity of a point in the first image with a point in the second image. The characteristics of the matrices, the runtimes of the original and the proposed vectorized version and the speedup ($Speedup = \frac{Time_{original}}{Time_{vectorized}}$) for the many-core and multicore machines, can be seen in Table 1.

Considering the performance for the two architectures, the execution time (seconds) for pairing two images varied considerably, both for the *Original*

Table 1. Comparison of the execution time (seconds) of the *Original* and *Vectorized* versions for many-core and multicore machines (only one core was used).

Imagem	Characteristics			Many-core			Multicore		
	#Lin	#Col	#Iter	Original	Vectorized	Speedup	Original	Vectorized	Speedup
alamo18	1069	3306	3097	74.680	3.917	19.07	13.828	0.985	14.03
eifell	387	1917	121	0.686	0.097	7.07	0.136	0.031	4.39
essighaus	951	898	3698	23.299	1.357	17.17	4.214	0.348	12.11
miduomo02	2932	4369	1081	91.820	3.769	24.36	16.870	1.028	16.41
neubrandeburg	2142	3526	2380	119.171	5.089	23.42	21.931	1.347	15.14
notredame	3026	3297	2087	136.469	5.474	24.93	24.994	1.448	17.26
pantheon2	2083	4195	1093	63.395	2.764	22.94	11.694	0.714	16.38
sanmarco2	2454	3213	501	26.026	1.123	23.17	4.703	0.297	15.83
startgarder	3044	4339	786	68.277	2.737	24.94	12.643	0.734	17.22
startgarder3	4028	4484	3004	356.535	13.655	26.11	65.500	3.727	17.57

and *Vectorized* version. The reason for this behavior is that the time to match two images is proportional to the size of the matrix and the number of iterations to find the optimal match. The performance of the *Vectorized* version is significantly better than the *Original* one. The main reason for the excellent performance of the *Vectorized* version was the efficient use of the available 512-bit SIMD instructions, since only one machine core is used.

The speedups average obtained was ≈21 and ≈14.5, respectively, for many-core and multicore machines. However there was a great variation in performance depending on the size of the matrix and the number of iterations. For example, the worst speedup was 7.07 (many-core) and 4.39 (multicore) for the *eifell* matrix and the best was 26.11 (many-core) and 17.57 (multicore) for the *startgarder*3 matrix. The matrices with the shortest execution times obtained the worst speedups, while the best speedups were obtained by the matrices with the longest execution times. In small matrices, the execution time of instructions that were not vectorized has a greater weight in the total execution time, affecting performance.

Although the performance of the vectorization in the two architectures was very different, when comparing different matrices with similar *Original* execution times the performance was similar. For example, the *Original* multicore execution time for the *notredame* matrix was 24.99 s achieving a speedup of 17.26. In turn, the *Original* execution time for the *essighaus* matrix in the many-core machine was 23.29 s and the speedup 17.17.

When comparing the performance of the auction algorithm in the many-core and multicore machines a double impact due to the faster processor speed of the multicore machine can be observed. The higher speed of the multicore processor has produced shorter run times than the many-core machine. On the other hand, this higher clock reduced the speedups of the vectorization of the multicore machine when compared to the many-core. Finally, the excellent performance of the vectorization has two main reasons: execution of the main instructions in blocks due to the removal of deviation instructions and non-execution of instruction blocks due to the use of the vectorized conditional instructions.

Impact of the Size of the Matrices and the Number of Iterations on the Runtimes. This subsection analyzes the impact of the size of the matrices and the number of iterations on the performance of the vectorization. It was necessary to use an application that simulates the movement of particles, over time, within a 3D environment with different speeds, disturbed by random noises. This application allows the creation of matrices of the same size but that require different number of iterations to find the optimal value.

Matrices of sizes 2000 × 2000, 4000 × 4000 and 8000 × 8000 were generated with different number of iterations and the matching of these particles between two instants of time was performed using the original and vectorized auction algorithm. The execution times and speedup can be seen in Table 2. Results show that the vectorization performance improves with the increase in the size of the matrix and in the number of iterations. For example, for the 2000 × 2000 matrix, the speedups of the matrices with 4341 and 12735 iterations were 16.5% and 29.3% higher than those of the matrix with 3100 iterations in the many-core machine, while for the multicore machine it was 20.3% and 37.8% higher.

Similarly, speedups improved according to the increase in the size of the matrices. For example, for the many-core architecture speedups ranged from 18.35 (2000 × 2000 matrix with 3100 iterations) to 29.48 (8000 × 8000 matrix with 44227 iterations), whereas for the multicore architecture ranged from 11.87 to 19.84. One reason for this behavior is that the increase in the size of the matrix augments the amount of data to be vectorized in relation to the part that cannot be vectorized, which improves the performance in relation to the original version. On the other hand, the increase in the number of iterations improves the performance of the vectorized conditional instructions, since the number of associations decreases monotonically. Actually, these conditional statements had a great impact in the auction algorithm performance's since in the initial iterations most persons are associated with objects. Therefore, in subsequent iterations, only few persons are associated, so that for most of the iterations, many instructions are not executed due to vectorized conditional instructions.

Table 2. Iterations, Runtimes (seconds) for *Original* and *Vectorized* codes and Speedup (only one core of each architecture was used).

Matrix		Many-core			Multicore		
Size	Iterations	Original	Vectorized	Speedup	Original	Vectorized	Speedup
2000 × 2000	3100	87.10	4.75	18.35	15.56	1.31	11.87
	4341	116.16	5.44	21.37	20.72	1.45	14.28
	12735	332.16	14.00	23.73	60.06	3.67	16.36
4000 × 4000	4479	497.71	22.27	22.35	89.34	6.36	14.04
	8760	920.24	35.46	25.95	166.24	9.66	17.21
	24652	2549.36	93.24	27.34	465.21	25.09	18.54
8000 × 8000	7447	3177.16	117.04	27.15	584.94	33.60	17.41
	12757	5381.02	192.29	27.98	994.81	54.09	18.39
	44227	15780.76	570.91	29.48	3389.08	170.79	19.84

Execution Times of the AVX-512 × AVX-2. Unlike many-core processors that rely on 512-bit vector instructions since their creation, only the most recent architectures of multicore processors have this technology. Different technologies were incorporated into multicore processors, such as SSE, SSE2, SSE3, SSE4, AVX, and AVX-2, until the AVX-512 vectorized instructions became a reality [6]. Therefore, this subsection evaluates the performance gain that the modern AVX-512 vectorized instructions can achieve when compared to the previous vectorized instruction set, AVX-2 which have 256 bits instructions.

For this experiment, only the multicore machine was used. To compare with the AVX-512 vectorized version proposed in this work, a complete AVX-2 vectorized version of the auction algorithm was implemented based on the work in [3], that presented only part of the AVX-2 vectorization of the auction algorithm. The speedup ($Speedup = \frac{Exec\_Time_{AVX-2}}{Exec\_Time_{AVX-512}}$) for the 10 matrices presented in Subsect. 6.1 was calculated. The average performance gain of the AVX-512 implementation considering all matrices were ≈1.66. The largest speedup obtained was 1.86 for the *startgarder* matrix, while the smallest was 1.28 for the *eifell* matrix. Moreover, the worst speedups were obtained for the smallest matrices (*eifell* and *essighaus*), while the best for the largest matrices (*miduomo*02, *notredame*, and *startgarder*). This same experiment was carried out with the artificial matrices presented in the last subsection and the average speedup considering all artificial matrices were ≈1.71. This result indicates that the AVX-512 version was able to achieve very good results considerably improving the performance of the AVX-2 implementation. Additionally, for larger matrices, the performance of the AVX-512 vectorization was close to reach its full potential.

6.2 Experimental Analysis of the Parallel Vectorization

The same many-core and multicore machines described in the beginning of this section were used. However, the objective now is to evaluate the performance of the auction algorithm when executing with multiple threads and, with this, take advantage of the several cores available in these architectures.

Performance Evaluation. Initially, the three matrices with the longest execution times presented in Table 1 (*neubrandeburg*, *notredame* and *startgarder*3) were used. The vectorized versions were executed increasing the number of OpenMP threads. For the many-core machine the two versions were executed with 2, 4, 8, 16, 32, 64, 128 and 256 threads, while for the multicore machine the two versions were run with 2, 4, 8, 16 and 32 threads.

Only the static loop scheduling policy was used [16]. Preliminary tests have identified that although execution is not uniform, there is not enough imbalance for dynamic scheduling policies take advantage. Additionally, thread affinity was enabled to determine the set of cores where the threads could be scheduled, helping to improve performance on NUMA systems [16]. Thus, only cores in the same local memory were chosen to avoid the non-local memory access overhead

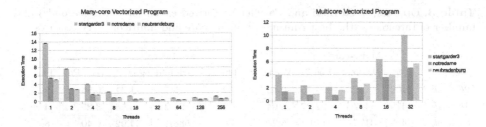

Fig. 3. Runtime (seconds) of Parallel *Vectorized* Multicore and many-core executions

whenever possible. The arithmetic mean of the execution times (in seconds) of the *Original* and *Vectorized* versions were calculated and can be seen in Fig. 3.

Analyzing the running times of the executions on the many-core machine (Fig. 3), it is possible to observe that there was an increase in performance for the *Vectorized* versions as the number of threads increased up to the limit of 64. However, as the size of the matrix remains constant as the number of cores increases, the amount of work for each core decreases. As the overhead remains constant for each unit of work, the efficiency decreases [10].

On the other hand, running times with 128 and 256 threads were worse than with 64 threads, despite the system having quad hyper-threading. The main reasons for the loss of performance from hyperprocessing are the absence of input/output operations and intensive use of the bus.

In turn, the behavior of the parallel version for the multicore machine (Fig. 3) was considerably worse. The *Vectorized* multicore version scale up only until 4 threads. The main reason for the lower scalability of the multicore execution, is the smaller amount of work to be parallelized. For example, the multicore *Vectorized* execution time for the *stargarder*3 matrix is only 2.07 s with 4 threads. Considering that this matrix has 3004 iterations, as can be seen in Table 1, the execution time for each iteration is only 0.000689 s. Thus, as the parallelism occurs within each iteration of the auction algorithm the fine granularity of the tasks limits its scalability.

Despite the better scalability and speedups of the auction algorithm in the many-core machine, the execution times were relatively more close in both architecture. On average, the best runtimes on the many-core machine were 2.5 times better than on the multicore machine.

Impact of the Size of the Matrices on Parallel Execution Times. To a better evaluation of the behavior of the parallel vectorized auction algorithm with the increase in the size of the matrix (coarse granularity), matrices of sizes 2000×2000, 4000×4000, 8000×8000 and 16000×16000 with 3100, 4479, 7447 and 9115 iterations, respectively, were used. The arithmetic average of 50 executions can be seen in Table 3. The results in the table clearly show the benefits of running the parallel version on both architectures. Considering the *Original* sequential version, the execution times on the multicore machine were

Table 3. Original, Vectorized and Parallel Vectorized execution times (seconds) and number of threads for the best runtimes in many-core and multicore architectures

Matrix		Many-core				Multicore			
Size	Iter.	Original	Vec	Vec+Par	Thread	Original	Vec	Vec+Par	Thread
$2k \times 2k$	3100	87.1	4.75	0.63	32	15.7	1.31	0.96	2
$4k \times 4k$	4479	497.7	22.27	2.04	32	91.2	6.56	3.25	4
$8k \times 8k$	7447	3177.1	117.04	5.23	64	586.1	34.92	10.40	8
$16k \times 16k$	9115	15783.8	570.97	20.99	128	3013.1	176.24	36.44	16

more than 5 times faster than on many-core architecture for all sizes of matrices. These results can be explained due to the higher clock frequency and a memory hierarchy more suitable to run sequential programs on multicore machine.

When analyzing the execution times of the *Vectorized* version in comparison with the *Original* one, the performance gain from running on the many-core machine was evident. The speedups ($Speedup = \frac{Execution\_Time_{original}}{Execution\_Time_{SIMD}}$) were $\approx$1.6 greater than the speedups of the multicore machine, in spite of both architectures having AVX-512 SIMD instructions. The main reason for this behavior is the fine granularity of the tasks for the multicore architecture when compared with the many-core architecture for the same matrix.

The execution times obtained with the *Vectorized Parallel* versions, as well as the number of threads to obtain these times show the best scalability of the many-core processor. Even starting from vectorized sequential times, on average, $\approx$3.4 times slower than those produced by the *Vectorized* sequential version on the multicore machine, the execution times on the many-core architecture were $\approx$1.7 times faster for all matrices. The better scalability of the vectorized parallel auction algorithm as the size of the matrix increase can be highlighted through the total speedup ($Total_Speedup = \frac{Execution_Time_{original}}{Execution_Time_{SIMD+Parallel}}$). For both systems, the speedup consistently increased as the size of the matrices increased. In the multicore, the lowest speedup was 16.44 while the highest speedup was 82.70. In turn, the performance in the many-core machine was quite impressive, being the lowest speedup 138.44 while the highest speedup was 751.97.

Performance Impact of Clock Down in the Xeon AVX-512 Architecture. While the frequency on the Xeon Phi machine is 1.4 GHz, Intel Xeon Platinum has a base frequency of 2.10 GHz and a max turbo frequency of 3.70 GHz. However, the max frequency that an application can achieve depends on the number of concurrently utilized cores and also the type of vectorization used [17]. The reason for this behavior is to reach the maximum possible frequency without overheating the processor [7]. Therefore, this subsection evaluates the performance impact of clock down in Intel Xeon Platinum machine on the Parallel Vectorized Auction Algorithm. The same matrix 8000 × 8000 used in the previous experiment were executed with the AVX-2 and AVX-512 vectorized versions

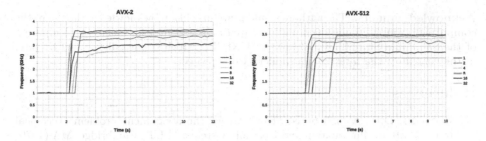

Fig. 4. Frequency of the cores as the number of threads increase

with 1, 2, 4, 8, 16 and 32 threads. The frequency of the cores for AVX-2 and AVX-512 vectorized versions were collected and are presented in Fig. 4.

As can be clearly seen, for both versions, the frequency decreases as the number of threads used increase. For example, in the AVX-2 version, the frequency with 2 threads was approximately ≈3.5 GHz, while the frequency with 16 threads was ≈3.0 GHz. Moreover, the frequency when executing the AVX-512 version were, in general, smaller than when executing with AVX-2, since the AVX-512 version enables twice the number of floating point operations and, thus, requires a lower frequency to avoid overheating. These variations in the frequency when increasing the number of threads and that depends on the size of the vectorized instructions has a directly impact in the performance of the applications and, consequently, in the scalability evaluation of Multicore architectures.

7   Conclusions

In order to take advantage of the full potential of many-core and multicore architectures, this work implemented and evaluated a vectorized version of the auction algorithm, as well as its parallel implementation in OpenMP, While the proposed vectorized algorithm was able to efficiently use the AVX-512 registers, the parallel version divides the workload between the available cores.

A series of experiments analyzed the vectorization performance in detail, as well as the efficiency of the parallel OpenMP implementation. Results show that it is possible to take advantage of the potential of both architectures. However, mainly due to the lower clock of many-core processors, the auction algorithm showed considerably better scalability in the many-core machine. While on the many-core machine the vectorized parallel version reached ≈750 of total speedup, on the multicore machine was ≈80. However, when we consider the execution time, the performance on the many-core machine was, on average, only ≈1.7 times better than on the multicore machine.

This excellent performance was only possible because the proposed implementation explored not only the multiple cores available in the two architectures, but mainly due to the efficient vectorization of the auction algorithm that was able to exploit the maximum potential of the AVX-512 instructions.

Acknowledgements. The authors would gratefully like to acknowledge the use of the computing resources maintained and operated by the Center for Scientific Computing of the São Paulo State University (NCC/UNESP), which is partially funded by Intel in the context of the Intel/Unesp Modern Code project.

References

1. Bertsekas, D.P.: A distributed algorithm for the assignment problem. Technical report, Lab. for Information and Decision Systems, M.I.T., Cambridge, MA (1979)
2. Bertsekas, D.P., Castañon, D.A.: Parallel synchronous and asynchronous implementations of the auction algorithm. Parallel Comput. **17**(6–7), 707–732 (1991)
3. Sena, A.C., Marzulo, L.A.J., Nascimento, A.P., Vasconcelos, C.N.: A malleable vectorized auction algorithm for modern multicore architectures. In: IEEE International Conference on High Performance Computing and Communications (HPCC), pp. 640–648 (2018)
4. Carpaneto, G., Martello, S., Toth, P.: Algorithms and codes for the assignment problem. Ann. Oper. Res. **13**(1), 191–223 (1988). https://doi.org/10.1007/BF02288323
5. Diaz, J., Muñoz-Caro, C., Niño, A.: A survey of parallel programming models and tools in the multi and many-core era. IEEE Trans. Parallel Distrib. Syst. **23**(8), 1369–1386 (2012)
6. Intel: Intel intrinsics guide. Technical report, Intel (2017)
7. Intel: Intel Xeon processor scalable family thermal mechanical specifications and design guide. Technical report, Intel (2019)
8. Kollias, G., Sathe, M., Mohammadi, S., Grama, A.: A fast approach to global alignment of protein-protein interaction networks. BMC. Res. Notes **6**(1), 1–11 (2013)
9. Kollias, G., Sathe, M., Schenk, O., Grama, A.: Fast parallel algorithms for graph similarity and matching. J. Parallel Distrib. Comput. **74**(5), 2400–2410 (2014)
10. Mackay, D.: Optimization and performance tuning for Intel® Xeon Phi^{TM} coprocessors. Technical report, Intel (11 2012)
11. Mark-Sabahi: a guide to auto-vectorization with Intel C++ compilers. Technical report, Intel, April 2012
12. Nascimento, A.P., Vasconcelos, C.N., Jamel, F.S., Sena, A.C.: A hybrid parallel algorithm for the auction algorithm in multicore systems. In: International Symposium on Computer Architecture and High Performance Computing Workshops (SBAC-PADW), pp. 73–78, October 2016
13. Reinders, J.: Intel AVX-512 instructions. Technical report, Intel (2017)
14. Sathe, M., Schenk, O., Burkhart, H.: An auction-based weighted matching implementation on massively parallel arch. Parallel Comput. **38**(12), 595–614 (2012)
15. Shokoufandeh, A., Dickinson, S.: Applications of bipartite matching to problems in object recognition. In: Proceedings of the ICCV Workshop on Graph Algorithms and Computer Vision (1999)
16. van der Pas, R., Stotzer, E., Stotzer, E., Terboven, C.: Using OpenMP - The Next Step: Affinity, Accelerators, Tasking, and SIMD. The MIT Press, Cambridge (2017)
17. Vladimirov, A.: A survey and benchmark of Intel Xeon Gold and Platinum processors. Technical report, Colfax Research (2017)
18. Wende, F., Noack, M., Steinke, T., Klemm, M., Newburn, C.J., Zitzlsberger, G.: Portable SIMD performance with OpenMP* 4.x compiler directives. In: Dutot, P.-F., Trystram, D. (eds.) Euro-Par 2016. LNCS, vol. 9833, pp. 264–277. Springer, Cham (2016). https://doi.org/10.1007/978-3-319-43659-3_20

Green Energy HPC Data Centers to Improve Processing Cost Efficiency

Jorge Lozoya Arandia[1]([✉])(iD), Carlos Jesahel Vega Gómez[1](iD), Alberto Coronado[1](iD),
Jesus Alejandro Gonzalez Garcia[2](iD), and Verónica Lizette Robles Dueñas[3](iD)

[1] School of Engineering and Technological Innovation, University of Guadalajara, Campus
Tonalá, 45425 Jalisco, Mexico
{jorge.larandia,alberto.coronado}@academicos.udg.mx,
Carlos.Vega@cutonala.udg.mx
[2] University of Flensburg, Flensburg, Germany
alejandro@elion.mx
[3] Data Analysis Center of the University of Guadalajara, Zapopan, Jalisco, Mexico
lizette@redudg.udg.mx

Abstract. The cost of processing in an HPC data center is one of the determining
variables for its implementation and operation, with energy consumption being
one of the most significant operating variables due to the high energy demand
required by the different elements that make up a HPC data center. This research
proposes the use of clean energy to operate HPC data centers, to allow optimization
of the efficiency of the processing operation in these spaces, considering their
service availability needs and the technology installed in a High performance
computer data center whit a medium capacity that seams to a regular equipment
installed in Latin America. The implementation of renewable energies, such as
solar energy, represents an option to make the effectiveness of energy consumption
more efficient in a data center, but since its availability is not stable, it is necessary
to implement it alongside other energy sources that allow an uninterrupted power
supply, to ensure constant data center operation. Determining the cost of HPC
processing is a metric that the different HPC centers of the world seek to make more
efficient in order to take advantage of the installed capacities to the maximum.
This cost has different variables that largely concern the operation of the data
center where the HPC equipment is housed. In this article we propose a model
that projects the cost of HPC processing based on capex implementation costs and
Opex operations.

Keywords: HPC data center · Solar energy · HPC processing cost

1 Introduction

With the arrival of the digital era, the need for infrastructure that supports telecommunications and data processing services has reached levels that have made them critical
to maintaining the applications that support this equipment, this situation makes the

© Springer Nature Switzerland AG 2022
I. Gitler et al. (Eds.): CARLA 2021, CCIS 1540, pp. 91–105, 2022.
https://doi.org/10.1007/978-3-031-04209-6_7

maintenance of the spaces that house these technologies a priority to operate the services housed. High Performance Computing (HPC) is a tool that allows the processing of large amounts of data through large amounts of parallel processing [1]. The HPC requires data centers where the teams that distribute and deliver these services are housed, in these spaces the conditions of infrastructure and electrical support are of vital importance for their adequate operation that allow them to carry out the required services according to the service level agreement (SLA).

For an HPC data center to offer quality services, it must have the necessary infrastructure to house the equipment that delivers those capabilities. HPC data centers, in general, represent high and constant energy consumption, since the equipment that comprise them must be energized 24 h a day, 365 days a year and support high priority services to carry out their functions with high availability. This requires uninterrupted energy support with the same service characteristics 24 h a day, 365 days a year, in order to take advantage of hosted services. HPC data centers worldwide account for 1 to 5% of global electricity use [2, 3]. This behavior in HPC processing energy consumption becomes a determining factor in the operation, energy consumption and its cost. An alternative to solving this problem is the use of renewable energy sources, which are cheaper in the long term [4]. Data centers provide a way in for off-site grid energy to power the infrastructure and to balance the inconsistent nature of renewable energy. The nature of variable workloads in data centers and prediction algorithms contribute to improved power and resource management, to use clean energy more effectively in data centers [5]. Therefore, to ensure supply, redundant energy sources and transition systems between them must be used to make automatic transitions without interruptions to the equipment, by means of batteries. Since clean energy is not consistent, it carries more challenges in its efficient usage [5].

In addition to the high energy consumption and the operating costs that result from it, another problem that faces HPC processing, with respect to data centers, is the high cost involved in planning and implementation. Therefore, it is desirable to have a tool that allows a plan to be developed, a model projecting both consumption and the total cost of owning a data center that meets the required service level agreements. Costs need to be broken down into their parts, which are generated by the energy consumption of the data center. It is proposed that the cost of HPC processing can be optimized by implementing renewable energies, through an analysis of the cost of energy consumption during Processing, and comparing it connected to the electricity grid and connected to an energy source, and determining its impact in the total cost of operations.

The implementation and operation of an HPC data center is made up of different variables that represent the equipment of data processing, storage, backup and network technologies, as well as building equipment such as power supply, air conditioning and sensor systems for operation and information and building security. Each of these elements in turn has different unique characteristics according to the space where they are implemented and their function, there are data centers in different geographical locations that require different cooling systems, security among other factors, in turn according to the purpose of use, these spaces can accommodate different processing, storage and high-speed network architectures for interconnection of equipment. The sum of these variables allows the design and operation of the HPC data center to be included in an analysis model for projections of its energy consumption.

Supercomputing in Latin America is a technology that has been developed alongside higher education institutions and industry, and the installed capacities are generally around 100 thera flops up to 500 thera flops, only in the case of Brazil it has capacities installed greater than this average. This research is based on the capabilities installed in the Center for Data Analysis and Supercomputing (CADS) of the University of Guadalajara, Mexico.

This article proposes a model for the analysis of energy consumption of an HPC data center (Fig. 1), comparing the use of different energy sources to analyze their costs and projections, through renewable energies. It is proposed that total energy consumption costs are optimized through the analysis of implementation and operation with renewable energies and projecting consumption and dimensioning capacities, linking this with their respective costs. The total cost of operation (TCO) is made up of the cost of implementation (CAPEX) plus the annual operating cost (OPEX). Extrapolating these costs and relating them to energy consumption and the implementation of the technologies necessary to deliver this energy to the data center helps form the model. These costs are compared with a data processing cost proposal, which allows deduction of a dimension of its impact on the cost of the processing capacity of an HPC Data Center, which is the main objective of an analysis center based on HPC.

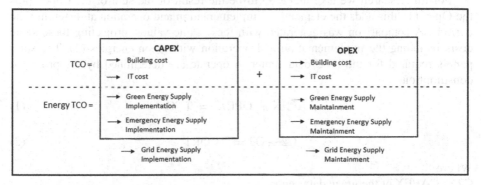

Fig. 1. TCO analysis focused on energy consumption costs in HPC Data Center.

The green data center model for HPC (Fig. 2) is made up of different elements that take into account the need to maintain uninterruptible power with high availability and include alternative energy sources. This model considers two main electrical power sources: one connected to the public electricity supply network and, another, a source of solar energy, which reaches a mains meter. The latter is connected to the internal electrical system and considered an energy transfer for a plant generator of energy, based on solid fuel, and its connection to the TI equipment is through a battery system that protects the equipment from the variation generated in these changes of energy source.

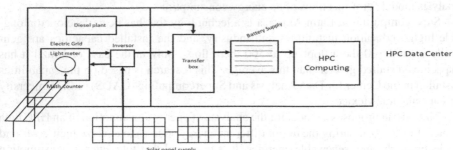

Fig. 2. Hybrid-powered green data center model.

Total Cost of Operation in a Data Center

Total operating cost (TCO) is defined as the financial calculation of the total direct and indirect costs of a data center and how any cost is subject to minimization (6). TCO's cost model is made up of the implementation costs, or capital expenses, (CAPEX): that is, the cost of building the data center, acquiring and installing its IT equipment (servers, network infrastructure, unit refrigeration, power distribution units, etc.), and the acquisition, installation and commissioning of the equipment necessary for the solar-wind hybrid system connected in each green data center.

For this research we take the TCO to be the result of the sum of the Capex plus the Opex (1), this adds the elements of implementation and operation at different time periods. A comparison was generated with these same values, projecting these same costs including the implementation and operation with green energies (2). The solar panels required for the HPC data center to operate are determined by the projected consumption.

$$CAPEX + OPEX = TCO \tag{1}$$

$$C2 + O2 = TCOR1 \tag{2}$$

Where:
C2 = CAPEX of the green data center
O2 = OPEX of the green data center
R1 = TCO total cost of operation of a green data center

The components of the CAPEX cost are made up of [7] For its analysis, a general cost per HPC node is considered, which includes all the network elements, connectivity and balancing necessary for its operation, plus the sum of the expenses associated with building construction costs (3).

$$CAPEX = \sum_{i=1}^{N_{dc}} \left(C_{IT} N_S^i + \underline{C} + C_{pv} N_{pv}^i \right) \tag{3}$$

Parameters

C_{IT}	Total cost of infrastructure per HPC Node
N_S^{ij}	Number of HPC nodes in the green data center, that the service is requested by as source of the request
C	Costs associated with building the data center
C_{pv}	Total cost of solar panels per unit area
N_{pv}^i	Number of solar panels installed in the green data center

OPEX

We defined the operating cost of an HPC data center in the same way, considering the structure of processing nodes and separating the costs from energy consumption, to this data we added an inflation rate.

The formula to analyze the Opex is:

$$\left(R_{inf} = \sum_{k=0}^{Lifespan} \left(1 + r_{inf}\right)^k \right) :$$
(4)

$$OPEX = C_e R_{inf} T \sum_{i=1}^{N_{dc}} \left(P_{IT} N_S^i - P_{pv}^i N_{pv}^i - P_w^i N_w^i \right) + \sum_{i=1}^{N_{dc}} \sum_{j=1}^{N_u} R_{inf} P_{sla}^j \lambda_{ij} e^{-\frac{\tau_j^{max}}{\tau_{ij}}}$$

$$+ C_M R_{inf} T \sum_{i=1}^{N_{dc}} N_S^i$$
(5)

Parameters

C_e	Energy cost (in dollars)
r_{inf}	Rate of inflation
T	Green data center operating time (in hours)
P_{IT}	Total energy consumption of IT infrastructure per HPC Node (including air conditioning, power distribution, and data network operation)
N_S^{ij}	Number of HPC Nodes in the green data center, that the service is requested by as Source of the request
P_{pv}^i	Green energy that can be generated in space (xi, yi) per unit area of solar panels
N_{pv}^i	Number of solar panels installed in the green data center
C_M	Maintenance and related services cost per HPC Node per hour of operation of the green data center
T	Green data center operating time (in hours)
r_{inf}	Rate of inflation

Node Processing Model in HPC

The energy consumption in an HPC data center is determined through processing capacities. The way to measure this capacity is the amount of computing assigned to a job that is used to deliver in a certain amount of time; the processing capacities in these data centers are determined by the infrastructure hosted in it. Processing was measured by the number of cores working together within each team, as a processor. These are called HPC processing nodes. A stochastic search, based on a genetic algorithm, was used to reduce IT power consumption and migration costs by considering energy-aware, virtual machine migration [8].

Each HPC processing node is made up of different elements that, together, allow its operation. In this article, they were divided into components that allow the analysis of its energy consumption as well as the cost of implementation and operation (Fig. 3). In this way, they comprise the air conditioning capacity required, the data network that makes up the data transmission and processing elements, and the electrical support elements.

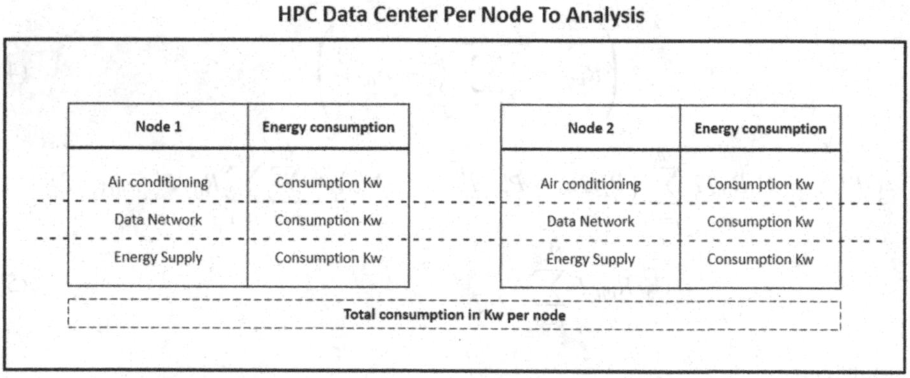

HPC Data Center Per Node To Analysis

Node 1	Energy consumption		Node 2	Energy consumption
Air conditioning	Consumption Kw		Air conditioning	Consumption Kw
Data Network	Consumption Kw		Data Network	Consumption Kw
Energy Supply	Consumption Kw		Energy Supply	Consumption Kw
Total consumption in Kw per node				

Fig. 3. Capex and Opex elements in HPC data center by nodes.

Node Processing Technology in HPC Model to Improve Energy Consumption

HPC processing technologies are currently very varied and different manufacturers have initiatives to reduce their energy consumption and optimize the operation in capacity processing [22], in this variety of technologies, high-performance network equipment is added. speed to interconnect processors and storage systems where processed data is enabled. These configuration variations make each HPC data center unique, even with the same technologies and capacities installed, the variation in geographic location makes renewable energy possibilities even more variable.

Due to this great variety, encompassing different points of energy consumption and alternative energy sources allows its analysis in a very specific way. For this research we are based on an architecture installed in the Center for Data Analysis and Supercomputing of the University of Guadalajara. For the implementation of renewable energy, it is necessary to determine the geographical location and the surrounding conditions for its implementation, and in terms of energy supply capacities, it also depends on the capacities installed in the HCP data center.

HPC data center, they depend entirely on the environmental conditions of the space where it is implemented, since the factors of heat, humidity and wind in the geographical position where it is located determine these factors. In the case of Mexico, supercomputing centers such as Abacus are in conditions of height and temperature, different from the CADS of the UDG, this means that each one has different energy consumption factors.

2 Development

The elements of TCO in Capex and Opex are defined by the architecture of the data center. For this article they were grouped into operation factors and those that have to do with energy consumption [7], each energy consumption behavior allows its optimization in the OPEX or CAPEX respectively. This must directly obey the HPC processing requirements defined in its design.

The analysis of capex is based on the elements (3) that confirm each node operation and are divided into those concerning implementation with solar panels and without solar panels. For this analysis we propose the operation and evaluation of the OPEX in the case of use of renewable energy whit solar panels and when the implementation doesn't have an alternative supply power. In order to analyze the behavior of energy consumption in relation to the cost, it is assigned a cost of processing.

The cost of processing is based on the implementation cost plus the operating cost divided by the operating time assigned to it, divided into the processing nodes (6). This proposal responds to a supercomputer architecture assigned in nodes for the distribution of the jobs to be processed. This tells us the cost of processing per hour.

$$\text{HPC processing cost} = (\text{Capex} + \text{Opex}) / \text{Processing Nodes} \qquad (6)$$

Green Energy Estimation Model for HPC Data Center
The analysis model by nodes in an HPC data center is defined by the components that provide the processing service; these are divided into those that have some energy consumption and those that are part of the building's facilities, assigned to analyze the operation cost of the HPC Data Center. The model to analyze CAPEX in an HPC data center is to assign each element that forms the total CAPEX to each HPC node Capex. The model to analyze the OPEX and to analyze each component off the Opex per HPC node. Processing was measured by the number of cores working together within each team, as a processor, and all cores into which it is divided is monitored; this core has different consumption according to the job assigned to the cores that comprise this node.

Processing Cost Allocation Model
The analysis of the total cost of a TCO data center allows differentiation of the elements that make it up. For this research it is proposed to separate the energy supply elements in the implementation and operation of the same, once these elements are differentiated we can generate different variables, such as implementing solar panels, and analyze their impact on the cost in the implementation and operation of the data center. In the case of an HPC data center it is proposed to be able to see this cost directly referenced to the processing capacities and how its use affects the main task of an HPC center, data processing.

To achieve this, an analysis of these elements was developed according to the HPC computing architecture hosted in the data center, which is based on Nodes (Fig. 4). The HPC architecture based on nodes, allows the use of processing in a differentiated way, with different sequences and exploitation logics, it does not necessarily use all of the installed capacities. In this way, each process has different costs and energy consumption, air conditioning and network capabilities. This analysis allows us to differentiate which is the CAPEX and OPEX by NODE and so we can identify the impact of the use of green energies directly, for each data processing in HPC.

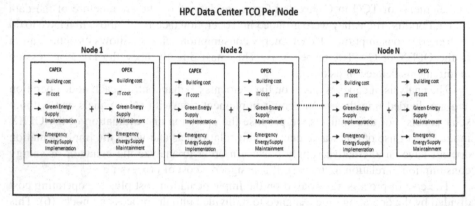

Fig. 4. TCO model per node.

3 Results

The results obtained were based on an HPC center design with 150 nodes and a data center that supports these services [12] once the algorithms were developed, they began by defining the costs of Capex and Opex, with energies connected to the public grid and with solar energy. These costs were considered for all the design factors for its operation in an uninterrupted way, in order to provide the computing capacities required for the HPC processing to operate correctly. When making the projection of implementation and operating costs connected to the public network, it is observed that the implementation costs are the same and their optimization is directly proportional to the design factors. Because they are only done once, they do not vary with time (Fig. 5). The Opex is increasing due to the increase in maintenance costs and variations in electricity consumption. The accumulated cost in five years represents a significant increase due to the electricity consumption rates paid annually.

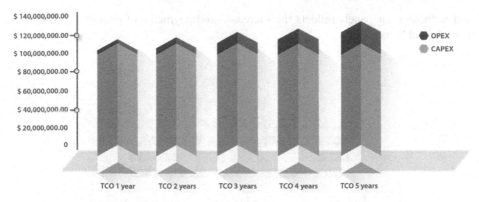

Fig. 5. Capex and Opex costs of data center, connected to the electricity grid 5-year projection.

Regarding the implementation of an alternative energy power system based on solar panels, the cost of implementation increases and it is important to take into account that this implementation depends on the solar energy capture capacity of the space and that it is intermittent. The factors considered in the implementation include the surface required to install the solar panels. During operation, it is observed that the accumulated costs are stable due to the low maintenance costs and those to which there are no increases in electricity rates.

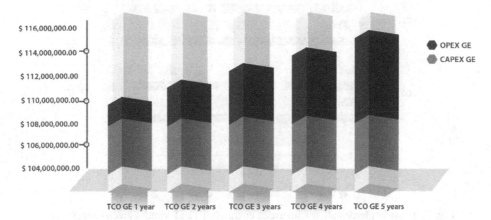

Fig. 6. Capex and Opex costs of data center with energy supply from solar panels 5-year projection.

To achieve a comparison of these implementations, five-year consumption projections are proposed, which are accumulated with the same factors considered in Capex and Opex. In this projection, the same capacities are compared in a number of nodes for the same HPC data center Fig. 6. This projection of implementation costs (see Fig. 6) reflects the increase that is implied when being able to install solar panels. An increase in stable operating costs is seen in both implementations but, in Fig. 7, the accumulated cost without solar panels reflects the increases and payments of energy consumption from the public network.

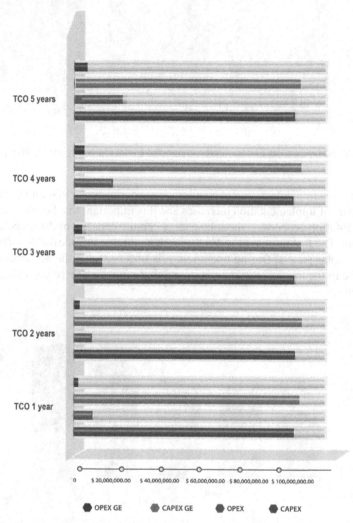

Fig. 7. Costs implementation with green energy (GE) and without green energy (GE).

Processing Cost Estimate per Node

The data comprising each node were analyzed and projected for 5 years, a projection with power from the electrical network and another connected to a network and solar panels, assuming that the supply complies with that projected, i.e. the solar radiation is the minimum expected in the design. In the first year, there is no variation with the

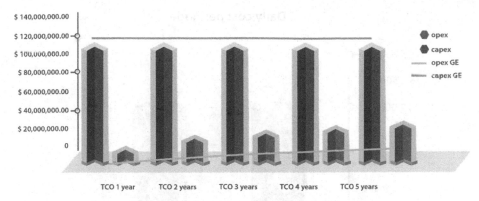

Fig. 8. GE Opex consumption without GE Opex.

two power sources and by generating 5-year projections, the operating costs with power supply from the electrical network increases (Fig. 9). This relationship is projected per node, as an accumulation in 5 years, and the cost of maintenance compared to the cost of energy consumption is shown in Fig. 10.

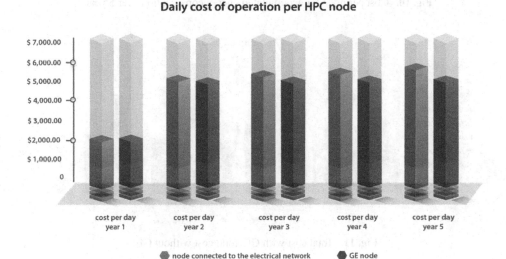

Fig. 9. Projected annual energy consumption.

Comparative

The total cost of operation (TCO) of an HPC data center was projected annulled for 5 years with green energies. In this case, for solar panels and without these energies connected to the public grid, the cost variation per year includes a projection of annual increase at current rates (Fig. 11).

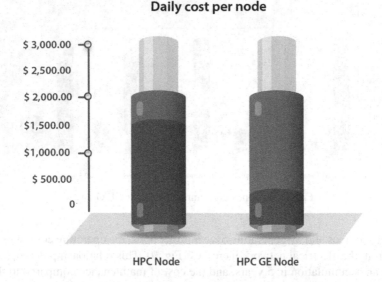

Fig. 10. Cost per node for accumulated energy consumption over 5 years.

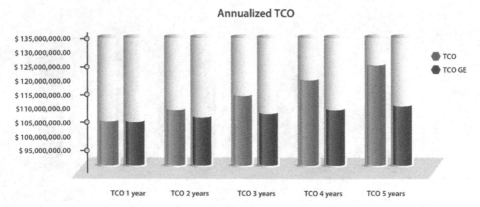

Fig. 11. Total cost with GE, total cost without GE.

Once the TCO of the data center has been identified, it can be analyzed and distributed by node. This allows observation of its operation according to the type of varying electrical energy sources, projecting it to 5 years (Fig. 12).

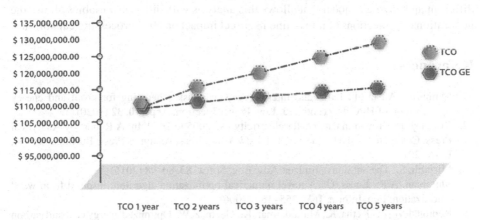

TCO per node de HPC

TCO 1 year   TCO 2 years   TCO 3 years   TCO 4 years   TCO 5 years

Fig. 12. Cost per node with GE and without GE.

4 Conclusions

In the implementation and operation of an HPC Data Center, the variables that make it up are very specific due to the technologies implemented in it, due to this the energy consumption can be varied. Being able to model these consumptions to analyze them and be able to consider the use of alternative energies for its operation, such as solar, allows to project behaviors and have elements to make decisions about processing costs that directly affect the obtaining of the best results in the use of the technologies hosted in the data center.

The analysis of the total cost of operation of an HPC data center can be determined in the costs of implementation and energy consumption, this allows determination of the impact of implementation of technologies of different kinds, for the supply of the required processing. Proposing a structure of the elements required for processing in HPC that helps us to set a cost per processing in nodes, allows us to identify the direct impact on the processing capabilities of the data center; the main purpose of an HPC data center being the maximum use of computing capacities. This proposed structure shows tangible values for the impact of the use of green energy in its operation. The architecture of computer nodes in HPC allows the analyzing of its energy consumption in a particular way, by including all the elements that comprise it and that have an energy consumption.

The implementation of green energy in the HPC data center represents a considerably higher initial investment than if this solution is not implemented (Fig. 8). This investment is not reflected in any savings in the first year of operation. The implementation of solar panels considerably improves the cost per processing node when it is projected for five operations, where a significant saving in energy consumption costs is seen (Fig. 12).

The implementation of solar panels for energy supply must consider all the technical elements for it, such as the required space and the level of annual solar radiation at the site to be installed. These factors generate different conditions for each data center; the operation also varies according to the installed architecture. This makes each data center different and having a model that allows this analysis with different variables allows the generation of projections of it to define its direct impact on HPC processing capabilities.

References

1. Mamun, S.A., et al.: Intra- and inter-server smart task scheduling for profit and energy optimization of HPC data centers. J. Low Power Electron. Appl. **10**, 32 (2020)
2. Koomey, J.: Growth in data center electricity use 2005 to 2010. In: A Report by Analytical Press, Completed at the Request of The New York Times; Analytics Press: Burlingame, CA, USA (2011)
3. Mirjalili, S.: The ant lion optimizer. Adv. Eng. Softw. **83**, 80–98 (2015)
4. Merabian, A.R., Lucas, C.: A novel numerical optimization algorithm inspired from weed colonization. Eco. Inform. **1**(4), 355–366 (2006)
5. Renugadevi, T., Geetha, K., Muthukumar, K., Geem, Z.W.: Optimized energy cost and carbon emission-aware virtual machine allocation in sustainable data centers. Sustainability **12**, 6383 (2020)
6. Koomey, J.: Ph.D. with Kenneth Brill, Pitt Turner, John Stanley, and Bruce Taylor. A Simple Model for Determining True Total Cost of Ownership for Data Centers. https://www.missio ncriticalmagazine.com/ext/resources/MC/Home/Files/PDFs/(TUI3011B)SimpleModelDete rmingTrueTCO.pdf
7. Latest Microsoft Datacenter Design Gets Close to Unity PUE. https://www.datacenterknowl edge.com/archives/2016/09/27/latest-microsoft-data-center-design-gets-close-to-unity-pue. Accessed 10 Jan 2020
8. Xu, H., Liu, Y., Wei, W., Xue, Y.: Migration cost and energy-aware virtual machine consoli-dation under cloud environments considering remaining runtime. Int. J. Parallel Prog. **47**(3), 481–501 (2019). https://doi.org/10.1007/s10766-018-00622-x
9. Shehabi, A., et al.: United States Data Center Energy Usage Report; Lawrence Berke-ley National Laboratory: Berkeley (2016). https://www.osti.gov/servlets/purl/1372902/. Accessed 10 Mar 2020
10. Bilbao, M., Alba, E.: Ga and pso applied to wind energy optimization. Master's thesis, Universidad Nacional de la Patagonia Austral, Universidad de Málaga (2009)
11. Tomašević, M., Lapuh, L., Stević, Ž, Stanujkić, D., Karabašević, D.: Evaluation of criteria for the implementation of high-performance computing (HPC) in Danube region countries using fuzzy PIPRECIA method. Sustainability **12**, 3017 (2020). https://doi.org/10.3390/su1 2073017
12. Gigler, B.-S., Casorati, A., Verbeek, A.: Financing the Future of Supercomputing, how to Increase Investment in High Performance Computing in Europe. European Investment Bank (2018). https://www.eib.org/attachments/pj/financing_the_future_of_supercomputing_ en.pdf. Accessed 5 Apr 2021
13. Michalakes, J., et al.: The weather research and forecast model: software architecture and performance. In: Proceedings of the Eleventh ECMWF Workshop on the Use of High Per-formance Computing in Meteorology, Reading, UK, 25–29 October 2004; World Scientific: Singapore, pp. 156–168 (2004)
14. University of Guadalajara. Data Analysis Center of the University of Guadalajara (2018). http://cads.cgti.udg.mx/
15. CINVESTAV. ABACUS: Laboratory of Applied Mathematics and High Performance Com-puting of the Department of Mathematics. ABACUS CINVESTAV (2021). https://www.aba cus.cinvestav.mx/inicio

16. Collins, J.R., Stephens, R.M., Gold, B., Long, B., Dean, M., Burt, S.K.: An exhaustive DNA micro-satellite map of the human genome using high performance computing. Genomics **82**, 10–19 (2003)
17. Aksanli, B., Rosing, T.: Providing regulation services and managing data center peak power budgets. In: Proceedings of the 2014 Design, Automation & Test in Europe Conference & Exhibition (DATE), Dresden, Germany, 24–28 March 2014, pp. 143–147 (2014)
18. Benini, L.; Micheli, G.D.: System-level power optimization: techniques and tools. ACM Trans. Des. Autom. Electron. Syst. (TODAES) **5**, 115–192 (2000)
19. Berl, A., Gelenbe, E., Di Girolamo, M.: Energy-efficient cloud computing. Comp. J. **53**, 1045–1051 (2010)
20. Bogdan, P., Garg, S., Ogras, U.Y.: Energy-efficient computing from systems-on-chip to micro-server and data centers. In: Proceedings of the 2015 Sixth International Green Computing Conference and Sustainable Computing Conference (IGSC), Las Vegas, NV, USA, 14–16 December 2015, pp. 1–6 (2015)
21. Brown, K., Bouley, D.: Classification of data center infrastructure management (DCIM) tools. In: Schneider Electric's Data Center, White Paper; Science Center: Foxboro, MA, USA (2014)
22. Chandler, B.: GPU-accelerated vision modeling with the HPE cognitive computing toolkit. Electron. Imaging **14**, 156–159 (2017). https://doi.org/10.2352/issn.2470-1173.2017.14.hvei-136

DICE: Generic Data Abstraction for Enhancing the Convergence of HPC and Big Data

Pablo Brox, Javier Garcia-Blas$^{(\boxtimes)}$, David E. Singh, and Jesus Carretero

University Carlos III of Madrid, Leganes, Spain
{pbrox,fjblas,dexposit,jcarrete}@inf.uc3m.es

Abstract. Today's data-intensive applications require access to multiple types of storage platforms, such as parallel file systems, distributed file systems, and in-memory data systems. In addition, many applications are demanding the processing of data streams. The goal is to develop mechanisms to integrate and hide the diversity of data sources from applications and improve data access performance.

In this work, we propose the implementation of a data container-based solution for data-intensive applications, which provides a high-level programming interface to different storage systems, commonly used in both HPC and HPDA environments. Our approach, DICE, hides the complexity of dealing with data from multiple sources, reducing the effort to access items transparently to end users and developers. The abstraction is based on a series of plugins that facilitate extension to other existing file systems.

Keywords: HPC · Big Data · Data abstraction

1 Introduction

For several years, I/O-intensive high-performance computing (HPC) has been primarily based on distributed object-based file systems that separate data from metadata management and allow each client to communicate in parallel directly with multiple storage servers. Exascale I/O raises the throughput and storage capacity requirements by several orders of magnitude, therefore we need to develop methods that can manage the network and storage resources accordingly. We presume that the systems already developed for data analytics are not

This work was supported by the EU project "ASPIDE: Exascale Programming Models for Extreme Data Processing" under grant 801091. This research was partially supported by Madrid regional Government (Spain) under the grant "Convergencia Big Data-HPC: de los sensores a las Aplicaciones. (CABAHLA-CM)". Finally, this work was partially supported by the Spanish Ministry of Science and Innovation Project "New Data Intensive Computing Methods for High-End and Edge Computing Platforms (DECIDE)" Ref. PID2019-107858GB-I00.

I. Gitler et al. (Eds.): CARLA 2021, CCIS 1540, pp. 106–119, 2022.
https://doi.org/10.1007/978-3-031-04209-6_8

directly applicable to HPC due to the fine-granularity I/O involved in scientific applications. Another weakness of existing systems is the semantic gap between the application requests and the way they are managed at the block level by the storage back-end.

The NESUS research network foresees in its Research Roadmap [12] that future applications will need more sophisticated novel interfaces that should be able to abstract architectural and operational issues from requirements for both storage and data. They should allow applications and services to easier manipulate storage and data, while providing the system with flexibility to optimize operation over a complex set of architectural and technological constraints. HiPEAC initiative recommends to address the issues of efficiency (maximizing power efficiency and performance through heterogeneous computer system design and catering for data locality), dependability and applications (bridging the gap between the growth of data and processing power; safety, predictability and ubiquitous availability of systems).

Data management challenge is currently addressed from multiple directions. However, there are two main approaches with a wide agreement [5]. First, data abstractions need to change given that traditional parallel file systems are failing on adapting to the new needs of applications and especially to their scalability characteristics. Abstractions such as object stores or key-values are positioning themselves in the lead to become the new storage containers such as Dynamo, BigTable or Cassandra. Second, data intensive HPC-based applications are becoming more necessary than ever in order to be able to analyze the huge amount of data.

This paper presents DICE[1], a Data container Interface for ExasCalE. The main contribution of this work is to detail the design principles of a generic I/O interface that unifies the access of parallel file systems in a single I/O interface. DICE hides the complexity of accessing different storage patterns (single file, multiple files in a single folder, etc.) by enabling data accesses using iterators. Additionally, with the objective of optimizing data accesses in massively large-scale applications, we show the integration with CLARISSE [9], an I/O manager that orchestrate data accesses.

The rest of the paper is structured as follows. Section 2 describes the design and implementation details of DICE. Section 3 summarizes the integration done for reducing I/O interference using DICE. Experimental results are shown in Sect. 4. In Sect. 5, we compare DICE with other existing approaches. Finally, Sect. 6 concludes the paper and discusses of future works.

2 Data Containers

The concept of data containers is introduced to reduce the complexity of accessing and creating data in different storage systems. These containers are high-level abstractions that provide a common interface, with a simple set of operations,

---

[1] Source code and examples available at https://gitlab.arcos.inf.uc3m.es/pbrox/dice.git.

to manage data items that belong to a dataset or a collection of datasets. In addition, they are designed to expose metadata that can be used to improve data locality or perform task scheduling in runtime. They can be categorized depending on their behavior: input, those used to read data, and output, the ones for writing data.

Fig. 1. DICE URI example.

The term dataset refers to a group of data elements that live in the same storage unit, and a collection is a group of datasets storing the same kind of data. Each dataset -or collection of them- is unequivocally identified by a uniform resource identifier (URI) that specifies the storage system and the dataset -or collection- path, Fig. 1 shows an example. Depending on their item type, datasets can be *binary*, whose data is written in a binary format, or *text*, whose data elements are in text format and separated by a determined character.

In general, the containers design pursues the following goals:

– Provide a common interface for different storage systems that ranges from in-memory storage to distributed file systems typically used for HPC and high-performance data analytics (HPDA) areas.
– Reduce the complexity for accessing individual data items from a dataset or a dataset collection.
– To expose metadata that can be exploited for improving data locality and task scheduling on runtime systems.

2.1 Input Containers

Input containers are the ones providing an interface to extract data from the storage system. They are designed to work with data elements already created that are going to be processed by the application, but they cannot be used to write new results. Depending on the cardinality, we distinguish them in two categories: *Collection Container*, which holds a collection of datasets, and *Dataset Container*, which manages a dataset. In addition, according to the item type, there are two input containers for each category: binary and text.

Regarding the access operators, the user can interact with the containers using an iterator-like scheme to traverse them. Depending on the type, iterators can be random access or sequential, and they behave similarly to pointers. Iterators are associated with a given element (*File* or data item) and can be

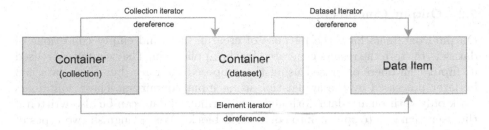

Fig. 2. Input containers hierarchy.

dereferenced to return it. Furthermore, they always provide the "++" operator to advance to the next element. Figure 2 shows the different iterators type and its hierarchy. A *Container* has two iterators, a collection one, which is always random access and is used to traverse and access its datasets; and an element iterator, which is not random access (can only be used sequentially) and goes through the elements of all the datasets in the collection. In the case of *File*, it only provides one iterator that behaves as the *Container* element iterator, but only for the elements of the dataset.

Other operations supported by all the input containers include obtaining all the beginning and ending iterators, retrieving its URI and the common comparison operators, "==", "!=". Moreover, the dataset container (*File*), and sometimes its iterator, also includes a function to retrieve the network names of the storage servers where the data, and its replicas, are located. Below you can find a broader description of the text and binary input containers and their main differences.

Text Containers. Text input containers work with datasets -or collections- whose data items are stored in text format and separated by a known character. The data items size is unknown and does not have to be equal for the same dataset. Its elements, those accessible by the element and *File* iterators, are retrieved as formatted strings, without the separator. Furthermore, as a data element may be stored in more -or less- than one storage block, elements are parsed each time the iterator is incremented. Because of it, the operation to retrieve the data location is only available for text input *Files*, as the iterator location can concern several overlapped blocks. In addition, the iteration range of a *File* can be limited within a determined interval, allowing to divide its processing.

Binary Containers. Binary input containers are designed for datasets -or collections- that store data items written in binary. Data items size is fixed and known for each dataset and, depending on the selected backend, usually matches with its internal block size. Its elements, those accessible by the element and *File* iterators, are retrieved in the form of raw (binary) blocks. As their size and offset is always known, it is possible to extend the get data location operation to the iterator level. In this way, binary input containers can obtain the network location of each data element inside the dataset.

2.2 Output Containers

Output containers have the purpose of creating new and empty collections of datasets to store the results generated by the application. They cannot be reused as input containers or erased using the proposed interface, but their data can be later processed by the application using input containers. These containers work only with binary data, although text-formatted data can be also written if the user manages to split it into equal-sized blocks. We distinguish two types of output containers depending on their purpose: *Flusher*, which is used to write chunks of data in new datasets, and *Movement Container*, used to merge several collections into a new one.

Flusher. Flusher containers are the ones designed to write new data on the supported storage systems. They are created over a collection URI -that can exist and store datasets or not- and allow the creation of newly named datasets inside it. Once a flusher is instantiated, the collection is created if needed but the user is not able to store any data until the *newfile* operation is called to create a new dataset. At that point, the flusher can be employed to write data in the selected dataset until the next *newfile* call. Figure 3 illustrates the process. Notice that after the *newfile* operation, the prior dataset cannot be modified, and there is no option to create a flusher over a single dataset.

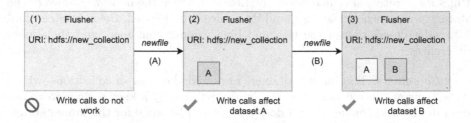

Fig. 3. Example of flusher life-cycle.

There are two different ways to write into a flusher: the POSIX-like function and the C++-like operator. For the first one, the user specifies a buffer and its size inside a *write* function call. The other method uses the flusher "<<" operator with a raw binary block or a C++ string. Both operations translate into direct write calls in the storage system API.

Movement Container. The Movement Container is conceived to move or gather all the datasets from several collections into a new one. It works for collections with different storage systems and data formats. However, the resulting collection will be located in a single backend and can be read with input containers from one data type (there are no input containers for mixed-format data). They are created over a collection URI -that can exist and store datasets or not-, and input collection containers (binary or text) can be attached to it using the "<<" operator. Later, when the user calls the *flush* operation, all the datasets from the attached collections are copied into the container URI using a *flusher*.

2.3   Storage Support for Containers

Containers are designed to act as a common front-end for those storage system frameworks that are tipically used in HPC and HPDA. This storage infrastructure includes alternatives such as: local node filesystems, large distributed storage filesystems, in-memory storage systems, etc. Containers unify those systems by exposing the same interface to access the storage capabilities of such components. This abstraction is provided by a set of software connectors for the supported storage systems.

The storage systems used for the containers can be classified in two categories: secondary storage systems and in-memory storage systems. The first category refers to those storage systems that are mainly targeted to long-term data storage. In this sense, those systems are not usually on the same nodes where the computations take place in a HPC platform. The second category, refers to those systems that are stored in main memory and mostly on the computation nodes. Specifically, in-memory systems are mainly targeted to store temporal data and to act as a proxy for other secondary storage systems. Figure 4 shows a schema that represents the relations among storage systems and containers. As observed, we initially plan to support POSIX and HDFS as secondary storage systems and IMSS (Hercules) as for the in-memory storage.

Each container is associated with a particular dataset, or collection of datasets, that is stored on a given storage infrastructure. Each dataset container uses a unique name, given as a Uniform Resource Identifier (URI), that refers both to the storage system and the specific dataset. While a collection container uses a set of URIs that can be defined implicitly (e.g. a directory URI) or explicitly (e.g. a list of URIs).

2.4   Interface

Containers are defined as C++ types, with its own set of associated member functions. There are two main categories of container types: input containers (Container_In) and output containers (Container_Out). The main method, as for any other C++ type, is the constructor. Both input and output containers share the same constructor interface. Listing 1.1 shows the constructor interfaces for containers.

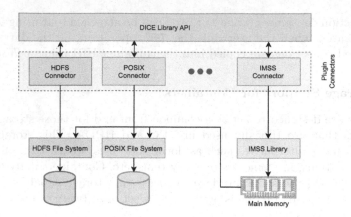

Fig. 4. Container architecture schema.

Listing 1.1. Container_In constructor prototypes.

```
1 //binary dataset/collection containers constructors
2 Container_In (std::string URI, size_t item_size, Options opt = {});
3 Container_In (std::vector<std::string> URIs, size_t item_size, Options
  ↪    opt = {});
4 Container_In (PatternString pattern, size_t item_size, Options opt =
  ↪    {});
5
6 //Text dataset/collection containers constructors
7 Container_In (std::string URI, std::string separator, Options opt =
  ↪    {});
8 Container_In (std::vector<std::string> URIs, std::string separator,
  ↪    Options opt = {});
9 Container_In (PatternString pattern, std::string separator, Options
  ↪    opt = {});
```

The main mandatory parameter of the containers constructor is the container URI, or set of URIs, that refers to the storage support for the dataset/collection. Dataset containers always require a single URI that correlates to a unique dataset located at the storage system. Whereas collection containers can be referred using a single URI for a collection, using a list of URIs correlating to individual datasets, or using a URI pattern that can be indexed into a list of individual datasets URIs.

Another mandatory parameter of the containers constructor is either the size of the item or the separator string. The size of the item is a mandatory parameter for some binary containers while the separator string is a mandatory parameter for all the text containers. Therefore, this parameter determines wheter the container is a binary or a text container.

The optional parameters are grouped into a single parameter list called Options. These options include the following configuration information:

– Back-end URI/set of URIs: This parameter is used for in-memory containers that have a backend support on a long-term storage system. Depending on the URIs provided for the in-memory container, this option can be provided in different formats. If the in-memory URI correspond to a collection, the back-end URI can be expressed in any of the different options stated for the container URI (a unique collection URI, a list of URIs or a pattern). However, the cardinality of both should be the same at the allocation time. For instance, if the URI of an output container is provided as a unique collection URI and the back-end is specified as a list, the number of elements of the list should be the same as the number of datasets allocated for that collection. Otherwise, if the in-memory URI correspond to a dataset, the back-end should also be provided as a unique dataset URI.

– Replication: This parameter setups the number of replicas per item at the container storage. This option cat take the following values: no replication (NONE), double replication (DMR) and triple replication (TRM).
– Distribution: This parameter configures the data distribution among the storage nodes. For instance, some of the values supported for this parameter are round-robin distribution (RR) or bucket distribution (BUCKET).
– Size: this parameter determines the necessary amount of memory that should be allocated for storing the data items in the corresponding storage system.

Listing 1.2 shows the C++ variadic interface for parsing the different suported option.

Listing 1.2. Container configuration options interface.

```
1  //Options constructor: Backend URIs
2  template <class... T>
3  Options (std::string URI, T... rest);
4  template <class... T>
5  Options (std::vector<std::string> URIs, T... rest);
6  template <class... T>
7  Options (PatternString pattern, T... rest);
8
9  //Options constructor: Redundancy
10 enum Replication {NONE, DMR, TMR}
11 template <class... T>
12 Options (Replication rep, T... rest);
13
14 //Options constructor: Distribution
15 enum Distribution {RR, BUCKET, ...}
16 template <class... T>
17 Options (Distribution dist, T... rest);
18
19 //Options constructor: Container size
20 template <class... T>
21 Options (size_t size, T... rest);
```

The proposed containers provides two ways for accessing the data items, through iterators and using a set of container member functions. Basically, they provide, following the definitions of the C++ standard, a random access iterator for accessing the different data items. This iterator supports the necessary operators stated for the random access iterator, i.e. it supports "++", "–", "–=", "+=" and "*" operators. Additionally, the containers also provide a set of member functions for operating directly with the storage system. Basically, the member functions provided by these containers are the following:

– get: This member function returns a data item/dataset identified by a data location structure. This data location is comprised by the ip of the nodes that stores a given data item and the index of the data item or a dataset in the corresponding dataset/collection ,respectively. Note that, for a data collection, the data location does not indicate any ip since it refers to a dataset that can be distributed.

- **write**: This function stores a data item on a given location on a dataset container.
- **get_dataloc**: This member function obtains the data location for a given data item/dataset identified by the index or its iterator.
- **range**: This member function allows to limit the iteration range of a *File* container within the specified interval (in bytes). In this way, the user can divide the data element processing between different threads or processes in a safe way.
- **size**: Returns the amount of allocated memory for a given container or the number of datasets part of a collection.

Listing 1.3 shows the interfaces for the supported member functions.

Listing 1.3. Container member functions

```
1  //Container methods: get
2  template <class T>
3  T get(Dataloc dataloc);
4
5  //Container methods: set
6  template <class T>
7  void set(Dataloc dataloc, T item);
8
9  //Container methods: get_dataloc
10 Dataloc get_dataloc(iterator it);
11 Dataloc get_dataloc(unsigned int index);
12
13 //Container methods: allocate
14 range(size_t begin, size_t end);
15
16 //Container methods: size
17 size_t size();
```

3   Reduction of I/O Interference

This section describes how the DICE interface has been interfaced with CLARISSE. CLARISSE is a middleware that provides I/O coordination and control [9]. Originally, CLARISSE only supported applications that perform I/O via MPI, and in this work we have extended this integration to applications that use the DICE interface. Figure 5 shows the coupled integration of this architecture. CLARISSE consists of three layers corresponding to data management, application control, and I/O scheduling policies. The data management layer (not used in this work) enables the creation of a storage buffer area used to share data between different applications. The I/O scheduling policy layer implements I/O scheduling policies that enforces an order when several applications simultaneously perform I/O on the same filesystem. The control layer includes functionalities for the coordination of I/O operations between different applications. Each application's DICE interface is connected to the control layer by

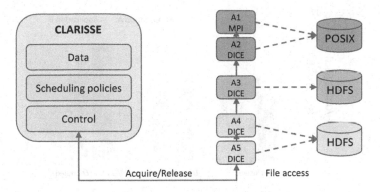

Fig. 5. Integration of CLARISSE into DICE. The CLARISSE control commands for coordinating the I/O are represented with solid lines. The I/O operations are represented with dashed lines.

means of an acquire/releases protocol (shown with solid lines in the figure). By means of this protocol, when an application performs an exclusive I/O operation, i.e. without any other application performing I/O at the same time, then this operation is immediately granted by CLARISSE. However, when several applications perform I/O simultaneously, then CLARISSE, by means of the control layer, imposes an I/O access order. Note that the integration of CLARISSE with the applications is done transparently, without introducing changes in the application code.

Five applications are shown in the Figure example, A1 is MPI-based and does not use containers, while the rest use DICE. Within this example A1 and A2 use the POSIX interface (via MPI and DICE, respectively) to access a file system that they share. A3 uses IMS, while A4 and A5 access data using HDFS. In this example, we assume that the physical file system is different for each interface. Thus, CLARISSE will independently schedule the I/O of A1 with A2 and A4 with A5. Note that in the case where both POSIX-based and HDFS-based file systems are based on the same physical device, combined scheduling of all four applications would be possible. Examples of scheduling policies are the delayed I/O [4], which allow to avoid that several applications perform I/O simultaneously, competing for bandwidth and increasing the risk of contention. Note that in this example, I/O is coordinated between DICE-based applications as well as between mixed MPI and DICE applications.

4   Evaluation

The experimental evaluation has been carried out in a cluster of 8 nodes with the following configuration. Each node has an Intel(R) Xeon(R) CPU E5-2603 v4 processor with 126GB DDR4 of RAM memory. All nodes are connected through a 10 Gbps network interface. The compiler used is GCC 8.0. After that, the source code has been compiled using both -O3 and -DNDEBUG flags.

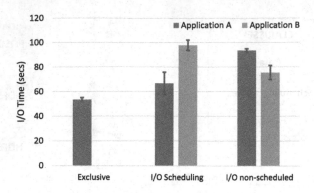

Fig. 6. I/O interference evaluation for two different applications performing a single I/O access.

Different experiments have been performed in a cluster using the *copydir* benchmark that copies the files from one directory into another one using containers. In our experiments, the directory size has two files with a total size per directory of 7.2 GB. Figure 6 shows the I/O access time of *cpydir* benchmark for three different scenarios: when only one application is exclusively executed (exclusive), when two applications are simultaneously executed using a I/O scheduling algorithm (I/O scheduling) and when two applications are simultaneously executed without I/O scheduling (I/O non-scheduled). The provided results are the average of five different executions. We can observe that when the I/O is scheduled, Application A has a higher priority, obtaining a I/O time that is close to the Exclusive scenario at expense of Application B that has a longer I/O time. When the I/O is not scheduled both applications perform the I/O at the same, creating interference that degrades the I/O performance of both of them.

Figure 7 shows the impact of the I/O scheduling on the overall application performance when two different tasks have three I/O phases with the same duration spaced 90 s. Each requests was performed by the *copydir* benchmark on a 7.2 GB directory and the results correspond to the average of five different executions. When the I/O is not scheduled, there are multiple overlaps between the I/O phases of both applications, producing a degradation on the performance in all the phases. By means of I/O scheduling, the first I/O accesses are spaced in time, avoiding the risk of further simultaneous (and interfering) I/O phases. This leads to a reduction in the overall I/O time of 14.8% and 10.9% for applications A and B, respectively.

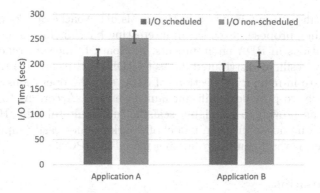

Fig. 7. I/O interference evaluation for two different applications performing multiple I/O accesses.

5 Related Work

VIDAS [11] proposes containers as data abstractions that allow consistent sharing of uniquely identified external storage resources, such as NFS or remote Amazon S3 objects, across virtualized environments. It differs from our proposal on its access interface, which is POSIX-like and does not support iterators. BitDew [7] offers a programmable environment for automatic and transparent large-scale data management and distribution on computer desktop grids. It uses the metadata to dynamically control the repartition and distribution of data, bridging the gap between desktop grids and P2P data sharing. Similarly to us, the users can add or replace according to their needs. ADIOS [10] provides a flexible approach for I/O within scientific codes by implementing a generic and simple API that relies on external XML description of the I/O characteristics (data types, transport methods as MPI-IO, POSIX-IO or HDF5, ...), supporting processing pipelines for service-oriented architectures. In contrast to our work, rather than using a URI, it depends on an XML external description of the storage system. Finally, in [1], Abbasi et Al. present Data Services, a set of system-level abstractions that encapsulate high-performance output data movement and manipulation for petascale systems. They aim to make it easier to develop, deploy and maintain per-site and per-run optimizations of I/O processes. Although it supports different storage back-ends, their approach is an external service in charge of the whole data output pipeline.

One of the main challenges of performance optimization in the I/O subsystem is avoiding the risk of I/O interference [6]. There are several solutions that address this problem on different levels of the platform architecture. At system level, shared-burst buffers are able to absorb bursty I/O traffic, although they are also susceptible to suffer performance degradation because of I/O interference [13]. A different approach for tackling this problem consists of predicting the application interference [2] and performing resource provisioning. Alternative solutions like [6], introduce I/O scheduling policies for coordinating the I/O access and avoiding contention. CLARISSE corresponds to this last category.

The scientific community is aware that tools like Apache Spark, and the RDD data model they propose, provides an interesting baseline for integration of scientific simulations in BDA environments. he Spark framework relies heavily in the concept of resilient distributed dataset (RDD) [14] to provide this functionality. RDDs are in-memory collections of data, and the operations on them are tracked in order to provide significant fault tolerance. According to its authors, the system has proven to be highly scalable and fault tolerant. However, the data abstraction and application model of Spark are not easily supported using MPI [8], which is the main programming model in HPC [3].

6   Conclusions

In this work, we have presented DICE, a generic data access abstraction for unifying HPC and Big Data worlds. DICE aims to simplify I/O accesses in data-intensive applications by using the well-known iterators objects. DICE takes advantage of modern C++ features that enables a generic code implementation, as the same time, reducing significantly the number of internal data copies. In this work, we also show the integration of CLARISSE, an I/O controller that enables the coordination of consecutive I/O accesses, avoiding interferences that increase the I/O latency. The combination of both solutions facilitates coexistence of both traditional HPC applications and Big data-based applications.

In the future, we plan to extend DICE to support other popular cluster-based file system such as Ceph (Rados) of BeeFS and cloud-based file systems such as Amazon S3. This feature will enable data analytics mixing local and remote storage subsystems.

References

1. Abbasi, H., Lofstead, J., Zheng, F., Schwan, K., Wolf, M., Klasky, S.: Extending I/O through high performance data services. In: 2009 IEEE International Conference on Cluster Computing and Workshops, pp. 1–10. IEEE (2009)
2. Alves, M.M., de Assumpção Drummond, L.M.: A multivariate and quantitative model for predicting cross-application interference in virtual environments. J. Syst. Softw. **128**, 150–163 (2017)
3. Caíno-Lores, S., Lapin, A., Carretero, J., Kropf, P.: Applying big data paradigms to a large scale scientific workflow: lessons learned and future directions. Future Gener. Comput. Syst. **110**, 440–452 (2018)
4. Carretero, J., Jeannot, E., Pallez, G., Singh, D.E., Vidal, N.: Mapping and scheduling HPC applications for optimizing I/O. In: Ayguadé, E., Hwu, W.W., Badia, R.M., Hofstee, H.P. (eds.) ICS 2020: 2020 International Conference on Supercomputing, pp. 33:1–33:12. ACM, Barcelona, Spain (2020)
5. Carretero, J., Zomaya, A.Y., Jeannot, E.: Ultrascale Computing Systems. Institution of Engineering and Technology (2019)
6. Dorier, M., Antoniu, G., Ross, R., Kimpe, D., Ibrahim, S.: CALCioM: mitigating I/O interference in HPC systems through cross-application coordination. In: IPDPS - International Parallel and Distributed Processing Symposium, pp. 155–164. Phoenix, United States (2014)

7. Fedak, G., He, H., Cappello, F.: Bitdew: a data management and distribution service with multi-protocol file transfer and metadata abstraction. J. Network Comput. Appl. **32**(5), 961–975 (2009). (Next Generation Content Networks)
8. Gropp, W., Thakur, R., Lusk, E.: Using MPI-2: Advanced Features of the Message Passing Interface. MIT press (1999)
9. Isaila, F., Carretero, J., Ross, R.B.: CLARISSE: a middleware for data-staging coordination and control on large-scale HPC platforms. In: IEEE/ACM 16th International Symposium on Cluster, Cloud and Grid Computing, CCGrid 2016, Cartagena, Colombia, 16–19 May 2016, pp. 346–355. IEEE Computer Society (2016)
10. Liu, Q., et al.: Hello adios: the challenges and lessons of developing leadership class i/o frameworks. Concurr. Comput. Pract. Exper. **26**(7), 1453–1473 (2014)
11. Llopis, P., Blas, J., Isaila, F., Carretero, J.: VIDAS: object-based virtualized data sharing for high performance storage I/O. In: Proceedings of the 4th ACM Workshop on Scientific Cloud Computing, Science Cloud 2013, pp. 37–44. Association for Computing Machinery, New York, NY, USA (2013)
12. Sousa, L., Kropf, P., Kuonen, P., Prodan, R., Trinh, A.T., Carretero, J.: A Roadmap for Research in Sustainable Ultrascale Systems. Carlos III University of Madrid (2018)
13. Thapaliya, S., Bangalore, P., Lofstead, J., Mohror, K., Moody, A.: Managing I/O interference in a shared burst buffer system. In: 2016 45th International Conference on Parallel Processing (ICPP), pp. 416–425 (2016)
14. Zaharia, M., et al.: Resilient distributed datasets: a fault-tolerant abstraction for in-memory cluster computing. In: Proceedings of the 9th USENIX Conference on Networked Systems Design and Implementation, pp. 15–28. NSDI (2012)

A Comparative Study of Consensus Algorithms for Distributed Systems

Kelsi Rado Van Dame, Thomas Bronson Bergmann, Mohamed Aichouri, and Maria Pantoja[✉] ⓘ

California Polytechnic State University, San Luis Obispo, CA 95116, USA
mpanto01@calpoly.edu

Abstract. Distributed Systems (DS) where multiple computers share a workload across a network, are used everywhere, from data intensive computations to storage and machine learning. DS provide a relatively cheap and efficient solution that allows stability with improved performance for computational intensive applications. Fundamental to DS is the consensus algorithm, necessary to agree on which server is the master, who has a lock and many other applications. Consensus algorithms are sometimes very difficult to understand and therefore implement correctly. In this paper we chose to complete a comparative study between three different consensus algorithms Raft, Paxos, and pBFT. We provided our implementation for the three algorithms with details of the assumptions taken. The goal of this study is to better understand the differences between the systems in terms of performance and assess the advantages and disadvantages of each. To test the performance of each program, we recorded consensus latency vs. node count and we present a summary of our results in this paper.

Keywords: Distributed consensus · Paxos · Raft · pBFT · Byzantine failure

1 Introduction

Despite the great prevalence and need for high performing consensus algorithms today, relatively few studies can be found regarding the comparative performance of distributed consensus. For this reason, in this paper we sought to compare differences in consensus latency vs node count in each of 3 algorithms: Raft [9], Paxos [4], and pBFT [1]. There are three main properties in distributed consensus algorithms; fault tolerance, liveness, and safety.

(a) Fault Tolerance. The profound difference between these algorithms is that Raft and Paxos are both intolerant of Byzantine failures, while pBFT, as the name might suggest, is tolerant. These failures take their name from the Byzantine Generals Problem, in which a group of generals is poised in separate locations around an enemy city. If the majority of generals attack the city in a synchronized manner, they can successfully conquer it, but they

© Springer Nature Switzerland AG 2022
I. Gitler et al. (Eds.): CARLA 2021, CCIS 1540, pp. 120–130, 2022.
https://doi.org/10.1007/978-3-031-04209-6_9

must first come to a consensus as to when they should launch the attack. The dilemma is that some of the generals may be unreliable. Their messages may be delayed, they may have fled the battle, or they may be traitors, sending false or inconsistent messages to the other generals. So the question then is, how can one be sure a majority consensus has been reached? If we apply the concept to distributed consensus, then each general represents a node and the majority of nodes need to reach consensus and execute the same action in order to avoid complete failure. Raft, Paxos, and pBFT are all capable of handling nodes that have crashed or gone offline but only pBFT is secure enough to handle the possibility of particularly malicious nodes that send false or inconsistent messages to other nodes. To put it in other terms, all three algorithms can ensure the liveness of a system by preventing nodes from indefinitely halting progress but only pBFT can ensure the safety of a system by preventing malicious nodes from improperly altering the network.

(b) Liveness. Liveness of the system is guaranteed through leader elections in Raft and Paxos, or equivalently by view changes in pBFT. Details of these processes can be found under the descriptions of each algorithm in the Implementation section. It is expected that the differences, between the leader elections in Paxos and Raft, and view changes in pBFT, will all have a significant impact on latency times but we expect the starkest divergence in latency to come from the assurance of safety in pBFT.

(c) Safety. Under the assumption that at least 2/3 of all system nodes, rounded up, are functioning properly, pBFT handles Byzantine faults by requiring all non-faulty nodes to agree in order to move beyond various stages of the algorithm. Functionally, this requires that every node sends a message to every other node three separate times so that each individual node in the system can confirm a 2/3 majority consensus. The equivalent processes in Raft and Paxos trust that any message received is valid. Therefore, a majority of messages need only be broadcasted and confirmed by one node, the leader, instead of by every node in the system. This difference means that, just to ensure safety, pBFT needs to send exponentially more messages as the number of nodes increases, while the number of messages sent in Raft and Paxos will increase linearly for each node in the system [2]. This design difference in pBFT, while important for Byzantine failures, is expected to cause the largest distinction in latency times between any of the algorithms. It is thus our goal to understand the extent by which these different design decisions in each of our three algorithms cause varying degrees of consensus latency at scale.

We provide all code for the three different consensus algorithm in the github [13] so readers can replicate results and implement their own consensus algorithms.

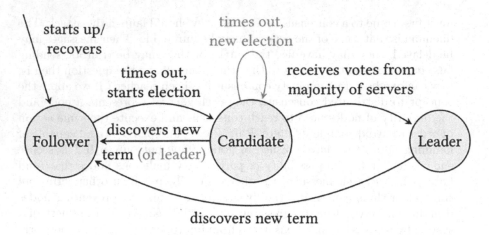

Fig. 1. Diagram showing the interactions between nodes during leader election [3]

2   Implementation

2.1   Paxos

Paxos [4–7] is the oldest of the consensus algorithms we are comparing and is considered to be the first consensus algorithm to be proven correct [11]. Here we will detail significant features of our Paxos implementation.

Voting. Choosing a leader in Paxos involves a 2-phase process where nodes are split into different categories. 'Proposer' nodes choose which nodes become candidates to be leader. 'Acceptor' nodes are used to confirm a single leader is elected. Although only one acceptor is necessary, multiple acceptors allow additional fault-tolerance in the case that a single acceptor fails. A client sends a proposer node a request to reach consensus, where the proposer assigns an id to the request so newer client requests have larger ids. After the request is received and an id has been assigned, the proposer reaches out to the acceptor nodes, asking each acceptor if the id is the largest it has seen. If it is the largest, the acceptor sends back a 'promise' stating that it would vote for that id if the proposer wants. If the proposer receives 'promises' from more than half of the acceptors, then the proposer sends a second message to all acceptors, asking them to vote for their id if it is still the largest. If most acceptors still find that id to be the largest, they send a vote to the proposer. Once a majority of acceptors vote on a single proposal, consensus has been reached and a new leader has been selected.

Safety features: There are several safety features to ensure that leader election does not cause multiple leaders to be elected or cause miscommunications. Only a node that has been proposed to be leader may become one. Instead of having every node in the election be a candidate to be leader, the proposer(s) choose which nodes become candidates. Only a single node is chosen. The second phase of our two phase election process ensures only one node chosen. This is because, unlike promises, an acceptor is only able to vote once for a new leader and since a majority of acceptors are necessary to win an election, there will never be a case where two different nodes could both be elected as leader or have a tie occur. These safety features along with others guarantees the State Machine Safety property. State machine Safety: If a node has applied a log entry at a given index to its state machine, no other server will ever apply a different log entry for the same index (as shown in Fig. 1).

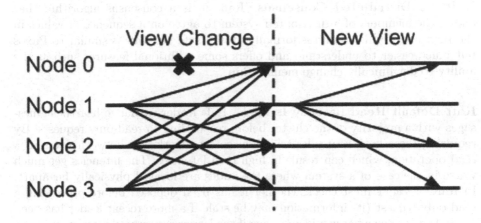

Fig. 2. View changing in pBFT taken from hyperledger [2].

Leader Failures. Normally, nodes expect consistent messaging from the leader with a built in timeout if the leader takes too long to send a message. In the case of a leader failure this timeout will occur, causing a new election with the proposer(s) choosing the candidates. Once a candidate receives a majority of votes from other nodes, it must ensure its logs are up to date before assuming the role as leader. Once leader, the node begins replicating its logs and sending them to the other nodes. Sending the replicated logs provides fault-tolerance for Paxos by allowing the other nodes to continue running and allow them to elect a new leader if this leader fails as well. This replication also provides scale by allowing clients to read from any available node.

Key Differences Observed. While developing our implementation of Paxos, we made several observations that may help explain the differences in performance between algorithms.

1. Unlike newer consensus algorithms like Raft, Paxos does not have a heartbeat style protocol to make sure all nodes are up to date. This allows out of date nodes to be elected as the leader. If this occurs, the leader will update itself before taking any actions as leader. Although this allows more possible nodes to become leader, it also slows down the algorithm by making the elected node wait until being up to date before being able to take actions as a leader.
2. Unlike in Raft, there will never be a tie from an election which aids in Paxos' speed as ties cause greater delays in leader election.

2.2   Raft

Raft for Distributed Consensus. Raft [9] is a consensus algorithm that allows the members of a distributed system to agree on a sequence of values in the presence of failures and is formally proven safe [3]. Raft is similar to Paxos but much easier to understand and offers some additional features such as the ability to dynamically change membership.

Raft Default Read Latency Is High. Raft leader exchange heartbeat messages with a majority of the cluster before responding to read-only requests. By requiring these heartbeats, Raft introduces a network hop between peers in a read operation, which can result in high read latencies. The latencies get much worse in the case of a system where the nodes are located physically far apart. In Raft, a leader must check whether it has been deposed before processing a read-only request (its information may be stale if a more recent leader has been elected). Let's see what would go wrong if the leader serves read requests without exchanging heartbeats. Consider the following sequence of events:

1. Assume all nodes: A, B, and C of the cluster have a key k whose value is set to V1. C is the leader to start with
2. Imagine C gets network partitioned from the other nodes A and B (but not from the client). This results in A and B electing a new leader, say A, while C still thinks it is the leader.
3. The client connects to A to perform an operation to update the value of key k to V2. This succeeds because the operation gets replicated to a majority of nodes - A and B.
4. The client now tries to read the value of key k from node C, which continues to think it is the leader and responds with the value V1 which is a stale read from the client's point of view. Therefore, without exchanging heartbeats before a read operation, a Raft leader that is partitioned away from the rest of the peers might serve stale reads, which would violate linearizability.

To summarize, Raft does provide linearizability on reads without any reliance on clocks, but this requires an additional round-trip to the majority of replicas on every read operation, which would result in potentially lower performance.

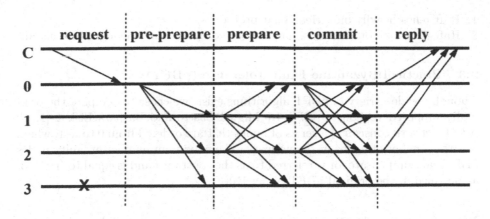

Fig. 3. Normal case operations of practical Byzantine Fault Tolerance taken from the original pBFT paper [1].

Raft Leader Leases. The Raft paper mentions that it is possible to rely on a form of time-based lease for Raft leadership that gets propagated through the heartbeat mechanism. And if we have sufficiently well-behaved clocks, it is possible to obtain linearizable reads without paying a round-trip latency penalty. Alternatively, the leader could rely on the heartbeat mechanism to provide a form of lease, but this would rely on timing for safety (it assumes bounded clock skew). A newly elected leader cannot serve reads (or initiate writing a no-op Raft operation, which is a prerequisite to accepting writes) until it has acquired a leader lease. During a leader election, a voter must propagate the longest remaining duration time of an old leader's lease known to that voter to the new candidate it is voting for. Upon receiving a majority of votes, the new leader must wait out the old leader's lease duration before considers itself as having the lease. The old leader, upon the expiry of its leader lease, steps down and no longer functions as a leader. The new leader continuously extends its leader lease as a part of Raft replication. Typically, leader leases have a short duration. The sequence of steps is as follows:

1. A leader computes a leader lease time interval
2. The timer for this time interval starts counting down on the existing leader
3. The leader sends the lease time interval to the followers
4. The followers receive the lease time interval and start their countdown.
5. Each node performs a countdown based on its monotonic clock

Overall, this sequence creates a time window where the old leader steps down and the new leader does not step up, causing an unavailability window which will reduce the performance.

Key Differences Observed. While developing our implementation of Raft, we made several observations that may help explain the differences in performance between algorithms.

1. Raft relies heavily on a Heartbeat protocol.
2. Raft allows tie on elections, and are solved by running the algorithm again.

2.3   Practical Byzantine Fault Tolerance (pBFT)

Though a wide variety of pBFT algorithms exist, we chose to compare the originally proposed version of pBFT by Miguel Castro and Barbara Liskov [1]. A pBFT network consists of a series of nodes that are ordered from 0 to n–1, where n is the number of nodes in the network. The maximum number of faulty nodes pBFT can compensate for is referred to as the constant f and is equal to $(n–1)/3$, as outlined in the original pBFT paper [10].

View Changes: As the network progresses, the nodes move through a series of views. A view is the period of time for which a given node is the leader of the network. Each node in the network continuously takes turns being the leader, starting with the first node. If the current leader, is producing invalid messages or simply not doing anything at all, it will eventually be suspected to be faulty by enough replicas to cause a view change. This is handled by timeouts and message consistency checks against different parameters kept as part of each node's state. View changing in pBFT is the equivalent process to handling leader elections in Paxos and Raft. The primary difference is that pBFT must account for malicious nodes during view changes. When a secondary node has determined that the current primary, or leader, of the view is faulty, it will broadcast a view change message to the network. If the primary is indeed faulty, all non-faulty nodes will broadcast view change messages. When the primary associated with the next view receives $2f + 1$ view change messages from different nodes, thereby assuring consensus despite potential bad actors, it will broadcast a new view message for all the nodes to begin the next view. When the secondary nodes receive the message, they will switch to the new view, and the new primary will start publishing blocks and sending messages. The primary, p, associated with a particular view is determined based on the view number, v, such that $p = v \bmod n$. A diagram depicting the view change process for a 4 node system is shown in Fig. 2 with node 0 being the current faulty primary and node 1 being the primary associated with the next view.

Normal-Case: During normal-case operation pBFT algorithm follows a series of five stages. Each node in the network must continually maintain the following information:

1. The list of nodes that belong to the network
2. Its current view number
3. Its current sequence number (the block it is working on)

4. The phase of the algorithm it is currently in (see "Normal-Case Operation")
5. A log of the blocks it has received
6. A log of all valid messages it has received from the other nodes

In the first stage, the client sends a request to the leader. For simplicity, it is assumed that the client waits for one request to complete before sending the next one. In the second stage, the pre-prepare stage, The current leader will create a block for the client's request and publish it to the network. Each node performs preliminary verification to ensure the block is valid (i.e. that the leader is not sending faulty messages) and adds the block to their log. This is also where a timeout may trigger a view change if the leader takes too long to produce a valid block. The leader then broadcasts a pre-prepare message to all of the nodes containing the ID of the block just published, the block's number, the primary's view number, and the primary's ID. Nodes, again validate the message and add the message to its internal log. This includes verifying the digital signature of the message, checking that the message's view number matches the node's current view number, and ensuring that the message is from the primary for the current view. This primes all nodes in the system to agree on which block to perform consensus on. In the third stage, the prepare stage, all secondary nodes will broadcast a prepare message to the rest of the network (including itself). Prepare messages, like pre-prepare messages, contain the ID and number of the block they are for, the node's view number and the node's ID. In order for any secondary node to move to the next phase, the node must receive and log $2f + 1$ prepare messages from different nodes that have the same block ID, block number, and view number. This consensus of at least $2/3$ of the system ensures protection against bad actors. This stage and the next is where a pBFT vastly expands the number of messages it must send over Raft or Paxos to ensure safety of the system. In the fourth stage, the commit stage, all nodes (primary and secondaries) broadcast a commit message to the whole network including itself. Commit messages, like the ones before, contain the ID and number of the block they are for, the node's view number and the node's ID. A node must receive and log $2f + 1$ matching commit messages from different nodes before it can safely commit the block. In the fifth, and final stage, a completion message from each node is set back to the client. A diagram of depicting normal- case operations of pBFT in a 4-node network is shown in Fig. 3. C refers to the client, node 0 refers to the current leader, and node 3 represents a malicious node.

Notable Assumptions: To ensure that only one block is considered at a time, nodes do not allow more than one pre-prepare message at a given view and sequence number.

# of nodes	Paxos	Raft	pBFT
50	8048ms	7888ms	10249ms
100	14122ms	13180ms	18782ms
200	25943ms	23630ms	42003ms
300	33010ms	29664ms	110967ms
400	39291ms	34693ms	337604ms

Fig. 4. Number of Nodes Vs Consensus Latency

3   Results

To compare performance between the three consensus algorithms, we decided to measure consensus latency vs. node count for each algorithm. We selected the various network sizes (node counts) to be 50, 100, 200, 300, and 400 to show trend lines as network size increased. The experiment was conducted locally on three different machines, one for each algorithm. The machine and network used are were provided by the XSEDE Program [14] and run on Bridges-2 CMU HPH [15]. The pBFT algorithm was run with a blocksize of 5000. Any extra time required for initialization of the network was not included when measuring latency. The following latency versus number of nodes data is represented in Fig. 4 and in Fig. 5 contains the raw data for our experiment. Generally Raft produced the fastest results with Paxos as a close second. Above, 50 nodes

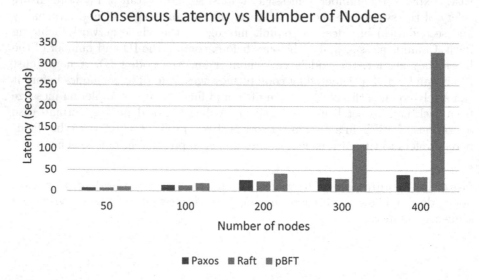

Fig. 5. Visualization showing the exponential rate of difference in latency between pBFT and the other algorithms

pBFT begins to increase latency dramatically when compared with either of the other two algorithms. Both Raft and Paxos appear to follow a more linear increase in latency as network size increases while pBFT follows more closely to an exponential rate of increased latency at scale. However, below 50 nodes, all three algorithms remain fairly comparable to each other in terms of latency. Below is a graph correlating consensus latency in seconds vs. number of nodes (network size) for each algorithm.

4   Conclusion

There is very few data comparing the performance of very popular and heavily used consensus algorithms. Through the process of completing this project, we realized that a comparison of consensus algorithms is less about comparing raw performance as it is to weighing the pros and cons of several smaller design decisions and optional additions. In this paper we provide the full implementation for three of the most heavily used consensus algorithms so DS developers can take inform decision on the best consensus algorithm for its system. One consideration that needs to be made with the results is that each algorithm was ran on a different machine, which may have slightly effected the data. From the results, we see that the Raft and Paxos are fairly close in runtime with Raft being a little faster. Similar runtimes between these two makes sense when considering Raft is heavily based on Paxos. However, we also see that the pBFT algorithm begins diverging in runtime starting at 300 nodes and is always slower than the other two. If one were to just look at the results, they would assume pBFT was the worst algorithm because it took so much longer. However with more knowledge of the pBFT algorithm, we understand this extra time comes with a more robust Byzantine fault tolerance, meaning it may be the most useful at certain tasks. So if your application has a high likelihood of nodes needing to restart frequently, Paxos may be the best option. However, if your application need a stronger practical guarantees of liveness, then Raft would be more appropriate. Or if your application is having a serious problem with nodes sending false messages, pBFT would be the way to go. These are just a few examples of the many considerations to be made when choosing between just these three algorithms.

References

1. Castro, M., Liskov, B.: Practical Byzantine Fault Tolerance. Massachusetts Institute of Technology (2019). http://pmg.csail.mit.edu/papers/osdi99.pdf 6 Dec 2020
2. Seeley, L.: Introduction to Sawtooth PBFT, Hyperledger (2019). https://www.hyperledger.org/blog/2019/02/13/introduction-to-sawtooth-pbft 6 Dec 2020
3. Howard, H., Mortier, R.: Paxos vs Raft: have we reached consensus on distributed consensus? University of Cambridge (2020). https://arxiv.org/pdf/2004.05074.pdf 2 Dec 2020
4. Lamport, L.: Paxos Made Simple, ACM SIGACT News (2001). https://lamport.azurewebsites.net/pubs/paxos-simple.pdf 3 Dec 2020

5. Lamport, L.: The part-time parliament. ACM Trans. Comput. Syst. **16**(2), 133–169 (1998)
6. Lamport, L.: Fast paxos. Distrib. Comput. **19**(2), 79–103 (2006)
7. Lampson, B.W.: The ABCD's of paxos. In: Proceedings of PODC 2001, ACM Symposium on Principles of Distributed Computing, p. 13. ACM (2001)
8. GXUI - A Go cross platform UI library (2015). https://github.com/google/gxui
9. Ongaro, D., Ousterhout, J.: In search of an understandable consensus algorithm. In: Proceedings of the 2014 USENIX Conference on USENIX Annual Technical Conference (USENIX ATC 2014), pp. 305–320. USENIX Association, USA (2014)
10. Bolosky, W.J., Bradshaw, D., Haagens, R.B., Kusters, N.P., Li, P.: Paxos replicated state machines as the basis of a high-performance data store. In: Proceedings of NSDI 2011, USENIX Conference on Networked Systems Design and Implementation, pp. 141–154. USENIX (2011)
11. Chandra, T.D., Griesemer, R., Redstone, J.: Paxos made live: an engineering perspective. In: Proceedings of PODC 2007, ACM Symposium on Principles of Distributed Computing, pp. 398–407. ACM (2007)
12. Hunt, P., Konar, M., Junqueira, F.P., Reed, B.: ZooKeeper: wait-free coordination for internet-scale systems. In: Proceedings of ATC 2010, USENIX Annual Technical Conference, pp. 145–158. USENIX (2010)
13. "Code Repository for the article" Paxos. https://github.com/tbbergmann/569Paxos Raft. https://github.com/theAichouri/Raft569 pBFT. https://github.com/mycalpoly/Practical-Byzantine-Fault-Tolerance-PBFT
14. Towns, J., et al.: XSEDE: accelerating scientific discovery. Comput. Sci. Eng. **16**(5), 62–74 (2014). https://doi.org/10.1109/MCSE.2014.80
15. Nystrom, N.A., Levine, M.J., Roskies, R.Z., Scott, J.R.: Bridges: a uniquely flexible HPC resource for new communities and data analytics. In: Proceedings of the 2015 Annual Conference on Extreme Science and Engineering Discovery Environment (St. Louis, MO, 26–30 July 2015). XSEDE15. ACM, New York, NY, USA (2015). https://doi.org/10.1145/2792745.2792775

OCFTL: An MPI Implementation-Independent Fault Tolerance Library for Task-Based Applications

Pedro Henrique Di Francia Rosso[1,2]([✉]) [iD] and Emilio Francesquini[2] [iD]

[1] Universidade Estadual de Campinas (UNICAMP), Campinas, SP, Brazil
p233687@dac.unicamp.br
[2] Universidade Federal do ABC (UFABC), Santo André, SP, Brazil
{pedro.rosso,e.francesquini}@ufabc.edu.br

Abstract. Fault tolerance (FT) is a common concern in HPC environments. One would expect that, when Message Passing Interface (MPI) is concerned (an HPC tool of paramount importance), FT would be a solved problem. It turns out that the scenario for FT and MPI is intricate. While FT is effectively a reality in these environments, it is usually done by hand. The few exceptions available tie MPI users to specific MPI implementations. This work proposes OCFTL, an implementation-independent FT library for MPI. OCFTL can detect and propagate failures; provides false-positive detection; exchanges a reduced number of messages during failure propagation; employs checkpointing to reduce the impact of failures; and has a reduced delay to detect sequential simultaneous failures in comparison to related works.

Keywords: Fault tolerance · High-Performance Computing · Message Passing Interface

1 Introduction

Message Passing Interface (MPI) is a message passing protocol specification frequently used to parallelize and distribute jobs in High Performance Computing (HPC). Among several implementations, Open MPI [10] and MPICH [4] are the most commonly employed by the HPC community. HPC applications typically run on large clusters and dedicated computing environments. In such environments, Fault Tolerance (FT) is a common concern justified by the large number of computing nodes which ultimately leads to an increased failure rate [8].

Even today, the development of fault-tolerant MPI applications is done manually, with some exceptions like ULFM and MPICH. User Level Failure Migration (ULFM) [3] is implemented inside Open MPI whereas MPICH has its own FT routines [4]. However, these approaches are not portable, nor easy to use, and are far from complete FT solutions. Building a portable and implementation-independent FT library, OCFTL (OmpCluster Fault Tolerance Library), is the

I. Gitler et al. (Eds.): CARLA 2021, CCIS 1540, pp. 131–147, 2022.
https://doi.org/10.1007/978-3-031-04209-6_10

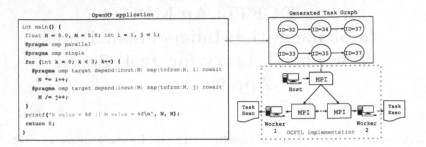

Fig. 1. Flow of the parallelization process.

main focus of this work. OCFTL can be used in a plug-and-use style with any standard-compliant MPI implementation. OCFTL uses MPI functions defined by the specification, and it does not rely on modifications to the MPI implementation itself, which makes it portable.

OCFTL provides mechanisms to detect and propagate failures, survive them and complete the program execution correctly even if in the presence of failures. This paper describes the rationale of OCFTL and the use of it in OmpCluster (https://ompcluster.gitlab.io), a project that focuses on easing parallel programming on HPC clusters using OpenMP (https://www.openmp.org/).

2   Background and Motivation

This work is inserted in the context of the OmpCluster research project, which aims at easing scientific programming for HPC clusters by leveraging the LLVM compiler infrastructure. This project aims at parallelizing applications with OpenMP tasks. These tasks are deployed by the runtime to the target cluster using MPI as shown in Fig. 1. An application execution flow follows: from an OpenMP program, the runtime system creates the tasks that have been previously described by the programmer using OpenMP directives, building a Directed Acyclic Graph (DAG) that models the dependencies between the tasks. Those tasks are then scheduled and distributed across the computing nodes (either CPU or CPU-GPU nodes) using MPI. When the execution completes, the final results are sent back to the main program. The MPI task distribution is based on an event system, where each MPI process implicitly communicates within this event system.

To provide fault tolerance for OmpCluster, we need to take into account failure detection and propagation, and failure mitigation. The first consists in the library being able to detect and propagate failures, making every process on the application achieve a consistent state (*i.e.*, knowing all the failures in the system). The second consists in reducing the impact of failures, a common way to do this is to restart the program whenever a failure happens, which would cause a significant overhead. The mitigation of this impact is essential to reduce the time spent dealing with failures.

2.1   Failure Detection and Propagation

One of the most common approaches found in the literature to detect failures in HPC system is through the use of a heartbeat message. In this detection system, each process is an `emitter` (it sends alive messages to other processes), but also, an `observer` (it receives alive messages from other processes). In this work, we employ a ring topology, where a process is an emitter to the next process in the ring and an observer for the previous process in the ring. There are two properties of interest to the heartbeat mechanism: the `period` (period of time between each alive notification), and the `timeout` (amount of time to wait between notifications from the observed process to declare it as failed).

This kind of heartbeat-based failure detection mechanism was used by ULFM [3], and Zhong et al. [22] which uses heartbeats as a secondary failure detection mechanism. Another important concept is failure propagation. To achieve a consistent state between all processes in the application, every process needs to know about every failure. To achieve that, the process that detects a failure broadcasts it to the remaining processes. This is done using a fault-tolerant broadcast. It is essential that every process receives the broadcast, so all of them have the same vision of the processes' states in the system, thus the necessity of a fault-tolerance broadcast.

ULFM [3] employs a broadcast based on HBA (hyper-cube), which consists of, from the starter process, sending the broadcast to k processes forward and k processes backward in the ring where N is the number of processes and $k = \lfloor log_2(N) \rfloor$. On the other hand, Zhong et al. [22] employ the use of circulant graphs, for instance the binomial graph BMG. In this case, the broadcast is sent by the process with rank k to processes with ranks $k + 2^0, k + 2^1, k + 2^2, ...$, forward and backward in the ring. In both cases, each process, except for the starter process, will replicate the broadcast the first time they receive it. One important thing to notice is that in this kind of broadcast, multiple messages will be received by each process, making it fault-tolerant.

2.2   Failure Mitigation

One can find in the literature several approaches, each with their own strengths and weaknesses, to failure mitigation. In this work, we employ checkpointing to deal with failures. In future works, we intend to employ replication as well.

Checkpointing is one of the most common failure mitigation techniques. It consists in saving program snapshots to a stable and reliable storage [13]. There are several categories of checkpointing. The category that more closely matches with the requirements of the OmpCluster project is the *application-level* category. In this type of checkpointing, applications are required to guide what data must be saved and loaded, giving total control of the checkpointing procedure to the application. In OmpCluster's case, the user is OmpCluster's runtime system itself. Examples of libraries that fall in this category include SCR [15], Veloc [16] and FTI [2]. Since Veloc allows the application to perform both coordinated and uncoordinated checkpointing[1] and SCR and FTI are strictly coordinated, Veloc was chosen as to be the checkpointing library for OCFTL.

3 Related Work

Fault tolerance and MPI are a frequent topic of research interest. Some works propose targeted MPI implementations. Open MPI, for example, refers users to a separate implementation, ULFM [3], as its main FT approach[2]. MPICH, on the other hand, has limited support to FT in the vanilla implementation for TCP-based communications https://wiki.mpich.org/mpich/index.php/Fault_Tolerance. However, it is not clear what behavior can be expected on other configurations such as Infiniband or shared memory.

ULFM proposes a FT chapter for the MPI specification. By this date, it is implemented inside Open MPI and relies on it. The authors propose functions to limit the impact failures have on the application execution, allowing users to invalidate and shrink communicators (modifying it to contain only alive processes), agree to something (e.g., a flag), and acknowledge that a failure happened. It uses the heartbeat failure detection mechanism and a hypercube-based algorithm (HBA) to propagate failure [5]. In a recent proposal [22], the authors employ a Binomial Graph (BMG) based algorithm for failure propagation. OCFTL also uses a heartbeat mechanism, however it does not employ any additional detection system such as discussed by Zhong (e.g. OS Signals) [22]. This lean mechanism makes our algorithm simpler and allows us to use a proven and scalable peer-to-peer topology for failure propagation based on Chord [7].

Reinit++ [12] is an approach that was tested with OpenMPI. Relying on simplicity, Reinit++ employs only a few additional data structures, and a single new function (MPI_Reinit) which allows recovery and restart after failures. Reinit++ authors claim improvements over ULFM and discuss a global recovery system (restarting the entire application). Reinit++ failure detection mechanism is based on a root node which monitors some daemon processes that, in turn, monitor application MPI processes, to do that, the authors extended OpenMPI runtime process manager.

Other works such as LFLR [20] and Fenix [11] use ULFM to allow recovery after failures. LFLR focuses on local recovery, dealing only with the restart of the failed component. Thus, no global restart of the program is required. In this sense, it is much closer to the approach followed by OCFTL. Similarly, Fenix uses procedures proposed by ULFM to perform process recovery. Additionally, Fenix supports different types of checkpoints (implicit, asynchronous, coordinated, and selective). Contrary to these approaches, OCFTL employs its own failure detection and propagation mechanisms [17], not relying on other libraries like ULFM and thus making it portable.

---

[1] Coordinated checkpointing requires synchronization of checkpoint functions in every process, while uncoordinated checkpointing does not require synchronization.

[2] https://www.open-mpi.org/faq/?category=ft#ft-future.

A hybrid FT approach was proposed to take into account failures in the Easy-Grid middleware (a framework for grid-type applications) using checkpointing and message logs, as well as self-healing properties [18]. On top of LAM/MPI and EasyGrid framework, the authors use those tools to detect and recover from failures. In this sense, OCFTL tends to be more generic, providing a more portable FT library as well as not relying on another tool.

MPI stages [19] proposes a brand-new MPI implementation with FT. However, it offers only basic MPI functionality as well as checkpointing. It is not clear how its failure detection and propagation system works. OCFTL, on the other hand, is based on the MPI specification, and can (and should) therefore be used with any MPI compliant implementation.

Finally, some works constitute the initial proposals for FT in MPI, that were later migrated to other projects. It is the case of LA/MPI [1] and MPI-FT [14]. As well as other projects focuses on old versions of MPI standard and are discontinued or outdated, like the FT-MPI [9].

4   An Implementation-Independent Fault Tolerance Library – OCFTL

OCFTL provides FT mechanisms compatible with any specification-compliant MPI implementation, such as OpenMPI and MPICH, employing user-level MPI functions only, making it easier to update as new MPI standards are released. To do so, OCFTL creates an additional thread for each MPI process to control the FT heartbeat through a main loop. This loop checks, on each iteration, if there are any messages to send or receive, or if there are any other FT procedures pending. Thus, OCFTL requires MPI to be initialized with MPI_THREAD_MULTIPLE. Finally, for the time being, OCFTL is implemented and focuses on C/C++ only.

4.1   Failure Detection

Our failure detection mechanism was inspired by ULFM's [5]. The algorithm was modified to work as a user-level library, relying on the standard MPI functions and proposing some improvements.

OCFTL presents important differences from ULFM's failure detection mechanisms. First, the failure propagation is performed using a modified broadcast based on the Chord algorithm [7] which is similar to BMG broadcast. In this approach, each process s sends messages to every process r such that $pos_r = (pos_s + 2^i) \ mod \ N$, where i goes from 0 to $\log_2(N)$, N is the size of the heartbeat ring, and pos_r and pos_s indicates the position of process r and s respectively. This is done once per process upon receiving the first broadcast from another process, replicating the broadcast $\log_2(N)+1$ times in total, which differentiates from the original chord-based algorithm, that avoids the message redundancy. Additionally, the expected time to achieve a consistent state is $\log_2(N)$ multiplied by the main loop iteration time. When a process fails, it is removed from the ring data structure present on every process.

OCFTL also provides *false positive* failure detection. This means that, when a process failure is detected but after a while, the process recovers (*e.g.* due to an intermittent network failure), the former observer will capture the message and start a procedure of adding it back to the ring. This is achieved using the broadcast procedure discussed before.

OCFTL also includes an optional initial procedure to shuffle the distribution of MPI processes throughout the heartbeat ring (this shuffling process only affects the heartbeat, not impacting on the applications). Often, MPI processes are distributed sequentially to the machines or rack, and when a failure occurs, if those MPI processes are observing other processes in the same machine/racks, the procedures taken by the heartbeat would take $(2(n-1)+1) \times hb_{to}$ to detect all failures, where hb_{to} represents the heartbeat timeout and n represents the total number of processes in the machine/rack. The shuffling procedure reduces the average time to detect failures since it spreads the MPI processes evenly across the ring, which reduces the probability of processes in the same machine or rack to appear sequentially on the ring. Assuming m machines with n consecutive processes each, $P_n = m \prod_{i=0}^{n-1} \frac{1}{(m*n)-i}$ represents the probability of having n consecutive process in the ring.

Since OCFTL is focused on HPC applications, which typically run on large clusters, we expect the number of failures to increase linearly with the number of machines. On the other hand, the time needed to detect and propagate a failure only increases at a logarithmic rate.

4.2 Handling Failures

To handle failures, we use checkpointing, and plan to add replication in the future. Checkpoint/restart consists of periodically saving states of the execution, and in case of failures, resuming the application from the last saved state.

To execute checkpointing, OCFTL leverages Veloc [16]. Veloc is a library that permits saving and loading checkpointing synchronizing or not the processes. It also provides an infrastructure that saves the process locally (same machine as the application process execution) and sends the checkpoint in background to a more reliable storage (like a distributed storage). In this work, OCFTL stands as an interface between the application and Veloc. Thus, the application depends on OCFTL's interface, making it possible to exchange the checkpointing library without the need to perform adaptations on the application code. This interface also provides the checkpoint interval calculation that takes into account the cost (δ) of the checkpoint (time to write it) and the MTTI (M) (Mean time to interruption) ($\theta = \sqrt{2\delta M}$) [21], which is directly connected to OCFTL's notification system, emitting a notification when a checkpoint is necessary.

OmpCluster, in particular, employs coordinated checkpointing, *i.e.*, every OmpCluster process is suspended during checkpointing and resumed after it is done. The loading process, for the time being, is still coordinated due to limitations of OmpCluster's runtime infrastructure. When these limitations are lifted, checkpointing will be uncoordinated, so loading will be limited to only a few specific processes. Since OCFTL focuses on a task-based runtime environment,

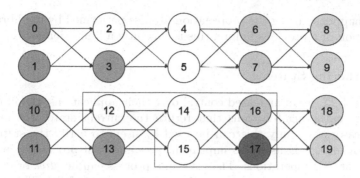

Fig. 2. Task restart procedure illustration

Fig. 2 illustrates a procedure to identify which tasks need to be restarted. The green shaded tasks have already been saved, *i.e.*, their output are available in saved checkpoints; the white tasks indicate executed but not saved; the blue tasks are in execution; the red one is a task that began its execution but suffered from a failure; and yellow tasks are the not yet executed tasks.

After identifying a failure of a process, the system will check if any task has failed, in the case of the Fig. 2, the task 17 failed. First, the system will wait for the currently executing tasks (6, 7 and 16) to finish, and then start a `restart` procedure. To define which tasks will be restarted, we evaluate each task that is a dependency or a dependent of the failed task, both directly or indirectly. This means that from the task 17, we recursively evaluate the dependencies and the dependents, repeating for each new task, and marking all tasks that were executed, but not saved, for restart. For the example of shown on Fig. 2, we evaluate the tasks 14, 15, 18 and 19 first, and after the tasks 16, 12, 13 and 10. From all those tasks, the ones that fill the requirements to restart are 12, 14, 15 and 16. This procedure avoids the overhead of restarting unnecessary tasks, if, for example, restarting all non-saved tasks from the last checkpoint taken.

4.3 Repairing Communicators

MPI provides optimized collective communications between processes. However, they require the participation of every process from a given communicator. In an environment with nodes that might experience failures, this can be a frequent cause of deadlocks.

To tackle this problem, we propose a repair function similar to `MPI_Comm_Shrink` (available in ULFM [3]). This function shrinks the set of processes to contain only alive processes (as determined by the failure detection mechanism described in Sect. 4.1). The shrinkage only completes successfully if all MPI processes have a coherent view of the communicator state, *i.e.*, they have the same view of the whole system regarding which processes are alive or dead. An inconsistent state (their view are not coherent) might be reached when a failure happens during the propagation process performed by the library after the detection of a previous failure, this is currently a limitation for this project.

4.4 Gathering States

To give OCFTL users increased control over their applications, the library provides state gathering functions that return the current state of a process or communicator. Not only this can be used by users to verify the state of execution, but also, it is useful to implement pre- and post-processing in OCFTL wrappers for MPI operations. The state of a process can be *alive* or *dead* while a communicator can be *valid* or *invalid* (when a process fails). This is used in OCFTL wrappers for MPI functions in the case of OmpCluster.

4.5 MPI Wrappers

One of the problems of using MPI with the possibility of failures is the behavior of MPI functions, which could deadlock if a failed process is participating. To tackle that, OCFTL employs function wrappers. This is achieved leveraging linker option "-Wl,--wrap=FUNCTION" available in the GCC and Clang compilers. This option redefines the symbol FUNCTION to two new symbols, for example, in the case of a MPI_Send function: the __real_MPI_Send, expressing the original MPI_Send function; and, the __wrap_MPI_Send, a custom implementation for MPI_Send. Any call in the code for MPI_Send will in fact be calling __wrap_MPI_Send. These wrappers could be created for any MPI function. In the particular case of OmpCluster, the functions MPI_Wait, MPI_Test (used as a loop condition), MPI_Barrier, MPI_Comm_free, MPI_Mprobe, MPI_Send and MPI_Recv were wrapped[3], but any MPI function could be wrapped in the same way.

The general solution for these wrappers is to use the non-blocking variant existent for almost every MPI function and loop test the associated MPI_Request object while verifying the other part of the communication. For example, Algorithm refalg:wrapspssend replicates the behavior of MPI_Send, waiting in the function while the operation does not complete. Line 3 replaces the blocking send for the non-blocking send, associating a request object to it. This request is tested in every loop iteration (lines 5 to 11), as well as the status of the destination is checked (lines 7 to 10). If the operation completes successfully (the test in line 6 completes), the function returns success, otherwise, if the destination process is not alive, the function returns an error and avoids the possible deadlock caused by an operation involving a dead process.

---

[3] OCFTL's wrappers source codes can be found in the library implementation, available at https://gitlab.com/phrosso/ftmpi-tests/-/tree/master/OCFTLBench/ftlib.

Algorithm 1. Wrapper function to `MPI_Send`.

```
1   int __wrap_MPI_Send(const void *buf, int count, MPI_Datatype datatype,
    ↪    int dest, int tag, MPI_Comm comm) {
2     MPI_Request w_send_request;
3     MPI_Isend(buf, count, datatype, dest, tag, comm, &w_send_request);
4     int test_flag = 0;
5     while (!test_flag) {
6       MPI_Test(request, &test_flag, status);
7       if (getProcessState(dest) != ProcessState::ALIVE) {
8         MPI_Request_free(request);
9         return ft::FT_ERROR;
10      }
11    }
12    return ft::FT_SUCCESS;
13  }
```

4.6 Notification Callbacks

Integration between OCFTL and applications is done using an event notification system. Currently, OCFTL has four types of notifications: `Failure`, `False-Positive`, `Checkpoint` and `CheckpointDone`. For the application to receive these notifications, it needs to register a callback function using the OCFTL method `registerCallback`. Whenever one of those notifications is triggered, OCFTL calls all registered function (one or more functions can be registered). The treatment for these callbacks is specific to each application using OCFTL, and specifies what should be done after a notification is received.

5 Experimental Results and Discussion

This section discusses the experiments performed to assess different MPI implementation behaviors and to benchmark OCFTL[4]. To execute the tests, OpenMPI v4.1 and MPICH v3.4.2 were used along with the respective recovery flags (`"--enable-recovery"` and `"--disable-auto-cleanup"`), initializing with `MPI_THREAD_MULTIPLE` thread level option. All tests were performed in the Santos Dumont supercomputer (SDumont, LNCC - Brazil). For the reported experimental results, the computing nodes named B710 featuring 64 Gb of RAM and 2xCPU Intel Xeon E5-2695v2 Ivy Bridge, each with 12 cores (24 threads) running at 2.4 GHz (3.2 GHz Turbo Boost) were used. The network interface is InfiniBand (56 Gb/s). The number of cores was selected according to each test.

5.1 MPI Behavior

Each MPI implementation has ample freedom to implement the MPI standard, so it is expected that different MPI implementations present different behavior in the presence of failures. To properly implement a fault tolerant solution in

---

[4] The tests and the library are available at: https://gitlab.com/phrosso/ftmpi-tests.

Table 1. Behavior of different MPI operations for MPICH and MPICH+UCX. (ok means program finished and to means program timed out)

	MPICH		MPICH+UCX	
	Kill P0	Kill P1	Kill P0	Kill P1
MPI_Allreduce	(ok/ok/-)	(ok/ok/-)	(to/to*/-)	(to/to*/-)
MPI_Barrier	(ok/ok/-)	(ok/ok/-)	(to/to/-)	(to/to/-)
MPI_Bcast	(ok/ok/-)	(ok/ok/-)	(to/to*/-)	(to/to/-)
MPI_Bsend	-	(ok/ok/-)	-	(to/to/-)
MPI_Gather	(ok/ok/-)	(ok/ok/-)	(to/to/-)	(to/to*/-)
MPI_Recv	-	(ok/ok/-)	-	(to/to*/-)
MPI_Reduce	(ok/ok/-)	(ok/ok/-)	(to/to/-)	(to/to*/-)
MPI_Send	-	(ok/ok/to)	-	(to/to/to)
MPI_Wait	-	(ok/-/-)	-	(to/-/-)

Representation: (Blocking/Non-Blocking/Synchronous)

Table 2. Behavior of different MPI operations for OpenMPI and OpenMPI+UCX. (ok means program finished and to means program timed out)

	OpenMPI		OpenMPI+UCX	
	Kill P0	Kill P1	Kill P0	Kill P1
MPI_Allreduce	(to/ok/-)	(to/ok/-)	(to/to/-)	(to/ok/-)
MPI_Barrier	(to/to/-)	(to/to/-)	(to/to/-)	(to/to/-)
MPI_Bcast	(to/ok/-)	(to/to/-)	(to/to/-)	(to/ok/-)
MPI_Bsend	-	(to/to/-)	-	(to/to/-)
MPI_Gather	(to/to/-)	(to/ok/-)	(to/to/-)	(to/to/-)
MPI_Recv	-	(to/ok/-)	-	(to/to/-)
MPI_Reduce	(to/to/-)	(to/ok/-)	(to/to/-)	(to/to/-)
MPI_Send	-	(to/ok/to)	-	(to/to/to)
MPI_Wait	-	(to/-/-)	-	(to/-/-)

Representation: (Blocking/Non-Blocking/Synchronous)

OCFTL, it was necessary to evaluate the behavior of each implementation in different critical execution scenarios.

To evaluate the behavior of different MPI distributions, point-to-point and collective operations were executed in all variations (blocking, non-blocking and synchronous when applicable) by two processes. Some operations have a source and a destination processes (*e.g.*, MPI_Send) while in others every process has both jobs (*e.g.*, MPI_Allreduce). Where applicable, two instances of the tests were being executed, one killing the MPI rank 0 and the other killing the MPI rank 1. Each run is considered unsuccessful if it times out, since the objective of these tests is to check if the operation deadlocks or not. The benchmark programs and runtime configurations are available on the Behavior folder of the aforementioned Git repository.

Tables 1 and 2 show the results of the experiments with a few MPI operations on MPICH and OpenMPI distributions with and without UCX[5], respectively. For both tables, each cell represents the results of each variation of an operation when applicable, in the order `Blocking/Non-Blocking/Synchronous`. Possible values are: `ok` if the program finished (with or without errors); `to` if the program timed out; and `(-)` if the variation does not exist.

Table 1 shows that for MPICH configured without UCX, the program finished for all tests, but the synchronous send. This was expected since MPICH in its basic configuration has support for failure detection. For MPICH with UCX, every program timed out after 5 s (a regular execution of the test program runs in less than 1 s). The `(*)` next a result means that the program does not time out during the target function, but on the execution of `MPI_Request_free` or on `MPI_Finalize` functions.

Table 2 shows that for Open MPI without UCX, most of the `Non-Blocking` operations the program finishes, while for `Blocking` operations every program times out. For the configuration with UCX, every program, but the `Non-Blocking MPI_Allreduce` (when the rank 1 process was killed) has failed.

These results show the importance of wrappers while working with fault tolerance and MPI. The idea of wrappers is replicating the function behavior with functions that not deadlock, and always check the other side of the communication, or the communicator state if it is a collective communication. This way, the behavior of these tests can be avoided.

5.2 Empirical OCFTL Performance Evaluation

This section evaluates the OCFTL under stressed MPI programs[6]. To perform such evaluations, we use the Intel MPI Benchmarks[7], which is a set of MPI benchmarks intended to test MPI distributions of the MPI standard.

This suit offers various subsets of benchmarks. These experiments leverage the MPI-1 subset, evaluating elementary MPI operations. It has point-to-point (P2P, where two processes communicate with each other) and collective (`coll`, where a set of processes communicates with the entire set of processes) operations. For this experiment, we choose the `ping-pong` as a P2P operation (since it is a `send-recv` operation), and the `allreduce` application as a `coll` operation (since it is an all-to-all operation). To limit the combinatorial explosion of 4 different MPI distributions with different heartbeat parameters, we chose only one benchmark of each type.

These experiments use 20 nodes with 24 processes each (480 processes in total). Discussions in this paper are limited to the tests with the `medium` size

---

[5] UCX is an optimized framework for communications between nodes in high-bandwidth and low-latency networks, which is commonly used with MPI.

[6] We consider an MPI program as `stressed` when it is overloaded by MPI message exchanges. Benchmarks are examples of stressed MPI programs, since they overload the MPI runtime with MPI operations to establish the limits of a MPI distribution.

[7] Available at https://github.com/intel/mpi-benchmarks.

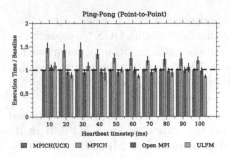

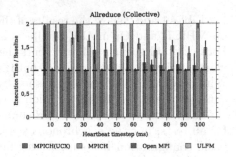

Fig. 3. PingPong benchmark for messages with 64 Kbytes size (*Note:* Bars overlapping the plot limits in Fig. 4 show a relation between tests and baseline ranging from 2.06 to 30.34.)

Fig. 4. AllReduce benchmark for messages with 64 Kbytes size (*Note:* Bars overlapping the plot limits in Fig. 4 show a relation between tests and baseline ranging from 2.06 to 30.34.)

of messages (64 Kbytes per message). But tests were also performed with a min length (0 Bytes per message) and large length (4 Mbytes per message)[8]. The number of internal repetitions of the operation, for each run, is 640 times (the default value for messages with 64 Kbytes). The npmin (minimum number of the participants in each benchmark) was also set to 480, meaning that for the P2P benchmark, there will be 240 pairs of processes, and every process will do the MPI operation collectively for the coll benchmark. This number of processes evaluates the limits of heartbeat parameters and the scalability of OCFTL.

Four MPI distributions were tested: MPICH with UCX, MPICH without UCX, Open MPI, and ULFM. For the first three, OCFTL was the FT approach, while for the last, it used the ULFM's detector. The experiment tested different values of heartbeat period, and the timeout was set to 100 times higher than the period. The baseline in the tests represents the execution of the benchmarks without fault tolerance support. Tests were executed 10 times and the confidence intervals are calculated using the Bootstrap method [6] with 10000 iterations. The Bootstrap method was chosen since we do not know, beforehand, the probability distribution of the data.

Figures 3 and 4 show the results for the messages with 64 Kbytes. P2P results shows that only MPICH without UCX has significant overhead. For the collective tests, Open MPI was the only distribution that did not show overheads. In particular, MPICH without UCX, showed a high overhead for lower values of the heartbeat period. One important aspect to notice is the total run time of the applications. Although MPICH showed higher overheads in the collective tests, it showed better performance (time wise) than Open MPI in all cases and ULFM (for values of heartbeat period higher than 40 ms). MPICH with UCX showed the best completion times among all distributions. Evaluating

---

[8] All test results are available in the aforementioned Git repository. Due to space limitations, here we show only results with the most significant overheads (*i.e.*, overheads for the remaining configurations is lower than those presented here).

the execution times of P2P, Open MPI was as good as ULFM, while MPICH with and without UCX performed worse. Since OCFTL can be used with any standard-compliant distribution, this portability allows us to choose the best distribution, where the difference in execution times between MPI implementations can easily surpass the overhead caused by OCFTL.

5.3 Internal Broadcast

To evaluate the internal broadcast, a comparison was made between our approach, BMG and HBA algorithms, where each broadcast was implemented within OCFTL to be evaluated.

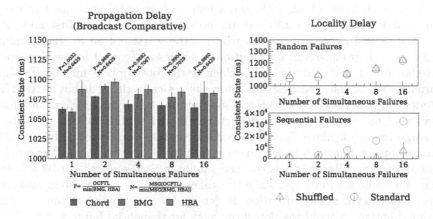

Fig. 5. Internal Broadcast comparison (left) and Locality delay results for standard and shuffle heartbeat initial positions (right). (*Note:* Error bars represent the 95% confidence interval calculated using Bootstrap with 10000 iterations [6].)

The objective is to evaluate the time to propagate a failure and the overhead they would impose on the application. So the tests monitored the total time needed to propagate a set of simultaneous failures to all remaining application processes. The total number of messages each broadcast has used to complete the propagation was also counted. The configuration for this experiment uses a total of 480 processes distributed over 20 nodes and evaluates cases for 1, 2, 4, 8, and 16 simultaneous failures. Each scenario consists of 10 samples.

Figure 5 (left) shows the comparison between the broadcasting algorithms. Our approach is marginally better than BMG and HBA (time taken to achieve a consistent state is practically the same for all of them) as the values of P (representing the performance relation between our approach and the best of BMG and HBA) are close to 1. The main difference is in the total number of messages (N in the figure). The proposed algorithm achieved the reduction of about 30% in most of the experiments (those represent received only broadcasts, messages lost during the execution and the broadcasts sent to already dead processes are not taken into account). These results show that our broadcast algorithm is a viable and better alternative to current state-of-the-art FT broadcasting algorithms.

5.4 Locality Problem

The rationale behind shuffling positions of the MPI rank in the ring is to solve the delay of multiple sequential failure detection. These tests evaluate two approaches: the standard, which does not shuffle the initial positions of the processes, and the shuffled, which is the approach we suggest that random shuffle the initial positions of the process in the ring. For this experiment, 480 processes were used over 20 nodes and each scenario consists of 10 samples.

This experiment proposes the evaluation of the detection delay by simulating simultaneous failures (1, 2, 4, 8, and 16 simultaneous failures) for two cases: sequential distribution of ranks over the nodes (*e.g.,* 0–23 in the first node, 24–49 in the second node, and so on), which is the worst option for the standard approach; and, round-robin distribution of processes (*e.g.,* 0 in the first node, 1 in the second node, and so on), which is the best option for the standard approach. The worst and best cases are theoretically defined, but as OCFTL includes a probability factor, this is not deterministic anymore. Figure 5 (right) shows that for random failures, the standard and shuffle options take about the same time to achieve the consistent state, while for sequential failures, the standard option follows a linear function that increases the time as the number of simultaneous failures increases. The shuffle option is shown to be a better choice for sequential failures, since the times to achieve a consistent state are less or equal to the standard option. In general, experiments show that shuffling is a good option to avoid the detection delay for sequential failures.

5.5 Checkpointing

Since OmpCluster is our case of study, the checkpoint was configured to run accordingly to the OmpCluster runtime. Whenever OmpCluster head process receives the checkpoint notification, a coordinated checkpoint occurs, saving all data future tasks will need. When a task fails, all the necessary data to run the tasks marked to restart (like discussed in Sect. 4.2) is restored. This system was tested with a blocked matrix multiplication application, in which, after some time, a checkpoint is taken, then, a failure is injected causing a failure to at least one task. So, based on the tasks' evaluation, all necessary data is loaded, and then, the tasks are restarted. All the tests ran successfully. A general MPI application (whose communication graph does not follow that of a task-based application such as that of OmpCluster) is still a work in progress. The current checkpointing algorithm is suited to task-based applications, but when working with other types of applications whose tasks are not well-defined, the programmer still needs to use the available checkpoint functions to use OCFTL.

5.6   Limitations

OCFTL is under development. Therefore, limitations described in this section are expected to be removed in the near future. The first observed limitation is present in the repair communicator procedure, in which, an inconsistent state of agreement between the processes occurs if a request to repair a communicator is made while OCFTL is in the middle of failure propagation, where processes will not agree with each other, and the procedure will not succeed. Concerning OmpCluster, there are two main limitations: the restarting of failed tasks is currently sequential, given OmpCluster's runtime limitations; and, OCFTL is not able to deal with failures in the head process (rank 0), since this process holds the OpenMP core, and if it fails, the application needs to be restarted.

5.7   Stand-Alone Use

This paper brings the discussion about OCFTL in the context of OmpCluster project. Although some solutions are specific for the project, the core of OCFTL can be used in a stand-alone way. The failure detection and propagation mechanisms, checkpointing, state gathering and communicator repair could be all used by other applications that leverages the task-based workflow paradigm. As Omp-Cluster deals with the FT notifications of OCFTL, the responsibility of dealing with each notification falls to the stand-alone application, which should be able to deal with each notification accordingly to its needs.

6   Conclusions and Future Work

Providing FT for MPI is a complex task. This paper proposes OCFTL, a FT library that focuses on the portability, compatible with any MPI standard-compliant distribution. OCFTL provides failure detection and propagation mechanisms, and although inspired by other FT MPI approaches, it does not rely on any of them. For checkpointing it employs Veloc, however the application only interfaces with OCFTL providing portability. It also provides the application with checkpoint interval calculation.

Results show that OCFTL wrappers can avoid deadlock of MPI operations in the presence of failures; that the portability of OCFTL can overcome the overhead it imposes to the different MPI distributions; that the internal broadcast reduces the number of messages employed while retaining FT characteristics; and, the delay when detecting simultaneous sequential failures can be reduced. It also demonstrates that OCFTL can be used in stand-alone mode with applications or systems other than OmpCluster.

This is an ongoing project, so as future works we plan to tackle the presented limitations, as well as improving the library, providing incremental checkpointing, support for FT in GPUs and FT for the head process of OmpCluster.

Acknowledgment. The authors are grateful to the Center of Petroleum Studies (CEPETRO-Unicamp/Brazil) and PETROBRAS S/A for the support to this work as part of BRCloud Project.

References

1. Aulwes, R., et al.: Architecture of LA-MPI, a network-fault-tolerant MPI. In: 18th International Parallel and Distributed Processing Symposium, Proceedings, Santa Fe, NM, USA, p. 15. IEEE (2004). https://doi.org/10.1109/IPDPS.2004.1302920
2. Bautista-Gomez, L., Tsuboi, S., Komatitsch, D., Cappello, F., Maruyama, N., Matsuoka, S.: FTI: high performance fault tolerance interface for hybrid systems. In: Proceedings of 2011 International Conference for High Performance Computing, Networking, Storage and Analysis, SC 2011. Association for Computing Machinery, New York (2011). https://doi.org/10.1145/2063384.2063427
3. Bland, W., Bouteiller, A., Herault, T., Bosilca, G., Dongarra, J.: Post-failure recovery of MPI communication capability: design and rationale. Intl. J. High Perform. Comput. Appl. **27**(3), 244–254 (2013)
4. Bosilca, G., et al.: MPICH-V: toward a scalable fault tolerant MPI for volatile nodes. In: SC 2002: Proceedings of the 2002 ACM/IEEE Conference on Supercomputing, p. 29. IEEE (2002)
5. Bosilca, G., et al.: A failure detector for HPC platforms. Intl. J. High Perform. Comput. Appl. **32**(1), 139–158 (2018)
6. Efron, B., Hastie, T.: Computer Age Statistical Inference, vol. 5. Cambridge University Press, Cambridge (2016)
7. El-Ansary, S., Alima, L.O., Brand, P., Haridi, S.: Efficient broadcast in structured P2P networks. In: Kaashoek, M.F., Stoica, I. (eds.) IPTPS 2003. LNCS, vol. 2735, pp. 304–314. Springer, Heidelberg (2003). https://doi.org/10.1007/978-3-540-45172-3_28
8. Elliott, J., Kharbas, K., Fiala, D., Mueller, F., Ferreira, K., Engelmann, C.: Combining partial redundancy and checkpointing for HPC. In: 2012 IEEE 32nd International Conference on Distributed Computing Systems, pp. 615–626. IEEE (2012)
9. Fagg, G.E., Dongarra, J.J.: FT-MPI: fault tolerant MPI, supporting dynamic applications in a dynamic world. In: Dongarra, J., Kacsuk, P., Podhorszki, N. (eds.) EuroPVM/MPI 2000. LNCS, vol. 1908, pp. 346–353. Springer, Heidelberg (2000). https://doi.org/10.1007/3-540-45255-9_47
10. Gabriel, E., et al.: Open MPI: goals, concept, and design of a next generation MPI implementation. In: Kranzlmüller, D., Kacsuk, P., Dongarra, J. (eds.) EuroPVM/MPI 2004. LNCS, vol. 3241, pp. 97–104. Springer, Heidelberg (2004). https://doi.org/10.1007/978-3-540-30218-6_19
11. Gamell, M., Katz, D.S., Kolla, H., Chen, J., Klasky, S., Parashar, M.: Exploring automatic, online failure recovery for scientific applications at extreme scales. In: SC 2014: Proceedings of the International Conference for High Performance Computing, Networking, Storage and Analysis, pp. 895–906. IEEE (2014)
12. Georgakoudis, G., Guo, L., Laguna, I.: Evaluating the performance of global-restart recovery for MPI fault tolerance. Technical report, Lawrence Livermore National Lab. (LLNL), Livermore, CA, United States (2019)
13. Koren, I., Krishna, C.: Fault-Tolerant Systems. Elsevier Science (2020). https://books.google.com.br/books?id=YrnjDwAAQBAJ
14. Louca, S., Neophytou, N., Lachanas, A., Evripidou, P.: MPI-FT: portable fault tolerance scheme for MPI. Parallel Process. Lett. **10**(04), 371–382 (2000)
15. Moody, A., Bronevetsky, G., Mohror, K., De Supinski, B.R.: Design, modeling, and evaluation of a scalable multi-level checkpointing system. In: SC 2010: Proceedings of the 2010 ACM/IEEE International Conference for High Performance Computing, Networking, Storage and Analysis, New Orleans, LA, USA, pp. 1–11. IEEE (2010)

16. Nicolae, B., Moody, A., Gonsiorowski, E., Mohror, K., Cappello, F.: VeloC: towards high performance adaptive asynchronous checkpointing at large scale. In: 2019 IEEE International Parallel and Distributed Processing Symposium (IPDPS), Rio de Janeiro, Brazil, pp. 911–920. IEEE (2019)

17. Rosso, P.H.D.F., Francesquini, E.: Improved failure detection and propagation mechanisms for MPI. In: Anais da XII Escola Regional de Alto Desempenho de São Paulo, pp. 45–48. SBC (2021)

18. da Silva, J.A., Rebello, V.E.F.: A hybrid fault tolerance scheme for EasyGrid MPI applications. In: Proceedings of the 9th International Workshop on Middleware for Grids, Clouds and e-Science, MGC 2011. Association for Computing Machinery, New York (2011). https://doi.org/10.1145/2089002.2089006

19. Sultana, N., Skjellum, A., Laguna, I., Farmer, M.S., Mohror, K., Emani, M.: MPI stages: checkpointing MPI state for bulk synchronous applications. In: Proceedings of the 25th European MPI Users' Group Meeting, pp. 1–11 (2018)

20. Teranishi, K., Heroux, M.A.: Toward local failure local recovery resilience model using MPI-ULFM. In: Proceedings of the 21st European MPI Users' Group Meeting, pp. 51–56 (2014)

21. Young, J.W.: A first order approximation to the optimum checkpoint interval. Commun. ACM **17**(9), 530–531 (1974)

22. Zhong, D., Bouteiller, A., Luo, X., Bosilca, G.: Runtime level failure detection and propagation in HPC systems. In: Proceedings of the 26th European MPI Users' Group Meeting, pp. 1–11 (2019)

Accelerating Smart City Simulations

Francisco Wallison Rocha[1]($\boxtimes$)(ID), João Cocca Fukuda[1]($\boxtimes$)(ID),
Emilio Francesquini[2]($\boxtimes$)(ID), and Daniel Cordeiro[1]($\boxtimes$)(ID)

[1] School of Arts, Sciences and Humanities, University of São Paulo, EACH–USP,
São Paulo, Brazil
`{wallison.rocha,joao.fukuda,daniel.cordeiro}@usp.br`
[2] Center for Mathematics, Computation and Cognition, Federal University of ABC,
CMCC–UFABC, Santo André, Brazil
`e.francesquini@ufabc.edu.br`

Abstract. Urban traffic simulations are of great importance for smart
cities research. However, city-scale simulators can be both process and
memory-intensive, and hard to scale. To speed up these simulations and
to allow the execution of larger scenarios, this work presents a set of
optimizations based on two complementary approaches. The first is an
approach inspired by SimPoint to estimate the results of new simulations using previous simulations. This technique consists of identifying
and clustering recurring patterns during a simulation, and then using a
representative (the centroid of the cluster) of the recurring patterns to
reconstruct the remaining ones. On a dataset with 216 time series, our
technique was able to estimate the original series (of the same simulation)
with an average error of 6.38×10^{-6}. Using only the trips which include
the centroids (50% of the total simulation), estimation of metrics such as
average speed and percentage of street occupancy rate, presented errors
of 1.2% and 30% respectively, with a speedup of 1.95 in execution time.
The second approach works on a lower level. In this approach we explore
alternative implementations to Erlang's ETS tables, a central data structure used by the InterSCity simulator, and a current performance bottleneck. These optimizations yielded a speedup of approximately 1.28 when
compared to the current version of the simulator.

Keywords: Smart cities · Simulation · SimPoint · Profiling

1 Introduction

Urban mobility is an aspect of great interest for citizens and government. It is
essential to ensure quality of life in large cities [11]. Nevertheless, cities like São
Paulo, Rio de Janeiro and New York face issues that are consequence of mobility
problems, such as heavy urban traffic, insufficient public transportation, and
pollution. Solving these problems requires innovative solutions. Generally, the
implementation such solutions is complex, so there is a need to test and evaluate
them before deploying [17].

© Springer Nature Switzerland AG 2022
I. Gitler et al. (Eds.): CARLA 2021, CCIS 1540, pp. 148–162, 2022.
https://doi.org/10.1007/978-3-031-04209-6_11

Computer simulations have been used by city planners and smart city researchers to investigate and validate solutions for mobility problems. Their use on large-scale in conurbation scenarios like São Paulo, however, can be challenging due to the amount of computational resources required for running larger simulations.

The InterSCSimulator [17] is a simulator written in *Erlang*, an actor-based programming language that simplifies parallel and distributed computing. The use of Erlang alone, however, is not enough to allow the execution of such large scenarios. The simulator has some limitations such as excessive memory usage, scalability with suboptimal speedup, and limited ability to employ all available resources, e.g. using at most 50% of the available processing power.

Long-running simulations is also a problem faced by hardware designers. To reduce the execution time of the simulation of new hardware architectures, Hamerly et al. [8] proposed the Simpoint technique. The goal of the SimPoint is to find and exploit the large scale behavior of programs. After a full execution of the simulation, representatives of patterns of the execution (called *simulation points*) are identified and reused to estimate results of future executions with different inputs. Clustering algorithms like K-means are used to identify the patterns and which parts of the simulation are represented by them.

Inspired by the Simpoint technique, this work proposes a two-level approach to improve the InterSCSimulator's performance. On a higher level, the execution of the simulation was changed to detect and reuse similar behaviour of parts of the simulation through data analysis on past executions. We call this higher level approach *Simulation Estimation by Data Patterns Exploration* (SimEDaPE).

On a lower level, application-level and VM-level profiling techniques were used to identify bottlenecks and optimize process and memory consumption. Using profiling tools from both inside and outside the Erlang's virtual machine (BEAM), we identify bits of code and language components that might hinder performance. This approach also takes advantage of the several profiling tools for Linux, the environment on which this simulation is run.

2   Related Works

The performance of urban traffic simulation was studied on different contexts. Different approaches employed by the existing simulators suffers from different types of problems.

Fu, Yu and Sarwat [6] present a scalable and distributed urban traffic simulator using a quadtree and Apache Spark. Ramamohanarao et al. [14] show a distributed simulator, which enables it to achieve greater scalability different from the others found in the literature by the author.

To accelerate autonomous vehicle simulations in a distributed environment Tang et al. [19] present an approach using Apache Spark. Gütlein, German and Djanatliev [7] built a large-scale multi-level urban transport traffic simulator framework, which offers the advantage of high performance, a more flexible level of detail, and a decent fit to the use case at the same time. Khunayn et al. [2] present algorithms for improving the scalability of smart city simulators.

Due to the large memory consumption by discrete event simulations, Lin and Yao [10] propose a reverse computing approach in their multithreaded discrete-event simulator. The proposed method is used for large-scale stochastic reaction-diffusion simulation to solve excessive memory consumption. Unlike this work, which aims to use the SimPoint technique to estimate the results of extensive simulations and consequently reduce memory consumption with these estimates.

Santana *et al.* [17] developed a simulator written in Erlang and scalable for urban traffic to meet the scalability challenges existing in previous works in the literature. Despite its highly scalable architecture, their developers reported that in order to increase the simulations capabilities of InterSCSimulator, it is necessary to face several challenges such as the final output file size, memory usage, distributed communication optimization and some performance bottlenecks such as CPU usage. In particular, they have shown a CPU usage of around 50% [17], which is far from optimal.

This work expands our previous efforts on the matter [15] by proposing an integrated two-level approach for accelerating the InterSCSimulator, with a new implementation for Erlang's ETS table and a new testbed for measuring the accuracy and performance of the proposed simulation estimation method.

3   SimEDaPE: Simulation Estimation by Data Patterns Exploration

The SimPoint technique was developed to accelerate hardware simulations. The use of SimPoint requires the definition of metrics that can summarize the behavior of the simulation. Computer architecture designers use metrics such as data cache misses, performance (IPC), and branch mispredictions [8].

By detecting which parts of the simulation behave similarly concerning these metrics, computer programs can be divided into various intervals of different sizes. Each interval has a certain amount of *basic code blocks*, *i.e.*, a section of code executed from start to finish with one input and one output. The form and number of times these blocks are executed define the behavior of the interval.

To compare the intervals and group those with similar behaviors, SimPoint defines a structure called *Basic Block Vectors* (BBV). A BBV is a vector of the size of the number of blocks that a given interval contains. Each cell in the vector represents a basic block of code. Cell values are defined by the number of times your blocks are executed in that interval.

After generating the *Basic Block Vectors* for each interval, it is now possible to compare them with each other. To compare two different BBVs X and X', Hamerly *et al.* [8] use the *Manhattan* distance. After extracting the information on how many times each basic code block is executed and transforming it into BBV, the clustering process is performed. In this process, some clustering algorithm is used. In particular, Hamerly *et al.* chose the *K-means* algorithm with the distance of *Manhattan* to cluster BBVs with similar patterns.

After performing the entire clustering process, the simulation points that best represent each group of *Basic Block Vectors* are collected. Each simulation point has an execution weight that indicates the percentage of overall program execution that the SimPoint represents. Later, in new executions, the technique will execute these simulation points and use the weights previously assigned to estimate the remainder of the simulation that each point represents. Thus, it is not necessary to run the entire simulation.

The InterSCSimulator has limitations related to the distribution of tasks between processes, excessive memory usage, and a maximum CPU processing power usage of 50%. These limitations make it difficult to simulate large scenarios such as the city of São Paulo with more than 12 million inhabitants. To improve the simulator's performance, we took inspiration from SimPoint. In this work, we propose the *Simulation Estimation by Data Patterns Exploration* (SimEDaPE) technique to speed up InterSCSimulator and consequently reduce excessive memory usage. SimEDaPE analyzes the simulation event data produced by InterSCSimulator, identifying the simulation patterns, clustering them, selecting the representative (we also call here *simulation points*) for each cluster, and estimating the remaining data.

InterSCSimulator receives a map and set of trips (origin-destination pairs) as input. Through observations, we realized that streets and avenues have similar behavior in certain intervals of the simulation time (this occurs throughout the entire simulation). The behavior of a road is defined according to the flow of vehicles through it. With the vehicle flow we were able to extract the different metrics (*e.g.*, average speed or occupation rate of a road) from the simulation. Moreover, we can segment the traffic of a street into time intervals throughout the simulation, which can then be clustered according to their behavior.

After generating these intervals, we cluster them with similar intervals, regardless of the street from which they were extracted. To compare these intervals for clustering, we regard them as time series. The specific time series used for comparison are generated from the events (vehicles entering and leaving the road) of each interval, thus representing the flow of vehicles.

After the clustering is done, we select a representative for each cluster. These representatives are then mapped to each of the time series of its cluster. These mappings allow us to transform our representative (simulation point) into any other time series in the same cluster. Later, a new simulation similar to the original, can be run partially. That is, there is no need to simulate all the input trips. Due to the partial simulation, not all time intervals or partial intervals will be generated. Therefore we employ the simulation points and mappings created in the previous step to estimate the remaining intervals, thus decreasing the overall simulation time.

Our adaptation of the SimPoint technique, SimEDaPE, to the context of the InterSCity simulator was guided by metrics for traffic simulation such as average vehicle speed, distance traveled, road's occupation rate, etc. In the next sections we explain the three phases that compose SimEDaPE (time series extraction, clustering, and estimation) in more detail.

3.1   Time Series Extraction

SimPoint [8] uses *Basic Block Vectors* (BBV) to represent and compare the intervals of basic blocks. In SimEDaPE, behaviors are represented by time series. Time series are constructed using the events of entry and exit of vehicles into and from a road in a certain time interval.

For each street, a time series s with an undefined size is created. In chronological order, when there are n input events e_i at time i in the street, the value of position s_i of the time series is incremented ($series_i = series_{i-1} + n$) and when n output events at the instant of time i happen the value of that position is decremented ($series_i = series_{i-1} - n$), thus generating the flow of vehicles for that road. This flows allows the visualization of periods that may represent, for example, traffic jams, times with a smoother flow, among other information.

3.2   Clustering

To compare and cluster BBVs by similarity, Harmely *et al.* [8] use the Manhattan or Euclidean distance (shown in Fig. 1a) and the K-means clustering algorithm. SimEDaPE, on the other hand, uses distinct distance and cluster algorithms due to the nature of the data (BBVs *vs.* time series) used to represent the simulation behavior. To compare time series it employs Dynamic Time Warping (DTW) [1] (Fig. 1b) and Shape Based Distance (SBD) [13]. For clustering, it uses K-means and K-shape. This choice was guided by the findings of the study performed by Paparrizos and Gravano [13]. In their study, using a dataset of 48 time series, they compared DTW and SBD with the Euclidean distance. This study aimed at determining which technique is the best to compare time series. For this dataset, DTW was better than the Euclidean distance for 60% of the time series, equivalent in 4% and worse in the remaining 36% (considering an accuracy of 0.788). Furthermore, considering SBD and Euclidean distance, SBD provided better results for 62% of the time series, equivalent in 25% and worse in 13% (considering an accuracy of 0.795).

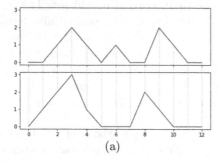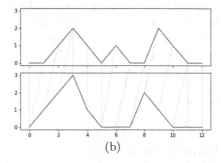

(a)   (b)

Fig. 1. Example of association of points from two time series using Euclidean distance (a) and DTW distance (b).

We choose the K-shape algorithm with SBD because its asymptotic complexity $O(m \log(m))$ is less than that of K-means with DTW which is $O(m^2)$ [13], where m is the size of the time series. Before clustering can be done, however, a normalization of the obtained time series is performed. The rationale for this normalization is two-fold. First, the time series extracted from the simulation events can be of different lengths. To correct that we perform a linear interpolation on the shorter series to make all of the series' sizes uniform. The second reason is that time series can behave similarly but on different scales. For example, consider a time series of one street with capacity for 80 vehicles compared to another with capacity for 20. Both can have a traffic jam, but with different number of vehicles. So, to achieve better clustering results, we apply a scale transformation to each time series, which allows us to compare data in the same amplitude. In this work, the normalization is described by $w' = \frac{w - \bar{x}}{\sigma}$, where w' is the normalized series, w is the series to normalize, $\bar{x}$ is the average of all the values in w, and σ is the standard deviation of the same values.

3.3 Estimation

After clustering, the next step is to determine the simulation points. These are chosen as the centroids of each simulation cluster (similar to what is done by [8]). The centroid of a cluster is the element (time series) with the shortest average distance to all other elements of the same cluster.

Finally, to estimate a time series from the simulation point (the cluster centroid), we used the warping path calculated using DTW. The warping path is the element-by-element association with the shortest distances between two series. The warping path is used to map simulation points into series in the cluster. In subsequent simulations, this same warping path is used to warp the simulation point into each series. Equation 1 shows how the simulation point is warped to estimate each series, where u_j is the element at position j in the series to be estimated, d_{ij}^2 is the distance between element c_i in the cluster and the element u_j in the series. Furthermore, it is necessary to apply scale reversal to return the series to its original amplitude using the equation: $w = w' \cdot \sigma + \bar{x}$.

$$u_j' = \begin{cases} c_i - \sqrt{d_{ij}^2 - d_{ij-1}^2}, & \text{if } u_j \geq c_i \\ \sqrt{d_{ij}^2 - d_{ij-1}^2} + c_i, & \text{if } u_j < c_i \end{cases} \tag{1}$$

4 Low-Level Performance Optimizations

We conducted a series of low-level performance profiling and optimizations on the code of InterSCSimulator. To investigate processing and memory bottlenecks, we employed VM-level and application-level profiling techniques.

InterSCSimulator is written in Erlang, a functional programming language used in the implementation of large-scale applications. Erlang programs are executed in BEAM, the Erlang Virtual Machine. Effective profiling of Erlang applications must take into account the operations carried out by the VM as well the operations from the application itself.

The profiling tools from application-level (outside the virtual machine) are the same as for any other compiled language [3,5,16]; tools such as *operf* and *linux-perf*. They analyse the stack frame and called functions' memory addresses from running processes to measure performance. Then they read the virtual machine's built-in functions' symbol tables to translate those functions' memory addresses into function names. This means that any code made purely in Erlang (namely the simulation's code) will not be known to these tools. They are meant for checking for BEAM's built-in components that are impacting the simulation throughout the code base like data structures or functions.

The tools from inside BEAM, however, give a better overview as to where some of these bottlenecks occur [9,18]. Erlang's built-in tools such as `fprof`, `eprof` and `cprof` were used as they are immediately accessible from a clean install and their single purpose design allows for an easier deployment, and use.

VM-Level Profiling. The profiling tools used inside BEAM were chosen mainly by their ease of use and their output's usefulness when put together with the profiling tools from outside the VM.

Fperf was the first of three tools. It allows for a more in-depth performance analysis than the other two built-in tools used, but its output is not immediately useful. It's format is not understandable by humans without the help of the documentation and the size is considerably big for it to be read as plain text.

That being said, with the help of *erlgrind*, it is possible to view the output's data on *KCacheGrind*, a graphical visualizer for *Valgrind*'s output format mainly intended for C profiling. *KCacheGrind* annotates time spent on functions and call graph visualization with *graphviz*. This is useful for with an *fprof* output, it is possible for Erlang's function call to be analysed and profiled in a more intuitive way.

Cprof and *eprof* have less capabilities and return less data. Both *cprof* and *eprof* count function calls, but *eprof* also measures the accumulated time spent on each of those function calls. They allow for faster and simpler profiling as their output is easily understood. They were mainly used to make simple benchmarks and to verify some assumptions about specific parts of code and optimization ideas.

Application-Level Profiling. On the application-level profiling, the tool of choice was *linux-perf* (or just *perf*). The *record* and *report* functions were used to gather execution information of the program and all other programs also running on the system using the -*a* flag. This is necessary as the simulation framework makes use of Erlang's multi-process facilities, and not all of these processes were in the scope of the profiling tool's single process profiling.

Our application-level profiling detected performance degradation on functions relying on multi-process synchronization using Erlang's ETS data structure. On SimDiasca version 2.4.0 and Erlang OTP version 24.0.3, on a simulation of 6440 trips (24 h simulation time, 13 s real time), about one fourth (25.25%) of the whole execution time was spent on synchronization functions.

The other identified functions that were degrading the performance of the simulation was the *ETS* tables functions. They made up about 5.89% of the whole execution time.

The synchronization was required for the nature of the SimDiasca (the simulation framework utilized), and so it was deemed out-of-scope. The *ETS* was then chosen as the best target for optimization.

4.1 Optimizations

ETS is the Erlang Term Storage. It allows for multiple tables, each containing a set of values (or terms) kept inside tuples that can be accessed by matching any of its elements from any process so long as this process has the identifier of the table. The tables are identified by an atom.

The most used *ETS* table throughout the simulation was the *list_streets* table. It keeps track of all simulations' streets and their status like maximum speed and current capacity (structure of *list_streets* in Listing 1).

Every iteration of the simulation, every vehicle has to get the information about the current and next streets on its trajectory and possibly update the current capacity of these streets to compensate for the car either leaving or entering it. This causes heavy usage of the table during runtime.

NIF. The first optimization was a custom storage library made using Erlang's Native Implemented Functions (NIFs) interface to substitute the *list_streets* table for a more specific solution.

The *NIF*-implemented storage library has only the necessary functions for the storage to work (`lookup`, `insert`, `update_element`, and `update_counter`), removing any unnecessary multi-table storage support that might hinder the performance (as there is only one table for this implementation).

It also changed the storage strategy itself so instead of allowing a search in any position of the structure for an element that matches, it uses a hash table with the `Vertices` element as key, as it is the only element used for this purpose.

This yielded better results as seen in Sect. 5.2, but as it was an outside function, it had its limitations. Due to Erlang's garbage collection, the library had to create its own environment to store *Eterms* (Erlang's C interpretation of an Erlang variable) and manage copying terms from the program into its own environment for storage and from its own storage to the program's for access. This caused some unintended overhead.

```
1   { Vertices,   Id, Length, StorageCapacity,
2     Freespeed, Count, Lanes, {}, IsCycleway,
3     IsCyclelane, Inclination, CountOnlyBikes }.
```

Listing 1: Structure of the street stored in *list_streets* *ETS* table

BIF. Creating our own *BIF* (built-in function) was another attempt to get even closer to the virtual machine and work around the problems outlined in the previous section. This approach makes use of the internal functions of the *ERTS* (Erlang Runtime System) along with access to the processes' own term environment for even faster insertions, lookups, and updates. This required modifications to the BEAM's source code to add a new module which implements the functions.

The *BIF* does not need to create or identify existing environments (as the *NIF* implementation does); instead, it uses the process' environment. However it needs to take care of the stored terms' reference counting because of the Erlang VM's garbage collector. It does this by storing a self-managed copy of the tuple.

Just-in-Time Compilation. The last optimization to the simulation was the update from Erlang OTP from version 20 to 24, which comes by default with a just-in-time compiler, allowing for a great performance boost without directly modifying the framework or the simulation's code. Some breaking changes were introduced between versions 20 to 24 of Erlang OTP. This required some modifications to InterSCity simulator components to remove deprecated functions and update functions calls to the new environment API.

5   Experimental Results

Experimental results were obtained using a scenario with more than $100,000$ trips in a region of 36 roads. This scenario was used in our experiments to test the performance of the Low-level performance optimizations and to generate a dataset with more than 216 time series of size $11,600$, distributed into 36 clusters to be used with SimEDaPE. The machine used to run the experiment has 8 GB RAM and an Intel Core i7-7500U CPU 2.70 GHz quad-core processor.

5.1   SimEDaPE

In this section, two experiments are presented. The first experiment aims to determine how good our technique is to transform our simulation point into a series of its own cluster. Additionally, it shows us the accuracy of the technique to estimate new metrics based on the same simulation.

The second experiment shows how good our technique is for estimating metrics such as average speed, percentage of vehicles, etc., from simulations similar to the first one which was used to extract the simulation points. Moreover, it also explores possible simulation speedup opportunities created by our technique.

First Experiment. Figure 2 shows Cluster C_{12} with a sample of two time series. In red, we highlight the centroid c_{12} and in green, the time series s_{13} (the time series in the same cluster which is the farthest from the centroid). We have chosen this cluster because the time series s_{13} has the greatest distance to its centroid compared to all the time series of all the clusters, thus being the worst

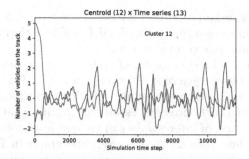

Fig. 2. Series with the longest distance from its centroid among all clusters.

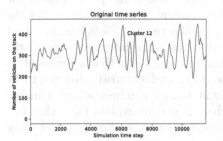
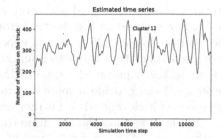

(a) Original time series s_{13} of cluster c_{12}

(b) Estimated time series s_{13} from the centroid of cluster c_{12}

Fig. 3. Estimate of the series with the longest distance to the centroid.

case. The *x-axis* represents the simulation time steps, and the *y-axis* represents the number of vehicles on the road in that moment. All series are normalized using the *z-score*. z-score is a standardization method used to transform normal variants into standard score format [12].

Figures 3a and b show the result of the reverse process. Given a centroid in red (Fig. 2) and the signature of a series, we compute an estimate for the original series (Fig. 3a) from the same scenario of a simulation. Figure 3b shows the estimate from the centroid. Equation 1 was used to estimate the time series and then $w = w' \cdot \sigma + \bar{x}$ to reverse the scale normalization. The estimation error on a series of n values is given by $E = \sum_{i=1}^{n} |s_i - s'_i|$, where s_i is a value of the original series and s'_i its estimation. The error of the estimated series (Fig. 3b) in relation to the original series (Fig. 3a) was 4.66812×10^{-5}. For the complete simulation, the biggest error was 0.00015, the mean error was 6.28048×10^{-6} with a standard deviation of 1.69169×10^{-5}.

Second Experiment. In this experiment, we show the capability SimEDaPE has to estimate metrics of interest for simulations different from the original simulation (source of the simpoints and related information such as warping paths, means, and standard deviations). In the second simulation, we changed the simulated scenario with the inclusion of new traffic lights in 11% of the streets. The number, origin, and destination of the trips are the same, and the same simulation time was kept (24 h). SimEDaPE's performance is shown by running 19 partial and one complete scenarios.

In Fig. 4, the errors of the estimates of each sample for the metrics of average speed (Fig. 4a) and percentage of street occupancy rate (Fig. 4b) are presented. The percentage corresponds to the number of trips performed in relation to the full simulation. SimEDaPE presents estimation results that vary in accuracy depending on the metric of interest. As can be seen in Fig. 4a, the biggest error of the estimates is less than 2.5%. However, the graph in Fig. 4b shows that the biggest error is above 30% (for estimates calculated by partial simulations ranging from 15 to 50% of the trips composing the full simulation). Furthermore, one could expect that an inverse proportionality between the percentage of the total simulation executed and error would be present. However, this is not the case. For example, in Fig. 4a, the error for partial scenario 20% is less than that for partial scenario 25%. It was expected that the more information from the complete simulation, the better our estimate. We hypothesize that a combination of some key trips (at the time of the selection of which road trips are to be executed) can provide a more accurate result than a combination of a higher number of irrelevant trips. Further research is needed to explain this behavior.

In Fig. 5, we show the execution time of the simulation applying our technique with samples of trips from 5% to 100%. Using the metric estimation information for each sample gives us a sense of how long we can speed up the simulation. For example, if we want to estimate the percentage of street occupancy rate in the simulation with a maximum error of 30%, then we can select a sample of size 50% (containing all the trips that make up the simulation points) which would give us a speedup of 1.95. Additionally, we would have an error of about 30% for estimating the percentage of street occupancy rate and an error of 1.2% for calculating the average speed.

An important point to consider is whether it is better to apply our technique or run the entire simulation. We can divide our technique time into four steps: clustering, warping path calculation, partial simulation execution, and simulation estimation. The clustering step takes 159.31 s and the warping path

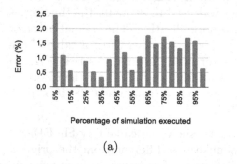

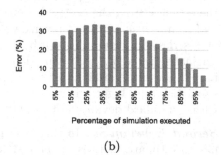

(a)   (b)

Fig. 4. Estimate of the average speed (a) and percentage of street occupancy rate (b).

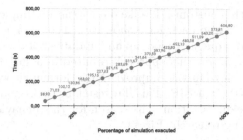

Fig. 5. Execution time of the samples of the trips of the complete simulation.

calculation approximately 9511 s. These execution times are considerable, however they are executed only once, and can be leveraged to estimate an arbitrary large number of new simulations amortizing their cost. Figure 6 shows the time for the execution steps of the partial simulation and the simulation estimation. These last two steps can vary according to the size of the new simulation to be estimated. In this experiment, the estimation time was 7.46 s on average.

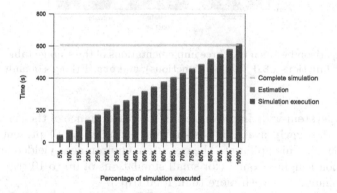

Fig. 6. Time spent on each step of the SimEDaPE application.

In the graph shown in Fig. 6, we can see how the cost of calculating the warping path can be high when compared to the time needed to run the full simulation (about 16× longer). Usually, the clustering step takes longer than calculating the warping path. However, due to the number of clusters selected for this experiment (36) and the number of iterations of the K-shape algorithm (8), we were able to reduce the time considerably (159, 31 s). Moreover, compared to the rest of the execution, the estimation step is very fast (7.46 s on average) and is not a bottleneck for the execution of the estimation.

5.2 Low-Level Optimizations

Our profiling analysis demonstrated that an important portion of the execution time was spent in Erlang's ETS tables. A first attempt to alleviate this issue was done using NIFs with a custom ETS-like data structure implementation. Experimental results of this approach have shown a speedup of 1.2 for a benchmark composed of a mixed sequence of lookup and update operations. When evaluated with the InterSCSimulator, this approach resulted in a speedup of 1.28.

Next, in an attempt to further improve the performance, we moved the implementation from a NIF to a BIF. This did result in performance gains, with the exception of the `lookup` function. The reason for this behavior is still unknown and a topic of ongoing research (Fig. 7).

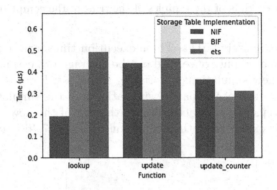

Fig. 7. Comparison between the three implementations of the storage table. `NIF` (native implemented functions), `BIF` (built-in functions), and `ets` (Erlang's default ETS implementation).

Another, system-wide improvement in the performance of the simulation was done using the newly available just-in-time compiler (JIT) present in Erlang OTP version 24. This update to the execution environment yielded speedups on the simulation ranging from 2 (for small simulations of up to 10 trips) up to 4.5 (for larger simulations with more than 1000 trips).

The speedups obtained by the use of a JIT compiler can be explained by the fact that all the code executed by the simulation is affected, including Erlang's ETS tables, the InterSCity simulator itself as well as all the libraries on which it depends. It is worth noting that a JIT-based approach has already partially been done before, but only for some components (including *ETS* [4]) in order to improve performance.

6   Conclusions

This work presents a two-level approach to improve the performance of a smart city simulator (InterSCSimulator). In this work we propose an adaptation of the Simpoint technique which we call Simulation Estimation by Data Patterns Exploitation (SimEDaPE). Using this technique, we show how to speed up smart city simulations by reusing knowledge acquired from previous simulations. Data from previous simulations are analysed to detect roads that behave similarly according to a given metric, and this information is used to infer how clusters of similar roads should behave in new simulations. The performance obtained with SimEDaPE was improved with several low-level optimizations conducted through a deep profiling analysis at both the application and VM-level.

The results shown by SimEDaPE are encouraging. Estimates of new metrics on an already-run simulation, show average errors of 6.28×10^{-6} (with a standard deviation of 1.69×10^{-5}). The biggest error was 0.00015. When the precision of the simulation itself is taken into account, errors of this magnitude are negligible. To evaluate the performance of the approach in a new simulation, we modified 10% of the roads including new traffic lights in the simulation. We observed a variation of accuracy in the results according to the metric ranging, for the studied metrics, from 1.2% to approximately 30%. We also presented a trade-off analysis between metric estimation accuracy and the simulation speedup.

The performance gains provided by SimEDaPE were further improved with the optimizations provided by the second part of our work: improved implementation of the ETS tables as a NIF, and as a BIF as well as the new version of the simulator, compatible with a JIT compiler.

In future works, we intend to validate the simulator using real-world mobility patterns (to be obtained with partners from the public sector). We also intend to improve the pre-processing step of SimEDaPE using multithreading. Additionally, another point to be considered is a study for the use of other forms of estimation, such as the use of Principal Component Analysis (PCA) and metrics that improve the warping path estimation.

Acknowledgment. This research is part of the INCT of the Future Internet for Smart Cities funded by CNPq proc. 465446/2014-0, Coordenação de Aperfeiçoamento de Pessoal de Nível Superior - Brasil (CAPES) - Finance Code 001, FAPESP proc. 14/50937-1, and FAPESP proc. 15/24485-9.

References

1. Berndt, D.J., Clifford, J.: Using dynamic time warping to find patterns in time series. In: Proceedings of the 3rd International Conference on Knowledge Discovery and Data Mining, AAAIWS 1994, Seattle, WA, pp. 359–370. AAAI Press (1994)
2. Bin Khunayn, E., Karunasekera, S., Xie, H., Ramamohanarao, K.: Exploiting data dependency to mitigate stragglers in distributed spatial simulation. In: Proceedings of the 25th ACM SIGSPATIAL International Conference on Advances in Geographic Information Systems, SIGSPATIAL 2017. Association for Computing Machinery, New York (2017). https://doi.org/10.1145/3139958.3140018
3. Binder, W., Hulaas, J., Moret, P., Villazón, A.: Platform-independent profiling in a virtual execution environment. Softw. Pract. Exp. **39**(1), 47–79 (2009). https://doi.org/10.1002/spe.890
4. Fritchie, S.L.: A study of erlang ETS table implementations and performance. In: Proceedings of the 2003 ACM SIGPLAN Workshop on Erlang, pp. 43–55 (2003)
5. Fritchie, S.L.: DTrace and erlang: a new beginning. In: Erlang User Conference (2011)

6. Fu, Z., Yu, J., Sarwat, M.: Demonstrating GeoSparkSim: a scalable microscopic road network traffic simulator based on apache spark. In: Proceedings of the 16th International Symposium on Spatial and Temporal Databases, pp. 186–189. Association for Computing Machinery, New York (2019). https://doi.org/10.1145/3340964.3340984

7. Gütlein, M., German, R., Djanatliev, A.: Towards a hybrid co-simulation framework: HLA-based coupling of MATSim and SUMO. In: 2018 IEEE/ACM 22nd International Symposium on Distributed Simulation and Real Time Applications (DS-RT), Madrid, Spain, pp. 1–9. IEEE (2018)

8. Hamerly, G., Perelman, E., Lau, J., Calder, B.: SimPoint 3.0: faster and more flexible program phase analysis. J. Instr. Level Parallelism $7(4)$, 1–28 (2005)

9. Karlsson, S.: Exploring the Elixir ecosystem testing, benchmarking and profiling (2015). https://hdl.handle.net/20.500.12380/219742. Accessed 13 Apr 2021

10. Lin, Z., Yao, Y.: Parallel discrete event simulation of stochastic reaction and diffusion using reverse computation. In: 2015 IEEE International Conference on Smart City/SocialCom/SustainCom (SmartCity), Chengdu, China, pp. 643–648. IEEE (2015). https://doi.org/10.1109/SmartCity.2015.142

11. Martins, T.G., Lago, N., de Souza, H.A., Santana, E.F.Z., Telea, A., Kon, F.: Visualizing the structure of urban mobility with bundling: a case study of the city of são paulo. In: Anais do IV Workshop de Computação Urbana, pp. 178–191. SBC (2020)

12. Mohamad, I.B., Usman, D.: Standardization and its effects on k-means clustering algorithm. Res. J. Appl. Sci. Eng. Technol. $6(17)$, 3299–3303 (2013)

13. Paparrizos, J., Gravano, L.: K-shape: efficient and accurate clustering of time series. In: Proceedings of the 2015 ACM SIGMOD International Conference on Management of Data, SIGMOD 2015, pp. 1855–1870. Association for Computing Machinery, New York (2015). https://doi.org/10.1145/2723372.2737793

14. Ramamohanarao, K., et al.: Smarts: scalable microscopic adaptive road traffic simulator. ACM Trans. Intell. Syst. Technol. (TIST) $8(2)$, 26 (2017)

15. Rocha, F.W., Francesquini, E., Cordeiro, D.: An approach inspired by simulation points to accelerate smart cities simulations. In: XII Escola Regional de Alto Desempenho de São Paulo. Sociedade Brasileira de Computação (2021). https://doi.org/10.5753/eradsp.2021.16703

16. Rosà, A., Chen, L.Y., Binder, W.: Actor profiling in virtual execution environments. In: Proceedings of the 2016 ACM SIGPLAN International Conference on Generative Programming: Concepts and Experiences, pp. 36–46 (2016)

17. Santana, E.F.Z., Lago, N., Kon, F., Milojicic, D.S.: InterSCSimulator: large-scale traffic simulation in smart cities using erlang. In: Dimuro, G.P., Antunes, L. (eds.) MABS 2017. LNCS (LNAI), vol. 10798, pp. 211–227. Springer, Cham (2018). https://doi.org/10.1007/978-3-319-91587-6_15

18. Ślaski, M., Turek, W.: Towards online profiling of Erlang systems. In: Proceedings of the 18th ACM SIGPLAN International Workshop on Erlang, pp. 13–17 (2019)

19. Tang, J., Liu, S., Wang, C., Liu, C.: Distributed simulation platform for autonomous driving. In: Peng, S.-L., Lee, G.-L., Klette, R., Hsu, C.-H. (eds.) IOV 2017. LNCS, vol. 10689, pp. 190–200. Springer, Cham (2017). https://doi.org/10.1007/978-3-319-72329-7_17

High Performance Computing
and Artificial Intelligence

Distributed Artificial Intelligent Model Training and Evaluation

Christina Monahan, Alexander Garcia, Evan Zhang, Dmitriy Timokhin, Hanson Egbert, and Maria Pantoja(✉) ⓘ

California Polytechnic State University, San Luis Obispo, CA 95116, USA
mpanto01@calpoly.edu

Abstract. Machine Learning (ML) and in particular Neural Networks (NN) are currently being used for different image/video processing, speech recognition and other tasks. The goal of supervised NN is to classify raw input data according to the patterns learned from an input training set. Training and validation of NN is very computationally intensive. In this paper we present an NN infrastructure to accelerate model training, specifically tuning of hyper-parameters, and model inference or prediction using distributed systems techniques. By accelerating model training, we give ability to researchers to obtain a large set of potential models to use and compare in a shorter amount of time. Automating this process not only reduces development time but will provide an easy means for comparing results for different classifiers and/or different hyper-parameters. With a single set of training data, our application will run different classifiers on different servers each running models with tweaked hyper-parameters. To give more control over the automation process the degree by which these hyper-parameters will be tweaked can be set by the user prior to running. The prediction step in most ML algorithms can also be very slow, especially on video prediction where current systems calculate their inference predictions on an entire input video, and then evaluate accuracy based on human annotations of objects of interest within the video. To reduce this bottleneck, we also accelerate and distribute this important part of the ML algorithm development. This process involves sending to each server the data; the model weights; and human annotations within the video segmentation. Our efficient distribution of input frames among each node greatly reduced the amount taken for testing and to generate accuracy metrics. To make our implementation robust to common distributed system failures (servers going down, lost of communication among some nodes, and others) we use heartbeat/gossip style protocol for failure detection and recovery. We tested our infrastructure for fast testing and inference of ML on video with data generated by a group of marine biologists researching the behavior of different marine species on the deep sea. Results show that by using our infrastructure times improved by a factor of 15.

Keywords: Machine learning · Neural network · Distributed computing · HPC

© Springer Nature Switzerland AG 2022
I. Gitler et al. (Eds.): CARLA 2021, CCIS 1540, pp. 165–176, 2022.
https://doi.org/10.1007/978-3-031-04209-6_12

1   Introduction

Neural Networks (NN) have been hugely successful in many classification tasks, from winning the game of Go against the best human player to early skin cancer detection [11]. Traditional NN are trained to produce a point estimate by optimizing a set of tunable parameters, the optimization is typically carried out using some form of gradient descent. When configuring a model for a machine learning application, there is often no clear-cut optimal way to structure the model. Different base model structures can train at different rates and classify data with differing degrees of accuracy and precision. It's often beneficial for programmers training a machine learning application to be able to compare the performance of their model when using different types of parameters and model configurations. For example, when training a sequential model, programmers can choose to compare the performance of standard Recurrent Neural Networks (RNN) layers versus Long Short Term Memory (LSTM) or Gated Recurrent Units (GRU) layers. They can also test the performance of any of these versus 1-D convolutional layers, or more complex architectures such as transformers. Even within each of these layers, further optimizations can be made by tuning different hyper-parameters, such as by changing the learning rate, error function, batch size, and number of epochs. There is currently not a best way to choose these, so hyper-parameter tuning often employs guess and check to see if changing a hyper-parameter affects the model's performance, and every developer group has their own initial favorites to try. The problem is that, since training a model can be very time consuming, making one small change and having to wait for a long time to see how the change affected the performance is undesirable for someone looking to efficiently tune their model.

Hyper-parameter tuning in NN has been researched before. In [4] Schikuta et al., created a data parallel neural network implementation. They ran comparative analysis of a multi-threading instance, two different parallelization approaches and a concurrent implementation. They identified the concurrent implementation using GoLang [6] to have the best execution time. In [1], the ATM (Auto-Tuned Model) project presents a distributed, collaborative, scalable system for automated machine learning. The team introduced 'Tune' as an open source framework for distributing model selection for hyperparameter tuning in python. In [8] an internet of things (IoT) device structure is used to run neural networks. They describe how IoT devices can use neural networks to get precise predictions, using small neural networks on the inside of the device, and deep neural networks that run on the cloud when predictions are uncertain. In [9], the researchers describes how to implement failure detection on a distributed NN. This allows each node to give progress to a master node on its prediction status. If a node is taking too long the master can redirect that node's job to a working node. We can do this using heartbeats pings from workers to master.

The **main contributions** of our work are twofold. **First**, distribute hyperparameter tuning on a cluster to improve training, similar problem as stated in [1] but using different libraries (Tensorflow [12] and Keras) and programming languages (GoLang [6]), to improve the flexibility, speed, and scalability of the

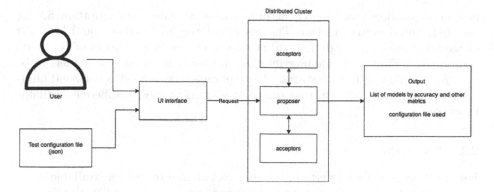

Fig. 1. System infrastructure

system. We make the system robust by adding failure detection and consensus protocol. This will mitigate the parallelism delays in building models. Furthermore, our solution will provide the capability to customize the configuration file to specify which models and hyperparameters a user prefers to use. The user should be able to either create a new configuration using the client program or provide a configuration file for the distributed system to run. The output of the application would be a list of models ranked by validation and accuracy. **Second**, we consider the problem that rises when one must perform large scale model prediction. An example of such a scenario is providing recommendations on Amazon. When a page is loaded, Amazon provides the user with unique recommendations for items related to the ones on that page. There is a ML model that is making these recommendations in the background and considers all the potential users of the system. This process needs to be scalable. The code for our implementation and validation to allow reproducibility can be found in these two references, [5] (distributed parameter and model training library) and [10] (inference acceleration).

2   Implementation Auto Tuning for ML Training

Since our primary goal is to build a distributed application, we need to use a programming language that allows us to exploit distributed paradigms. We choose to use Go programming language [6] since it has native support for concurrency with the use of channels which we will leverage for all communication. The basic infrastructure of our software is explained in Fig. 1. Failure detection will be monitored via a heartbeat function using a Gossip style protocol [16]. Additionally, our planned solution will manage membership using Paxos style protocol [17] to replicate processes across the servers to eventually select the optimal configuration. Furthermore, our solution will provide the capability to customize the configuration file to specify which models and hyper-parameters a user prefers to use while training. The user should be able to either create a new configuration using the client program or provide a configuration file for the distributed system to run. The output of the application would be a list of models ranked by validation and accuracy. Our system consists of two main components. First, a simple user interface for users to choose the models to be used for training with some starting hyperparameters. Second, a back end fault-tolerant distributed system that distributes training jobs to different available processes.

2.1 Front End

For the front end user interface, the user can choose to use the available models/hyperparameters or to import a saved configuration from a file. For the first option, as illustrated in Fig. 2 the user can select from the available models and hyperparameters by selecting each checkbox next to the option. All selected items will be added to their configuration and saved as a JSON file to be used by the back end. From the same user interface, the user can also import their models and hyperparameter file.

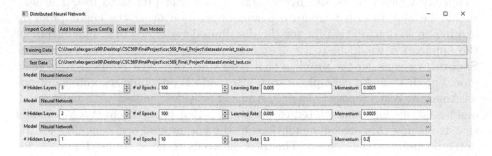

Fig. 2. Front end UI

2.2 Back End

The back end gets a user's configuration and runs several neural networks with the user model as a base to help compare the outcomes of the network with different hyperparameters. We leverage the concurrency in Go, by generating a system of channels to send and receive messages between servers within the environment.

Heartbeat/Gossip. To support failure detection every worker process that is started by the master to complete the training job is started with its own heartbeat table. Using a gossip approach to failure detection, every worker node also monitors two neighbor nodes heartbeat tables. If a node is identified as failed it is labeled that it has 'died' and the job will be sent to another worker process.

Paxos. For consensus our implementation uses a Paxos [17] style election algorithm, employing one master 'proposer' process, two shadowmasters processes, and multiple worker 'acceptor' processes to execute functions in parallel while providing fault tolerance. The master process distributes the training jobs to workers, monitors work completion and handles failed workers. The master process records its progress to an internal log which is saved to stable storage ultimately providing a persistent state for recovery. This internal log and the values are committed to the commitLog are backed up on a file in the directory. When a proposer failure is detected, the two shadowmasters are running processes that remain synchronized and ready to take over as the primary master upon failure. For achieving consensus using the before mention Paxos style algorithm, we select certain nodes (at random) identify as a proposer or acceptor. Acceptors will vote in the consensus algorithm. Once consensus is reached the proposal is committed to stable storage in a CommitLog, which is output to a file in the current directory. The file consists of lines of commits, formatted (id command message), where id is the committed proposal, and the rest corresponds to functions and arguments that were proposed to be performed but not adopted.

Recovery. There are two Shadowmaster servers that read from a CommitLog as the persistent state after a failure/restart - which will ensure it resumes service exactly where it left off. If the master is not heard from within 2 s, a shadowmaster will begin the process to continue the next task in sequence from the commitlog - becoming the master. This ensures a consistent state through failure and providing recovery from a complete system shutdown.

Libraries. Extensive amount of time was spent attempting to use external libraries to identify and use a predefined machine learning algorithm. GoLearn [13] was not compatible with any of the team members systems. GoNet [14] libraries are functional but proved not to be a strong training network. After several attempts at integrating GoML [15] cluster, linear, and Bayesian models without success, we successfully implemented a single machine learning model which we will use to auto tune the hyperparameters and train on. Additionally, Go does not have native support for GUIs, so are using an external library to produce our front end as well. In particular, the library ui [18] provides cross platform support, making it a great option for creating a user interface.

3   Accelerated Prediction/Inference Implementation

We focus on a specific machine learning problem, which is making video metric generation faster. Current systems use a single neural network to predict on frames in a video. This process can become slow based on how many frames are in the video and how large of a network is used. We target network speeds by loading the model multiple times on separate nodes and we make each node handle a segment of the entire length of the video. The distributed video prediction starts with a Golang [11] script whose steps are listed next (also explained in Fig. 3:

in

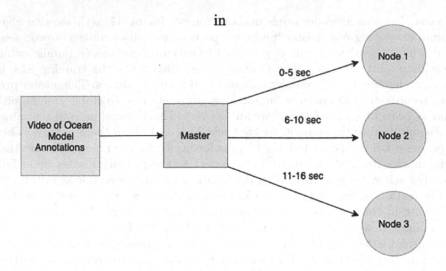

Fig. 3. Prediction distribution

1. The script reads in the video.
2. Video length is split by the number of nodes
3. Nodes are started and receive their individual configurations.
4. Each Node loads in the model and the human annotations for their segment
5. The script waits for the nodes to finish.
6. Metrics are aggregated and written as a CSV.

To execute the script a user must specify a video as in
go run hub.go video1.mp4 model_weights.h5.

The script will find the video either by finding it in the local directory or downloading it from an external server. The video metadata are then extracted, which contain the length, width, and height of the video. The script will also retrieve all the human annotations for that video from a database, which will be used to evaluate the model predictions.

Using this information the script divides the video into segments, based on how many nodes it has access to. Once this is completed, the script will start the number of specified nodes and send each node the segment it is responsible for and any configuration files used during the prediction process. The configuration file contains things such as the model path, the size of frames the model takes his input, the confidence the model needs to make a prediction, and the length of how long a concept needs to be tracked. The work done by each node consist of the following actions, Fig. 4:

- Access the video and model weights from a local path, or it will download them from an external server.
- Execute a python script for prediction on a video. This script will open the model and load in its weights file, then open the video. The model will make a prediction on every 10th frame.

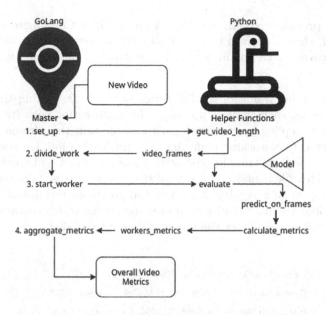

Fig. 4. Prediction system architecture

- If a prediction has higher confidence, then specified in the configuration file, it will track the prediction using openCV. This python script follows the same process as a neural network running on a single node.
- Once this node finishes predicting on its segment of the video, it will have generated a CSV file of tracked objects.
- Shares CSV file with nodes that are responsible for the video segments before and after the video segment that it worked on. These nodes are considered neighbors in the system. We share the tracked objects that appear at the very last part of the segment and the very beginning of the segment. Each node will compare its tracked objects at the very end of the video segment and the very beginning with its neighbors. If there is an object that appears at the last frame of a segment and at the first frame of another segment with closely overlapping boxes, we count this as a single object by communicating to the other neighbor that it has found the same object. This process checks both ends of a given node's video segment and allows for an object that appears in two consecutive segments to be counted only once.
- Once this check has been completed, the nodes are responsible for generating the metrics for their segment.
- The nodes compare the human annotations with the model generated annotations. If a human annotation overlaps with a model annotation, it is the same object, and is at the same time, we classify it as a true positive. If a model annotation doesn't overlap with anything, or it does overlap but is of a different object, it is a false positive. If a human annotation doesn't overlap with anything, then it is a false negative.

– Generate precision, recall, and the F1 score. Once these metrics have been generated, they are saved to a CSV file. After everything is done, the node communicates to the main script that it finished and sends its metric file name.

The main script waits for all the nodes to finish generating their metrics. During this time, each node is updating the main script with its progress. If a node has not replied to the master within a certain time frame that node's job is redirected to a working node that has finished its job. Once all the video segments have their metric file generated, the main script will create an overall metrics file. This file contains the sum of the true positives, false positives, and false negatives. Then is recalculates an overall precision, recall, and F1 score for the entire video. We are left with an overall metric file which contains F1 scores, precision, etc. for each object the model is trying to predict.

#1 Default Results - Runtime: 282.76544 s, Accuracy: 65.20%

#1 Double Epoch Results - Runtime: 597.94749 s, Accuracy: 70.40%

#1 Half Epoch Results - Runtime: 125.34542 s, Accuracy: 54.00%

#1 Double Learning Rate Results - Runtime: 285.95292 s, Accuracy: 69.20%

#1 Half Learning Rate Results - Runtime: 288.01739 s, Accuracy: 57.80%

#1 Double Momentum Results - Runtime: 279.84725 s, Accuracy: 63.60%

#1 Half Momentum Results - Runtime: 294.09015 s, Accuracy: 64.40%

#2 Default Results - Runtime: 277.21928 s, Accuracy: 68.00%

#2 Double Epoch Results - Runtime: 564.87490 s, Accuracy: 74.60%

#2 Half Epoch Results - Runtime: 123.18619 s, Accuracy: 58.60%

#2 Double Learning Rate Results - Runtime: 268.17048 s, Accuracy: 64.60%

#2 Half Learning Rate Results - Runtime: 276.84927 s, Accuracy: 58.00%

#2 Double Momentum Results - Runtime: 277.53344 s, Accuracy: 66.60%

#2 Half Momentum Results - Runtime: 263.84605 s, Accuracy: 63.40%

#3 Default Results - Runtime: 40.57651 s, Accuracy: 12.20%

#3 Double Epoch Results - Runtime: 91.89485 s, Accuracy: 11.00%

#3 Half Epoch Results - Runtime: 15.50504 s, Accuracy: 18.20%

#3 Double Learning Rate Results - Runtime: 43.10625 s, Accuracy: 11.40%

#3 Half Learning Rate Results - Runtime: 40.94053 s, Accuracy: 11.00%

#3 Double Momentum Results - Runtime: 42.30688 s, Accuracy: 13.60%

#3 Half Momentum Results - Runtime: 43.72060 s, Accuracy: 11.40%

Fig. 5. Output on the UI

4 Results

After building the application, we test it with various configurations and failure situations in our system to make sure that a worker processes can be restarted and that if a master process fails, the system can reelect a new master process and continue execution from where the previous master left off.

4.1 Manual Adjustment Testing

Once a machine learning algorithm, model, and data were identified, several test and evaluation cycles were conducted with individual hyper-parameter adjustments to identify if the Neural Network training and predictions were operational. All cycles led to identifying the optimal initial state for our model to begin the training and predictions. A few of the critical adjustments we needed to perform included the number hidden layers, number of output layers, type of problem, number of epochs, learning rate, and momentum and others. Adjusting the number of Hidden Layers to multiple variations from 1 single layer up to 100 layers, the optimal initial state of our program this project identifies is to set it at 100 layers with 32 nodes each. The number of epochs illustrated that the model is working when tested on the same training data set. Furthermore, as the learning rate increased, the prediction results did not; so, the model is set to 0.005 learning rate initially. Lastly, the momentum factor remained at 0.005, as variations showed no impact. All these tests and manual adjustments conducted during the development of this program - are the exact reason why software like the one being developed in this paper is needed.

4.2 Hyper-parameter Scopes

Every hyper-parameter has an identified range for adjustments to be tailored for the individual users data set. The following settings are available. Within the User Interface (UI), as seen in Fig. 2, the adjustable hyper-parameters have the following range:

- Number of Hidden Layers = 1–10,000
- Number of Epochs = 1–10,000
- Learning Rate = 0.0–1.0
- Momentum = 0.0–1.0

4.3 Model Variations

With the implemented model variations this program adjusts the hyper-parameters based on the selections in the user interface. There are individual variations identified, which the results provide insight for further training, the code is written so adding extensions for further Model parameter and configuration adjustment is a relatively easy task left to the reader. For prove of concept for this paper we added 7 hyperparameters that can be tuned automatically.

- Model 1: Original model as user specified.
- Model 2: Double the number of Epochs specified.
- Model 3: Half the number of Epochs specified.
- Model 4: Double the Learning Rate specified.
- Model 5: Half the Learning Rate specified.
- Model 6: Double the Momentum specified.
- Model 7: Half the Momentum specified.

Results of the parameter auto tuning are shown in Fig. 5. A complete list of the parameters is shown to the user so they can choose their optimal one. Since we run the auto-tuning as a distributed system the time taken to generate all values on Fig. 5 are same as the ones required to run just one of the models with a fixed value for the hyperparameters.

Test Recovery. To test the recovery and replication of nodes, we use a timer to manually kill nodes in our main thread and then start the node back up to observe that the system still works, and the node has rejoined the cluster.

4.4   Inference Results

We ran the testing process multiple times using a different number of nodes in the process. Our results are recorded below in a Fig. 6, which describes the clock time taken to complete and the CPU time to complete. The dataset we used contained around 28,000 frames. Thus, they were evenly divided into the nodes used to process them (using Eq. (1)). EX: 1 Node = each node has 28000 Frames, 2 Nodes = each node has 14000 frames each etc....

Number of Node	real time	user time	sys time
1	15m30.142s	0	0
2	7m54.320s	12m14.407s	2m23.794s
4	3m42.546s	5m21.247s	0m47.679s
8	1m55.715s	2m43.043s	0m22.821s
16	1m27.738s	1m57.978s	0m20.264s
32	1m1.505s	1m20.076s	0m15.529s

Fig. 6. Execution time

In Fig. 6, the real time column measures how long the metrics took to be calculated in real time. When we had two workers it took over seven minutes to calculate the overall metrics. We were able to get this time down to just over 1 min using 32 workers. The user time is the amount of time the CPU was doing work for the master or node's job. The system time is the amount of time the CPU was performing system calls for the kernel on the program's behalf. Note, these last two times should be multiplied by the number of nodes to give a better estimation of the real performance of the model's time, as we ran only one worker at a time.

$$Node\_Frames = \frac{Video\_Frames}{Number\_Of\_Frames} \tag{1}$$

In Fig. 7 we present a graph depicting the relationship between number of nodes used and the time taken in seconds to complete the prediction task. As the number of nodes used increases, the performance improves. The performance improvement from 1–4 nodes is quite dramatic but after that it starts to plateau. This is most likely since the prediction tasks require the same setup before predicting across each node and since the time taken for actual predictions becomes negligible the improvement seen also decreases.

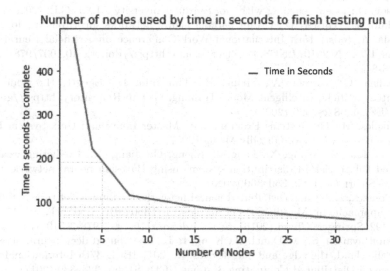

Fig. 7. Scalability

5   Conclusions

In this paper we developed a functional software tool for tuning hyperparameters, including an entire user interface, that allows fast and robust testing and evaluating of ML algorithms. We integrated the training of a neural network with a Paxos consensus algorithm to not only accelerate training but also provide failure recovery and coordination to the system. We also improve the model's predictive speed by distributing the task among many nodes and or go routines.

Possible future work could be to build a model API, similar to the one used in Tensorflow [12] serving, which is a simple model serving mechanism that runs on a webserver and is uses POST requests. In this way each node would not have to run the model per say but could reference replica API's and produce metrics. Furthermore, we could include generalization of our metrics to other kinds of loss functions such as Mean Squared Error (MSE).

References

1. Liaw, R., Liang, E., Nishihara, R., Moritz, P., Gonzalez, J.E., Stoica, I.: Tune: a research platform for distributed model selection and training (2018). arXiv arXiv:1807.05118
2. Swearingen, T., Drevo, W., Cyphers, B., Cuesta-Infante, A., Ross, A., Veeramachaneni, D.: ATM: a distributed, collaborative, scalable system for automated machine learning. In: 2017 IEEE International Conference on Big Data (1905), pp. 151–162 (2017). https://doi.org/10.1109/BigData.2017.8257923
3. Stinson, D.: Deep Learning with Go. Purdue University, M.S.E.C.E. (2020)
4. Schikuta, E., Turner, D.: Go for parallel neural networks. In: Rojas, I., Joya, G., Catala, A. (eds.) 15th International Work-Conference on Artificial Neural Networks, IWANN 2019, LNCS. Springer, Cham. https://doi.org/10.1007/978-3-030-20518-8
5. Monahan, C., Garcia, A., Zhang, E., Timokhin, D., Egbert, H.: Code Distributed Artificial Intelligent Model Training. Github Repository. https://github.com/Ezhang98/csc569 (2020)
6. Tsoukalos, M.: Go Systems Programming: Master Linux and Unix System Level Programming with Go. O'Reilly Media (2017)
7. Du, Y., Liu, Y., Wang, X., Fang, J., Sheng, G., Jiang, X.: Predicting weather-related failure risk in distribution systems using Bayesian neural network. IEEE Trans. Smart Grid **12**, 350–360 (2020)
8. De Coninck, E., et al.: Distributed neural networks for internet of things: the big-little approach. In: Mandler, B., et al. (eds.) IoT360 2015. LNICST, vol. 170, pp. 484–492. Springer, Cham (2016). https://doi.org/10.1007/978-3-319-47075-7_52
9. Teerapittayanon, S., McDanel, B., Kung, H.T.: Distributed deep neural networks over the cloud, the edge and end devices. In: 2017 IEEE 37th International Conference on Distributed Computing Systems (ICDCS), pp. 328–339 (2017)
10. Monahan, C., Garcia, A., Zhang, E., Timokhin, D., Egbert, H.: Code distributed artificial intelligent model evaluation for replication. Github Reposit. (2020) https://github.com/hi4a4/distributedmodelevalulation
11. Google Research Research Blog: AlphaGo: Mastering the ancient game of Go with Machine Learning, 27 January 2016
12. Abadi, A., et al.: Large-scale machine learning on heterogeneous systems (2015). Software available from tensorflow.org
13. Machine Learning Library in GoLang https://pkg.go.dev/github.com/golang-basic/golearn (2014)
14. Go module implementing multi-layer Neural Network https://pkg.go.dev/github.com/dathoangnd/gonet (2020)
15. Go Module for Machine Learning (2019). https://github.com/cdipaolo/goml
16. Demers, A., et al.: Epidemic algorithms for replicated database maintenance. In: PODC 1987 (1987)
17. Lamport, L.: Paxos made simple. ACM SIGACT News (Distributed Computing Column) **32**, 4 (Whole Number 121), December 2001
18. GXUI - A Go cross platform UI library (2015). https://github.com/google/gxui

Large-Scale Distributed Deep Learning:
A Study of Mechanisms and Trade-Offs
with PyTorch

Elvis Rojas[1,2]([✉]), Fabricio Quirós-Corella[4], Terry Jones[3],
and Esteban Meneses[1,4]

[1] Costa Rica Institute of Technology, Cartago, Costa Rica
[2] National University of Costa Rica, Pérez Zeledón, Costa Rica
erojas@una.ac.cr
[3] Oak Ridge National Laboratory, Oak Ridge, TN, USA
trjones@ornl.gov
[4] National High Technology Center, San José, Costa Rica
{fquiros,emeneses}@cenat.ac.cr

Abstract. Artificial intelligence is a transforming technology for creating new scientific discoveries, services, and products. Its full potential is achieved when massive data repositories and large-scale computing systems are available. Both factors are becoming easier to obtain daily as sensor networks constantly create open-data archives, and Moore's law still makes supercomputing power more accessible. However, as deep learning models become larger to tackle data complexity, researchers must determine how to speed up training in those models. This paper uses an experimental approach to try to understand the algorithms and trade-offs associated with distributed deep learning. This study used the Summit supercomputer at Oak Ridge National Laboratory to determine that existing distributed deep learning mechanisms scale in execution time. However, as more nodes are used, accuracy degrades significantly. To solve this, several hyper-parameters must be tuned. The results show that optimizing those parameters is a nontrivial task. We also evaluated the impact of other scaling techniques, such as mixed precision and adaptive parameter optimization.

Keywords: Distributed deep learning · Performance · Scalability

Notice: This manuscript has been authored by UT-Battelle, LLC, under contract DE-AC05-00OR22725 with the US Department of Energy (DOE). The US government retains and the publisher, by accepting the article for publication, acknowledges that the US government retains a nonexclusive, paid-up, irrevocable, worldwide license to publish or reproduce the published form of this manuscript, or allow others to do so, for US government purposes DOE will provide public access to these results of federally sponsored research in accordance with the DOE Public Access Plan (https://energy.gov/downloads/doe-public-access-plan).

I. Gitler et al. (Eds.): CARLA 2021, CCIS 1540, pp. 177–192, 2022.
https://doi.org/10.1007/978-3-031-04209-6_13

1   Introduction

The recent wave of artificial intelligence (AI) methods spearheaded by deep neural networks has permeated many fields in science, engineering, and business. Several recent studies [5,6,14] highlight the importance of AI for scaling science, boosting international competitiveness, improving health technologies, ensuring fair access to information, and many other desirable outcomes. Data science, high-performance computing (HPC), and AI complement each other by combining advanced data management, computing, and information extraction capabilities, respectively. Therefore, it is crucial to understand the interaction between these areas to realize their combined potential.

Because Moore's law is still true, the resulting increase in computational power and ease of deploying sensors in greater numbers coupled with open-data initiatives permit access to massive data repositories, and AI frameworks become more sophisticated. In particular, deep learning (DL) models are becoming larger to cope with increased data complexity. Training a DL model with thousands or millions of parameters is a difficult computational problem. To address this challenge, DL model training could be decomposed into a distributed approach. However, there are many design decisions and trade-offs when attempting this. This paper explores the details using an experimental approach.

Different distributed training (DT) mechanisms derive from the particular data parallelism approach. This study focuses on the performance (Training time performance) and scalability analysis of various DT mechanisms of PyTorch, such as Distributed Data Parallel (DDP), Horovod (HVD), DeepSpeed (DSP), and FairScale (FSC). These DT mechanisms implement different algorithms and data parallelism techniques. Therefore, it is important to determine how much benefit each mechanism offers. Furthermore, this study included four convolutional neural network (CNN) models: ResNet50, ResNet1010, VGG16, and VGG19. These CNNs are all run with different depths to evaluate their role together with DT mechanisms.

The contributions of this paper are as follows:

- a survey of the most popular PyTorch DT mechanisms describing the most important details for their implementation (Sect. 3);
- an analysis of the performance offered by the different DT mechanisms when scaling on several GPUs and a study of the effects of using different CNNs with the different DT mechanisms (Sect. 5.1);
- a study of the trade-offs between CNN learning and the GPU scaling using all the DT mechanisms and CNNs included in this paper (Sect. 5.2); and
- a performance analysis of two advanced optimization approaches in DT: one related to the floating-point precision of the data (i.e., automatic mixed precision [AMP]), and another related to the updating of the weights of a CNN (i.e., Adaptive Summation [AdaSum]) (Sects. 5.3 and 5.4).

2   Related Work

Within the existing state-of-the-art AI literature is a study that explores the fundamental DT approaches, such as the data-parallel and the model-parallel methods [8]. The study explores the most popular distributed DL (DDL) frameworks by comparing their parallelism implementation. Other work [18] provides an evaluation to the PyTorch DDP module. Also, a recent study [17] provides a taxonomy with a compact overview of the wide range of principles and characteristics that significantly impact how the DDL systems operate. This study includes aspects related to parallelism, optimization, and scheduling techniques.

That same study also introduces the need of having standardized AI benchmarks to evaluate the performance of DDL systems because using processing metrics, such as GPU utilization or training sample throughput, is not useful in practice [17]. The DAWNBench benchmark [4] analyzes the performance of different DL tasks by improving training and inference time. It explores different optimizations, such as multi-GPU in TensorFlow and PyTorch. DeepBench [1] is another tool that considers neural network libraries for benchmark operations and workloads that are important to both DL training and inference. Additionally, this benchmark evaluates the performance of all-reduce operations. MLPerf [20] is a performance benchmark that evaluates DL workloads, including image classification, object detection and segmentation, reinforcement learning, translation, and recommendation. Deep500 [3] is a benchmarking infrastructure that enables data-parallel DT to potentially scale to thousands of cores. It compares distributed variants of Stochastic gradient descent and loss functions, including TensorFlow's native parameter server, and HVD. AIBench [9] corresponds to an extensible, configurable, and flexible end-to-end AI benchmark that measures and evaluates DL technologies of different application scenarios, such as search engines, social networks, and e-commerce. Unlike these benchmarks which evaluate the training performance or model learning, our study focuses on analyzing the scalability and the computing performance of DDL systems.

3   Background

3.1   Deep Learning Neural Network Models

Artificial neural networks (ANNs) are adaptive systems with an architecture inspired by the neural cortex of the human brain. ANNs incorporate artificial neurons, which are computation units that process the input information and generate an output of interest according to the neural network configuration. ANNs are converted into a deep neural network when more than one hidden layer is added to the interconnected layers structure to solve more sophisticated AI problems [8]. The most common deep neural networks studied from a performance perspective are the convolutional neural networks (CNNs). These models consider convolutional filters as hidden layers, such as VGGNet and ResNet models, which are used for image classification and recognition. These are very computationally intensive and could take days to complete. Therefore, the idea is to adapt parallel and distributed algorithms, which can run much faster and drastically reduce training time [13]. For example, VGG-D and VGG-E are CNNs of 16 and 19 weight layers with 138 million and 144 million parameters, respectively. Their implementations contain several significant modifications that allow training and evaluation on multiple GPUs [28]. On the other hand, ResNet50 and ResNet101 are residual convolutional network configurations with 50 weight layers of 25.6 million parameters and 101 weight layers of 44.5 million parameters, respectively. ResNet models alleviate the training of deeper CNNs by using shortcut connections that skip one or more layers by performing identity mapping [12,29]. Additionally, ResNet models could support an all-reduce communication scheme to efficiently synchronize, average, and exchange model updates across participating GPUs [21].

3.2 Deep Learning Frameworks

A DL framework is a software tool that allows the design, construction and execution of CNNs easily and quickly by hiding the low-level implementation details through high-level programming interfaces. Current DL frameworks provide highly optimized parallelization mechanisms to train and validate CNNs. Furthermore, these frameworks allow the optimized use of multi-GPUs through libraries such as cuDNN and NCCL to speed up training. Nowdays there is a great variety of DL frameworks such as: PyTorch, TensorFlow, MXNet, Caffe, Deeplearning4j, Chainer and many others. Each of these DL frameworks performs the execution of the CNN implementing different techniques and algorithms, so these frameworks can vary in complexity of use, performance, and the type of applications in which they can be efficient.

We focus this study on PyTorch which is based on the Torch framework. PyTorch bases its operation on tensor computing to use the power of GPUs and implements techniques such as reverse-mode auto-differentiation to optimize at both the functional and neural network layer level [18,24].

3.3 Distributed Deep Learning Training

The most recent DT mechanisms have formed a shift toward the data parallelism strategy for scaling out DL systems. To achieve its objective, DT encompasses a series of processes, algorithms, and hardware resources. Figure 1 shows a general view of how some of these elements interact with each other. They can be grouped into four large sections: Parallel Data Loader, Training Loop, Data Parallel Process, and HPC System. This study focuses mainly on the Data Parallel Process in which the different DT mechanisms are implemented. However, we also experimented with factors that directly influence the Training Loop process, such as learning rate (LR) or batch size. For the HPC System process element, distributed hardware factors result in performance benefits, including libraries optimized for GPUs. We focused our work on the PyTorch library, which allows the implementation of different mechanisms of DDL training based on data parallelism, including DDP, HVD, DSP, and FSC.

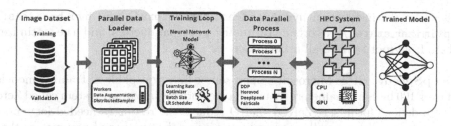

Fig. 1. DT process.

Distributed Data Parallel: PyTorch offers a DDP module to parallelize and easily scale training across several processes and devices. Each process has its own model replica and local optimizer in which every model copy will be fed with a different subset of input data samples and in which the gradients will be averaged across processes to update the model locally. DDP ensures training correctness by maintaining gradient communications to keep all model replicas synchronized [18].

To develop a multinode DT with DDP, the function `DistributedData Parallel(model, device_ids)` must be implemented to parallelize the model by splitting the input across the specified devices. However, it is first necessary to set the back-end communication type, the initialization mechanism, and the number of processes participating in the job (`world_size`). The NVIDIA Collective Communication Library (NCCL) was used as communication back end because it offers better performance with optimized collective operations when using GPUs. Also, an environmental variable mechanism was used as the initialization mechanism. These mechanisms along with the `world_size` are parameters of the `torch.distributed.init_process_group()` function that is used to initialize the distributed process. Also, PyTorch provides a `DistributedSampler` to slice the data among processes and synchronize them to avoid overlapping batches.

Horovod: HVD is an open-source library that makes DDL fast and easy to use with TensorFlow, Keras, PyTorch, and MXNet. HVD is based on a ring all-reduce algorithm for averaging gradients and communicating those model updates to all nodes. HVD uses the NCCL that introduces the ability to run ring all-reduce across multiple machines. Furthermore, HVD can be used with the AdaSum algorithm to improve the data parallel training of DL models by allowing users to scale to more training workers without penalizing LR and convergence stability [27].

When HVD works with PyTorch, it wraps the optimizer with `hvd.DistributedOptimizer()`. Then, it uses all-reduce (`hvd.allreduce()`) operations to combine gradient values before applying gradients to the model weights. The `loss.backward()` instruction is performed in parallel to compute the all-reduce operations that are executed after each gradient. HVD also uses the instruction `hvd.broadcast_parameters()` and `hvd.broadcast_optimizer_state()` to broadcast model-state parameters and the optimizer state from root rank to all other processes.

DeepSpeed: DSP is Microsoft's open-source library capable of training models of over 100 billion parameters by using a memory optimization system called Zero Redundancy Optimizer (ZeRO). ZeRO reduces the resources needed for model and data parallelism while massively increasing the number of parameters that can be trained [26]. This system consists mainly of two sets of optimizations that face different challenges. The first one, ZeRO-DP, removes memory state redundancies across data-parallel processes by partitioning model states. ZeRO-R aims to reduce the residual memory consumption by identifying and removing activation replication during the forward and backward propagation [25].

To implement DSP, it must first be initialized with the `deepspeed.initialize()` command with the following parameters: CNN, model parameters, the training dataset, and other arguments. This initialization will return a new version of each of the parameters. In a distributed execution environment, it is necessary to take the PyTorch DDP implementation as a base because the command `init_process_group()` must be replaced with `deepspeed.init_distributed()`, including the same parameters. Additionally, within the training cycle, the instructions `loss.backward()` and `optimizer.step()` must be replaced by `model.backward(loss)` and `model.step()`, which are versions of the model generated in the DSP initialization process.

FairScale: FSC is PyTorch's library that extends the latest DT and scaling techniques for high performance. The FSC library includes three different implementations to reduce the memory redundancy in model states: the Optimizer State Sharding (OSS), Sharded Data Parallel (SDP), and Fully Sharded Data Parallel (FSDP). OSS shards (i.e., fragments) the model optimization state in different ranks based on the parameter size. SDP and FSDP both implement techniques and algorithms that allow the model parameters and optimizer state to be sharded across data parallel workers, reducing gradients. To increase batch size without loss of accuracy, FSC implements AdaScale [2].

FSC can be implemented in a simple way based on DDP codes by wrapping the optimizer and CNN. To implement OSS, the optimizer must be wrapped with the OSS function from the `fairscale.optim.oss` library. Using SDP (`ShardedDataParallel()`) or FSDP (`FullyShardedDataParallel()`) requires the replacement of the `DistributedDataParallel()` function with either of the two implementations. However, there is a difference between the two: the model and optimizer are required when implementing SDP, and only the model is required when implementing FSDP. Therefore, this must be used before declaring the optimizer to properly initialize FSDP.

Table 1. Computer program versions.

Software tool	Version
Python	3.7.0
PyTorch library	1.7.1
HVD library	0.21.0
DSP library	0.4.3
FSC library	0.3.7
CUDA library	10.2.8
CuDNN library	7.6.5
NCCL	2.6.4

Table 2. Experimental configurations and software.

Item	Value
DL framework	PyTorch
DT mechanism	DDP, HVD, DSP, FSC
Network models	ResNet50-101, VGG16-19
Optimizer	Adam
LR scheduler	ReduceLROnPlateau
Batch size	32
Epochs per training	200
Dataset	Cifar100, ImageNet

4 Methodology

System Description: The experiments conducted in this study used the Oak Ridge Leadership Computing Facility's Summit supercomputer at Oak Ridge National Laboratory. Summit is ranked second in the world according to the latest TOP500 list from June 2021. This supercomputer has a theoretical performance of 200 PFlops with a power consumption of 10,096 kW. Summit consists of 6,608 nodes, each with six NVIDIA Tesla V100 GPUs and two IBM POWER9 22C CPUs. Table 1 lists all versions of software used in the experiments.

Experimental Configurations: The experiments developed in this study used the PyTorch framework as the main tool for executing DT based on data parallelism. With few modifications, PyTorch allows the implementation of mechanisms to execute DT or its optimization. The mechanisms implemented to execute the DT are DDP, HVD, DSP, and FSC. Additionally, some of the popular CNN types were included, such as ResNet50, ResNet101, VGG16, and VGG19. According to the type of experiment, the DT mechanism and the type of CNN vary. The experiments performed were based on scaling on GPUs using up to 40 Summit nodes, which is equivalent to 240 GPUs. We scaled in GPUs to analyze different variables associated with DT, such as: (1) the performance of DT mechanisms, (2) the performance of the different CNN in DT, (3) the trade-off between neural network learning (i.e., accuracy) and GPU scaling, and (4) the performance trade-off of DT mechanisms with different floating-point precisions and different batch sizes. We use the term performance to refer to training time performance. Finally, the experiments shared default parameters, such as batch size, number of training epochs, image dataset, optimizer, and LR scheduler. Also, each reported value is an average value as a result of running 10 replica trainings. If an experiment uses other parameters, then they will be specified in the experiment description. Table 2 summarizes the experiment parameters.

It is important to clarify that this study does not intend to fully optimize scaling to large numbers of GPUs. Large-scale DT requires significant effort to

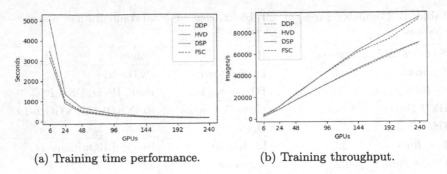

(a) Training time performance.   (b) Training throughput.

Fig. 2. ResNet50 performance scaling up to 240 GPUs.

compensate for the loss of statistical efficiency by manipulating several hyper-parameters. For this, tuning techniques should be used, such as auto-tuning, scaling up and warming up the LR, auto-tuning the batch size, auto-tuning the momentum, and other regularization techniques. Furthermore, the effectiveness of these tuning techniques is specific to the problem, so each DL implementation has its own tuning [16]. We aim to understand the mechanisms and explore the trade-offs in scaling the training phase of DL models.

5   Experimental Results

5.1   Scalability Study

The first experiment performed consisted of studying the scalability of the different DT mechanisms taking into account different CNNs. We measured the time of the DT with different numbers of GPUs. To calculate the training times, only the training cycle was included. Figure 2 shows DT performance using ResNet50 with the CIFAR100 dataset. Figure 2a shows how performance increases as the number of GPUs increases. However, when reaching 144 GPUs, the average time per training is similar among all four DT mechanisms. The worst performance is presented by HVD with six GPUs (one node). When the number of GPUs is increased, its performance improves and becomes comparable with the other DT mechanisms. This HVD behavior is expected because the DT mechanism is optimized to scale to many GPUs distributed in multiple nodes. On the other hand, the difference in performance between DDP and FSC is almost impercep-tible, but they differ in the throughput generated by each framework. Figure 2b shows the throughput (i.e., average number of images processed per second) gen-erated by each of DT mechanism. In all the executions, the number of images processed increases almost linearly with respect to the number of GPUs. Fur-thermore, there is a notable difference between the throughput of HVD-DDP and the throughput of DSP-FSC. This difference indicates that performance is not closely related to throughput. For example, although the performance between DDP and FSC is similar in Fig. 2a, Fig. 2b shows that the throughput of these two DT mechanisms is different.

Table 3. Performance of DT mechanisms and DL models in DT scaling on GPUs (time units are seconds).

GPU	DDP				HVD				DSP				FSC			
	R50	R101	V16	V19	R50	R101	V16	V19	R50	R101	V16	V19	R50	R101	V16	V19
CIFAR100																
6	4416	8200	1830	2107	5060	9060	2785	3049	3167	5580	1465	1704	3485	5952	2230	2534
24	1207	2252	557	609	1349	2345	738	927	901	1544	502	542	1029	1640	750	850
48	624	1118	282	322	678	1186	383	472	461	802	267	291	493	872	376	428
96	342	640	165	185	364	645	207	251	263	429	158	170	279	477	164	176
144	236	445	116	135	237	418	141	194	211	313	136	156	194	320	160	180
192	199	357	110	116	194	353	117	157	155	245	103	111	176	280	108	118
240	162	287	85	96	154	288	95	120	134	200	90	94	141	240	111	112
ImageNet																
240	3479	3125	1799	1925	3398	3722	3371	3454	3254	3552	3025	3151	2175	2083	2333	2234

Table 3 shows the performance data (i.e., run time) of the four DT mechanisms with the four CNNs. Furthermore, the table is divided into two sections that show the performance of the CIFAR100 and ImageNet datasets. Only 25 epochs were run with ImageNet because of the large dataset size, and only 240 GPUs were used. By scaling with CIFAR100 up to 240 GPUs in all cases, there is a notable reduction in execution time. This behavior is the same for all DT mechanisms. DSP has the best performance with all CNNs. However, the training times do not present significant differences that allow us to establish that a DT mechanism is really superior in performance. With respect to the CNN, in all cases, the models with more layers (e.g., ResNet101, VGG19) tend to generate a lower performance, which is normal because they have a greater number of parameters. These results indicate that the CNN similarly influences training performance, regardless of the DT mechanism used. Performance with the ImageNet dataset is similar to CIFAR100 in regards to the particular CNN type. However, in this case, the best performance was obtained by FSC. Although the dataset is an additional element that affects training and results, it does not affect the functioning of the DT mechanisms.

Finally, to analyze the performance according to the number of GPUs, the percentage by which the training time is reduced for each DT mechanism and CNN was calculated. The training time of six GPUs was taken as a basis. The average time reduction results were 70.6, 84.9, 91.8, 93.7, 95.1, and 95.8% for 24, 48, 96, 144, 192, and 240 GPUs, respectively. These results show that with few GPUs, the best average performance is achieved. For example, with 96 GPUs, a reduction of more than 90% is obtained, and doubling the number of GPUs to 192 GPUs can only reduce the time by around 3%. It can be concluded that the increase in the number of GPUs does not ensure the increase in performance.

5.2   Accuracy and Scaling Trade-Off

In addition to the training performance, how well the models are trained must be considered. A great performance is not enough if adequate accuracy and error

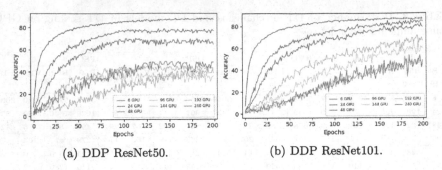

(a) DDP ResNet50.   (b) DDP ResNet101.

Fig. 3. Accuracy of training scaling up to 240 GPUs.

reduction results are not obtained. To analyze the performance of the accuracy, we performed a series of experiments to adjust some hyperparameters to avoid overfitting or underfitting. First, we determined which LR scheduler provided the best results. The following types were tested: `LambdaLR`, `MultiplicativeLR`, `StepLR`, `MultiStepLR`, `ExponentialLR`, and `ReduceLROnPlateau`. The LR scheduler selected was `ReduceLROnPlateau` because it produced the best results. This LR scheduler checks a certain metric, and if there is no improvement for a specific number of epochs (`patience`), the LR is reduced. We used the loss as a metric varying the patience and with the other parameters by default. Second, experiments were conducted with LRs of 0.1, 0.01, 0.001, and 0.0001; patients of 10, 20, 30, 40, and 50; and scaling up to 240 GPUs. After finding the appropriate LR and patience for each case, 10 repetitions were performed for each case to obtain the averaged results. In all experiments, we make sured that the results obtained were valid by accounting for the training accuracy, validation accuracy, training loss, and validation loss.

Figure 3 shows the DDP accuracy behavior with ResNet50 and ResNet101 scaling up to 240 GPUs. Accuracy behaves similar with both CNN. Figures 3a and 3b show that using a deeper CNN does not generate significant differences in accuracy and only increases training time. This behavior can vary with different hyperparameters or datasets. On the other hand, in both figures, the effect on accuracy produced by the increase in the number of GPUs is notable. There is a clear reduction in accuracy as the number of GPUs scales. This is an unwanted effect because with large batch sizes, the gradients are averaged and the LR per sample is smaller. To solve this, the LR usually must be scaled up; however, this can cause the divergence of other model parameters [15, 22]. To try to reduce this unwanted effect, sophisticated optimization and autotuning techniques that are beyond the scope of this study must be applied. This is similar behavior to that generated with large batch sizes or when scaling on GPU without optimizing the batch size [10,11]. Additionally, in both figures, the accuracy is more stable with few GPUs and becomes unstable when scaling.

Table 4 shows the behavior of the accuracy of all the experiments performed. The training accuracy and validation accuracy are displayed for each DT mech-

Table 4. Accuracy of DT mechanisms and DL models scaling on GPUs .

	R50	LR	R101	LR	V16	LR	V19	LR	R50	LR	R101	LR	V16	LR	V19	LR
GPU	DDP								HVD							
6	87/66	α	86/68	β	75/64	α	69/58	β	73/68	α	69/63	α	71/60	α	65/54	α
24	78/63	β	79/65	β	74/61	α	64/55	β	70/65	α	67/61	α	63/55	α	53/46	α
48	69/59	β	74/60	β	61/55	β	56/50	β	68/63	α	63/59	α	45/44	α	30/31	α
96	44/40	β	40/37	β	48/45	γ	52/45	γ	63/59	α	65/61	α	48/47	α	36/32	α
144	35/34	β	47/40	γ	46/45	γ	47/37	γ	61/56	α	68/61	α	42/40	α	40/36	α
192	38/37	β	55/50	γ	37/33	γ	27/26	γ	57/55	α	60/58	α	36/30	α	26/25	α
240	48/40	γ	48/40	γ	46/40	γ	35/27	γ	57/53	α	73/64	α	32/27	α	28/20	α
	DSP								FSC							
6	71/59	β	72/63	β	74/62	β	70/64	β	86/75	β	79/67	β	77/5 9	β	73/60	β
24	72/63	β	68/60	β	70/63	β	68/57	β	81/76	β	77/74	β	75/63	β	71/64	β
48	66/54	β	61/57	β	52/45	β	51/43	β	77/55	β	75/68	β	71/61	β	70/65	β
96	65/55	β	60/51	β	44/40	β	42/37	β	52/45	β	51/50	β	48/42	β	55/65	β
144	58/51	β	63/56	β	45/41	β	40/36	β	50/44	β	47/42	β	54/44	β	55/50	β
192	60/50	β	64/60	β	41/38	γ	39/37	γ	37/33	α	40/37	α	42/39	β	40/35	β
240	54/48	γ	52/45	γ	40/38	γ	33/31	γ	45/42	α	45/40	α	43/40	β	38/33	β

LR: $\alpha = 0.01$, $\beta = 0.001$, $\gamma = 0.0001$

anism and CNN. Additionally, the initial LR is shown for each case. The initial LR reported varies, depending on the case (e.g., number of GPUs, DT mechanism, and CNN) and was obtained in previous experiments. Patience for each case is not reported, but it does vary depending on the case. In all cases, the accuracy is degraded at some level. However, with HVD using ResNet50 and ResNet101, the accuracy suffered less degradation when scaling on GPUs. This is because HVD is a more mature and optimized DT mechanism. Furthermore, DSP is a DT mechanism oriented to model training with billions of parameters and memory efficiency. This proves that the problem of accuracy degradation when scaling is not directly associated with the DT mechanism or the type of CNN and is related to the optimization of the hyperparameters that participate in training and synchronizing the processes. On the other hand, the LR shows a behavior pattern in which the LR is higher when the number of GPUs is lower, and as the GPUs are scaled, the LR must be decreased to maintain adequate accuracy results. Regarding CNN, our results show that CNN with more layers can generate slightly lower accuracy compared with the version with fewer layers. Additionally, there are no significant differences between the ResNet and VGG CNN, so their use will depend on the type of problem to be solved and the desired performance.

5.3 Mixed-Precision Distributed Training

Mixed precision training considers an autocasting mechanism that chooses the precision for GPU operations to improve performance while maintaining accuracy. To test the effect of mixed precision in DT training we used NVIDIA's APEX library [23]. We used two APEX utilities: AMP through `apex.amp` and

Table 5. Execution time (in seconds) AMP.

	ResNet50			VGG16		
GPU	Base	MO1	MO2	Base	MO1	MO2
6	4416	4896	4239	1830	2214	1820
24	1207	1316	1147	557	623	516
48	624	685	603	282	337	276
96	342	375	328	165	195	158
144	236	259	227	116	157	114
192	199	215	188	110	118	96
240	162	177	154	85	101	83

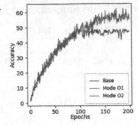

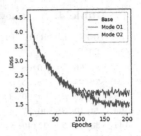

Fig. 4. Acc. VGG16   **Fig. 5.** Loss VGG16

a module wrapper for DT similar to DDP through `apex.parallel`. Other functionalities, such as fused optimizers or fused layer normalization, were not tested. AMP provides four mixed precision modes (O0, O1, O2, and O3) that can be selected through the `opt_level` parameter during AMP initialization, `amp.initialize(model,optimizer,opt_level)`. The O0 and O3 modes are not true mixed precision and are useful for establishing accuracy and speed base cases. Thus, they were not considered in the experiments. The O1 mode provides mixed precision by modifying the Torch functions and Tensor methods to cast the inputs according to a whitelist-blacklist of the model. The whitelist is performed in FP16, and the blacklist is performed in FP32. The O2 mode is considered "almost FP16" mixed precision. This mode casts the model weights to FP16, modifies the model's forward method to cast input data to FP16, and implements dynamic loss scaling.

We modified a DDP implementation, and trainings were run with ResNet50 and VGG16. Table 5 shows the results of the experiments. The base performance is the same as the performance reported in Table 3 for ResNet50 and VGG16 with DDP. With both CNNs, the O2 mode presents a slight improvement in performance, reducing the training time compared with the base time. The O1 mode slightly increased the training time. Figures 4 and 5 show the accuracy and loss of VGG16 trainings. Figure 4 shows the accuracy obtained in the trainings. The O1 mode and the O2 mode both increased the accuracy. The loss shown in Fig. 5 also reflects a decrease in the error with both modes. This same experiment was performed with ResNet50; however, neither mode had a significant effect, and accuracy and loss behaved similarly. We were able to verify that manipulating the precision of the floating values can improve performance and accuracy. However, not all cases will show improvement. Only by experimenting with those optimizations can it be determined whether there is real improvement.

5.4   Adaptive Summation in Distributed Training

When the batch size increases with the number of GPUs, there is usually a degradation in the convergence stability. This results in a loss in accuracy. To solve this situation, techniques such as AdaSum [19] with HVD or Adascale [15] with FSC have been developed. To experiment with this type of technique, we conducted

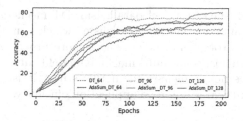

Fig. 6. AdaSum DT.

Table 6. HVD AdaSum training results.

DT type	LR	AT/AV	Time(s)	Throughput
64 DT	0.01	60/50	190	68992
64 AdaSum	0.01	70/59	1452	7040
96 DT	0.001	74/61	185	69248
96 AdaSum	0.001	80/71	1081	9472
128 DT	0.001	64/54	170	77696
128 AdaSum	0.001	69/58	906	11520

an experiment that implemented AdaSum in HVD training. The experiment consisted of running trainings with and without AdaSum and increasing the batch size by 64, 96, and 128. For a proper comparison, the hyperparameters did not vary when training with the same batch size. Before performing 10 repetitions to obtain the average results, experiments were performed to find the appropriate LR for each case. Additionally, the trainings were run with only 128 GPUs because of an HVD AdaSum restriction, which limits the number of processes to powers of two. Consequently, the trainings were run with 32 nodes and reducing from six to four GPUs per node.

Figure 6 shows the behavior of the average accuracy in the different trainings. The figure groups the results that we wanted to compare by color. For example, the results of a DT without AdaSum with a batch size of 128 vs. a DT with AdaSum with the same batch size are displayed as DT_128 (red dotted line) and AdaSum_DT_128 (red solid line). With AdaSum, accuracy was improved in the three batch size comparisons. Using batch sizes of 96 and 128, AdaSum generated lower accuracy values in early epochs. However, accuracy improved after epoch 150. In these same batch sizes without AdaSum, the training stabilized and did not increase the accuracy after a certain epoch. The HVD accuracy behavior was stable compared with DDP results (e.g., Fig. 3) because of the `all_reduce` mechanism that it implements. Table 6 summarizes the information that resulted from the experiments. The table shows the LR used, the maximum training accuracy with respect to the maximum validation accuracy (AT/AV), the average training time, and the images processed per second (i.e., throughput). The table does not report the loss results, although those values were considered to determine the correctness of the results. The difference in performance observed in training with AdaSum and without AdaSum is clear. Training time is increased by 86.9, 82.8, and 81.23% for batch sizes of 64, 96, and 128, respectively. Undoubtedly, the differences in performance are significant and the increase in accuracy is also evident, so using this type of technique in training will depend on user needs and the available hardware.

6 Discussion

Model Parallelism. The experiments performed in this work were based on the data parallelism strategy. However, the memory constraints of the systems require other strategies to be considered, such as model parallelism. DT mechanisms, such as DSP, provide functionality for model parallelism, which can be implemented relatively easy. Also, PyTorch implements the remote procedure call framework, which provides mechanisms for multi-machine model training [18]. Although those strategies were not implemented in this study, it is necessary to study and experiment with them to improve application efficiency.

Beyond Traditional Parallelism. Data parallelism and model parallelism are both techniques that increase the performance of DL training. However, new techniques have emerged to optimize the use of hardware resources and increase performance, especially when the model is too large for one GPU. One of these techniques is known as *pipeline parallelism*. In this technique, the layers of a model are divided into stages that can be processed in parallel. There are implementations in PyTorch (`torch.distributed.pipeline`), DSP (`deepspeed.pipe`), and FSC (`fairscale.nn.Pipe`). Pipeline parallelism is just the beginning because this technique is being combined with other techniques, such as hybrid parallelism, to further increase its efficiency.

High-Level PyTorch. Given the need to reduce application development times and coalesce the many libraries with different functionalities, high-level frameworks have emerged. Keras for TensorFlow is an example. These frameworks hide low-level details, allowing more efforts to be focused on experimentation. PyTorch Lighting was developed based on PyTorch [7] and is a high-level, lightweight PyTorch wrapper for AI research. It supports a variety of plugins to further speed up distributed GPU training, including `DDPPlugin`, `DDPShardedPlugin`, and `DeepSpeedPlugin`. Also, PyTorch Lightning offers advanced optimizations to improve throughput, memory efficiency, and model scaling. All these functionalities in the same framework make this type of implementation very attractive for users who want to optimize their development times.

7   Concluding Remarks

DDL promises to extend the impact of complex AI methods by speeding up their training. However, there are several issues, trade-offs, and design decisions associated with achieving this goal. This paper explores some of those issues and presents the counterbalances of existing mechanisms for scaling DDL. We used the Summit supercomputer to collect experimental results. Despite the most popular mechanisms having good scalability in execution time with their base configuration, there is a significant accuracy degradation as more nodes are used. Several strategies can alleviate a low accuracy level, including hyperparameter optimization. Additionally, we explored other available scalability strategies, mixed precision, and adaptive parameter optimization.

In future work, we intend to extend this study by using approaches based on model and pipeline parallelism. Additionally, it is necessary to study and experiment with the main optimization approaches for scaling in GPUs, accounting for both hyperparameter optimization techniques and approaches based on optimization algorithms, such as ZeRO, along with the idea of studying the DT of CNN with billions or trillions of parameters.

References

1. Baidu-Research: DeepBench. https://github.com/baidu-research/DeepBench
2. Baines, M., et al.: Fairscale: a general purpose modular pytorch library for high performance and large scale training (2021). https://github.com/facebookresearch/fairscale
3. Ben-Nun, T., Besta, M., Huber, S., Ziogas, A.N., Peter, D., Hoefler, T.: A modular benchmarking infrastructure for high-performance and reproducible deep learning. In: 2019 IEEE IPDPS, pp. 66–77. IEEE(2019)
4. Coleman, C., et al.: Dawnbench: an end-to-end deep learning benchmark and competition. Training **100**(101), 102 (2017)
5. Droegemeier, K.: 2016–2019 progress report: advancing artificial intelligence R&D, a report by the artificial intelligence research & development interagency working group, November 2019
6. Fagnan, K., Nashed, Y., Perdue, G., Ratner, D., Shankar, A., Yoo, S.: Data and models: a framework for advancing AI in science, December 2019. https://doi.org/10.2172/1579323, https://www.osti.gov/biblio/1579323
7. Falcon, W.A., et al.: Pytorch lightning. GitHub, March 2019. https://github.com/PyTorchLightning/pytorch-lightning
8. Farkas, A., Kertész, G., Lovas, R.: Parallel and distributed training of deep neural networks: a brief overview. In: 2020 IEEE 24th INES, pp. 165–170. IEEE (2020)
9. Gao, W., et al.: AIbench: an industry standard internet service AI benchmark suite. arXiv preprint arXiv:1908.08998 (2019)
10. Goyal, P., et al.: Accurate, large minibatch SGD Training imageNet in 1 hour (2018)
11. Gupta, S., Zhang, W., Wang, F.: Model accuracy and runtime tradeoff in distributed deep learning: a systematic study (2016)
12. He, K., Zhang, X., Ren, S., Sun, J.: Deep residual learning for image recognition. In: Proceedings of the IEEE Conference on Computer Vision and Pattern recognition, pp. 770–778 (2016)
13. Hegde, V., Usmani, S.: Parallel and distributed deep learning. In: Tech. report, Stanford University (2016)
14. Hey, T., et al.: US Department of Energy, Advanced Scientific Computing Advisory Committee (ASCAC), subcommittee on AI/ML, data-intensive science and high-performance computing, final draft of report to the committee, September 2020
15. Johnson, T.B., Agrawal, P., Gu, H., Guestrin, C.: AdaScale SGD: A user-friendly algorithm for distributed training. In: ICLR (2020)
16. Koliousis, A., Watcharapichat, P., Weidlich, M., Mai, L., Costa, P., Pietzuch, P.: Crossbow: scaling deep learning with small batch sizes on multi-GPU servers. Proc. VLDB Endow. **12**(11), 1399–1412 (2019)
17. Langer, M., He, Z., Rahayu, W., Xue, Y.: Distributed training of deep learning models: a taxonomic perspective. IEEE Trans. Parallel Distrib. Syst. **31**(12), 2802–2818 (2020)
18. Li, S., et al.: Pytorch distributed: experiences on accelerating data parallel training. arXiv preprint. arXiv:2006.15704 (2020)

19. Maleki, S., et al.: Scaling distributed training with adaptive summation. In: Proceedings of Machine Learning and Systems 3 (MLSys 2021) (2020)
20. Mattson, P., et al.: MLPerf training benchmark. arXiv preprint arXiv:1910.01500 (2019)
21. Mikami, H., Suganuma, H., Tanaka, Y., Kageyama, Y., et al.: Massively distributed sgd: Imagenet/resnet-50 training in a flash. arXiv preprint arXiv:1811.05233 (2018)
22. Mikami, H., Suganuma, H., U-chupala, P., Tanaka, Y., Kageyama, Y.: Massively distributed SGD: ImageNet/ResNet-training in a flash (2019)
23. NVIDIA: Apex (a pytorch extension), July 2021. https://nvidia.github.io/apex/
24. Paszke, A., et al. Pytorch: an imperative style, high-performance deep learning library. In: Proceedings of the 33rd International Conference on Neural Information Processing Systems (2019)
25. Rajbhandari, S., Rasley, J., Ruwase, O., He, Y.: Zero: Memory optimizations toward training trillion parameter models. In: SC20, pp. 1–16. IEEE (2020)
26. Rasley, J., Rajbhandari, S., Ruwase, O., He, Y.: Deepspeed: system optimizations enable training deep learning models with over 100 billion parameters. In: Proceedings of the 26th ACM SIGKDD, pp. 3505–3506 (2020)
27. Sergeev, A., Del Balso, M.: Horovod: fast and easy distributed deep learning in tensorflow. arXiv preprint. arXiv:1802.05799 (2018)
28. Simonyan, K., Zisserman, A.: Very deep convolutional networks for large-scale image recognition. arXiv preprint. arXiv:1409.1556 (2014)
29. Zagoruyko, S., Komodakis, N.: Wide residual networks. arXiv preprint. arXiv:1605.07146 (2016)

Wind Prediction Using Deep Learning and High Performance Computing

Jaume Manero[1]([envelope]) [iD], Javier Béjar[1,2] [iD], and Ulises Cortés[1,2] [iD]

[1] Department of Computer Science, Universitat Politècnica de Catalunya,
Barcelona, Spain
jaume.manero@upc.edu, {bejar,ia}@cs.upc.edu
[2] Barcelona Supercomputing Center, Barcelona, Spain
http://www.bcs.com

Abstract. Deep Learning Convolutional Neural Networks have been successfully used in many applications. Its versatility lies in reducing the number of parameters to train while maintaining or improving the feature representation capabilities offered by other architectures. Due to its success, Convolutional Networks have become the architecture of choice for image and video processing applications. The application of Convolutional Networks to wind time series is still limited, being an area with high potential for developing new approaches. This paper explores several deep learning models and applies them to wind time series for multi-step forecasting. The time series used for the experimentation are multidimensional time-stamped multi-variate meteorological data. We use a large dataset of wind data from the National Renewable Laboratory with 126,692 wind sites, requiring the use of High Performance Computing. The experimentation results show how Convolutional Networks are a valid approach for wind time series forecasting.

Keywords: Wind forecasting · Time series · Deep learning · CNN · Convolutional networks · Multi-step forecasting · HPC

1 Introduction

Wind energy generation is a field where forecasting future production is a crucial process, as intermittence of renewable sources impacts the stability of the grid. The accurate prediction of future wind behaviour determines the energy output of wind-generated electricity.

Wind can be represented by a time series of multiple meteorological observations. These series are usually multi-variate as they contain several meteorological measures, like temperature, humidity or pressure.

Wind prediction based on time series is a challenging problem due to its nature, as wind formation is heavily dependent on local features like terrain ruggedness, climate structure or closeness to the sea. Moreover, wind time series present non-stationary and non-linear characteristics, challenging linear statistical methods for their prediction. Deep learning approaches, as they can represent

© Springer Nature Switzerland AG 2022
I. Gitler et al. (Eds.): CARLA 2021, CCIS 1540, pp. 193–207, 2022.
https://doi.org/10.1007/978-3-031-04209-6_14

non-linearity, show good representation ability with non-linear time series. However, the application of deep learning to wind prediction is not as widespread as the traditional methods [22], this work contributes by reducing this gap, proposing new deep learning approaches tailored explicitly to wind and verifying them in a wide area dataset.

There are two major approaches for time series forecasting, predicting a time step in the future (single-step prediction) or a sequence of steps (multi-step prediction). In this context, the prediction consists in the generation of a sequential horizon of length H, like $\widehat{Y} : (\widehat{y}_1, \ldots, \widehat{y}_H)$, which can be considered a regression problem and approached with different methods, like recursive prediction, multiple direct regression, or multiple-output regression [2].

However, the existing literature is overwhelmingly using single-step prediction, generating a lack of comprehensive research in multi-step models [26]. This research contributes to this area and proposes several multi-step approaches on wind time series by leveraging the deep learning recognition ability with sequences.

Most of the existing literature about applying deep learning to wind series is limited to small data sets (one single wind park, only a few wind sites), restricting the generalization of the conclusions. In this work, our contribution consists of a detailed and extensive test of different approaches on a broad set of data, as the experiments use the NREL (National Renewable Laboratory) wind dataset, which has 126,692 wind sites distributed across the USA geography.

Existing works use several DL architectures, like Multi-Layer Perceptron (MLP) and, to some extend, RNN (Recurrent Neural Networks) (See Sect. 2). However, we find only a few analyses of the effectiveness of convolutional networks on wind time series.

Convolutional Neural Networks (CNN) share or surpass the capabilities of MLP with lesser complexity and more stable fitting characteristics [20]. The objective of this work is to understand the performance of this deep learning architecture and which parameters and features make this approach more effective in wind forecasting. The research conclusions contribute to a better understanding of the application of deep learning to wind prediction.

This article contributes to the wind forecasting field in three significant areas.

(a) It is a first deep learning approach with multi-step forecasting applied to wind.
(b) A unique broad analysis of the application of deep learning on a large wind dataset
(c) An in-depth research regarding the applicability of convolutional networks to wind time series prediction

The outline of this paper is as follows. In Sect. 2 we describe some relevant related works. In Sect. 3, we perform a theoretical analysis of the forecasting using a Multiple-Input Multiple-Output (MIMO) approach, followed by a description of the application of CNN architectures to time series prediction. In Sect. 4, we describe the experimental setup and an analysis of the data, followed by Sect. 5 which contains a complete description of the experimentation with different convolutional architectures focusing on the details of each architecture and its results. Finally, in Sect. 6, we examine and discuss the results and the conclusions of all this research

2   Related Work

We can find deep learning applications to wind prediction in the literature, with most experiences based on multi-layer perceptron approaches, like the ones found in [5,15,21,22]. Convolutional networks are applied with lower intensity in some relevant articles.

Diaz in [7] develops several deep learning models and one CNN based on the Alexnet architecture that shows promising results but at the expense of heavy computing resources consumption. In [22] there is a comparison between different deep learning approaches where CNN shows some promising performance.

Most of these experiences are single-step, as they predict only one point in the future. Single-step allows for a more straightforward determination of the prediction error being less complicated to implement than multiple-step [27].

However, this work is about multiple-step prediction, where the output of a prediction is a sequence of values, as we believe is a better suited approach when using neural networks. There are several models to implement a multiple step strategy, but with some controversy on which one is the best method, as there are contradictory literature results. For instance, Kline in [16], through some experimentation, concludes that single output methods are superior to multiple-step approaches, while Bontempi and Taieb in [1,4,26] show evidence of the opposite.

3   Theoretical Background

3.1   Time Series Wind Prediction

A time series is a sequence of vectors formed by a fixed number of values, representing an observation. For instance, a wind time series is a sequence of a vector containing values like wind speed, temperature, humidity, direction, or pressure.

$$T : (t_1, \dots, t_N) \text{ where } t_i \text{ is a vector} \tag{1}$$
$$t_i : (v_1, \dots, v_n)$$

The DL architectures used in this work are created with a MIMO approach, as they are fed with sequences in windows $X : (x_i, \dots, x_l)$ of length l (lag) from the continuous time series and produce as an output another sequence $\widehat{y} : (\widehat{y}_1, \dots, \widehat{y}_H)$ of length H, which is the horizon to predict.

Convolutional architectures for time series receive as input 2D matrices. Each matrix is composed of a sequence of lag steps times the number of variables in the time series.

We find three effective approaches for multiple-step ahead forecasting, direct, iterated or recursive, and MIMO methods. This work is based on the MIMO approach, as we obtained better results while optimizing the computing resources for the analysis. The MIMO prediction consists of learning a model that defines a dependency between the input and output sequences.

$$f : (t_1, \cdots, t_n) \rightarrow (\widehat{y_1}, \cdots, \widehat{y_H}) \tag{2}$$

The MIMO method obtains a sequence of values as an output.

3.2 Convolutional Networks

Convolutional networks burst into the pattern recognition field in 1989 [19], transforming the way computing science understands artificial vision. Since then, and mainly due to the success of Alexnet [17], VGG16 and VGG19 [24], ResNet [13] and GoogleNet [25] at the Imagenet challenge [10], convolutional networks have become the method of choice for pattern recognition in images. They are responsible for the revolutionary advances in this area.

These convolutional networks manage the large image matrixes in a more efficient way than fully connected networks. To implement the MIMO approach with a CNN network, we combine one or several CNN layers followed by an MLP network. The CNN layers extract the input matrix features, and the MLP performs the regression to obtain the output sequence. In this paper, we use a CNN architecture with one-dimensional convolutions to process the multi-variant input sequences. One element of these sequences is a bi-dimensional matrix of depth lag and height length equal to the number of meteorological variables available.

There is some confusion on the use of two terms, kernel and filters. For a one-dimensional convolution, we must set both the kernel size and the number of filters. The kernel is the matrix of weights, or convolution window, used for the convolutional operation, where filters are the number of parallel operations (convolutions) that performed on the input data, each one with a kernel of the predetermined length, in a way, filters define the dimensionality of the output space of the convolution. The Convolutional operation has an issue when it operates on the sequence border, as the operation may use elements outside the matrix bounds. To solve this issue, we use padding. Padding consists of adding virtual cells outside the sequence or matrix to allow for a complete convolution operation. It can be classified into three approaches: *valid, same* or *causal*. Padding *valid* consists of working without additional virtual cells. The convolution avoids the operation *out of bounds*. The output sequence length will be smaller than the input as the convolution avoids working outside the border cells by skipping them. Padding *same* adds virtual cells at the beginning and end of the sequence (for 1d convolutions). With this strategy, the output length is similar to the input length. Padding *causal* only pads the beginning of the sequence. In this way, the convolution can work with the first elements. This approach causes an implicit dilation as the input sequence is delayed (dilated) by the padding length. In this work, we use *causal* padding when possible. However, for separable convolutions, this padding approach is not available, so we use *same* approach in this case.

Convolutional Networks Refinements. Convolutional Networks have been subjected to different refinements, generating variants that show good adaptability to specific conditions. We will use several of these refinements in our experimentation, which are:

- **Separable convolutions** are a subtle variation of convolutions and successfully used in image recognition [6]. This variant reduces the number of operations to be performed by the network from the standard convolutional approach. This reduction generates a stable training phase, and for some applications, there is a slight improvement in the accuracy. Separable convolutions split the convolutional operations into two steps that combine two kernels instead of one operation with a single kernel.
- **Skip and Residual connection models.** Deep fully connected networks are notoriously difficult to train. The vanishing/exploding gradient was initially addressed using intermediate normalisation layers, which assures convergence with a large number of layers, but then the issue of degradation appears. This problem can be partially reduced using the dropout technique. Dropout eliminates some connections in the network randomly and helps avoid the strong connections to take over the whole net, by closing some paths (dropout) the weak connections survive. Another technique to protect training consistency in a vanishing/exploding gradient situation is to modify the architecture of the network using *skip* and *residual* connections [13].
- **Stacked and multi-head models.** Stacked models are those that combine elementary network blocks formed by several individual convolutional layers. This idea is extensively used for image recognition applications, for example in the VGG or ResNet architectures, which obtained the best results in the Imagenet challenge in 2014 and 2015 [13, 24].
- **Gradient Boosting based ensembles.** An ensemble combines several learners to achieve higher accuracy than each of them isolated, this is not a new idea, as the universal statistical principle of *the Wisdom of the crowds* was laid out as early as Classical Greece. There are several ways to combine learners by Bagging the data (reducing variance by creating several sets of data to train the algorithm) or by Boosting, which consists of several models sequentially in a chain, and each new model fits the residual error from the previous models. Gradient Boosting was first defined in [11] using the gradient optimization algorithm to obtain the residual values. This algorithm consists of learning a function on the data and then fitting alternative learners on the residual or error value. In this case, this function becomes a kind of loss function L that can be optimized. Gradient Boosting is extensively used in Decision Trees but can be applied to any kind of learners, including neural networks [3].

4   Experiment Setup

In this section, we describe the experimentation performed with several convolutional architectures. First, we describe the data, followed by the general experimental setup, and then we analyse each of the experiments.

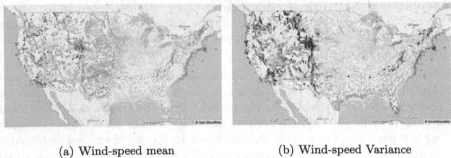

(a) Wind-speed mean   (b) Wind-speed Variance

Fig. 1. Variance and mean of the 126,692 NREL sites. The geography defines different site topologies with several combinations of mean and variance

4.1   Data

The data used in this work has been made available by the United States National Renewable Energy Laboratory [8]. The NREL dataset is the largest existing wind dataset, with seven years long measurements sampled every 5 min for 126,692 wind sites. The dataset contains the following data dimensions. The weather variables contained in the dataset are T: Temperature in Kelvin at 2 m, W_s: Wind speed in m/s at 100 m high, P_a: Barometric pressure, P_a at surface level, ρ: Air Density in Kg/m^2, W_d: Wind Direction in degrees.

The NREL dataset was generated by synthesizing a Numerical Weather Model and adjusted with real data obtained from some testing points where real data was available and used those real observations for validation purposes [8].

The sites are distributed across the US geography and show considerable heterogeneity as wind regimes differ depending on terrain, latitude, and specific orography. Figure 1 illustrates the mean and variance of the wind speed across all map sites. The resulting geographical distribution is aligned with the wind resource studies currently made for the US geography [9]. We apply pre-processing transformations commonly for neural networks. Firstly, the angle corresponding to the wind direction is transformed into its sine and cosine. Secondly, the data is averaged hourly, and finally, the data is z-standardized. This normalization consists of adjusting the values' scale to a mean of zero and a variance (σ^2) of one.

The seven years of data are split into three datasets, five years of data are used for training, and the other two years are divided into test and validation data (one year each). This data is then converted to examples consisting of overlapped time windows of length *lag*. For instance, with *lag* 12, the number of examples for training is 43,810 and for test and validation is 8,755 each.

4.2   Experimental Framework

The objective is to find a result by applying the prediction to the whole dataset (126,692 sites), this approach is resource consuming, and we found that it is statistically valid (according to a Kolmogorov-Smirnov test) to use a subset of sites (if the sample has at least 2,000 sites). In this way, for some experiments, we used this subset of sites.

This work is relevant for the comprehensive testing of the models on many wind locations, in general, related works only apply the algorithms to a limited set of sites due to the complexity of accessing large datasets of wind time series. The combination of considerable computing resources and the validation of results on the NREL dataset is a crucial combination that differentiates this work.

The process of experimentation has been done in three steps.

- Calculate baselines for comparison
- Analyse and select best Multi-step approach
- Develop and run experiments with convolutional and variant architectures

For an experiment, the prediction accuracy is measured with R^2 (coefficient of determination) for each time step. To evaluate the accuracy of the multi-step prediction, we use $\sum R_t^2$ for all predicted time steps. A perfect regression for a single time step is R^2 of 1, and for the 12 steps is 12. For a poor regression, it can even be negative.

4.3 Technical Assessment and HPC Requirements

From the software point of view the deep learning experimental architectures have been developed from scratch using Python 3.6, and using some add-on standard packages, being the most relevant:

- Machine Learning platform: Tensorflow 1.14.0
- Deep learning library: Keras 2.2.4
- Scikit-learn machine learning library: 0.21.4
- Statistical support: statsmodels 0.11

The size of the dataset and the nature of the algorithms has recommended to use an HPC resource for experimentation, and have been supported by a NVIDIA GPU based computer at the Super Computing Centre [23]. The HPC resource used is the *Minotauro* cluster which is build with BULL and it has 39 bullx R421-E4 servers, each composed of:

- 2 Intel Xeon E5-2630 v3 (Haswell) 8-core processors, (each core at 2.4 GHz, and with 20 MB L3 cache)
- 2 K80 NVIDIA GPU Cards
- 128 GB of Main memory, distributed in 8 DIMMs of 16 GB – DDR4 @ 2133 MHz - ECC SDRAM –
- 1 PCIe 3.0 × 8 8GT/s, Mellanox ConnectX®-3FDR 56 Gbit
- 4 Gigabit Ethernet ports.

The full HPC machine provides a Peak Performance of 250.94 TERAFLOPS distributed as 226.98 TERAFLOPS (K80) + 23.96 TERAFLOPS (Haswell).

4.4 Hyper-parameter Tuning and Optimization

One of the characteristics of convolutional networks is that they require less trainable parameters than fully connected networks. However, the size of these models generates complex and, sometimes, counter-intuitive combinations of parameters, making the obtention of the optimum combination a complex exercise if done randomly or by intuition.

The naive method for parameter optimisation consists of iteratively testing different combinations of parameters until a reasonably good one is found. This approach is time-consuming and yields poor results when the parameter space is nontrivial. For this reason, it is required to rely on a structured approach to parameter exploration to obtain sensible results on this type of architectures.

In this work, we used a structured approach based on Sequential Model-Based Optimization (SMBO) plus an adaptation of the Sequential Model-Based Algorithm Configuration (SMAC) developed by Hutter et al. in [14]. This approach has been selected because it is effective and can work with categorical parameters. This method uses a Bayesian strategy that consists of setting a quality criterion to estimate the results. This function is used to steer the exploration of the configuration space to obtain the parameters with the best accuracy results. To approximate and reproduce this theoretical function, we use a Random Forest approach.

Some parameters are manually set, like the optimizer, fixed to an Adaptive Gradient Descent (Adamax), all methods use early stopping and we set a maximum number of epochs to 200, this number may be low, however we verified that no architecture reached the limit as the training converged earlier.

5 Experimentation

We performed the experimentation in three phases. First, we verified the best approach for multi-step regression. Then, we developed a Random Forest baseline for comparison with the deep learning models, and finally, we experimented with several deep learning convolutional architectures that we analyzed and discuss in the next sections.

5.1 Multiple Input Multiple Output (MIMO) Approach

As it has been discussed in Sect. 3, there are three major approaches to predict an output sequence from an input sequence, which are: recursive, direct or MIMO approach. We have designed an experiment to compare the results and obtain the best approach for wind time series.

The experimentation consists of using recursive prediction, direct regression (multiple models in parallel), and multiple output regression or MIMO (one model for the whole sequence) over the same data set.

The conclusion from these tests is that the multiple-regression approach shows the best behavior. Its results are marginally better than with the direct approach but using significantly fewer resources. A recursive MLP scores 7.109 R^2, a direct approach 7.241 R^2 and MIMO 7.254 R^2. To verify if the three distributions are statistically significantly different, we perform a one-way ANOVA test on the three distributions, which rejects the hypothesis that they are the same. We apply the Tukey's Honestly Significant Difference (HSD) test to verify the significance of the means of the distributions, which also rejects the hypothesis that are the same. In this way, we can assure that the MIMO approach represents statistically significant improvements over the other two methods.

With these results, we have concluded that MIMO is the best approach to define the architectures, and we have chosen to develop all architectures as MIMO. To generate an output sequence, we use a combination of Convolutional and MLP blocks. The first block is a set of convolutional layers (of different types) followed by an MLP network that produces the output sequence. In this way the convolutional layers perform the feature extraction phase, and the MLP the regression. The network processes as input sequences of length *lag* and produces a sequence of length *horizon*. All models are defined with a *horizon* of 12 h.

5.2   Common Parameters in all Architectures

This section describes the common parameters to all the convolutional networks that define different features of the architecture.

Firstly, in all the models, we need to select the length of the input matrices. This length defines how long are the training input sequences. We call this length *lag*. This value impacts the prediction accuracy and must be optimised for each architecture in the hyperparameter searching process. The difference between the different optimal values has not been large (6–18 h). This result aligns with the nature of wind formation described in the literature [12,18] (Table 1).

We use four different convolutional architectures, vanilla (also called classic), separable, separable with skip and separable residual. All of them are based on layers using one-dimensional convolutions, tested with a variable number of layers and using padding *causal* for vanilla convolutions and padding *valid* for separable convolutions.

The main structural parameters are the *filters* length and the *strides*. The combination of them describes how the convolution operation is performed. *Kernel size* determines the size of the mask for the convolution. *Depth Multiplier*, is a parameter that multiplies the channels after the convolution, impacting the behaviour of the network.

The Activation function is relevant for each layer as well. We have identified Exponential Linear Units (ELU) and Leaky Rectified linear function (leaky ReLU) as the best performing. Both activations use a delta parameter that shapes the function, preferably a number between 0.2 to 0.4.

ELU and leaky ReLU avoid the zero dying issue when weights become close to zero or negatives. In this experimentation, the data is z-normalized, thus has negative values, which are better captured by these two activation functions.

Table 1. Models designed for the experimentation (L = layers)

Model	Description
Random forest	MIMO baseline
CNN classic	CNN 1,2,3,4,5,6,7,8 layers
CNN separable	CNN sep 1,2,3,4,5,6,7,8 layers
CNN skip	CNN skip 1,2,3,4,5,6,7,8 layers
CNN residual	CNN res 1,2,3,4,5,6,7,8 layers
CNN multi head	2,3,4 Parallel heads
CNN GB	Gradient boosting for separable and classic

Other parameters impact other network components, like *dropout*, which can be defined for each layer connection. We have experimentally observed its impact on model accuracy. *Dropout* is added to each connection in the convolutional networks and the MLP layers.

There are relevant differences between the best and the worst models of an experiment. In some cases, this difference is over 10% of the resulting error.

However, many combinations of parameters generate results very close to the best, with minimal differences. In the results table (see Table 2), we present the best result for some of the architectures, but it has to be noted that some other parameter combinations obtain quasi-optimal models with accuracies just some hundredths apart from the optimal.

5.3   Classic Convolutional Architecture

The Classic convolutional models are built with one-dimensional convolutional layers. We have developed six architectures with a depth of one to eight sequential layers (see Table 2).

The most relevant parameters in these architectures are *filters* and *strides* which define the convolution, *depth multiplier* which modifies the output channels, *drop* for each channel, and the architecture of the MLP component, number of layers, number of neurons and drop.

5.4   Separable Convolutional Architecture

Separable models (see Sect. 3.2) perform the convolution in a two-step process. They reduce some computational costs and have shown the best results in the experiments. The best results appear in structures with two and three layers, as the accuracy deteriorates with more layers.

For both architectures, separable and classic, we can observe that by including dropout in the layers, the accuracy increases, the best dropout values vary, and are usually between 0.3 and 0.5. The best values for filters and kernels usually decrease for deeper layers. For the classic convolutions, the best stride is one, while strides of three or four for separable convolutions offer the best results. Regarding the activation functions, ELU and leaky RELU units are superior to other functions. Finally, the optimal number of layers is two or three in all the structures.

Furthermore, we have developed a simple Gradient Boosting approach using the separable architecture, where we sequentially fit five models. In this algorithm, each model is sequentially fitted with the error residual of the previous ones. We obtain the best performance with this approach, as the results show improvement over the models without Gradient Boosting (see Table 2). Furthermore, this improvement is more significant for the validation dataset as it reduces the variance of the results.

5.5   Adding Skip and Residual Connections to the Models

We have added skip and residual connections to the classic convolutional models and tested them with one to eight layers. The skip and residual connections link the layers sequentially.

The results are slightly less accurate than the ones obtained with classic and separable convolutional models, but these additional connections bring stability to the network as they show better results in deeper architectures

5.6   Multi-head Architectures

Multi-head architectures consist of combining several convolutional layers in parallel and, after the convolutions are performed, the output is concatenated and fed to the MLP. We have tested three multi-head models with two, three and four heads in parallel.

The results (See Table 2) show as the best performing model the multi-head architecture with three heads. The results are not better than the ones from separable or classic architectures (but very close).

These results seem to confirm that for wind time series the most complex architectures, in general, do not outperform the simpler ones. Analysing only the multihead architectures is the one with three heads the best performing, with results that are over two and four heads.

Table 2. Model Experimentation R^2 results for each best model, (T): Test data, (V): Validation data, (Dev): Deviation, (Mean): Mean value

Model	Mean-T	Dev-T	Mean-V	Dev-V
RF	6.770	±0.805	6.532	±0.737
MLP	7.253	±0.793	6.953	±0.731
RNN-GRU	7.147	±0.798	6.822	±0.735
CNN - 2l	**7.226**	±0.800	**6.908**	±0.736
CNN - 2l GB	**7.232**	±0.794	**6.959**	±0.731
CNN-sep 1l	7.301	±0.798	6.991	±0.752
CNN-sep 2l	**7.321**	±0.797	**6.988**	±0.745
CNN sep 2l GB	**7.341**	±0.796	**7.043**	±0.753
CNN-skip 1l	6.935	±0.799	6.671	±0.730
CNN-skip 2l	**7.223**	±0.798	**6.904**	±0.738
CNN-res 1l	6.862	±0.796	6.602	±0.735
CNN-res 2l	**7.136**	±0.806	**6.834**	±0.739
CNN-MH 2Heads	7.145	±0.792	6.829	±0.731
CNN-MH 3Heads	**7.170**	±0.796	**6.854**	±0.735

6   Discussion and Conclusions

We obtained a set of conclusions for our work that can be summarized in the next subsections.

6.1   MIMO is a Reliable Approach for Deep Networks

We tested several approaches for the regression, and we chose the MIMO approach for its superior accuracy and better use of computing resources. Usually, in time series modelling, the output is single-step, however, aligned with works like [1], we believe that for Deep Learning applications, MIMO offers a higher potential than just a single point prediction.

6.2   Convolutional Networks are Superior to Baselines

Wind prediction from time series is a challenging problem due to the complexity of the wind time series. In addition, the variability of results, depending on the site characteristics, makes it necessary to test the algorithms on a broad spectrum of sites. Our approach has been to use a single algorithm but trained on each site. All the convolutional architectures have improved the baseline statistical method, showing the feasibility of applying deep learning architectures to the wind forecasting problem.

Regarding the convolutional networks, we can see that with classic convolutions and adding separable convolutions. The results are superior. The circumstance that using separable convolutions improves the classic convolutional operation is already observed in image recognition tasks [6]. Still, there is no reference for this result for the time series.

In the experimentation, we have reviewed the impact of several parameters. We conclude that the number of parameters requires a structured approach for the hyperparameter setting as the number of combinations is very high. Finally, ensemble approaches improve the accuracy with best results than classic or simple separable convolutions. Finally, a gradient boosting algorithm approach showed the best results.

An initial question was how long the examples should be or, in other words, to infer the future steps, how long must the input sequence be?. In our work, we obtained that the best input sequence is six to eighteen hours long. We can rephrase this outcome by saying that wind has little memory. The wind we have now around us does not have helpful information to predict the wind in a longer timeframe, from six to eighteen hours. The short memory of wind explains why the architectures are not very deep (as the sequences are not very long) and is aligned with the wind formation processes as described by the earth sciences [18].

7 Future Work

We foresee several future lines of work related to this research. The first, which has been outlined in the conclusions, is testing architectures for series sampled with shorter periods, the NREL dataset has five minutes steps, thus requiring other sources of data for this experimentation that are not readily available. The increased amount of data requires architectures with new parameters and more complex structures, where the use of skip and residual connections may obtain better results than simpler ones.

This work line must look into what makes the wind more predictable when using more information as input. Another area for experimentation is detecting wind ramps or gusts, using series sampled with very high frequency, in the scale of seconds. With these wind time series, which are challenging due to the massive amount of data required, the deep learning architectures can apply its feature extraction capabilities to model these rare and essential wind phenomena. Another area to analyze is how adding weather forecasts improves the results, creating hybrid models that predict using the time series information and weather forecasting input.

Finally, as we have obtained some promising results with a simple gradient boosting method, we believe that additional experimentation with more complex combinations of algorithms could lead to new models with increased performance. We are currently pursuing these and other related questions.

Acknowledgements. The authors would like to thank the Barcelona Supercomputing Center (BSC) for the usage of their resources and the United States National Renewable Laboratory (NREL) for the use of its Wind Toolkit (wind datasets). We would also like to thank the anonymous reviewers for providing valuable comments that helped to improve the quality of this paper. Prof. U. Cortés is a member of the Sistema Nacional de Investigadores (level III) (CONACyT-Mexico).

References

1. Ben Taieb, S., Bontempi, G., Atiya, A., Sorjamaa, A.: A review and comparison of strategies for multi-step ahead time series forecasting based on the NN5 forecasting competition. arXiv e-prints arXiv:1108.3259, August 2011
2. Ben Taieb, S., Sorjamaa, A., Bontempi, G.: Multiple-output modeling for multi-step-ahead time series forecasting. Neurocomputing **73**(10–12), 1950–1957 (2010). https://doi.org/10.1016/j.neucom.2009.11.030
3. Bengio, Y., Roux, N.L., Vincent, P., Delalleau, O., Marcotte, P.: Convex neural networks. In: Weiss, Y., Schölkopf, B., Platt, J.C. (eds.) Advances in Neural Information Processing Systems 18, pp. 123–130. MIT Press, Cambridge (2006)
4. Bontempi, G.: Long term time series prediction with multi-input multi-output local learning. In: Proceedings of the 2nd European Symposium on Time Series Prediction (TSP), ESTSP 2008, January 2008
5. Cao, Q., Ewing, B.T., Thompson, M.A.: Forecasting wind speed with recurrent neural networks. Eur. J. Oper. Res. **221**(1), 148–154 (2012). https://doi.org/10.1016/j.ejor.2012.02.042
6. Chollet, F.: Xception: Deep learning with depthwise separable convolutions. CoRR abs/1610.02357 (2016). http://arxiv.org/abs/1610.02357
7. Díaz, D., Torres, A., Dorronsoro, J.R.: Deep neural networks for wind energy prediction. In: Rojas, I., Joya, G., Català, A. (eds.) Advances in Computational Intelligence, pp. 430–443. Springer, Cham (2015). https://doi.org/10.1007/978-3-319-19258-1_36
8. Draxl, C., Clifton, A., Hodge, B.M., McCaa, J.: The wind integration national dataset (wind) toolkit. Appl. Energy **151**, 355–366 (2015)
9. Elliott, D., Holladay, C., Barchet, W., Foote, H., Sandusky, W.: Wind energy resource atlas of the united states, March 1987. (editor: NREL). https://rredc.nrel.gov/wind/pubs/atlas/
10. Fei-Fei, L., Deng, J., Li, K.: Constructing a large-scale image database. J. Vision **9**(8), 1037 (2009). https://doi.org/10.1167/9.8.1037
11. Friedman, J.H.: Stochastic gradient boosting. Comput. Stat. Data Anal. **38**(4), 367–378 (2002). https://doi.org/10.1016/S0167-9473(01)00065-2
12. Giebel, G., Brownsword, R., Kariniotakis, G., Denhard, M., Draxl, C.: The State-Of-The-Art in Short-Term Prediction of Wind Power: A Literature Overview, 2nd edn. ANEMOS.plus (2011). https://doi.org/10.11581/DTU:00000017. (Project funded by the European Commission under the 6th Framework Program, Priority 6.1: Sustainable Energy Systems)
13. He, K., Zhang, X., Ren, S., Sun, J.: Deep residual learning for image recognition. In: 2016 IEEE Conference on Computer Vision and Pattern Recognition (CVPR), pp. 770–778, June 2016. https://doi.org/10.1109/CVPR.2016.90

14. Hutter, F., Hoos, H.H., Leyton-Brown, K.: Sequential model-based optimization for general algorithm configuration. In: Coello, C.A.C. (ed.) Learning and Intelligent Optimization, pp. 507–523. Springer, Heidelberg (2011). https://doi.org/10.1007/978-3-642-25566-3_40

15. Khodayar, M., Kaynak, O., Khodayar, M.E.: Rough deep neural architecture for short-term wind speed forecasting. IEEE Trans. Indust. Inform. **13**(6), 2770–2779 (2017). https://doi.org/10.1109/TII.2017.2730846

16. Kline, D.: Methods for multi-step time series forecasting with neural networks, chap. 12, pp. 226–250. Information Science Publishing, January 2004. https://doi.org/10.4018/978-1-59140-176-6.ch012

17. Krizhevsky, A., Sutskever, I., Hinton, G.E.: Imagenet classification with deep convolutional neural networks. In: Pereira, F., Burges, C.J.C., Bottou, L., Weinberger, K.Q. (eds.) Advances in Neural Information Processing Systems 25, pp. 1097–1105. Curran Associates Inc., New York (2012)

18. Landberg, L.: Meteorology for Wind Energy. Wiley, Hoboken (2015). https://doi.org/10.1002/9781118913451

19. Le Cun, Y., Jackel, L.D., Boser, B., Denker, J.S., Graf, H.P., Guyon, I., Henderson, D., Howard, R.E., Hubbard, W.: Handwritten digit recognition: applications of neural network chips and automatic learning. IEEE Commun. Mag. **27**(11), 41–46 (1989). https://doi.org/10.1109/35.41400

20. LeCun, Y., Bengio, Y.: Convolutional networks for images, speech, and time-series. In: Arbib, M.A. (ed.) The Handbook of Brain Theory and Neural Networks, pp. 1–14. MIT Press, Cambridge (1995)

21. Liu, Z., Gao, W., Wan, Y.H., Muljadi, E.: Wind power plant prediction by using neural networks. In: IEEE Energy Conversion Congress and Exposition (ECCE), pp. 3154–3160, September 2012. https://doi.org/10.1109/ECCE.2012.6342351

22. Manero, J., Béjar, J., Cortés, U.: "Dust in the wind...", deep learning application to wind energy time series forecasting. Energies **12**(12), 2385 (2019). https://doi.org/10.3390/en12122385

23. Martorell, J.M.: Barcelona supercomputing center: science accelerator and producer of innovation. Contrib. Sci. **12**(1), 5–11 (2016). https://doi.org/10.2436/20.7010.01.238

24. Simonyan, K., Zisserman, A.: Very deep convolutional networks for large-scale image recognition. In: 3rd International Conference on Learning Representations, ICLR 2015, San Diego, CA, USA, 7–9 May 2015, Conference Track Proceedings, pp. 1–14 (2015), http://arxiv.org/abs/1409.1556

25. Szegedy, C., et al.: Going deeper with convolutions. CoRR abs/1409.4842 (2014). http://arxiv.org/abs/1409.4842

26. Taieb, S.B., Atiya, A.F.: A bias and variance analysis for multistep-ahead time series forecasting. IEEE Trans. Neural Netw. Learn. Syst, **27**(1), 62–76 (2016)

27. Venkatraman, A., Hebert, M., Bagnell, J.A.: Improving multi-step prediction of learned time series models. In: Proceedings of the Twenty-Ninth AAAI Conference on Artificial Intelligence, pp. 3024–3030. AAAI 2015, AAAI Press (2015)

An Analysis of Neural Architecture Search and Hyper Parameter Optimization Methods

David E. Puentes G.[1]([⊠]) [iD], Carlos J. Barrios H.[1] [iD], and Philippe O. A. Navaux[1,2] [iD]

[1] SC3UIS, CAGE Universidad Industrial de Santander, Bucaramanga, Colombia
david.puentes1@correo.uis.edu.co
[2] Informatics Institute - Federal University of Rio Grande Do Sul, Porto Alegre, Brazil

Abstract. The growing interest for Deep Learning has leading the develop of methods for Neural Architecture Search (NAS) and Hyperparameter Optimization (HPO). Generally, architectures are designed in an iterative and expensive process of trial and error, besides being restricted to designer creativity and its specific knowledge about the topic. This paper presents an analysis and discussion about the frequent algorithms used to automate neural networks' design and tuning of its hyperparameters. Similarly, Floating Point Operations per Second (FLOPS), training time, and network complexity are complementary objectives to accuracy in classification, conceiving the performance as the sum of precision and computational consumption. This study seeks to pinpoint possible future directions to reduce human intervention in constructing machine learning models and understanding Artificial Neural Networks.

Keywords: Hyperparameter optimization · Deep learning · Artificial neural network · Computing performance · Automated machine learning

1 Introduction

Machine learning seeks to provide machines with the ability to learn without being explicitly programmed, seeking to emulate the human learning process. Artificial neural networks (ANN), for instance, take the neuron as the processing unit that per-forms basic tasks, but by connecting (synapses) with other neurons, they can solve more complex tasks [1]. Although ANN has gained popularity and success in different applications, there are still challenges, such as searching for neural architectures (NAS) or hyperparameter optimization (HPO). The definition of the architecture and its hyper-parameters are critical tasks that condition the performance of the models and are often conducted manually, depending on the professional background and experience, which makes their use difficult for non-experts.

To solve this problem of interest to academia and industry, Automated machine learning (AutoML) has emerged to automate the ML pipeline within a constrained computing budget, from data preparation and feature engineering to model generation and evaluation. Specifically, the aim is to build optimal neural architectures and calibrate their hyperparameters in the generation of the models, for which different strategies have

© Springer Nature Switzerland AG 2022
I. Gitler et al. (Eds.): CARLA 2021, CCIS 1540, pp. 208–217, 2022.
https://doi.org/10.1007/978-3-031-04209-6_15

been used to tackle these problems jointly or in isolation. Both consist firstly of defining a search space delimited by learning-related parameters (learning rate, batch size, epoch, etc.) (HPO) or model-related parameters (number of layers, number of neurons per layer, etc.) (NAS). Secondly, a search space exploration strategy and, finally, an evaluation method. For complex networks with large volumes of data, the last phase is often highly costly as it involves configurations that are not necessarily competitive and consume resources. The paper is structured as follows: Sect. 2 gives an overview of NAS and HPO. In Sect. 3, it lists some optimization algorithms and their applications. An occurrence analysis and discussion are present in Sect. 4, exposing a trend in the applications and algorithms. Finally, in Sect. 5, it reports the conclusions and suggestions for future works.

2 Architecture and Hyper-parameters Optimization Overview

Deep Learning models are becoming increasingly complex and computationally expensive, demanding strategies that take advantage of the limited resources without restricting their performance [2]. The success of Deep Learning is mainly due to the originality of the neural architectures that skilled, creative professionals have designed with access to adequate resources for experimentation [3].

To reduce human intervention in the design of neural networks, the Neural Architecture Search aims to find a suitable architecture with the best performance and the lowest cost, which can be considered an optimization problem [4]. The NAS recognizes three fundamental dimensions: Search Space, Search Strategy, and Performance Estimation Strategy. Search Space delimits, in the first instance, the number of architectures to build, so that very narrow spaces limit the configuration possibilities, while those with greater amplitude led to evaluate more alternatives and consequently consume more resources. In addition, the space dimensions are given by the designer, i.e., a bias is introduced at the outset that limits the possibility of evaluating innovative designs.

Search Strategy establishes how the search space is to be examined with an exploration-exploitation balance. The goal is to find the best architecture rapidly while avoiding rapid convergence to suboptimal. Finally, machine learning aims to train a model and evaluate its accuracy on previously unseen data. However, this procedure is unsustainable in searching for Deep Learning architectures considering the number of alternatives generated and volumes of data used. Performance estimation consists of avoiding the complete training of the network and predicting the behavior of the accuracy measurements instead [4].

Once the neural architecture is defined, it is possible to improve its performance by automatically defining the values of the parameters of the learning algorithm (Hyperparameters). The optimization of hyperparameters reduces human effort when using machine learning and improves its performance and reproducibility. Hyperparameter configurations may work differently depending on the dataset under analysis [3, 4]. Formally the problem is defined as:

Let A be a machine learning algorithm with N hyperparameters, where the domain of the n-th hyperparameter is Λn. Therefore, the total configuration space is given by $\Lambda = \Lambda_1 \times \Lambda_2 \times \Lambda_3 \times \ldots \Lambda_N$. A vector of hyperparameters is expressed by $\lambda \in \Lambda$, and A_λ is the algorithm A instantiated in the vector λ. Given a data set D, the objective is (Eq. 1):

$$\lambda^* = argminE_{(D_{train}, D_{valid}) \sim D} V(L, A_\lambda, D_{train}, D_{valid}) \tag{1}$$

where $V(L, A_\lambda, D_{train}, D_{valid})$ measures the loss of algorithm A fitted on the hyperparameters λ for the training set D_{train} and evaluated on the set D_{valid}. In practice, it is not possible to access all observations in the population, so the expected value is used to perform the performance estimation. However, the loss function with respect to the hyperparameters cannot be optimized using the classical gradient-based methods since it is a black box function [4]. Some of the commonly used alternatives to address both NAS and HPO are presented in the following section.

3 Optimization Methods

The Neural Network performance primarily depends on its architecture, training process and data availability, therefore, its maximization is not a trivial work as there is no function that relates hyperparameters and performance (black box problem). These kinds of problems are so difficult that an optimal solution cannot be found by exact methods in a reasonable time. In this context, it is preferable to rely on iterative, novel and alternative optimization approaches to achieve approximate solutions with a balance between diversification (exploring new solutions) and intensification (exploiting current knowledge) [3].

3.1 Bayesian Optimization

Bayesian optimization is an optimization approach that has gained popularity as it facilitates the integration of prior knowledge about the possible behavior of the black-box function, in addition to its performance in instances of reduced search spaces [5, 6]. SmartTuning proposed by [7] is a strategy based on the LeNet-5 architecture to jointly optimize accuracy, training time, and inference memory usage. SmartTuning is a workflow composed of three modules: Tuning Controller (TC) to control the overall SmartTuning process starting with training data definition, validation, search space configuration, and objective weighting. BO Engine (BOE) to perform the optimization of the objective function and, finally, Performance Collector (PC) to collect the performance metrics. Similar [8] develop a scaled strategy for the assessment of landslide susceptibility. The authors used Random Forest to identify the main input features, reduce the dimensionality and avoid overlearning due to the reduced number of observations. Subsequently, they trained a convolutional network adjusted with Bayesian Optimization and compared the performance with artificial neural networks and support vector machines, demonstrating its superiority by including spatial correlations.

3.2 Population-Based Algorithms

Population-based algorithms start from an initial population of solutions that is collectively improved. NAS and HPO are initial proposals of architectures and hyperparameters that are improved until an approximate solution is reached, or a given stopping criterion is met. Particle Swarm Optimization (PSO) is an example inspired by collective behavior in flocks or shoals to establish a global response through the interactions between the agents (particles), changing the speed and location of each particle according to the individual experience and the global information of the swarm [9, 10]. [11] approaches NAS using a PSO algorithm with modifications in the definition of the position and speed of particles, demonstrating that combining both the best global and local position leads to a better exploration and exploitation of the search space. Subsamples and a unique period are taken, entirely training only the best architecture. Similarly [12] stated that it is paramount to minimize the fitness function evaluation time and proposed a linear model to rank the hyperparameter configurations and prematurely stop training once the rankings stabilize. They also stated that a suitable PSO variant should contain few particles to reduce the number of instances to train and generations.

[13] proposed a multilevel optimization strategy, where the first level defines the search space for the network architecture, while the second level determines the hyper-parameters associated with each of the layers. In turn, they employ sigmoid-like inertia to generate the initial population and guide the search, avoiding early convergence. Inter-estingly, the hierarchical strategy proposed by these authors recognizes that NAS and HPO are different and complementary problems, first building an architecture that is then calibrated.

Another family of population-based algorithms is evolutionary algorithms, named after the biological theory of evolution and natural selection proposed by Charles Darwin. The ideas of this theory are intuitively transferred to optimization, where the members of a population (current solutions) evolve in each iteration (generation). Those who provide the best fit are assigned as the next generation's parents [10, 14]. The fitness level of each member is given by the value of an objective function, for instance, the maximization of an image classification accuracy metric in the case of CNN (Fig. 1).

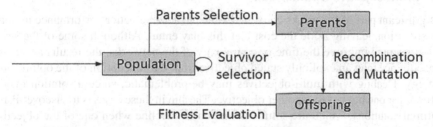

Fig. 1. General frameworks for evolutionary algorithms

For each architecture or configuration candidate is necessary to evaluate a fitness function, that is, an expensive training and evaluation process where could be included unpromising alternatives, a disappoint for this kind of algorithms. [15] proposed an asyn-chronous computational component (cache) to accelerate the evaluation of the fitness of the individuals, where each individual is placed on an available GPU and don't have to wait until the evaluation of the current one finishes. Also, they propose a variable-length encoding strategy and crossover operator, allowing to include skip connections to promote deeper CNN.

Frequently, NAS and HP are studied in popular datasets with the objective to do a benchmark. However, also there are some applications in practical situations as [16–18] for diseases or diagnostic, face recognition [19] or stock markets prediction [20].

3.3 Reinforcement Learning

Reinforcement Learning (RL) like evolutionary methods try to mimic a biology conduct, in this case the learning. Humans modify its behavior based on the outcomes of its decisions, reinforcing the actions with a positive response and forgetting those with a negative response (Fig. 2). It is critical to emphasize that RL does not maximize the reward to receive, but it tries to improve by changing its decisions, in a similar sense to Markov Chain [21].

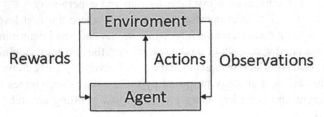

Fig. 2. General framework for Reinforcement Learning

For example, for HPO an agent can pick different hyperparameter values sequentially and tune the setup until it achieves the best accumulative reward [22]. Additionally, they propose a method to dynamically limit the model horizon by measuring its impact over policy.

3.4 Multi-objective Optimization

A significant part of the works consulted aimed to achieve better performance in image classification, leaving aside the cost that this may entail. Although some of the strategies presented improve the time or complexity of the networks, the results are more a consequence than an explicitly stated objective from the conception of the optimization strategy. Dealing with multi-objectives may be problematic, since a solution may be optimal for one but not for another objective. The aim in these cases is to discover Pareto Optimal solutions, which are solutions that do not decline when one of the objectives may be improved.

Architecture design is tackled by [23] with a genetic algorithm based on evolutionary learning to find the arrange with the better accuracy and compact network. Also, suggest an incremental learning proposal, where, taking account that offspring shares characters with the parents, then it could be initialized with the synaptic parent weights, demonstrating promise results to build compact architectures that would be applied in practical cases. On the other hand, [16, 24, 25] propose multi-objective models to optimize the pressure and the number of floating-point operations (FLOPS). [16] used a training strategy that takes advantage of previously identified patterns to guide the progressive search using a Bayesian learning model and a genetic algorithm to explore the search space. The work by [24] focused on optimizing the number of blocks, layers per block, and the growth rate of each block for the DenseNet [26] architecture. The authors used a particle swarm and proposed an encoding strategy that starts with the definition of the number of blocks to encode the other hyperparameters in vectors of fixed length subsequently.

4 Occurrence Analysis

The occurrence analysis was performed in Scopus in May 2021 using a combination of terms related to Deep Learning, Hyperparameter Optimization, Neural Networks, and Parameter Tuning. In a complementary way, a bibliometric analysis was performed supported by VosViewer software. The study shows the existence of five clusters according to keywords occurrence in the documents.

4.1 Cluster 1: Applications

The first keyword cluster is related to the different HPO and NAS applications. Image analysis and processing are the top topics, leaving straggler applications like speech recognition, natural language processing or pattern recognition. At the same time, the images studied usually come from popular datasets for benchmark or medical diagnosis, allowing diversifying the applications and study areas. Figure 3 shows the principal applications.

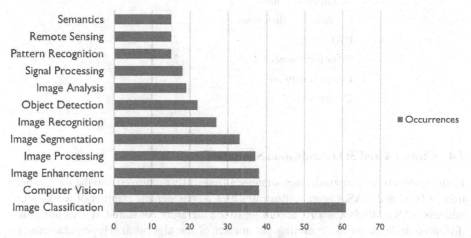

Fig. 3. Application occurrence. Occurrence indicates the number of documents where a keyword is used

4.2 Cluster 2: Learning

Similar to the first cluster, the second cluster confirms the interest in performance comparison with state-of-art in image analysis, emphasizing classification accuracy. Additionally, references to classic backpropagation, gradient-based algorithms, activation functions, learning rates, and data augmentation suggest the existence of a relationship with studies covering training acceleration and the hyperparameters that influence it.

4.3 Cluster 3: Multi-objective

When building a neural network and tuning its hyperparameter is not enough to obtain the best fit. It is also necessary to find a solution with reasonable costs and complexity levels that allow its implementation in industrial or commercial applications. The third cluster includes these considerations within multi-objective optimization, related to evolutionary optimization, PSO, HPO, and NAS. Table 1 shows that hyperparameter optimization is the main topic where multi-objective optimization is employed. As for search strategies, evolutionary algorithms and PSO are preferred over Bayesian Optimization, achieving competitive performance (minimal cost, complexity, and maximum accuracy).

Table 1. Occurrence multi-objective optimization

Keyword 1	Strength
Hyperparameter optimization	7
Neural architectures	6
Evolutionary algorithms	3
PSO	2
Classification accuracy	2
Complex networks	2
Computational costs	1

4.4 Cluster 4 and 5: Optimization Strategies

Both clusters refer to optimization strategies frequently employed and the joint conception of HPO and NAS. Figure 4 illustrates how a considerable number of works jointly address NAS and HPO, where, according to the literature consulted, it does not usually differentiate between the operating parameters of the algorithm (Hyperparameters) or those of design (Architecture). On the other hand, Bayesian optimization as well as genetic algorithms are the most frequent strategies, a behavior that can be explained by the background and previous knowledge about these strategies. Contrary to this, reinforced learning as expressed by it is an incipient and promising study area in automatic architecture design.

Likewise, there is a significant interest in strategies aiming to identify the best hyperparameter configuration. These strategies can be tested using *ad-hoc* architectures or established architectures that have demonstrated remarkable performance in the literature. For the sample analyzed ResNet (38) [27], VGGNet (31) [28], and AlexNet (21) [29] are the most studied architectures, and CIFAR and MNIST are the datasets generally used for model training and test.

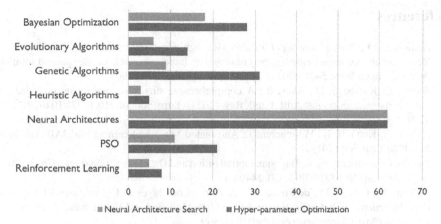

Fig. 4. Optimization strategies occurrence

5 Conclusion

Deep Learning has demonstrated its potential to solve different problems with excellent results. However, its design and hyperparameter influence its performance and change depending on the task to solve. The designing and tuning of such architectures require human expertise and creativity within a fixed computing budget. The present study introduces an analysis of different optimization techniques for HPO and NAS and literature keywords occurrences to present a general picture of the state of the art and possible future directions. In the first place, there is an array of different search strategies or optimization methods with their respective variations, where the evolutionary algorithms appear as the most commonly used strategy. Furthermore, there is a growing enthusiasm for alternatives like Bayesian Optimization and Reinforcement Learning to tackle black-box optimization.

Concerning applications, as shown in Sect. 4, image classification has received greater attention, leaving straggle applications as natural language processing, object detection, or audio analysis, among others. In general, the studies have two focuses: doing a benchmark to compare strategies that raise classification accuracy records using well-known datasets such as CIFAR or MNIST or medical applications on the disease diagnosis. This trend opens a range of opportunities to explore if the building patterflopsns or architectures expose similar performance in other datasets or practical problems. On the other hand, accuracy classification tends to be the unique or principal objective to optimize with the different search strategies. In contrast, multi-objective models consider the performance in a broader sense, considering the computational budget and network complexity.

Future research should explore multi-objective strategies, including alternative objectives like energy consumption or memory requirement and FLOPS or network complexity. The reduction of human intervention requires building adaptive search spaces to reject poorly promising networks. Finally, would delimit the search space and, consequently, reduce the time to find an optimal neural network.

References

1. Bishop, C.M.: Neural Networks for Pattern Recognition (1995)
2. Ren, P., et al.: A comprehensive survey of neural architecture search: challenges and solutions. ACM Comput. Surv. **54**(4) (2021). http://arxiv.org/abs/2006.02903
3. Akay, B., Karaboga, D., Akay, R.: A comprehensive survey on optimizing deep learning models by metaheuristics. Artif. Intell. Rev. (2021). https://doi.org/10.1007/s10462-021-099 92-0
4. Hutter, F., Kotthoff, L., Vanschoren, J.: Automated Machine Learning | MLJAR Automated Machine Learning (2019)
5. Archetti, F., Candelieri, A.: Bayesian Optimization and Data Science. Springer, Cham (2019). https://doi.org/10.1007/978-3-030-24494-1
6. Brochu, E., Cora, V.M., de Freitas, N.: A Tutorial on Bayesian Optimization of Expensive Cost Functions, with Application to Active User Modeling and Hierarchical Reinforcement Learning (2010). http://arxiv.org/abs/1012.2599
7. Li, X., Zhang, G., Zheng, W.: SmartTuning: selecting hyper-parameters of a ConvNet system for fast training and small working memory. IEEE Trans. Parallel Distrib. Syst. **32**(7), 1690–1701 (2021). https://doi.org/10.1109/TPDS.2020.3040723
8. Sameen, M.I., Pradhan, B., Lee, S.: Application of convolutional neural networks featuring Bayesian optimization for landslide susceptibility assessment. Catena **186** (2020). https://doi.org/10.1016/j.catena.2019.104249
9. Li, Y., Xiao, J., Chen, Y., Jiao, L.: Evolving deep convolutional neural networks by quantum behaved particle swarm optimization with binary encoding for image classification. Neurocomputing **362**, 156–165 (2019). https://doi.org/10.1016/j.neucom.2019.07.026
10. Smith, J.E.: Introduction to evolutionary computing, vol. 28 (2015)
11. Lawrence, T., Zhang, L., Lim, C.P., Phillips, E.-J.: Particle swarm optimization for automatically evolving convolutional neural networks for image classification. IEEE Access **9**, 14369–14386 (2021). https://doi.org/10.1109/ACCESS.2021.3052489
12. Wang, Y., Zhang, H., Zhang, G.: cPSO-CNN: an efficient PSO-based algorithm for fine-tuning hyper-parameters of convolutional neural networks. Swarm Evol. Comput. **49**, 114–123 (2019). https://doi.org/10.1016/j.swevo.2019.06.002
13. Singh, P., Chaudhury, S., Panigrahi, B.K.: Hybrid MPSO-CNN: multi-level particle swarm optimized hyperparameters of convolutional neural network. Swarm Evol. Comput. **63** (2021). https://doi.org/10.1016/j.swevo.2021.100863
14. Tian, Z., Fong, S.: Survey of meta-heuristic algorithms for deep learning training. In: Optimization Algorithms - Methods and Applications (2016)
15. Sun, Y., Xue, B., Zhang, M., Yen, G.G., Lv, J.: Automatically designing CNN architectures using the genetic algorithm for image classification. IEEE Trans. Cybern. **50**(9), 3840–3854 (2020). https://doi.org/10.1109/TCYB.2020.2983860
16. Lu, Z., et al.: Multiobjective evolutionary design of deep convolutional neural networks for image classification. IEEE Trans. Evol. Comput. **25**(2), 277–291 (2021). https://doi.org/10.1109/TEVC.2020.3024708
17. Lee, S., Kim, J., Kang, H., Kang, D.Y., Park, J.: Genetic algorithm based deep learning neural network structure and hyperparameter optimization. Appl. Sci. **11**(2), 1–12 (2021). https://doi.org/10.3390/app11020744
18. Houreh, Y., Mahdinejad, M., Naredo, E., Dias, D.M., Ryan, C.: HNAS: hyper neural architecture search for image segmentation. In: ICAART 2021 - Proceedings of the 13th International Conference on Agents and Artificial Intelligence, vol. 2, pp. 246–256 (2021)

19. Zatarain Cabada, R., Rodriguez Rangel, H., Barron Estrada, M.L., Cardenas Lopez, H.M.: Hyperparameter optimization in CNN for learning-centered emotion recognition for intelligent tutoring systems. Soft. Comput. **24**(10), 7593–7602 (2019). https://doi.org/10.1007/s00 500-019-04387-4
20. Chung, H., Shin, K.-S.: Genetic algorithm-optimized multi-channel convolutional neural network for stock market prediction. Neural Comput. Appl. **32**(12), 7897–7914 (2019). https:// doi.org/10.1007/s00521-019-04236-3
21. Sutton, R., Barto, A.: Reinforcement Learning: An Introduction (2015)
22. Wu, J., Chen, S., Liu, X.: Efficient hyperparameter optimization through model based reinforcement learning. Neurocomputing **409**, 381–393 (2020). https://doi.org/10.1016/j.neucom. 2020.06.064
23. Chen, J., et al.: A fast evolutionary learning to optimize CNN. Chin. J. Electron. **29**(6), 1061–1073 (2020). https://doi.org/10.1049/cje.2020.09.007
24. Wang, B., Sun, Y., Xue, B., Zhang, M.: Evolving deep neural networks by multi-objective particle swarm optimization for image classification. In: GECCO 2019 - Proc. 2019 Genetic and Evolutionary Computation Conference, pp. 490–498 (2019). https://doi.org/10.1145/332 1707.3321735
25. Gülcü, A., Kuş, Z.: Multi-objective simulated annealing for hyper-parameter optimization in convolutional neural networks. PeerJ Comput. Sci. **7**, 2–27 (2021). https://doi.org/10.7717/ peerj-cs.338
26. Huang, G., Liu, Z., Van Der Maaten, L., Weinberger, K.Q.: Densely connected convolutional networks. In: Proceedings - 30th IEEE Conference on Computer Vision and Pattern Recognition, CVPR 2017, vol. 2017-January, pp. 2261–2269 (2017). https://doi.org/10.1109/CVPR. 2017.243
27. He, K., Zhang, X., Ren, S., Sun, J.: Deep residual learning for image recognition. In: IEEE Conference on Computer Vision and Pattern Recognition, CVPR 2016, pp. 770–778 (2016). https://doi.org/10.1109/CVPR.2016.90
28. Simonyan, K., Andrew, Z.: Very deep convolutional networks for large-scale image recognition (2015)
29. Krizhevsky, A., Sutskever, I., Hinton, G.: ImagiNet classification with deep convolutional neural networks. In: Advances in Neural Information Processing Systems, pp. 1097–1105 (2007)

High Performance Computing
Applications

Solving the Heat Transfer Equation by a Finite Difference Method Using Multi-dimensional Arrays in CUDA as in Standard C

Josefina Sanchez-Noguez[1], Carlos Couder-Castañeda[2]([✉])(iD),
J. J. Hernández-Gómez[2](iD), and Itzel Navarro-Reyes[3]

[1] Universidad Nacional Autónoma de México, Facultad de Estudios Superiores,
Naucalpan de Juárez, Mexico
[2] Instituto Politécnico Nacional, Centro de Desarrollo Aeroespacial,
Mexico City, Mexico
ccouder@ipn.mx
[3] Instituto Politécnico Nacional, Escuela Superior de Física y Matemáticas,
Mexico City, Mexico

Abstract. In recent years the increasing necessity to speed up the execution of numerical algorithms has leaded researchers to the use of co-processors and graphic cards such as the NVIDIA GPU's. Despite CUDA C meta-language was introduced to facilitate the development of general purpose-applications, the solution to the common question: How to allocate (cudaMalloc) two-dimensional array?, is not simple. In this paper, we present a memory structure that allows the use of multidimensional arrays inside a CUDA kernel, to demonstrate its functionality, this structure is applied to the explicit finite difference solution of the non-steady heat transport equation.

Keywords: CUDA C · Multiarrays · Heat transfer.

1 Introduction

Today, the use of Graphic processing units (GPUs) to accelerate scientific applications is very common alongside the multi-core architectures to speed up a huge range of engineering applications to reduce their computing time. NVIDIA GPUs initially used to improve the performance of video games were not accessible to develop general purpose applications; nevertheless, with the introduction of CUDA (Compute Unified Device Architecture), the power of GPUs for scientific and engineering applications was unleashed by extensions to C language [12].

For this reason, GPUs have become part of the most powerful supercomputers on earth (see http://www.top500.org). Notwithstanding this remarkable fact, the usage of GPUs in scientific computation using low-level tools as CUDA C is a

This work was partially supported by the project IPN-SIP 20210291.

© Springer Nature Switzerland AG 2022
I. Gitler et al. (Eds.): CARLA 2021, CCIS 1540, pp. 221–235, 2022.
https://doi.org/10.1007/978-3-031-04209-6_16

complex task because it requires a high knowledge of the GPU architecture to obtain the best speed-up benefits.

Nowadays, hundreds of scientific applications have been migrated to GPU, so it is impossible to mention all of them, but the most current and representative ones that have been benefited for drastic speed ups in their computing times [17] would be applications for: flows in porous media [5], graph compression [6], MPI combined libraries for image processing [4], query speed up in databases [16], multi-physics modelation [7], solving Boltzmann transport equations [13], CFD code speed up in non-uniform grids [19], direct modeling of gravitational fields [3], reconstructing 3D images [20], propagating acoustic waves [11], solving Lyapunov equations for control theory [8], studies of convective turbulence [2], radiative transport modelling [1], computation of Lagrangian coherent structures [9], just to mention some of them.

Due to the complexity that could represent porting applications for their GPU processing, techniques to generate parallel code through directives expressing parallelism such as OpenACC (https://www.openacc.org/) have been developed, which permits introducing parallelism inside the source code and delegates to the compiler the task to generate the CUDA kernel automatically. OpenACC follows the development of parallel applications paradigm like OpenMP that is oriented to multi-core architectures [18].

Despite the kindnesses offered by programming based on directives, such applications are still being developed with low-level language, basically because of the preference of taking full control in the development, as well as to avoid the dependence of compilers supporting OpenACC.

The motivation of this paper arises during the development of an application based on finite difference method to solve the heat transfer equation, to facilitate the implementation of algebraic expressions. As established by [10], the main difficulty when implementing a finite-difference code on a GPU comes from the computational stencil. For example, a fourth-order spatial operator, the thread that handles the calculation of point (i, j, k) needs to access the arrays points $(i+1, j, k)$, $(i+2, j, k)$, $(i-1, j, k)$, $(i-2, j, k)$, $(i, j+1, k)$ and so on. This implies that 13 accesses to the memory are needed on the GPU to approximate fourth-order finite difference, which is a very high value, keeping in mind that access to global memory is slow compared with shared memory. For this reason, the use of shared memory could be very convenient to minimize access latency.

The structure developed in this work consists of defining two pointers, one with multi-indices that are used to access data inside the CUDA kernel, and the other which has data in a unidimensional form to be able to copy them. This is necessary due to the GPU architecture. This paper is organized as follows. Section 2, is given the code to create bi-dimensional arrays to use them inside a kernel. Section 3, is given the code to create three-dimensional arrays to use them inside a kernel. Section 4, is applied the structures developed to the solution of the non-steady heat transfer equation by the finite difference method in 2D and 3D. Section 5, the performante test are carried out considering the use of shared memory. Finally, Sect. 6 presents our conclusions.

2   Bidimensional Arrays

The essence to create a 2D array in CUDA so that both [][] indices can be used inside the kernel, is similar to create a continuous dynamic memory 2D array for CPU, which is shown in Listing 1.1; we use as an example the `float` type, but any primitive type could be used.

Listing 1.1. Continuous memory allocation for a 2D array in C on CPU.

```
float ** Get_Memory_Continuous_2D_float(int n, int m){
  float ** A = NULL;
  int i,j;
  cudaMallocHost((void***)&A,n*sizeof(float*));
  if (A == NULL)
    puts("Error_cudaMallocHost_first_level"),
    exit (-1);
  cudaMallocHost((void**)&A[0],n*m*sizeof(float));
  if (A[0] == NULL) puts("Memory_second_level"), exit (-1);
  for (i=1; i<n; i++)
    A[i] = A[0] + i * m;
  return A;
}
```

The function shown in Listing 1.1 is a contiguous allocation of memory for a 2D array, and we shall use it as the main structure to create a 2D array in CUDA, as shown in Listing 1.2. The function `Array_2D_GPU` has 4 parameters: one pointer to a pointer variable (**), one pointer to a pointer to a pointer (***), as well as two integers. The ** (P) pointer is used to receive the address of the pointer that points to the array in its contiguous form, which shall be used to transfer data between CPU and GPU. The *** (M) pointer shall receive the address of the P pointer which shall allow the usage of two indices [][] inside the kernels, that are the other two integer kind parameters of the `Array_2D_GPU` function: n and m denote the number of rows and columns respectively.

Listing 1.2. Contiguous memory allocation in CUDA C for a 2D array on GPU.

```
void Array_2D_GPU(float **P, float ***M, int n, int m)
{
  int i; float ** P_M, ** dev_M;
  P_M = (float **) malloc(n*sizeof(float*));
  if(P_M == NULL){ printf("\nMemory_error"); exit(-1); }
  cudaMalloc((void**)&P_M[0],n*m*sizeof(float));
  if(P_M[0]==NULL){ printf("\nMemory_error"); exit(-1); }
  for (i=1; i<n; i++)
    P_M[i] = P_M[0] + i * m;
  cudaMalloc((void***)&dev_M,n*sizeof(float*));
  if(dev_M==NULL){ printf("\nMemory_error"); exit(-1); }
  cudaMemcpy(dev_M,P_M,n*sizeof(float*),
    cudaMemcpyHostToDevice);
  *(P) = P_M[0];
  *(M) = dev_M;
}
```

The code shown in Listing 1.2 features two pointers: P_M and dev_M. The first one is used to transfer data between CPU and GPU, and the second one is used to handle the array using the indices ([][]) inside the kernel. The main idea behind this contiguous memory allocation for a 2D array of m x n is as follows:

- To create a first level pointer array (float *) of size n in CPU.
- In the first location of P_M[0] array, allocate memory for m x n elements in GPU.
- To assign to each element of P_M[i], the memory address of the element in the m x i location (creating the 2D array).
- To create a first level pointer array (float *) of size n in GPU.
- To transfer the memory addresses assigned to P_M[i] to GPU, i.e. copy the content of P_M to dev_M, where dev_M could be used inside a CUDA kernel as a 2D array.

The last point is very important because, paradigmatically, it only considers transfers of primitive data to GPU, however, memory addresses can also be transferred.

3   Tridimensional Arrays

Analogously to the 2D array creation, in the 3D case, it is also necessary to assign continuous memory. In Listing 1.3 we assign continuous memory for a 3D array in the CPU memory. Taking this code as the base, we shall build its CUDA equivalent showed in Listing 1.4.

Listing 1.3. Contiguous memory allocation in C for a 3D array on CPU.

```
float *** Get_Memory_Continuous_3D_float(int n, int m, int z)
{
  float *** A = NULL;
  float *p = NULL;
  int i,j,k;
  cudaMallocHost((void****)&A,n*sizeof(float**));
  if (A==NULL){printf("\nMemory_problem"); exit(-1);}
  cudaMallocHost((void***)&A[0],n*m*sizeof(float*));
  if(A[0]==NULL){printf("\nMemory_problem");exit(-1);}
  for(i=1; i<n; i++)
    A[i] = A[0] + i*m;
  cudaMallocHost((void**)&A[0][0],n*m*z*sizeof(float));
  if(A[0][0] == NULL){printf("\nMemory_problem");exit(-1);}
  for(j=1; j<(n*m); j++)
    A[0][j] = A[0][0] + j*z;
  return A;
}
```

Analogous to the structure used for the 2D multi-array, we define a function Array_3D_GPU with five parameters (two pointers and three integers), where the pointer to a pointer P_M is likely used to create the structure that shall transfer data between CPU and GPU. Now dev_M is a **** pointer which shall be used to handle the 3D array inside the kernel. The three integers, m, n and z are the indices of the array. The algorithm to create an array of size m x n x z proceed as follow:

- Allocate a second level pointers array (float **) of size n in CPU through P_M.
- In the first location of P_M[0], to allocate memory for m x n pointers elements in CPU.

- To assign to each element of P_M[i], the memory address of the element in the m x i locality.
- To create a first level pointers array (float *) of size n in GPU in the pointer P_M[0][0].
- To assign to each element of P_M[0][j], the memory address of the element in the j x z locality.
- In the pointer dev_M, to assign n elements of type float **.
- In the pointer dev_M_2D, to assign $n \times m$ elements of type float *. Then to transfer the $n \times m$ elements of type float * from P_M[0] to dev_M_2D.
- To assign *(P) = P_M[0][0].
- To assign to each element P_M[i], the memory address of the element in the $m \times i$ location.
- To transfer the n elements of type float ** from P_M to dev_M.

Listing 1.4. Contiguous memory allocation in CUDA C for a 3D array on GPU.

```
void Array_3D_GPU(float ** P,float **** M,int n,int m,int z)
{
 int i, j;
 float *** P_M = NULL, *** dev_M = NULL;
 float ** dev_M_2D = NULL;
 cudaMallocHost((void****)&P_M,n*sizeof(float**));
 if(P_M == NULL){printf("\nError Host Pointers"); exit(0);}
 cudaMallocHost((void***)&P_M[0],n*m*sizeof(float*));
 if(P_M[0]==NULL){ printf("\nError Host Pointers"); exit(0); }
 for (i=1; i<n; i++)
  P_M[i] = P_M[0] + i * m;
 cudaMalloc((void**)&P_M[0][0],n*m*z*sizeof(float));
 for (j=1; j<(n*m); j++)
  P_M[0][j] = P_M[0][0] + j * z;
 cudaMalloc((void****)&dev_M,n * sizeof(float **));
 cudaMalloc((void***)&dev_M_2D,n * m * sizeof(float*));
 if(dev_M== NULL){printf("\nError dev Pointers 3D"); exit(0); }
 if(dev_M_2D==NULL){ printf("\nError dev Pointers 2D");
 exit(0); }
 cudaMemcpy(dev_M_2D,P_M[0],n*m*sizeof(float*),\ cudaMemcpyHostToDevice);
 *(P) = P_M[0][0];
 for (i=0; i<n; i++)
  P_M[i] = dev_M_2D + i * m;
 cudaMemcpy(dev_M,P_M,n*sizeof(float**), cudaMemcpyHostToDevice);
 *(M) = dev_M;
}
```

4   Application to the Non-steady Heat Transport Equation

4.1   2D Case

The bidimensional non-steady heat transport equation is expressed as,

$$\frac{\partial T}{\partial t} = C \left(\frac{\partial T^2}{\partial x^2} + \frac{\partial T^2}{\partial y^2} \right), \quad 0 \le x, y \le 1, t \ge 0. \tag{1}$$

Applying an explicit finite difference scheme to the Eq. (1) and rearranging terms to obtain explicitly temperature at time $l+1$, $T_{i,j}^{l+1}$ [14], we obtain the algebraic equation:

$$T_{i,j}^{l+1} = T_{i,j}^l + C\Delta t \left(\frac{T_{i+1,j}^l - 2T_{i,j}^l + T_{i-1,j}^l}{\Delta x^2} + \frac{T_{i,j+1}^l - 2T_{i,j}^l + T_{i,j-1}^l}{\Delta y^2} \right). \quad (2)$$

Computational domain shall be a square that simulates a 1×1 plate, meshed with a $\Delta x = 0.003333333$ and $\Delta y = 0.005$, therefore $n_x = 301$ and $n_y = 201$, initial conditions were imposed as:

$$f(x,y) = \begin{cases} 1: \text{if } 0.05 \leq (x - 05)^2 + (y - 0.5)^2 \leq 0.01 \\ 0: \text{otherwise} \end{cases} \quad (3)$$

and Dirichlet boundary conditions

$$\alpha_0(y) = \alpha_1(y) = \beta_0(x) = \beta_1(x) = 0.0. \quad (4)$$

For the solution of the Eq. (2) were implemented three kernels versions named: 2D-1-1, 2D-1-2, 2D-2-2. The name structure is 2D-X-I, where X is the array dimension and I is the number of indices used inside the kernel and 2D refers to the dimension of the equation solved. T and Tn is the temperature in time l and $l + 1$ respectively, and the kernels are called for every iteration in time [14].

The 2D-1-1 kernel is showed in Listing 1.5, as can be seen, determine the boundary point (perimeter points) is not trivial, in fact, if it is established n_x and n_y as the number of points in the x and y direction respectively, the elements at the boundaries can be determined with the following conditionals: $l \bmod n_x = 0$, left side; $(l - 1) \bmod n_x = 0$, right side; $0 \leq l < n_x$, up side; $n_x n_y - (n_x + 1) \leq l < n_x n_y - 1$, down side; where l is the lineal index in the rows direction.

Listing 1.5. Kernel 2D using unidimensional array T with just one index 1.

```
--global-- void kernel(float *T, float *Tn, int nx, int ny,\
  float dt, float C, float dx2, float dy2)
{
  int l;
  l = blockIdx.x * blockDim.x + threadIdx.x;
  float Txx;
  float Tyy;
  if(l>nx && l<((nx*ny-1)-nx) && !((l%nx)==0 || ((l+1)%nx == 0)))
  {
    Txx = (T[l+1] -2.0f*T[l] + T[l-1])/dx2;
    Tyy = (T[l+nx] -2.0f*T[l] + T[l-nx])/dy2;
    Tn[l] = T[l]+dt*C*(Txx+Tyy);
  }
}
```

In Listing 1.6, is shown the kernel 2D-1-2 that uses two indices, simplifying the conditional (if), to make all the calculations over the interior points, nevertheless, the boundary conditions handle is still a little bit difficult, and can be established as: $(i \times n_x + j) \bmod n_x == 0$, left side; $(i \times n_x + j - 1) \bmod n_x == 0$, right side; $0 \leq (i \times n_x + j) < n_x$, up side; $n_x n_y - (n_x + 1) \leq (i \times n_x + j) < n_x n_y - 1$, down side; where i and j are the indices.

Listing 1.6. Kernel 2D using unidimensional array T with two indices (i,j) .

```
__global__ void kernel(float *T, float *Tn, int ny, int \
nx, float dt, float C,   float dx2, float dy2)
{
  int i,j,l;
  j = blockIdx.x*blockDim.x+threadIdx.x;
  i = blockIdx.y*blockDim.y+threadIdx.y;
  float Txx;
  float Tyy;
  if( (j > 0) && (j<(nx-1)) && (i > 0) &&  (i < (ny-1)))
  {
    l = i*nx+j;
    Txx = (T[l+1] -2.0f*T[l] + T[l-1])/dx2;
    Tyy = (T[l+nx] -2.0f*T[l] + T[l-nx])/dy2;
    Tn[l] = T[l]+dt*C*(Txx+Tyy);
  }
}
```

In Listing 1.7, is shown the proposed kernel 2D-2-2 using the temperature is a bidimensional array inside the kernel, to make it possible it is necessary to allocate T and Tn using the function listed in 1.2. The programability is improved and less prone to errors; the indices inside the kernel are very clear, and the boundary conditions are easily managed as: $j == 0$, left side; $j == n_x - 1$; $i == 0$, up side; $i == n_y - 1$, down side.

Listing 1.7. Kernel 2D using bidimensional array T with two indices (i,j).

```
__global__ void kernel(float **T, float **Tn, int ny, int\
nx, float dt, float C, float dx2, float dy2)
{
  int i,j;
  j = blockIdx.x*blockDim.x+threadIdx.x;
  i = blockIdx.y*blockDim.y+threadIdx.y;
  float Txx;
  float Tyy;
  if( (i > 0) && (i<(ny-1)) && (j > 0) && (j < (nx-1)))
  {
    Txx = (T[i][j+1] -2.0*T[i][j] +T[i][j-1])/dx2;
    Tyy = (T[i+1][j] -2.0*T[i][j] +T[i-1][j])/dy2;
    Tn[i][j] = T[i][j]+dt*C*(Txx+Tyy);
  }
}
```

4.2 3D Case

The tridimensional non-steady heat transport equation, is expresed as,

$$\frac{\partial T}{\partial t} = C \left(\frac{\partial T^2}{\partial x^2} + \frac{\partial T^2}{\partial y^2} + \frac{\partial T^2}{\partial z^2} \right) \quad 0 \leq x,y,z \leq 1, t \geq 0 \tag{5}$$

Applying an explicit finite difference scheme to the Eq. (1) and rearranging terms to obtain explicitly temperature at time $l + 1$, $T_{i,j,k}^{l+1}$:

$$T_{i,j,k}^{l+1} = T_{i,j,k}^l + C\Delta t \left(\frac{T_{i+1,j,k}^l - 2T_{i,j,k}^l + T_{i-1,j,k}^l}{\Delta x^2} + \frac{T_{i,j+1,k}^l - 2T_{i,j,k}^l + T_{i,j-1,k}^l}{\Delta y^2} \right.$$
$$\left. + \frac{T_{i,j,k+1}^l - 2T_{i,j,k}^l + T_{i,j,k-1}^l}{\Delta z^2} \right). \qquad (6)$$

In the same manner for the solution of the Eq. (6) were implemented three kernel versions named: 3D-1-1, 3D-1-3, 3D-3-3. The name structure is 3D-X-I, where X is the array dimension and I is the number of indices used inside the kernel and 3D refers to the dimension of the equation solved.

The 3D-1-1 kernel is showed in Listing 1.8, in this case, it is even more complex to determine the points on the boundary, for a 3D problem, there are 6 faces, if it is established n_x, n_y and n_z as the number of discrete points in the x, y and z direction respectively, the elements at the boundaries can be determined with the following conditionals: $l \mod n_x == 0$, left face; $(l+1) \mod n_x == 0$, right face; $0 \leq l < n_x n_y$, front face; $n_x n_y (n_z - 1) \leq l < n_x n_y n_z - 1$, back face; $l \mod n_x n_y < n_x$, top face; $l - (n_x * n_y) + nx \mod n_x n_y < n_x$, bottom face, where l is the lineal index in the rows direction.

Listing 1.8. Kernel 3D using a unidimensional array T and one index l. .

```
__global__ void kernel(float *T, float *Tn, int ny, int \
nx, int nz, float dt, float C, float dx2, float dy2, float dz2)
{
  int l;
  float Txx;
  float Tyy;
  float Tzz;
  l = blockIdx.x * blockDim.x + threadIdx.x;
  if( l > (nx*ny) && l < ((nx*ny)*(nz-1)) && !((l%nx)==0 \
  || ((l+1)\%nx == 0)) && !((l%(nx*ny) < nx) || \
    (((l-(nx*ny)+nx)%((nx*ny))<nx) ) ))
  {
    Txx = (T[l+1]    -2.0f*T[l] +T[l-1])/dx2;
    Tyy = (T[l+nx]   -2.0f*T[l] +T[l-nx])/dy2;
    Tzz = (T[l+nx*ny] -2.0f*T[l] +T[l-nx*ny])/dz2;
    Tn[l] = T[l]+dt*C*(Txx+Tyy+Tzz);
  }
}
```

In Listing 1.9, is shown the kernel 3D-1-3 that uses three indices, improving the readability of the code, nevertheless, however boundary points have to be found as: $j + n_x(i + kn_y) \mod n_x == 0$, left face; $(j + n_x(i + kn_y) + 1) \mod n_x == 0$, right face; $0 \leq j + n_x(i + kn_y) < n_x n_y$, front face; $n_x n_y (n_z - 1) \leq j + n_x(i + kn_y) < n_x n_y n_z - 1$, back face; $j + n_x(i + kn_y) \mod n_x n_y < n_x$, top face; $j + n_x(i + kn_y) \mod n_x n_y - n_x$, bottom face, where j, i, k, are the indices in the x, y and z directions respectively.

Listing 1.9. Kernel 3D using a unidimensional array T and three indices (i,j,k).

```
__global__ void kernel(float *T, float *Tn, int ny, int \
nx, int nz, float dt, float C, float dx2, float dy2, float dz2)
{
int i,j,k,l;
j = blockIdx.x * blockDim.x + threadIdx.x;
i = blockIdx.y * blockDim.y + threadIdx.y;
k = blockIdx.z * blockDim.z + threadIdx z;
float Txx;
float Tyy;
float Tzz;
if( (j>0) && (j<(nx-1)) && (i > 0) \
&& (i < (ny-1)) && (k>0) && (k<(nz-1)) )
{
l = j+i*nx+k*(nx*ny);
Txx = (T[l+1] -2.0f*T[l] +T[l-1])/dx2;
Tyy = (T[l+nx] -2.0f*T[l] +T[l-nx])/dy2;
Tzz = (T[l+nx*ny] -2.0f*T[l] +T[l-nx*ny])/dz2;
Tn[l] = T[l]+dt*C*(Txx+Tyy+Tzz);
}
}
```

In Listing 1.9, is depicted the proposed kernel 3D-3-3, using a tridimensional array inside the kernel, to use T and Tn as tree- dimensional arrays is necessary to create the arrays using the method Listed in 1.4 , with this, the finite difference finite method is easy to implement, and the boundary conditions are easily managed as: $j == 0$, left face; $j == n_x - 1$, right face; $z == 0$, front face; $z == n_z - 1$, back face; $i == 0$, top face; $i == n_y - 1$, bottom face, where j, i, k, are the indices in the x, y and z directions respectively.

Listing 1.10. Kernel 3D using three-dimensional array T with three indices (i,j,k).

```
__global__ void kernel(real ***T, real ***Tn, int ny, int nx, int nz,
real dt, real C, real dx2, real dy2, real dz2) {
    int i, j, k;
    j = blockIdx.x * blockDim.x + threadIdx.x;
    i = blockIdx.y * blockDim.y + threadIdx.y;
    k = blockIdx.z * blockDim.z + threadIdx.z;
    real Txx;
    real Tyy;
    real Tzz;
    if ((i>0) && (i<(ny - 1)) && (j>0) && (j<(nx-1)) &&
    (k>0) && (k<(nz - 1))) {
        Tzz = (T[i][j][k + 1] - 2.0 * T[i][j][k] + T[i][j][k - 1]) / dz2;
        Txx = (T[i][j + 1][k] - 2.0 * T[i][j][k] + T[i][j - 1][k]) / dx2;
        Tyy = (T[i + 1][j][k] - 2.0 * T[i][j][k] + T[i - 1][j][k]) / dy2;

        Tn[i][j][k] = T[i][j][k] + dt * C * (Txx + Tyy + Tzz);
    }
}
```

5   Performance Test

It is well known that the use of shared memory to cache data in multiprocessors could improve the performance of several algorithms written in CUDA [15]. Shared memory contained in every stream multiprocessor is much faster than global memory. In fact, shared memory latency is about 100x lower than the global memory latency. Shared memory is allocated per thread block, so all threads in the block have access to the same shared memory; in a finite difference problem the use of share memory can increase the performance because the number of accesses to global memory are reduced.

For the kernel 2D-2-2, was added the use of shared memory. In fact, the implementation of shared memory is clear and easy to implement also providing a readable code structure. The 2D-2-2 kernel implementation with shared memory is shown in Listing 1.11 and can be seen two shared memory arrays are used, `tile` and `tilen`, the first one is used to store the data from the global memory and make the operations internally, while `tilen` have an additional shadow region to store the values required to complete the finite difference operations, thus reducing the number of accesses to global memory. For the kernel 3D-3-3, the shared memory implementation is carried out in the same way and the coding is show in Listing 1.12.

Listing 1.11. Kernel 2D using bidimensional array T with two indices (i,j), and using shared memory.

```
__global__ void kernel_shared(real **T,real **Tn,int ny,int nx,real dt,
real C,real dx2,real dy2) {
  int i, j, l, m; real Txx; real Tyy;
  __shared__ real tile[tiley + 2][tilex + 2];
  __shared__ real tilen[tiley][tilex];
  j = blockIdx.x * blockDim.x + threadIdx.x;
  i = blockIdx.y * blockDim.y + threadIdx.y;
  if ((i >= 0) && (i <= (ny - 1)) && (j >= 0) && (j <= (nx - 1)))
    tile[threadIdx.y + 1][threadIdx.x + 1] = T[i][j];
  if ((i > 0) && (i < (ny - 1)) && (j > 0) && (j < (nx - 1))) {
    if (threadIdx.x == (blockDim.x - 1))
      tile[threadIdx.y + 1][threadIdx.x + 2] = T[i][j + 1]; // right
    if (threadIdx.y == (blockDim.y - 1))
      tile[threadIdx.y + 2][threadIdx.x + 1] = T[i + 1][j]; // down
    if (threadIdx.x == (0))
      tile[threadIdx.y + 1][threadIdx.x] = T[i][j - 1]; // left
    if (threadIdx.y == (0))
      tile[threadIdx.y][threadIdx.x + 1] = T[i - 1][j]; // up
  }
  __syncthreads();
  if ((i > 0) && (i < (ny - 1)) && (j > 0) && (j < (nx - 1))) {
    m = threadIdx.x + 1;
    l = threadIdx.y + 1;
    Txx = (tile[l][m + 1] - 2.0 * tile[l][m] + tile[l][m - 1]) / dx2;
    Tyy = (tile[l + 1][m] - 2.0 * tile[l][m] + tile[l - 1][m]) / dy2;
    tilen[l - 1][m - 1] = tile[l][m] + dt * C * (Txx + Tyy);
  }
  if (j == 0)
    tilen[threadIdx.y][threadIdx.x] = 0.0; // Dirichlet condition
  if (j == (nx - 1))
    tilen[threadIdx.y][threadIdx.x] = 0.0;
  if (i == 0)
    tilen[threadIdx.y][threadIdx.x] = 0.0;
  if (i == (ny - 1))
    tilen[threadIdx.y][threadIdx.x] = 0.0;

  if ((i >= 0) && (i <= (ny - 1)) && (j >= 0) && (j <= (nx - 1)))
    Tn[i][j] = tilen[threadIdx.y][threadIdx.x];
}
```

Listing 1.12. Kernel 3D using three-dimensional array T with three indices (i,j,z), and using shared memory.

```
__global__ void kernel_shared(real ***T,real ***Tn,int ny,int nx, int nz,
real dt,real C,real dx2,real dy2,real dz2) {
int i, j, k, q, r, s;  real Txx;  real Tyy;  real Tzz;
  __shared__ real tile[tiley + 2][tilex + 2][tilez + 2];
  __shared__ real tilen[tiley][tilex][tilez];
  j = blockIdx.x * blockDim.x + threadIdx.x;
  i = blockIdx.y * blockDim.y + threadIdx.y;
  k = blockIdx.z * blockDim.z + threadIdx.z;
if ((i>=0)&&(i<=(ny-1))&&(j>=0)&&(j<=(nx - 1))&&(k>=0)&&(k<=(nz-1)))
tile[threadIdx.y+1][threadIdx.x+1][threadIdx.z+1] = T[i][j][k];
if((i>0)&&(i<(ny-1))&&(j>0)&&(j<(nx-1))&&(k>0)&&(k<(nz-1))) {
if(threadIdx.x==(0)) tile[threadIdx.y+1][threadIdx.x][threadIdx.z+1]=T[i][j-1][k];
if(threadIdx.x==(blockDim.x-1))
tile[threadIdx.y+1][threadIdx.x+2][threadIdx.z+1]=T[i][j+1][k];
if(threadIdx.y==(0))
tile[threadIdx.y][threadIdx.x+1][threadIdx.z+1]=T[i-1][j][k];
if(threadIdx.y==(blockDim.y-1))
tile[threadIdx.y+2][threadIdx.x+1][threadIdx.z+1]=T[i+1][j][k];
if(threadIdx.z==(0))
tile[threadIdx.y+1][threadIdx.x+1][threadIdx.z]=T[i][j][k-1];
if(threadIdx.z==(blockDim.z-1))
tile[threadIdx.y+1][threadIdx.x+1][threadIdx.z+2]=T[i][j][k+1];
}
__syncthreads();
  if ((i>0)&&(i<(ny-1))&&(j>0)&&(j<(nx-1))&&(k>0)&&(k<(nz-1))) {
  q = threadIdx.x + 1;  r = threadIdx.y + 1;  s = threadIdx.z + 1;
  Txx = (tile[r][q+1][s] - 2.0 * tile[r][q][s] + tile[r][q-1][s])/dx2;
  Tyy = (tile[r+1][q][s] - 2.0 * tile[r][q][s] + tile[r-1][q][s])/dy2;
  Tzz = (tile[r][q][s+1] - 2.0 * tile[r][q][s] + tile[r][q][s-1])/dz2;
  tilen[r-1][q-1][s-1] = tile[r][q][s] + dt * C * (Txx + Tyy + Tzz);
  }
  if (j == 0)
    tilen[threadIdx.y][threadIdx.x][threadIdx.z] = 0.0;
  if (j == (nx - 1))
    tilen[threadIdx.y][threadIdx.x][threadIdx.z] = 0.0;
  if (i == 0)
    tilen[threadIdx.y][threadIdx.x][threadIdx.z] = 0.0;
  if (i == (ny - 1))
    tilen[threadIdx.y][threadIdx.x][threadIdx.z] = 0.0;
  if (k == 0)
    tilen[threadIdx.y][threadIdx.x][threadIdx.z] = 0.0;
  if (k == (nz - 1))
    tilen[threadIdx.y][threadIdx.x][threadIdx.z] = 0.0;
  if ((i>=0)&&(i<=(ny-1))&&(j>=0)&&(j<=(nx-1))&&(k>=0)&&(k<=(nz-1)))
    Tn[i][j][k] = tilen[threadIdx.y][threadIdx.x][threadIdx.z];
}
```

The numerical experiments were carried on a mid-range card, RTX 2060 Super with 8 GB of global memory with CUDA 11.4. For the 2D Case, the Block size was configured in different sizes: 4×4, 8×4, 8×8, 16×8, 16×16, 32×16 and 32×32. The notation used is XD−I, where X is the dimension of the array used inside the kernel, and I the number of indices used and the S indicates the use of shared memory.

The computing time where obtained after 20,000 time steps, with a mesh configuration of, $301 \times 201 = 60501$, the experiments were carried out in double and single precision. The computing times were estimated in milliseconds (ms) as the average of several executions.

Figure 1 is depicted the behavior of the computing times obtained using different versions of the 2D kernels in single precision varying the threads block size (warp size), as can be observed the structure 2D-2 does not introduce latency, therefore the performance is very similar compared with the other ones versions. The use of shared memory does not improve performance, this is because many memory moves are required in the finite difference method in proportion to the number of operations.

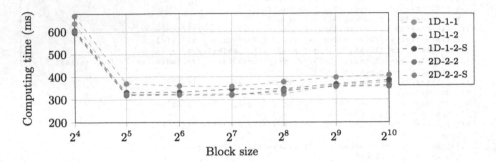

Fig. 1. Performance of the computation time in milliseconds, obtained by testing different configurations of 2D kernels in single precision.

For the double precision case, the behavior of the computing times are depicted in Fig. 2, in this case there are no significant differences among the kernels, even the use of shared memory does not improve the performance.

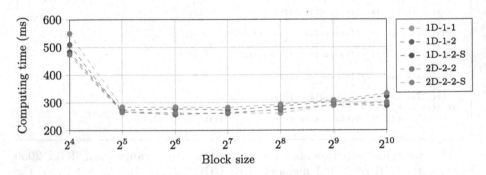

Fig. 2. The Behavior of the computing time, obtaining testing different setups of the 2D kernels in double precision.

For 3D case the sizes of the Blocks are: $4 \times 4 \times 4$, $8 \times 4 \times 4$, $8 \times 8 \times 4$, $8 \times 8 \times 8$ and $16 \times 8 \times 8$. Figure 3 depicts the behavior of the computing times for the versions of the 3D kernel and can be observed a slightly improved performance when shared memory is applied in some cases.

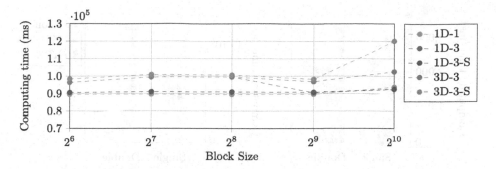

Fig. 3. Computational time performance in milliseconds, obtained by testing different configurations of the 3D kernels in single precision.

The computing times obtained for the double precision case are depicted in Fig. 4, can be observed, a slight drop in performance for the structure proposed when the block size is 2^9, however, the performance is very similar in all the cases, even using shared memory.

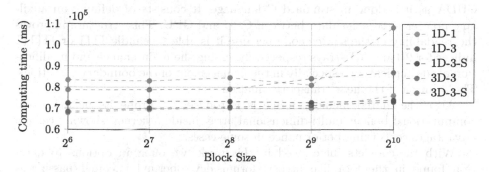

Fig. 4. Performance of the computation time in milliseconds, obtained by testing different configurations of the 3D kernels in double precision.

Finally, we compared the computational times obtained with the kernels: 2D-2-2-S with a block size of (16×8), and 3D-3-3-S with a block size of $(8 \times 8 \times 8)$, against its sequential counterpart with two Intel processors, a Xeon E5-2630V4 and an I5-4200U. For the 2D case, the results show that the CUDA code running on the RTX 2060 card is 90.30X and 11.96X faster in single and double precision respectively with respect to the serial code running on the Xeon processor, and 8.27X and 7.63X faster than the I5 in single and double precision respectively.

For the 3D case, the CUDA code is 10.49X and 14.67X faster in single and double precision respectively with respect to the Xeon processor. With respect to the I5 8.64X and 8.07X times faster in single and double precision respectively (see Fig. 5).

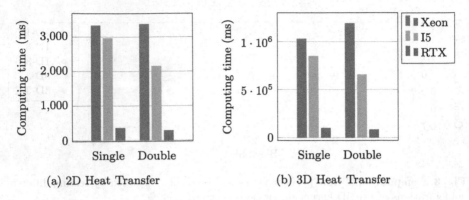

(a) 2D Heat Transfer   (b) 3D Heat Transfer

Fig. 5. Comparison between computation times and both single and double precision (Intel Xeon E52630V, Intel 5I5-4200U, and RTX2060 card), for 2D case (a) and 3D case (b).

6   Conclusions

This paper introduced a data structure that allows creating multi-arrays in CUDA as it is done in standard C language. It consists of defining an auxiliary pointer to transfer data between CPU and GPU. This structure improves the readability of the source code because it is able to handle [] [] or [] [] [] indices for 2D and 3D arrays respectively, easing the maintenance and modification of the application, especially in the management of the boundary conditions. The solution of the heat transport equation

Also, the shared memory usage is introduced to probe its behavior and computational benefit multi-dimensional array inside a kernel, showing certain advantages concerning performance in some cases.

With the codelets introduced in this work, we offer an options to question found in the fora like https://forums.developer.nvidia.com/t/passing-a-multidimensional-array-to-kernel-how-to-allocate-space-in-host-and-pass-to-device/10853.

Finally, it is necessary to mention that the performance results obtained, could vary, depending on the architecture and application.

References

1. Al-Refaie, A.F., Yurchenko, S.N., Tennyson, J.: GPU accelerated INtensities MPI (GAIN-MPI): a new method of computing Einstein-A coefficients. Comput. Phys. Commun. **214**, 216–224 (2017)
2. Calore, E., Gabbana, A., Kraus, J., Pellegrini, E., Schifano, S., Tripiccione, R.: Massively parallel lattice-Boltzmann codes on large GPU clusters. Parallel Comput. **58**, 1–24 (2016)
3. Couder-Castañeda, C., Ortiz-Alemán, C., Orozco-Del-Castillo, M., Nava-Flores, M.: Tesla GPUs versus MPI with OpenMP for the forward modeling of gravity and gravity gradient of large prisms ensemble. J. Appl. Math. **2013**, 1–7 (2013)

4. Galizia, A., D'Agostino, D., Clematis, A.: An MPI-CUDA library for image processing on HPC architectures. J. Comput. Appl. Math. **273**, 414–427 (2015)
5. Huang, C., Shi, B., He, N., Chai, Z.: Implementation of multi-GPU based lattice Boltzmann method for flow through porous media. Adv. Appl. Math. Mech. **7**(1), 1–12 (2015)
6. Kaczmarski, K., Przymus, P., Rzazewski, P.: Improving high-performance GPU graph traversal with compression. Adv. Intell. Syst. Comput. **312**, 201–214 (2015)
7. Krol, D., Harris, J., Zydek, D.: Hybrid GPU/CPU approach to multi-physics simulation. Adv. Intell. Syst. Comput. **1089**, 893–899 (2015)
8. Köhler, M., Saak, J.: On GPU acceleration of common solvers for (quasi-) triangular generalized Lyapunov equations. Parallel Comput. **57**, 212–221 (2016)
9. Lin, M., Xu, M., Fu, X.: GPU-accelerated computing for Lagrangian coherent structures of multi-body gravitational regimes. Astrophys. Space Sci. **362**(4), 1–11 (2017). https://doi.org/10.1007/s10509-017-3050-y
10. Michéa, D., Komatitsch, D.: Accelerating a three-dimensional finite-difference wave propagation code using GPU graphics cards. Geophys. J. Int. **182**(1), 389–402 (2010)
11. Nakata, N., Tsuji, T., Matsuoka, T.: Acceleration of computation speed for elastic wave simulation using a graphic processing unit. Explor. Geophys. **42**(1), 98–104 (2011)
12. Owens, J., et al.: A survey of general-purpose computation on graphics hardware. Comput. Graph. Forum **26**(1), 80–113 (2007)
13. Priimak, D.: Finite difference numerical method for the superlattice Boltzmann transport equation and case comparison of CPU(c) and GPU(CUDA) implementations. J. Comput. Phys. **278**(1), 182–192 (2014)
14. Recktenwald, G.W.: Finite-difference approximations to the heat equation. Mech. Eng. **10**(01), 1–10 (2004)
15. Rosen, P.: A visual approach to investigating shared and global memory behavior of CUDA kernels. Comput. Graph. Forum. **32**(3 PART2), 161–170 (2013). https://doi.org/10.1111/cgf.12103
16. Strohm, P., Wittmer, S., Haberstroh, A., Lauer, T.: GPU-accelerated quantification filters for analytical queries in multidimensional databases. Adv. Intell. Syst. Comput. **312**, 229–242 (2015)
17. Vuduc, R., Czechowski, K.: What GPU computing means for high-end systems. System **8**, 10 (2011)
18. Wienke, S., Terboven, C., Beyer, J.C., Müller, M.S.: A pattern-based comparison of OpenACC and OpenMP for accelerator computing. In: Silva, F., Dutra, I., Santos Costa, V. (eds.) Euro-Par 2014. LNCS, vol. 8632, pp. 812–823. Springer, Cham (2014). https://doi.org/10.1007/978-3-319-09873-9_68
19. Xu, C., et al.: Collaborating CPU and GPU for large-scale high-order CFD simulations with complex grids on the Tianhe-1a supercomputer. J. Comput. Phys. **278**(1), 275–297 (2014)
20. Zhang, T., Du, Y., Huang, T., Li, X.: GPU-accelerated 3D reconstruction of porous media using multiple-point statistics. Comput. Geosci. **19**, 79–98 (2014)

High-Throughput of Measure-Preserving Integrators Derived from the Liouville Operator for Molecular Dynamics Simulations on GPUs

Luis Rolando Guarneros-Nolasco[1]([✉]) [iD], Pedro Navarro-Santos[2] [iD],
Jorge Mulia-Rodríguez[3] [iD], Felipe Rodríguez-Romero[4] [iD],
and Roberto López-Rendón[5] [iD]

[1] Tecnológico Nacional de México/I. T. Orizaba, Av. Oriente 9 852, Col. Emiliano Zapata, 94320 Orizaba, México, Mexico
luisguarneros@gmail.com
[2] CONACYT - Universidad Michoacana de San Nicolas de Hidalgo, Edif. B-1, C.U. Francisco J. Mugica S/N, 58030 Morelia, Mexico
pnavarrosa@conacyt.mx
[3] Laboratorio de Biotermodinámica Molecular, Facultad de Ciencias, Universidad Autónoma del Estado de México, Av. Instituto Literario 100, 50000 Toluca, Mexico
jmr@uaemex.mx
[4] Laboratorio de Venómica Computacional, Facultad de Ciencias, Universidad Autónoma del Estado de México, Av. Instituto Literario 100, 50000 Toluca, Mexico
felipefrr@yahoo.com.mx
[5] Laboratorio de Bioingeniería Molecular a Multiescala, Facultad de Ciencias, Universidad Autónoma del Estado de México, Av. Instituto Literario 100, 50000 Toluca, Mexico
rlopezre@gmail.com

Abstract. Molecular dynamics simulation is currently a theoretical technique eligible in simulating of a wide range of systems, from soft condensed matter to biological systems. Excellent outcomes have resulted from using this technique; however, the implementation of this approach remains computationally expensive to some extent. Novel computing technologies may help reducing the computational simulation time, particularly, by using Graphical Processing Units (GPUs). Calculations on GPUs make possible to carry out simulations of large and complex molecular systems at a significantly reduced time. In this manuscript, the implementations of measure-preserving geometric integrator in the canonical ensemble coded in Compute Unified Device Architecture (CUDA) language are presented. The performance and validation of our High-throughput Molecular Dynamics (HIMD) code was done by calculating the thermodynamic properties of a Lennard-Jones fluid. From our tested systems, an excellent agreement was achieved with the reported of literature, compared with calculations carried out on Central Processing Units (CPUs). The implementation of the HIMD code performs time integration on Nosé-Hoover chains (NHC) faster in comparison to the NHC method implemented in LAMMPS code tested with one CPU vs one GPU. Along this work, the scope and limitations in performing simulations by using our HIMD code under rigorous statistical thermodynamics in the canonical ensemble are discussed and analyzed.

© Springer Nature Switzerland AG 2022
I. Gitler et al. (Eds.): CARLA 2021, CCIS 1540, pp. 236–249, 2022.
https://doi.org/10.1007/978-3-031-04209-6_17

Keywords: Molecular Dynamics (MD) · Graphical Processing Units (GPUs) · Nosé-Hoover Chains (NHC) · Canonical Ensemble (NVT)

1 Introduction

The accelerated use of molecular simulation methodologies, such as molecular dynamics (MD) simulations, have motivated the increasing interest in the implementation of rigorous algorithms in modern supercomputing technologies, which is a difficult task. Due to the purely numerical nature of the MD methodology, which emerges from the laws of statistical mechanics requiring the use of efficient schemes to sample the phase space, as well as maintaining control of thermodynamic variables at large scales of time and length. Nowadays, the combination of powerful computational technologies along with the strict laws of statistical mechanics placed in a same simulation code present a great challenge.

From a conceptual perspective, MD simulations (based on the integration of Newton's equations of motion) are considered numerical experiments that provide the means to sample the thermodynamic space of a given system through its evolutionary dynamic. In MD simulations, these spaces, so-called thermodynamic ensembles, are characterized according to the type of physical variables that must be evaluated. The simplest case is, e. g., when it is required to maintain the energy constant, this thermodynamic experiment is known as microcanonical ensemble (NVE). Herein, the thermodynamic condition is to not only maintain the energy constant (E), but also the volume (V) and number of particles (N). However, for comparisons with experimental conditions, it is often convenient to perform simulations at constant temperature, which lead us to explore the condition of the studied system in the canonical ensemble (NVT). In this case, the thermodynamic condition is to maintain the temperature constant (T), as well as the volume (V) and number of particles (N). The NVT ensemble is somewhat more difficult to generate than the NVE ensembles because kinetic energy fluctuations must generate the correct distribution function corresponding to the ensemble, in such a way, controlled temperature algorithms comprise one of the fundamental parts in MD simulations.

Generally, the Newtonian MD scheme is modified to maintain the temperature constant through tools called thermostat algorithms (TAs). An efficient thermostat must meet certain requirements given by the statistical mechanics e.g. a canonical distribution of speeds, be ergodic, etc. Not only speed averages are important, in some cases (e.g. solids) the pressure (volume) or temperature of the system can oscillate undesirably fluctuating (for dispersions) away from the average. Several strategies to improve simulations at the canonical ensemble have been suggested in the literature [1]. The simplest method is through the periodic scaling of velocities; this method is computationally cheap and numerically stable. However, it does not guarantee that a canonical space distribution will be obtained, but it is still commonly used. The lack of ergodicity for some thermostat algorithms, or for different temperature ranges, can lead to a dynamic that does not correctly reproduce the expected thermodynamic properties [2].

Simulating a thermal bath is not a simple task. To achieve an accurate and efficient integration in the constant-temperature ensemble, additional variables may be added to create a "thermostat" which controls the temperature of the simulated system [3].

These variables, or extended degrees of freedom, regulate the time-averaged values of temperature in order to reproduce as accurate as possible the phase space in the considered ensemble; the use of these types of methods should be used with caution. For example, the mass of extended variables must be carefully chosen, because of they affect spontaneous fluctuations in the system. Lippert et al. exposed computational challenges that involved controlling the temperature of a system using external degrees of freedom [4]. The extended degrees of freedom generally evolve on timescales much longer than those of particle motion; this could result in numerical inaccuracy if the numerical precision employed is insufficient.

Several TAs have been developed to make use of the extended phase space of the system of interest by adding an extra dimension, which take into account the interaction of the system with the environment. Between the most TAs highly cited are the Berendsen method [5], Andersen method [6], Nosé formulation [7]. According to these ideas, Hoover reformulates the Nose scheme-giving rise to the well-known Nosé-Hoover (NH) method [8]. The design of new schemes to control the temperature is a subject that is in constant evolution with the proposal of new and more sophisticated equations.

Undoubtedly, the TAs based on the NH formalism are currently the most popular isothermal simulation method. However, its disadvantage is that their equations are non-Hamiltonian in structure due to the non-canonical coordinate transformation, which precludes the use of symplectic integration schemes, [9] so that, the NH thermostat has the ergodicity problem, the failure of this approach under the conditions usually used in molecular dynamics calculations were clarified by Martyna et al. [10]. They proposed that the shortcomings of the NH algorithm could be overcome by connecting a chain of thermostats to construct a NH chain (NHC). Figure 1 shows schematically the construction of the NHC method.

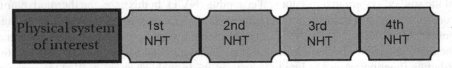

Fig. 1. Schematic representation of the NHC method and its operating. The temperature of the physical system (red box) is controlled by the mechanism of the NHC equations (all four green boxes). The first Nosé-Hoover thermostat (1st NHT) in the chain is coupled to the physical system, the second (2nd NHT) is coupled to the first Nosé-Hoover, the third (3rd NHT) is coupled to the second thermostat, the (4th NHT) is coupled to the third thermostat Nosé-Hoover, and so on, until forming a collective system of Nosé-Hoover chains (NHC). (Color figure online)

By using non-Hamiltonian equations of motion, such as NHC equations, the numerical integrator should be consistent with a non-Hamiltonian generalization of Liouville's theorem [11]. Meaning that, the integrator must be symplectic, conserving exactly the invariant phase-space volume, having an approximate energy conservation and time reversibility between other properties. A numerical integrator that achieves these features is known as a "measure-preserving" algorithm. These numerical algorithms are based on the decompositions of exponential operators, and the error in the total energy of the bounded system. These algorithms also represent the explicit integration of non-Hamiltonian dynamical systems. So far, Tuckerman et al. [12] have developed a consistent, classical and statistical theory of certain non-Hamiltonian dynamical systems. In addition, they have developed a "systematic way" of designing equations of motion of extended molecular dynamics known as the MTK equations, which are the origin of the NHC method.

MTK algorithms are already applicable to a wide range of scientific problems expanding their applications in several areas, such as, physical chemistry [13] and materials engineering [14] just to mention a few. The implementation of the MTK algorithms is not trivial and its evaluation is computationally expensive. So far, major MD codes such as, LAMMPS [15] have implemented the MTK algorithms. It is well-known that these codes have implemented the most advanced acceleration schemes of parallel computing and obtained the maximum performance of efficiency on clusters of CPUs. However, its routines to maintain the temperature under the MTK scheme are still programmed in CPUs.

On the other hand, with the advantage of graphics processing units (GPUs), the field of High-throughput MD (HIMD) becomes a fundamental tool for pharmaceutical research [16]. The GPUs offer massive numerical calculation capabilities, which have revolutionized both molecular simulation techniques and the reaching of groups of researchers in an accelerated manner. Nowadays, it is possible to have a workstation with a GPU along with the computing power of hundreds, or thousands, of laptops together. ACEMD [17] is the unique code of MD optimized to run on multiple GPUs architecture, and it is also one of the world's fastest MD platforms. Moreover, ACEMD works with Langevin type thermostats, and to date, it does not have implemented the MTK algorithms. A complete MD code is a very complex machine consisting of a diversity of statistical ensembles, force fields, integration algorithms, etc. Our group has undertaken the project of generating new MD code with methodologies implemented on GPUs that other codes do not take into account, as is the case of the NHC thermostat presented in this work.

The state-of-the-art HIMD reports that little effort has been directed to the efficient implementation of MTK algorithms on GPUs. The motivation for the use of integrators that explicitly preserve the measurement of the space phase, arise as a need to have an efficient tool that guarantees ergodic sampling at large scales of time and length. Nowadays, this task is only possible by using GPUs. Herein, we show the performance of measure-preserving geometric integrator in the canonical ensemble coded on GPUs, under the scheme of the MTK algorithms, which are the basis of the NHC thermostat. This HIMD code can simulate more than one million Lennar-Jones (LJ) type point particles, achieving up to 0.27 ns/day. In smaller systems, of an order of 30,000 particles, we achieved a production up to 30 ns/day. Most of the typical simulation results reported where the NHC method is widely exploited do not exceed 30,000 atoms, this may be due to the high computational cost and complexity of the method. The capabilities of our HIMD (https://gitlab.com/luisguarneros/himd) code break with this paradigm making possible the simulation of larger systems with longer times.

2 Methodology

It is well-known that a symplectic integrator conserves the Hamiltonian and therefore achieves stable integration over a long time. Due to the existence of a value that is completely conserved by the approximated propagator, these numerical methods are based on the decomposition of exponential operators. A system that preserves the generalized phase-space metric, will be consistent with the generalization of Liouville's theorem. The details of the Liouville operator algorithms derivation for non-Hamiltonian systems, such as NHC thermostat, can be found in original papers [18–20], therefore we will only outline the main NHC equations.

To generate a sampling of the canonical distribution (NVT), Hamilton's equations must be supplemented by a mechanism that allows the system to exchange energy with its surroundings. One popular method to mimic the influence of the surroundings in MD is referred to as the extended phase space approach. As previously mentioned, the Nosé-Hoover method is one of the best schemes to generate a canonical distribution, unfortunately its implementation presents ergodicity problems. The failure of this approach was solved by Martyna et al., introducing the NHC thermostat [9, 10]. The main idea beyond the NHC thermostat is the physical position and momentum variables of the particles in the system are coupled to additional phase space variables that mimic the effect of the surroundings by controlling the fluctuations in the instantaneous kinetic energy.

The NHC thermostat [9, 10] is a non-Hamiltonian MD scheme for generating the canonical ensemble. In this method, the ordinary phase space is extended to include a set of M thermostat variables $\eta_1, \ldots \eta_M$ and their conjugate momenta $p_{\eta_1}, \ldots p_{\eta_M}$; which serve to drive the fluctuations of the kinetic energy in such a way that they average the proper canonical value. These variables act as a heat bath coupled to the system. The NHC thermostat contains a conserved quantity, which guarantees the stability of the algorithm which is given by

$$H' = H(p, r) + \sum_{k=1}^{M} \frac{p_{\eta_k}^2}{2Q_k} + k_b T \left[dN \eta_1 + \sum_{k=2}^{M} \eta_k \right] \tag{1}$$

where $H(p, r)$ is the Hamiltonian of the physical system. When $M = 1$, the NHC system reduces to the simpler Nosé-Hoover system [8], which does not generate the corresponding canonical distribution.

3 Results

3.1 Code Validation

In this section, the results the implementation of the NHC thermostat on GPUs are presented. Firstly, we performed the validation of our code simulating a system composed of 864 particles of LJ fluid. A comparison with the data of the literature is included, we showed that the equilibrium properties are the same for the simulation time considered here, but our data was calculated on GPUs while those of literature are calculated by using CPUs architecture.

Figure 2 shows the equilibrium properties of LJ fluid in bulk phase testing the effective implementation of the NHC algorithm on GPUs. The comparison between literature data (calculations in CPUs) from Johnson et al. [21] and simulation data from this work (calculations in GPUs) is presented. Particularly, Fig. 2A shows the behavior of the potential energy (U^*) as a function of density (ρ^*) for a wide range of temperatures, from T* = 2.0 to T* = 6.0 (values are plotted in reduced units), error bars are also included. Meanwhile, Fig. 2B shows the behavior of the pressure (P^*) as a function of density (ρ^*) for a wide range of temperatures, from T* = 2.0 to T* = 6.0. In both cases, the perfect agreement between the values reported previously by using CPUs and the data obtained from our code by using GPUs is observed. These results show that, the canonical ensemble given by the NHC algorithm correctly reproduce the thermodynamic properties of a typical LJ fluid in equilibrium.

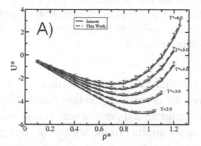 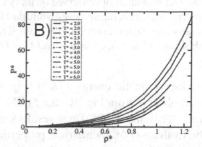

Fig. 2. Equilibrium properties of LJ fluid in bulk phase: **(A)** Potential energy vs. density. The blue line corresponds data from Johnson et al. [21], which was calculated on CPUs, while the red dotted line represents simulation data from this work calculated on GPUs. The symbol of the error bars is included in our calculations; **(B)** Pressure vs. density. The continuous lines correspond to the data reported by Johnson et al. [21], while the data with symbols corresponds to the data obtained in this work. All units are dimensionless. (Color figure online)

According to the Boltzmann distribution for that system, the energy profile obtained from a thermostat, must be entirely consistent with the canonical ensemble. To verify this rule, the evolution of the conserved quantity (ΔU) was evaluated by using the Eq. (1) for LJ fluid at $T^* = 2.0$, $\rho^* = 0.7$, and $N = 864$, these results are plotted in Fig. 3A. The instantaneous (ΔU) is defined as $|(U_i - U_0)/U_0|$ and the cumulative average (ΔU) is denoted by $\Delta U = \frac{1}{N_c} \sum_i |(U_i - U_0)/U_0|$, where i runs over the number of configurations, N_c. U_i is the total energy of the whole system including the thermostat, however, no drift in the conserved quantity was observed for any of the simulations as it was expected. Figure 3B shows a symmetrical density distribution for this system, which is characteristic for LJ fluid. This result is very consistent with implementations made by our group using CPUs [18, 19].

As the NHC motion equations are incorporated into the calculation, the simulation time increases due to the coupling of the thermostats, this caused the ergodicity of the dynamics to increase when increasing the available phase space of the dynamics. The implementation on GPUs of complex methods such as the NHC should be completed with caution. For this reason, the main purposes by using GPUs in MD simulations is to break the time/length scales, then be able to simulate larger systems for longer times preserving the correct application of the laws of statistical mechanics. To demonstrate the effectiveness of the NHC algorithm implemented in our code, the evolution of T^* (Fig. 4A), the reduced kinetic energy (K^*) (Fig. 4B), as well as the distribution of

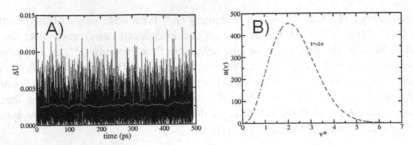

Fig. 3. (A) Evolution of conserved quantity (ΔU) as a function of simulation time (ps). The red line represents the averaged energy while the black line represents instant energy; (**B**) Histogram of cumulative momentum distribution obtained from a trajectory calculated using the NHC method. For this case $T^* = 2.0$, $\rho^* = 0.7$, and $N = 864$. (Color figure online)

the reduced kinetic energy $f(K^*)$ (Fig. 4C) are analyzed in the canonical ensemble. We can observe from Fig. 4C that $f(K^*)$ follows the correct distribution dictated by the canonical ensemble [18]. These results show an adequate comparison with similar results in the evaluation of geometrical properties that are applied to the algorithms designed to maintain the temperature in the canonical ensemble. It is important to emphasize the conservation of temperature shows no drifting, calculations using only CPUs presented in this section were performed running an in-house code.

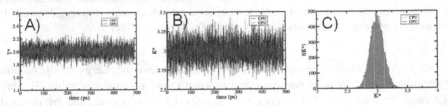

Fig. 4. Sampling of temperature between CPUS and GPUs platforms; (**A**) Evolution of the reduced temperature (T^*) of the system at equilibrium; (**B**) The behavior of the reduced kinetic energy (K^*); (**C**) The numerical distribution reduced kinetic energy $f(K^*)$ for the same system is shown. All thermodynamic properties are reported dimensionless.

To analyze the efficiency of the NHC method, we conducted a comparative study among the most popular methods used to maintain the constant temperature in Molecular Dynamics implemented in LAMMPS (version Aug-2018), which is one of the most widely used MD codes worldwide. LAMMPS includes fixes that can create a chain of thermostats coupled to a particle thermostat, to the best of our knowledge, it is only implemented on CPUs and using other accelerating packages other than using GPUs. Furthermore, there is not a routine of the NHC developed on GPUs, which is the main goal of this work.

To carry out the following analysis, two important considerations were taken into account. Firstly, we conducted a comparative study of 864 LJ particles to analyze the evolution of temperature using the NHC algorithm comparing the results obtained using the LAMMPS code. As expected, there was no difference between both codes. The simulations were carried out using NHC = 4 and $T^* = 2$. For this case study, the average temperature calculated between both codes was $\langle T^* = 1.99 \rangle$, with a standard deviation of ± 0.06 and ± 0.05 for LAMMPS and for our HIMD code respectively, these results can be shown in Fig. 5A.

Secondly, the behavior of the calculated temperature is analyzed employing four of the best methods designed to maintain temperature in MD simulations, namely, the NHC, NH, Berendsen and Langevin, these results are shown in Fig. 5B. In general, it is observed that all these methods maintain the imposed temperature through the simulation time, unlike the NH method, which showed a large oscillation at the beginning of the simulation (~25 ps of simulation time), this behavior has already been documented in other works [10]. As in the previous case, the average temperature calculated was of $\langle T^* = 1.99 \rangle$, which is in excellent agreement with the imposed temperature that is $T^* = 2$. The standard deviation ranged between ± 0.05 and ± 0.08 among the four analyzed methods, the lowest standard deviation of T* is found by using our HIMD-NHC simulations meanwhile the largest values are found employing the NH algorithm implemented on CPUs.

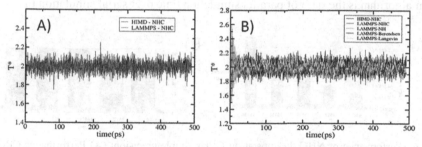

Fig. 5. Comparison between different approaches used to maintain constant temperature in MD. These tests were performed with a system of 864 particles type LJ. (**A**) Sampling the evolution of temperature using the NHC approach between our HIMD software and LAMMPS (version Aug-2018) software. Both tests were performed using NHC = 4. (**B**) Sampling the evolution of temperature using the most popular methods to maintain constant temperature in a MD, such as, Nose-Hoover (NH), Berendsen, Langevin and NHC performed with LAMMPS and HIMD. The simulation for NHC is the same as shown in Fig. 5A. Note that the simulations of LAMMPS were performed on CPUs compiled version Aug-2018, while the simulations of our HIMD code were performed on GPUs version 1.0. The evolution of each thermostat is identified with a different color as seen in the Figure.

3.2 Code Performance

After demonstrate that our HIMD code reproduces quite well the thermodynamic properties in phase equilibria for LJ fluid in bulk phase, we will present in this section the performance of our code compiled under different GPUs architectures. The benchmark tests are based on the LJ system. These benchmarking simulations were conducted on our cluster Olinka, which is equipped with several GPUs ranging from GTX-780 to GTX-2080 models.

The maximum number of atoms that can be evaluated on GPU is based on its hardware, mainly its memory size. Another factor keep in mind is, the parameters of the MD methodology, in the case of the NHC method, the number of thermostats and the control of the masses of the extended systems. Götz et al. [22] showed the maximum number of atoms that one GPU supports according to its memory capacity; for instance, the GPUs cards, such as, GTX-295 (895 MB), Tesla C1060 (4.0 GB), Tesla C2050 (3.0 GB) and Tesla C2070 (6.0) support 19200, 45200, 38100, 53050 atoms respectively. In this work we showed that by using a GPU model GTX-1080 (8.0 GB of memory) can simulate approximately 1 million atoms.

To know the advantages of the NHC thermostat on GPUs, e.g., high efficiency, high speed and low cost the execution time per step of MD and the speedup measured both parameters as a function of the number of particles, as shown in Fig. 6. We can observe from Fig. 6A that, the computational cost of time per step increased exponentially by processing only on CPUs. As the number of particles increased, the time per step also increases. When the processing task is done by the GPUs, the computational cost of time per step is basically constant. Speedup in Fig. 6B is measured as the ratio of wall time elapsed for carrying out a specific simulation. From this concept, the maximum speedup of an algorithm is the ratio of parallel simulation time over serial simulation time.

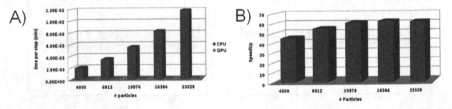

Fig. 6. Performance of NHC thermostat on GPUs simple precision: (**A**) Performance CPU vs. GPU of time per step as a function of particles number; (**B**) Speedup of NHC thermostat as a function of particle number. These tests were measured in the GPUs model GTX-1080 for a system of 4000, 6912, 10976, 16384 and 23328 particles. The Speedup obtained by migrating the NHC algorithms to GPUs, approached 60 times faster than the CPU version.

In numerical simulations, the performance of GPUs is very low when the number of particles is small because of bottleneck and connectivity problems. The maximum efficiency of GPUs is reached when the number of particles is large. It is worthy to mention that there are different schemes to measure the performance of a code, in this work, the performance of our code is based on the measurement of speedup. Herein, it was observed during a system of 4000 particles where a speedup of 45 was achieved. Meanwhile, a system of 23328 achieved a speedup of 60, and therefore, the speedup achieved went from a system of 4000 particles to a system of 23328 in the order of 15. These tests were measured in a GPU model GTX-1080. A speedup of this magnitude is significant because of the wide applications of MD simulations to biological systems. Certainly, our code does not have the capabilities to simulate biological systems yet, however, the acceleration achieved in our code is comparable with other jobs where they obtain accelerations of the same order of magnitude as ours, in different systems, not only biological ones. According to this data, we observe that the performance of our code is very successful, achieving an acceleration 60 times greater than the CPU version of our code. It is important to mention that acceleration increases using multiple GPUs. The philosophy in the development of our HIMD code is to obtain the best optimal performance using the lowest number of GPUs. This serves as an advantage for our users, as they will not require large GPUs clusters to execute our code. Currently, our code exploits the maximum capabilities only on one GPU.

The performing tests of the NHC thermostat was carried out using different GPUs architecture. This performance was based on different NVIDIA GPUs, exploring from first generation Tesla (2007–09), Fermi (2010–11), Kepler (2012 14), to Maxwell (2015–16) architectures. In Fig. 7, a complete analysis of the performance of NHC thermostat is shown. Figure 7 shows that the best performance of the NHC thermostat is achieved using GTX 1080 GPU cards, resulting in a production of 62 ns/day. In fact, it is documented that the best performance of the accelerated versions of the several MD codes are reached on a GTX 1080 GPU [20]. These experiments were achieved in single GPUs version of our code for a system of 10976 particles type LJ.

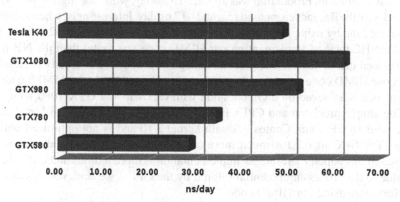

Fig. 7. Performance evaluation and benchmarking of the NHC thermostat in different GPUs architectures. The performance of our code was tested on a system of constituted by 10976 LJ type particles using simple precision.

From this version of our code, it can simulate up to 1.2 million particles, the benchmarking production is presented in Fig. 8. Simulating more than one million particles is a challenge that keeps many research groups hands on. This size of systems is the maximum that a GPUs supports, due to the capacity of the memory. GPUs with greater memory capacity could simulate larger systems, and of course with a higher ns/day production. Figure 8A shows the decay of ns/day production as the particle number increases. This behavior is normal due to the cost of calculating the forces. The maximum size that we manage to simulate is about 1.2 million LJ particles, obtaining only 0.27 ns/day on GPUs model GTX-1080. This is clearly displayed in Fig. 8B. Figure 8C shows an example of the configuration of this system, which measures approximately 40 nm.

Once we observed the great performance of our HIMD code, we proceeded to do a comparative analysis on the performance between HIMD and a few methods of

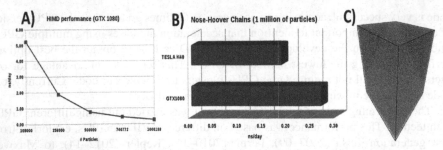

Fig. 8. HIMD of NHC thermostat performance on GPUs; (**A**) Maximum performance on a GPUs GTX-1080; (**B**) Comparisons of production in ns/day between two GPUs architectures to simulate one million LJ particles; (**c**) A snapshot of a system composed by one million particles.

LAMMPS (version Aug-2018) implemented to control the temperature in a simulation. The result is shown in Fig. 9. According to our measurements, the NH method achieved the lowest simulation. Production was about, ~15 ns/day, while the highest performance obtained with the Berendsen method reached ~17 ns/day. Interestingly, when simulations were carried out by using our implemented HIMD code, it produces 62 ns/day. Therefore, the NHC method implementing our HIMD code was faster than the NH method implemented in LAMMPS. The great advantage of production in ns/day is clearly evident in our HIMD code regarding the production obtained by the LAMMPS code. This performance is achieved on a Olinka node with GPUs model GTX-1080 with CUDA 10 using simple-precision and CPUs Intel(R) Xeon(R) CPU E5-2603 v3 @ 1.60 GHz 6-core with 16 GB Ram, Centos 7.8 with kernel 3.10 and is not optimized with Intel VTune. The NHC method is much more complex compared to the other approaches analyzed in this paper, therefore its implementation is more tedious and difficult. However, due to the processing potential offered by the GPUs, we achieved this difference in performance using our HIMD code.

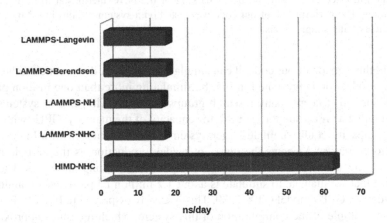

Fig. 9. Performance of different usually employed in MD, namely, Langevin, Berendsen, Nose-Hoover, and NHC. The measurement of the performance of these methods was carried out by using the LAMMPS (version Aug-2018) software in its CPU version, while the performance of our HIMD-NHC code is in its GPUs version.

4 Discussion

The key contribution of the HIMD codes is to accelerate the research in both simple and complex systems. We think that new computational algorithms and strong collaborations between chemists, physicists, biologists, mathematicians, engineers, and medical professionals will reinforce this research area. However, the problems and challenges related to biomolecules, which are often expensive in the sense of numerical simulation, open a breach with a major question difficult to answer. A question that has not been fully addressed to date is: How can the kinetic properties be reproduced correctly using MD to see extent simulations be accelerated by these simulations techniques [23]. This question falls on the different schemes used to control the temperature, which are classified by four types of methods being: Constraint methods, Weak coupling methods, Stochastic methods, and Extended system methods. Each one has advantages and disadvantages in its operation. Each of these methods presents artifacts, which are not fully understood yet. Several groups remain dedicated to trying to explain the effect of these anomalies generated by the movement equations themselves. An exhaustive analysis of these artifacts in the NHC method is beyond the scope of this work.

In this study, we focused only on extended the NHC method being the most popular. The main advantage of this method is that its movement equations solve the ergodicity problems presented by its predecessor method, the NH method. The condition of ergodicity is inviolable in statistical mechanics, which means that all states with the same energy are visited with equal probability in the long-time limit. A disadvantage, not yet fully proven, with this type of method is the coupling of the extra degrees of freedom that represent a heat bath, which can cause spurious energy oscillations, and can be controlled by an inertia parameter. A deep analysis of these effects goes beyond the scope of our work.

Herein, we present a new tool to enable HIMD simulation under a strict methodology based on the NHC method. The accurate simulation in the canonical ensemble is a problem of great scientific importance. With this proposed software, it is possible to perform simulations in order to be able to test predictions that serve as a point of reference of real experiments, in such a way that, promising results may be achieved. With molecular simulation methods, the laws of statistical mechanics must be comply, having to describe with precision the statistical ensemble under study, in this case the canonical ensemble. In view of this, it is demonstrated how to combine the most advanced supercomputing technologies in conjunction with the highest technologies that generate integrators that preserve measurements of the phase space for the canonical set at very low computational cost. The potential of GPUs is clear to do this task, allowing explicitly to evaluate precisely the simulation of simple systems under the scheme of the NHC thermostat. Thus, exceeding the exact temperature modeling at large scales with respect to other temperature control algorithms. Accelerated molecular dynamics on GPUs as provided by our HIMD platform should be of wide interest for many computational scientists as it provides performance comparable to that achievable on standard CPU supercomputers in a laboratory environment. Even research groups that have access to High-Performance Computing can find a useful tool in our code, which can run simulations locally for longer periods of time and with greater flexibility.

Finally, we think that the race to have more and better MD codes written to use the GPU technology is in constant developing, needing more innovation in this sense. It is very likely that our routines of the NHC method will be incorporated into the LAMMPS code, in order to take advantage of all the machinery of this code.

5 Conclusions

The evolution and innovation of the development of MD software on GPUs is constantly expanding. However, the use of GPUs acceleration of condensed-phase matter MD simulations is still developing. The pressure to achieve maximum performance has led to the use of approximations in statistical methodologies trying to avoid a real rigorous validation. The development of MD routines coded on GPUs seem to be an established and extremely active field. However, very few codes can be considered ready for production and likewise very few achieve the desired goal of making direct comparisons with real experiments, without making approximations. Regardless, the current benefits of GPUs are enticing, and this is driving both code and hardware development. Despite the substantial progress made in the development of the code, the difficulty in programming GPUs devices persists. Programming complex algorithms such as the NHC thermostat makes some groups choose to implement simpler thermostats, which are efficient at long times; an example being the NH and Langevin thermostats. With constant anticipated release of new technology, NVIDIA© will undoubtedly bring more competition in the development of more efficient software with more demanding implementations, such as, those discussed in this article. It is anticipated that with the release of newer versions of GPUs, MD codes will evolve rapidly, while research with these methodologies will increase exponentially in the coming years, the limitation of implementing complex methodologies such as those presented in this article are a latent challenge. We will continue to increase the capabilities of our software in the near future, adding sophisticated schemes to take into account electrostatic and van der Waals interactions.

Acknowledgments. All simulations reported in this study and the development of our HIMD code were performed using the Supercomputer OLINKA, located at the Laboratory of Molecular Bioengineering at Multiscale (LMBM), at the Universidad Autónoma del Estado de México. L.G.N. acknowledges CONACyT México for supporting his postdoctoral stay at the Tecnológico Nacional de México. P.N.S. thanks CONACYT for the research position under the Catedras-CONACYT program.

References

1. Tapias, D., Sanders, D.P., Bravetti, A.: Geometric integrator for simulations in the canonical ensemble. J. Chem. Phys. **145**, 084113 (2016)
2. Hoover, W.G., Sprott, J.C., Hoover, C.G.: Ergodicity of a singly-thermostated harmonic oscillator. Commun. Nonlinear Sci. Numer. Simul. **32**, 234–240 (2016)
3. Martyna, G.J., Tuckerman, M.E., Tobias, D.J., Klein, M.L.: Explicit reversible integrators for extended systems dynamics. Mol. Phys. **87**, 1117–1157 (1996)

4. Lippert, R.A., et al.: Accurate and efficient integration for molecular dynamics simulations at constant temperature and pressure. J. Chem. Phys. **139**, 164106 (2013)
5. Berendsen, H.J.C., Postma, J.P.M., van-Gunsteren, W.F., DiNola, A., Haak, J.R.: Molecular dynamics with coupling to an external bath. J. Chem. Phys. **81**, 3684–3690 (1984)
6. Andersen, H.C.: Molecular dynamics simulations at constant pressure and/or temperature. J. Chem. Phys. **72**, 2384–2393 (1980)
7. Nosé, S.: A unified formulation of the constant temperature molecular dynamics methods. J. Chem. Phys. **81**, 511–519 (1984)
8. Hoover, W.G.: Canonical dynamics: equilibrium phase-space distributions. Phys. Rev. A **31**, 1695–1697 (1985)
9. Martyna, G.J., Tuckerman, M.E.: Symplectic reversible integrators: predictor–corrector methods. J. Chem. Phys. **102**, 8071–8077 (1995)
10. Martyna, G.J., Klein, M.L., Tuckerman, M.: Nosé-Hoover chains: the canonical ensemble via continuous dynamics. J. Chem. Phys. **97**, 2635–2643 (1992)
11. Tuckerman, M.E., Liu, Y., Ciccotti, G., Martyna, G.J.: Non-Hamiltonian molecular dynamics: generalizing Hamiltonian phase space principles to non-Hamiltonian systems. J. Chem. Phys. **115**, 1678–1702 (2001)
12. Tuckerman, M.E.: Statistical Mechanics: Theory and Molecular Simulation, 1st edn, 696 p. Oxford University Press (2013). ISBN-13: 978-0198525264
13. Andoh, Y., Yoshii, N., Yamada, A., Okazaki, S.: Evaluation of atomic pressure in the multiple time-step integration algorithm. J. Comput. Chem. **38**, 704–713 (2017)
14. Selcuk, S., Zhao, X., Selloni, A.: Structural evolution of titanium dioxide during reduction in high-pressure hydrogen. Nat. Mater. **17**, 923–928 (2018)
15. Plimpton, S.: Fast parallel algorithms for short-range molecular dynamics. J. Comput. Phys. **117**, 1–19 (1995)
16. Stanley, N., De Fabritiis, G.: High throughput molecular dynamics for drug discovery. In Silico Pharmacology **3** (2015). Article number: 3
17. Harvey, M., Giupponi, G., De Fabritiis, G.: ACEMD: accelerated molecular dynamics simulations in the microseconds timescale. J. Chem. Theory Comput. **5**, 1632–1639 (2009)
18. Tuckerman, M.E., Alejandre, J., López-Rendón, R., Jochim, A.L., Martyna, G.J.: A Liouville-operator derived measure-preserving integrator for molecular dynamics simulations in the isothermal–isobaric ensemble. J. Phys. A Math. Gen. **39**, 5629–5651 (2006)
19. Yu, T.-Q., Alejandre, J., López-Rendón, R., Martyna, G.J., Tuckerman, M.E.: Measure-preserving integrators for molecular dynamics in the isothermal–isobaric ensemble derived from the Liouville operator. Chem. Phys. **370**, 294–305 (2010)
20. Romero-Bastida, M., López-Rendón, R.: Anisotropic pressure molecular dynamics for atomic fluid systems. J. Phys. A Math. Theor. **40**, 8585–8598 (2007)
21. Johnson, J.K., Zollweg, J.A., Gubbins, K.E.: The Lennard-Jones equation of state revisited. Mol. Phys. **78**, 591–618 (1993)
22. Götz, A.W., Williamson, M.J., Xu, D., Poole, D., Le Grand, S., Walker, R.C.: Routine microsecond molecular dynamics simulations with AMBER on GPUs. 1. Generalized born. J. Chem. Theory Comput. **8**, 1542–1555 (2012)
23. Feig, M.: Kinetics from implicit solvent simulations of biomolecules as a function of viscosity. J. Chem. Theory Comput. **3**, 1734–1748 (2007)

An Efficient Parallel Model for Coupled Open-Porous Medium Problem Applied to Grain Drying Processing

Hígor Uélinton Silva📷, Claudio Schepke(✉)📷,
César Flaubiano da Cruz Cristaldo📷, Dalmo Paim de Oliveira📷,
and Natiele Lucca📷

Federal University of Pampa, Alegrete, RS, Brazil
{higorsilva.aluno,claudioschepke,cesarcristaldo,dalmooliveira.aluno,
natielelucca.aluno}@unipampa.edu.br

Abstract. Does estimated that between 10% to 25% of the loss of the grain crop occurs post-harvest. Drying grains is one of the most critical steps in grain processing for its proper conservation after harvest. Considering that grain mass is an amount of solid and empty spaces (holes) through which a fluid can pass, grain drying can be assumed to be a coupled open-porous medium problem. In this paper is proposed a mathematical and computer simulation model. It describes convection in a free flow with a porous obstacle applied to grain drying. A computational fluid dynamics scheme was implemented in FORTRAN using Finite Volume to simulate and compute the numerical solutions. The code is parallel implemented using OpenMP programming interface. There was a significant reduction in processing time. The total simulation time was eight times less for a multicore architecture (16 physical cores).

1 Introduction

The drying process does make to remove the moisture inside a material, commonly used in food production. Grain drying is the removal of the kernel humidity until the safe moisture content. It is usually 12–14 % on a wet basis [1]. They fall into two types of artificial dryers used in grain production: Bin and Portable Dryers. Bin Dryers, such as batch dryers, recirculating batch dryer bins, and continuous flow dryers usually work with lower airflow velocities than other kinds. Consequently, they are generally more energy-efficient. However, it is slower than most other types of dryers. Batch Dryer Bin is a cylindrical structure with a perforated floor, fulled by a grain spreader, a fan heater unit and, a sweep and an underfloor unloading auger, as shown in Fig. 1.

The heater fan starts when grains does place inside the bin and, as long as it does not achieve the lower average grain content moisture, the process does not finish [4]. All this process presents different drying zones: dry layer, drying layer, and wet layer, which do be taken into account to determine the drying period. The dry zone does locate on the bottom of the bin, and it is the first layer to be dried. The process finishes when the wet zone becomes dried.

© Springer Nature Switzerland AG 2022
I. Gitler et al. (Eds.): CARLA 2021, CCIS 1540, pp. 250–264, 2022.
https://doi.org/10.1007/978-3-031-04209-6_18

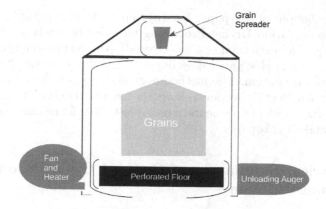

Fig. 1. Batch dryer bin.

Considering that the grain mass is an amount of solid and empty spaces (holes), through which a fluid can pass, the drying of the grain could assume as a problem of coupled open-porous media. Mathematical modeling and computer simulation are widely used to describe convection in a free flow with a porous obstacle. Many studies in the literature propose to predict the flow rate that passes through and around a porous medium. It uses Darcy's law formulation and its current modifications in the porous part, and the Navier-Stokes formulation in the open part [3]. However, one must take into account the abrupt change in free flow and porous media, creating a transition zone, as shown in Fig. 2.

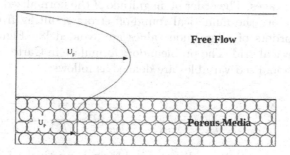

Fig. 2. Free porous flow

In our work, a Computational Fluid Dynamic scheme was implemented in FORTRAN using Finite-Volume to simulate and computing the numerical solutions. However, such kind of application demands quite a long execution time for any simple simulation. To reduce the execution time for an acceptable value, we explore the concurrency of instructions in Multi-Core and GPU architectures. These architectures could do adopted for numerical applications.

The contributions of this paper are: (a) to provide an application that allows the simulation of Grain Drying Processing for different kinds of grains; (b) to evaluate the parallel performance using OpenMP parallel programming interface.

The remainder of this paper does organize as follows. Section 2 presents the mathematical formulation. The methodology of development of the parallelization does detail in Sect. 3. Section 4 shows the numerical and performance results for the different parallel implementations. At last, Sect. 5 presents the conclusion and future work of this paper.

2   Numerical Simulation of Coupled Open-Porous Medium Problem

The mathematical formulation is present here, in which the physical problem adjusts the governing equation of a general model of fluid flow to one through and surrounding a porous media. The approach uses the Brinkman-Forchheimer modification for the Darcy equation to porous media, handling as a single domain problem. Despite applying a set of equations for each region (open and porous domain), the Single Domain approach validates a set of equations for all points in the whole domain [3,5].

In the present work following assumptions are made: Two-dimensional, unsteady, laminar flow of an incompressible and viscous flow has did considered; The porous medium is isotropic, uniform and homogeneous; One-domain approach is used for governing equations; The diameter of porous cylinder is sufficiently larger than the characteristics radius of the cylinder's pores.

Formulation of porous media problems using normalized variables can provide many advantages. The order of magnitude of the normalized variables is the same, and therefore the numerical round-off errors resulting from calculations with different orders of magnitude values are avoided [8]. Figure 3 shows the schematic numerical grid. The problem does formulate in Cartesian coordinates. The nondimensionalized variables are defined as follows:

$$x = \frac{\bar{x}}{d}, y = \frac{\bar{y}}{d}, u = \frac{\bar{u}}{u_0}, v = \frac{\bar{v}}{v_0}, p = \frac{\bar{p}}{\rho u_0^2}, T = \frac{\bar{T}}{T_c}, t = \frac{\overline{t u_0}}{d}, c = \frac{\bar{c}}{c_0}$$

where $\bar{x}$ and $\bar{y}$ are spatial coordinates, and their respectively $\bar{u}$ and $\bar{v}$ velocities components, u_0 is the velocity of injection, d is the diameter of the cylinder, $\bar{p}$ is the pressure, t is the time, and c is the dimensionless concentration. The velocity of fluid in the porous media v is related by the free fluid velocity by the Dupuit-Forchheimer equation $v = \varepsilon V$, where ε is the porosity and V is the velocity in the free fluid region. The governing equations for conservation of mass, momentum, and energy are given by equations:

$$\frac{1}{\beta} \frac{\partial p}{\partial \tau} + \frac{1}{\varepsilon} \frac{\partial u}{\partial x} + \frac{1}{\varepsilon} \frac{\partial v}{\partial y} = 0 \tag{1}$$

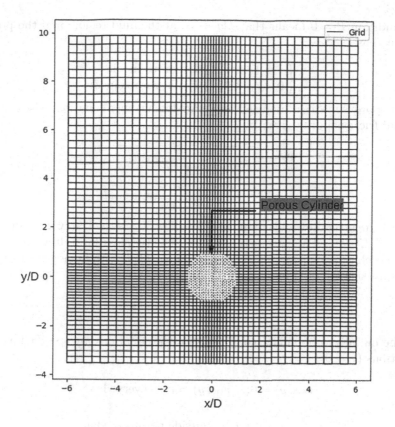

Fig. 3. Schematic numerical grid

$$\frac{\partial u}{\partial \tau} + \frac{1}{\varepsilon}\frac{\partial(uu)}{\partial x} + \frac{1}{\varepsilon}\frac{\partial(vu)}{\partial y} = -\varepsilon\frac{\partial p}{\partial x} + \frac{1}{Re}\left(\frac{\partial^2 u}{\partial x^2} + \frac{\partial^2 u}{\partial y^2}\right) + \varepsilon B\Phi_x \qquad (2)$$

$$\frac{\partial v}{\partial \tau} + \frac{1}{\varepsilon}\frac{\partial(uv)}{\partial x} + \frac{1}{\varepsilon}\frac{\partial(vv)}{\partial y} = -\varepsilon\frac{\partial p}{\partial y} + \frac{1}{Re}\left(\frac{\partial^2 v}{\partial x^2} + \frac{\partial^2 v}{\partial y^2}\right) + \varepsilon B\Phi_y + \varepsilon F_g \qquad (3)$$

$$\frac{\partial(T)}{\partial \tau} + \frac{1}{\varepsilon}\frac{\partial(uT)}{\partial x} + \frac{1}{\varepsilon}\frac{\partial(vT)}{\partial y} = \frac{1}{Pe}\left(\frac{\partial^2 T}{\partial x^2} + \frac{\partial^2 T}{\partial y^2}\right) \qquad (4)$$

P_e is the Péclet Number, defined by the expression $P_e = Lu/\alpha$. In the continuity equation, a time-dependent pressure term together with a multiplicative parameter nominated as artificial compressibility $1/\beta$. The numerical procedure is performed until the pseudo-transient turns negligible, Eq. 5. The regions of porous media and fluid are controlled by the parameters of Eqs. 2 and 3 as

$$B = \begin{cases} 0, & \text{outside porous media} \\ 1, & \text{inside porous media} \end{cases} \qquad (5)$$

the condition $B = 0$ means that $Da \to \infty$ at the fluid region, and the porosity is defined as

$$\varepsilon = \begin{cases} 1, & \text{outside porous media} \\ 0 < \varepsilon_0 < 1, & \text{inside porous media} \end{cases} \tag{6}$$

The porous media is modeled by Darcy-forchheimer equation, where Φ is the internal frictional drag given by

$$\Phi_x = -\frac{u}{Re.Da} + \frac{c_f}{\sqrt{Da}} u \sqrt{u^2 + v^2} \tag{7}$$

$$\Phi_y = -\frac{v}{Re \cdot Da} + \frac{c_f}{\sqrt{Da}} v \sqrt{u^2 + v^2} \tag{8}$$

in which Re is the Reynolds number of free flow, Da is the Darcy number defined as $Da = Kp/d^2$. The parameter c_f is a dimensionless form-drag constant. c_f is the Forchheimer coefficient and to a cylinder filled with homogeneous spheres the expression adopted by is:

$$C_f = \frac{1.75}{\sqrt{150\varepsilon^3}} \tag{9}$$

The initial and boundary conditions for the equations are specified as Initial conditions ($\tau = 0$):

$$u(x,y) = 0, \quad v(x,y) = v_i \quad \text{everywhere} \tag{10}$$

$$T(x,y) = \begin{cases} T_\infty, & \text{outside porous media} \\ T_p, & \text{inside porous media} \end{cases} \tag{11}$$

in which T_p is the temperature of the porous media.

The boundary conditions ($\tau > 0$):

$$u(x, -L_y) = 0, \; v(x, -L_y) = v_i, \; T(x, -L_y) = T_\infty \text{ at the inlet boundary} \tag{12}$$

$$u(x, L_y) = 0, \quad v(x, L_y) = v_i, \quad T(x, L_y) = T_\infty \quad \text{at the outlet boundary} \tag{13}$$

$$u(-L_x, y) = 0, \quad \left.\frac{\partial v}{\partial x}\right|_{(-Lx,y)} = 0, \quad T(-L_x, y) = T_\infty \quad \text{in the left side} \tag{14}$$

$$u(L_x, y) = 0, \quad \left.\frac{\partial v}{\partial x}\right|_{(Lx,0)} = 0, \quad T(L_x, y) = T_\infty \quad \text{in the right side} \tag{15}$$

The center of the cylinder is located at the origin of the Cartesian system as shown in Fig. 3. Thus the domain has length $2L_x$ and the height measuring $L_y = |2, 5(-L_y)|$.

The Finite Volume Method (FVM) is a widely used numerical technique [8]. In this method, the domain is divided up into discrete control volumes, where each node $P(i, j)$ is surrounded by a control volume. The boundaries of control volumes are positioned midway between adjacent nodes. Each control volume has width Δx and height Δy. As a consequence, the physical boundaries coincide with the control volume boundaries, as shown in the Fig. 4. Each point $P(i, j)$ is bounded by neighboring points placed at the interface between the two adjacent volumes named $n(i, j+\frac{1}{2})$, $s(i, j-\frac{1}{2})$ for North and South, $w(i-\frac{1}{2}, j)$, $e(i+\frac{1}{2}, j)$ for East and West. Similarly, points placed at the center of the neighboring control volumes are defined as $N(i, j+1)$, $S(i, j-1)$ for North and South, $W(i-1, j)$, $E(i+1, j)$ for East and West, see Fig. 5. In addition, the distances between the points W and P, and between points P and E, are identified by δx_w and δx_e, respectively. Similarly, the distances between the points N and P, and between points P and S, are identified by δy_n and δy_s.

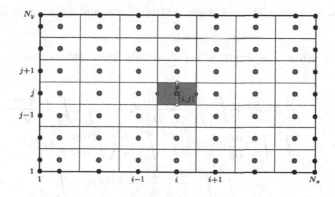

Fig. 4. Discrete control volumes inside of the domain

The main feature of FVM is that the conservation equations are integrated over the control volume based on the Fig. 5. Thus the continuity equation, Eq. 1 is integrated over the control volume as

$$\frac{1}{\beta \Delta \tau} \int_{\tau}^{\tau+\Delta\tau} \frac{\partial p}{\partial \tau} \Delta\Omega d\tau + \int_{s}^{n} \int_{w}^{e} \frac{1}{\varepsilon} \frac{\partial u}{\partial x} dxdy + \int_{s}^{n} \int_{w}^{e} \frac{1}{\varepsilon} \frac{\partial v}{\partial y} dxdy = 0 \qquad (16)$$

resulting in

$$\frac{\varepsilon}{\beta} \frac{\Delta\Omega}{\Delta\tau} \left(p_P^{\nu+1} - p_P^{\nu} \right) + \Delta y \left(u_e - u_w \right) + \Delta x \left(u_n - u_s \right) = 0 \qquad (17)$$

in which $\Delta\Omega = \Delta x \Delta y$ is the volume because $\Delta z = 1$ for simplicity.

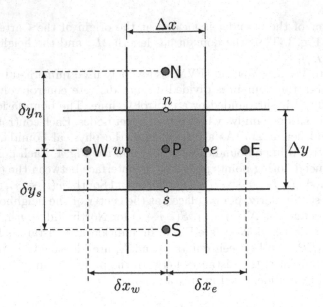

Fig. 5. Schematic figure of single control volume and neighboring points.

The momentum conservation, Eq. 2, in x-direction is integrated

$$\frac{1}{\beta\Delta\tau}\int_\tau^{\tau+\Delta\tau}\frac{\partial u}{\partial\tau}\Delta\Omega d\tau + \int_s^n\int_w^e\frac{1}{\varepsilon}\frac{\partial(uu)}{\partial x}dxdy + \int_s^n\int_w^e\frac{1}{\varepsilon}\frac{\partial(vu)}{\partial y}dxdy$$

$$= -\int_s^n\int_w^e\varepsilon\frac{\partial p}{\partial x}dxdy + \int_s^n\int_w^e\frac{\partial}{\partial x}\left(\frac{\varepsilon}{Re}\frac{\partial u}{\partial x}\right)dxdy$$

$$+ \int_s^n\int_w^e\frac{\partial}{\partial y}\left(\frac{\varepsilon}{Re}\frac{\partial u}{\partial y}\right)dxdy - \int_s^n\int_w^e\varepsilon B\Phi_x dxdy$$

resulting in

$$\frac{\Delta\Omega}{\Delta\tau}\left(u_P^{\nu+1} - u_P^\nu\right) + F_e u_e - F_w u_w + F_n u_n - F_s u_s = -\varepsilon\frac{p_e - p_w}{\Delta x}\Delta\Omega$$

$$+ D_e\left(u_E - u_P\right) - D_w\left(u_P + u_W\right) + D_n\left(u_N - u_P\right) - D_s\left(u_P + u_S\right) + \varepsilon B\Phi_x\Delta\Omega$$

$$(18)$$

in which $F_f = A_f u_f/\varepsilon$, $D_f = \varepsilon A_f/(Re\delta x_f)$ and f could be n, s, e, w.

In the same way, the momentum conservation equation in y-direction is integrated over the control volume

$$\frac{1}{\Delta\tau}\int_\tau^{t+\Delta\tau}\frac{\partial v}{\partial \tau}\Delta\Omega d\tau + \int_s^n\int_w^e \frac{1}{\varepsilon}\frac{\partial(uv)}{\partial x}dxdy + \int_s^n\int_w^e \frac{1}{\varepsilon}\frac{\partial(vv)}{\partial y}dxdy$$

$$= -\int_s^n\int_w^e \varepsilon\frac{\partial p}{\partial y}dxdy + \int_s^n\int_w^e \frac{\partial}{\partial x}\left(\frac{\varepsilon}{Re}\frac{\partial v}{\partial x}\right)dxdy$$

$$+ \int_s^n\int_w^e \frac{\partial}{\partial y}\left(\frac{\varepsilon}{Re}\frac{\partial v}{\partial y}\right)dxdy - \int_s^n\int_w^e \varepsilon B\Phi_y + \int_s^n\int_w^e F_g dxdy$$

resulting in

$$\frac{\Delta\Omega}{\Delta\tau}\left(v_P^{\nu+1} - v_P^\nu\right) + F_e v_e - F_w v_w + F_n v_n - F_s v_s = -\varepsilon\frac{p_n - p_s}{\Delta y}\Delta\Omega$$

$$+ D_e\left(v_E - v_P\right) - D_w\left(v_P + v_W\right) + D_n\left(v_N - v_P\right) - D_s\left(v_P + v_S\right) \qquad (19)$$

$$+ \varepsilon B\Phi_y\Delta\Omega + F_g\Delta\Omega$$

in which $F_f = A_f v_f/\varepsilon$, $D_f = \varepsilon A_f/(Re\delta y_f)$ and the subscript f could be n, s, e, w. The buoyancy therm is defined as

$$F_g = \frac{1}{Fr}\left(1 - \frac{1}{(T_n + T_s)/2}\right) \qquad (20)$$

Fr is the Froude Number is used in order to determine the resistance of the flow by moving around a body at a certain speed. The dimensionless number is the relation of the inertial and gravitational forces: $F_r = V/\sqrt{gd}$ The energy conservation as a function of temperature is integrated

$$\frac{1}{\Delta\tau}\int_\tau^{t+\Delta\tau}\frac{\partial T}{\partial \tau}\Delta\Omega d\tau + \int_s^n\int_w^e \frac{1}{\varepsilon}\frac{\partial(uT)}{\partial x}dxdy + \int_s^n\int_w^e \frac{1}{\varepsilon}\frac{\partial(vT)}{\partial y}dxdy$$

$$= \int_s^n\int_w^e \frac{\partial}{\partial x}\left(\frac{1}{Pe}\frac{\partial T}{\partial x}\right)dxdy + \int_s^n\int_w^e \frac{\partial}{\partial y}\left(\frac{1}{Pe}\frac{\partial T}{\partial y}\right)dxdy \qquad (21)$$

resulting in

$$\frac{\Delta\Omega}{\Delta\tau}\left(T_P^{\nu+1} - T_P^\nu\right) + F_e T_e - F_w T_w + F_n T_n - F_s T_s =$$

$$D_e\left(T_E - T_P\right) - D_w\left(T_P + T_W\right) + D_n\left(T_N - T_P\right) - D_s\left(T_P + T_S\right) \qquad (22)$$

in which $F_f = A_f v_f/\varepsilon$ and $D_f = A_f/(Pe\delta x_f)$.

After the integration of equations by finite volume, a system of sparse linear given by Eqs. 18, 19 and 22 is generated. However, the fluxes of the transported property through control volume faces must be properly calculated. For example, the flux coming out a control volume across a certain face must be equal to the flux coming in the adjacent control volume through the same face. Thus, the flux through a common face must be modeled. In the present work, the QUICK-scheme is used.

Quadratic Upstream Interpolation for Convective Kinematics, named QUICK-scheme is one of the methods highly used to solve convection problems, based on a conservative control volume integral formulation [6]. This safety is guaranteed by the good accuracy due to third-order spatial truncation error and first-order accurate in time. This method considers the weighted quadratic interpolation of three points upstream for the values of the cell face [8].

The choice of storing the properties (u, v, p and T) at the geometrical center of the control volume usually leads to non-physical oscillations and difficulties in obtaining a converged solution. Therefore the velocities must be estimated along cell face (w and e). Using some assumed interpolation profile, u_w and u_e can be formulated by a relationship of the form $u_f = f(u_{NB})$, in which NB denotes the u valued at the neighboring nodes. To ensure coupling between the pressure and velocity field, a second and third grid, which are staggered in the x-direction and y-direction relatives to the original grid, are used for the velocity components u and v, with the pressure being calculated in the original grid, as shown in Fig. 7. The temperature is also evaluated at the original grid. Note that, the u and v velocity components are evaluated, respectively, by red and yellow points, as shown in the Fig. 7. This procedure is known as a staggered grid. Thus, the Quick scheme is used and the velocity at the volume interfaces is calculated by a quadratic interpolation in the upwind scheme (Fig. 6).

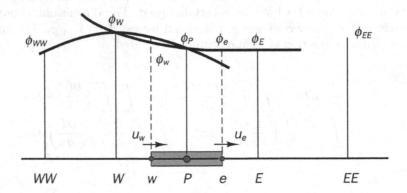

Fig. 6. Quick scheme interpolation for properties evaluated at the cell face

3   Methodology

In this section, we describe the parallel implementation of the coupled open-porous medium problem application. We list the parallel programming interfaces used and describe the procedures adopted to implement the discrete numerical simulation algorithm.

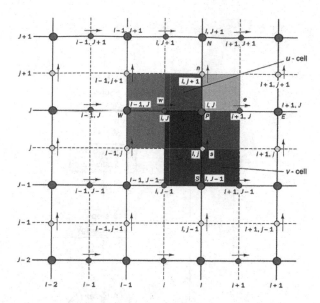

Fig. 7. Staggered grid: blue points are original grid, red and yellow points stands to local of evaluation of the u and v velocities components, respectively. (Color figure online)

3.1 The Algorithm

The flowchart of the application is presented in Fig. 8. The algorithm is composed essentially of a big loop where for each time step the physical properties are calculated. In this loop, the first step is to solve the quantity of movement. Next, is necessary to solve the continuity. The third step solves the energy. If necessary, the pressure needs to be calculated.

3.2 OpenMP Implementation

OpenMP is an API for shared and cross-platform parallel memory programming available in C/C++ and FORTRAN [7]. This API is based on the fork-join execution model, where a master thread starts executing and generates worker threads to run in parallel as needed or specified [2].

In our work, parallel threads were created to divide the computation of the loops of the routines called in the iterative step of the code. These loops run through the elements of the mesh. The directive !$omp parallel do is used to split the computation. Private variables are set, when data are restricted for each thread.

3.3 Experimental Setup

The computational environment used in this work for running the tests is composed by two Intel Xeon CPU E5-2650 processors, and one Nvidia Quadro M5000 GPU.

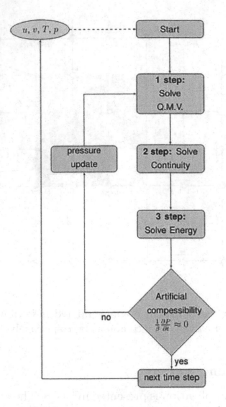

Fig. 8. Steps of the algorithm

For a better sampling of the application execution time, 30 executions were performed in order to obtain the average of the time for each of the test cases. In all cases, the number of iterations used was 20,000. Three case tests were defined to evaluate the performance of the parallel implementations: 51×63, 100×124, and 200×249 mesh sizes. The average results of the sequential executions obtained for these meshes were 310.833, 1258.613, and 837.340 s.

4   Experimental Results

This section presents some experiments performed for evaluating the numerical application results and the parallel directives adopted for CPU using OpenMP. For each case study, both the results representing the application's performance and the quality of its numerical results were highlighted when compared to the results generated by the original version.

4.1   Numerical Results

The porous cylinder is placed in an environment at forced flow. The initial temperature of the cylinder is equal to environment temperature $T\infty = T_p = 6$. At the bottom of domain, the fluid is injected with constant velocity $= 1.0$ at cold temperature $T = 1$. The present flow field is governed by four parameters namely, Reynolds number (Re), Péclet number (Pe), porosity (ε) and Darcy number (Da). These parameters were varied in the way to analyze a laminar flow behavior around a solid's circular cylinder and around and through a porous circular cylinder.

Figure 9 shows the velocity profile for different time steps. Initially, the flow is at low speed and the streamline is symmetrical around the cylinder. Note that, the streamlines penetrate the cylinder region due to the porous permeability. The cold fluid is injected into the inlet region of the domain. As a result, the cool fluid approaches the cylinder. A pair of vortices are formed and start to increase with time. The effect of the vortex is the mixture of the cold and heated region of the fluid flow.

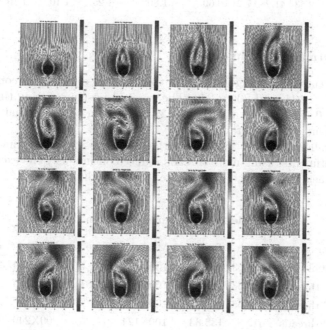

Fig. 9. Time evolution of streamlines for Re $= 100$, $\varepsilon = 0.7$ and $Da = 5.10^{-3}$.

4.2   Preliminary Performance Analysis

The code consists in pre-processing, iterative and post-processing steps. All these steps are explicitly invoked in the main routine. In the pre-processing step, configuration files are read, data are allocated and variables are initialized. The iterative step consists of a loop for the pseudo-time calculation. In this loop is called the routines solve_u and solve_v to solve momentum equation with quick scheme, solve_p to solve continuity equation, and solve_z to solve energy equation. At the end of the loop, the convergence is calculated and some variables are updated. The post-processing consists in writing the physical results in separate archives. These results are used after for plotting the output results using Python scripts.

A preliminary performance study was conducted using *perf* tool. Table 1 presents the 9 routines that more demand time for execution of the application. solve_u, solve_v, solve_p, and solve_z are essentially used to call other routines, including that spend more execution time like resv, resu, resz, upwind_v and upwind_u.

Table 1. Performance analysis with Perf tool

Routine	resv	resu	resz	upwind_v	upwind_u	solve_p	solve_u	solve_v	solve_z
% of time	42.53	41.28	7.21	2.60	1.80	1.25	1.10	1.10	0.45

4.3 Performance Evaluation

Table 2 presents the average execution time for three mesh size configurations: 51×63, 100×124, and 200×249. The pre and post processing time for these meshes was 0.122 s, 0.349 s, and 1.271 s. So, we can conclude that most of the time is demand for the iterative step.

The parallel OpenMP implementation provides execution time reduction. For all experiments, using more threads reduce continuously the execution time, including when hyperthreading is active (32 OMP threads).

Table 2. Performance: execution time

Configuration	Mesh	Time (s)	Mesh	Time (s)	Mesh	Time (s)
Sequential	51X63	301.79	100X124	1231.71	200X249	4830.54
2 OMP threads	51X63	167.52	100X124	655.81	200X249	2532.63
4 OMP threads	51X63	156.05	100X124	421.72	200X249	1632.77
8 OMP threads	51X63	138.33	100X124	271.25	200X249	979.65
16 OMP threads	51X63	110.22	100X124	182.96	200X249	628.77
32 OMP threads	51X63	97.61	100X124	194.87	200X249	605.18

Figure 10 presents the speed up related to the sequential execution. The results show that as larger the mesh is, the better is the speed up. For OpenMP, the best speed up was around 8, using 32 OpenMP threads.

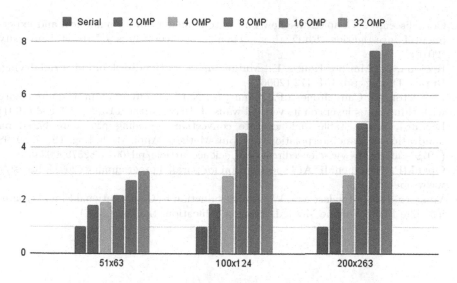

Fig. 10. Speed up related to the sequential execution

5   Conclusion and Future Works

In this paper, we provide an application for coupled open-porous medium problem. The model can be applied to grain drying. Some tests are conducted to prove the correctness. The implementation explores also efficient parallel implementations using OpenMP for Multi-core environments. We provide performance tests shown the scalability of the implementation for different sizes of threads and increase of speed up for larger meshes. The GPU implementation provided better results in relation to CPU.

In future works, the same parallel programming interfaces could be explored. For example, OpenMP could be used for GPUs according to the most recent specifications of the interface. In the same direction, other parallel task interfaces, like StarPU, can be adopted to explore multiple levels of parallelism.

Acknowledgements. This study was financed in part by the Coordenação de Aperfeiçoamento de Pessoal de Nível Superior - Brasil (CAPES) - Finance Code 001, Fundação de Amparo á Pesquisa do Estado do Rio Grande do Sul (FAPERGS), and Universidade Federal do Pampa.

References

1. Bala, B.K.: Drying and Storage of Cereal Grains. Wesley Blackwell, Hoboken (2017)
2. Chapman, B., Mehrotra, P., Zima, H.: Enhancing OpenMP with features for locality control. In: Proceedings of ECWMF Workshop Towards Teracomputing-The Use of Parallel Processors in Meteorology. Citeseer, PSU, Austrian (1998)

3. Cornelissen, P.: Coupled free-flow and porous media flow: a numerical and experimental investigation. Ph.D. thesis, Faculty of Geosciences - Utrecht University (2016)
4. Krokida, M., Marinos-Kouris, D., Mujumdar, A.S.: Handbook of industrial drying. Rotary Drying, pp. 151–172 (2006)
5. Le Breton, P., Caltagirone, J.P., Arquis, E.: Natural convection in a square cavity with thin porous layers on its vertical walls. J. Heat Transf. **113**(4), 892–898 (1991)
6. Leonard, B.: A stable and accurate convective modelling procedure based on quadratic upstream interpolation. Comput. Methods Appl. Mech. Eng. **19**(1), 59–98 (1979). https://www.sciencedirect.com/science/article/pii/0045782579900343
7. OpenMP: The OpenMP API specification for parallel programming (2021). https://www.openmp.org/
8. Versteeg, H.K., Malalasekera, W.: An Introduction to Computational Fluid Dynamics: The Finite Volume Method. Pearson Education, London (2007)

Author Index